OSF/Motif™:
Concepts and Programming

OSF/Motif™

Concepts and Programming

Thomas Berlage

GMD, Sankt Augustin

ADDISON-WESLEY PUBLISHING COMPANY

Wokingham, England • Reading, Massachusetts • Menlo Park, California
New York • Don Mills, Ontario • Amsterdam • Bonn
Sydney • Singapore • Tokyo • Madrid • San Juan

The programs in this book have been included for their instructional value. They have been tested with care but are not guaranteed for any particular purpose. The publisher does not offer any warranties or representations, nor does it accept any liabilities with respect to the programs.

Many of the designations used by manufacturers and sellers to distinguish their products are claimed as trademarks. Addison-Wesley has made every attempt to supply trademark information about manufacturers and their products mentioned in this book. A list of the trademark designations and their owners appears on page x.

Cover designed by Hybert Design and Type, Maidenhead
and printed by The Riverside Printing Co. (Reading) Ltd.
Printed in Great Britain by Mackays of Chatham PLC, Kent.

First printed 1991

British Library Cataloguing in Publication Data
Berlage, Thomas
  OSF/Motif : concepts and programming.
  1. Interfaces (Computers)
  I. Title
  004.6

  ISBN 0–201–55792–4

Library of Congress Cataloguing in Publication Data
Berlage, Thomas
    [OSF/Motif und das X-Window System. English]
    OSF/Motif : concepts and programming / Thomas Berlage.
      p.   cm.
    Translation of: OSF/Motif und das X-Window System.
    Includes bibliographical references and index.
    ISBN 0–201–55792–4
    1. X-Window System (Computer system) 2. Motif (Computer program)
  I. Title.
  QA76.76.W56B4613 1991
  005.4'3—dc20   90–28253
                                                           CIP

Preface

Graphical user interfaces play an important role in modern application programs. Unfortunately, programming them is a major task. Tools that support interface construction must be portable in order not to be outdated by the amazing pace of hardware innovation. Furthermore, users require a familiar standard interface for all applications because they are tired of constantly relearning basic operations.

OSF/Motif was designed by members of the Open Software Foundation as a standard interface for the years to come. It introduces important new concepts for anyone not familiar with the forefront of graphical interface technology. Nearly everyone involved in application development will be affected by this technology. A thorough understanding of the concepts and features of Motif is required in order to integrate it into an environment successfully.

This book aims to provide a solid background to the Motif technology for the following audiences:

- Programmers who want to learn Motif. This book is not only an introduction, but serves as a source of useful strategies even for the proficient programmer.

- Application designers who have to integrate Motif into their development work. They will gain an understanding of fundamentals as well as a detailed overview of functionality.

- Consultants who have to determine the impact of Motif on their customers' needs. This book provides an in-depth treatment as a basis for well-founded recommendations.

- Anyone interested in user interface technology. This book explains principles that are also relevant for other systems and outlines areas in which further research is worthwhile.

This book grew out of work in the Human-Computer Interaction research group at GMD (German National Research Centre for Computer Science). The project GINA is developing a framework for user interface construction as a part of the long-term project "Assisting Computer", which aims to provide more and better user support. We chose Motif as our standard base to concentrate on higher-level integration.

However, when we started working, no introductory material was available. This book reflects our experiences from the earliest technology snapshots to the release of version 1.1. Because of the sheer amount of detail involved, we also saw the need to abstract the fundamental concepts from the functional description. This book is therefore not simply a collection of features and examples, but teaches the concepts that will remain valid even if details change in future versions.

The book is divided into three parts, which cover different aspects of Motif while gradually introducing more detail:

- *Concepts.* The first part explains the basic concepts of the underlying technology.

- *Functionality.* The second part comprehensively covers the functionality of the Motif toolkit.

- *Programming.* The third part introduces four larger example programs, discussing how to extend the Motif functionality and how to interface Motif code and the application.

Different audiences will concentrate on different parts, but all parts are necessary for real understanding. At least a partially sequential reading is recommended. You can skip sections on the first reading, using the index to locate explanations of unknown terms.

Because of the amount of information involved, the book does not try to serve as a reference guide. For serious programming you need a number of further reference works (described in Appendix B). Fortunately there are several excellent books available for this purpose.

However, solid background information, advice and helpful hints are hard to find for Motif, to say the least. This book hopes to fill a gap in that respect.

This book covers both the 1.0 and 1.1 versions of Motif. Not all minor new features of 1.1 are described in order to avoid frequent version dependencies in the descriptions. Instead the book focuses on the larger part of the functionality which is common to both versions.

All the programs have been tested on Sun Sparcs, but you should not encounter serious difficulties on other platforms.

Acknowledgements

Many thanks to Peter Wißkirchen, who made this book happen, and to my colleagues for their patience.

Contents

PART TWO: FUNCTIONALITY

PART THREE: PROGRAMMING

List of Figures

Part
One

Concepts

Chapter 1

Architecture
and Design

1.1 Introduction

With computer hardware prices falling steadily every year, graphical user interfaces are becoming more and more popular. In the past, graphical user interfaces were difficult to program. Because each programmer created his or her own support library, external appearance and behaviour varied widely among different applications. Furthermore, different platforms had different window systems, making porting difficult. Tools were needed to create easily portable applications with a common user interface.

OSF/Motif was created to provide the functionality necessary to implement graphical user interfaces that would work identically on a wide variety of platforms, from high-end PCs to mini- and super-computers. Motif mainly consists of a *toolkit* for programmers, but there are other components. Details can be found in Section 1.2. The Motif toolkit provides programmers with the basic routines which enable them to include the most frequently used graphical interface elements in their programs.

A graphical user interface (see Figure 1.1 for a typical screen layout) has the following advantages over character-oriented displays:

- Graphical symbols, if carefully designed, are more easily recognized and memorized. The human brain simply has a much greater ability to absorb graphical information than to process character text.

3

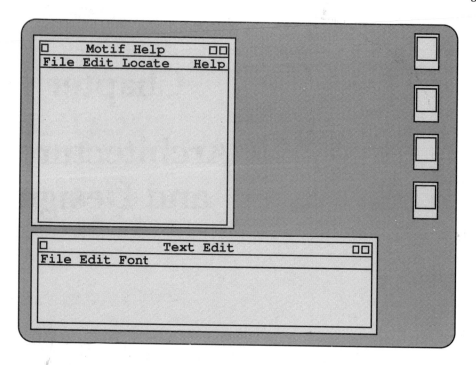

Figure 1.1: Layout of a Motif screen. On the left you see the windows of two different applications; on the right are icons representing applications whose windows are closed.

- A graphical user interface allows the user to set parameters and execute commands by *direct manipulation*. Invoking functions by direct physical interaction with instant visual feedback reduces learning time and gives the user a greater feeling of control over his or her computer.

Direct-manipulative interactions are controlled with a special pointing device such as a *mouse*. A user can specify locations on the screen by directly moving the mouse with his or her hand. A visible pointer on the screen constantly tracks the mouse's position. Depending on its position different actions can be initiated.

Why is programming graphical user interfaces so difficult? Graphical information is more extensive than text and requires more effort to specify it. Furthermore, direct manipulation dictates a radically different program structure compared with previous practice. The program must constantly monitor user actions which may concern one of many different visible components.

Motif drastically simplifies the programming of graphical user interfaces, because it combines the output and manipulation aspects of many commonly used interface elements.

Motif is for the most part independent of underlying hardware and system software because it is based on the *X Window System* developed at MIT. The X Window System provides the basic primitives in a hardware- and operating-system-independent way. On this basis Motif implements its own set of inter-active objects with a distinctive look and feel. The programmer can para-meterize and combine these elements to create a user interface.

The objects Motif provides actually originate from previous systems developed by DEC and Hewlett-Packard. Their respective features have been combined and improved. In addition, the behaviour was changed where necessary to make their respective user interfaces compatible with other systems such as the Presentation Manager from MicroSoft/IBM.

1.2 Architecture of Motif

Although the toolkit of interface objects is the central feature of Motif, there are a number of other components that make the whole product work. These components and their relationships are illustrated in Figure 1.2.

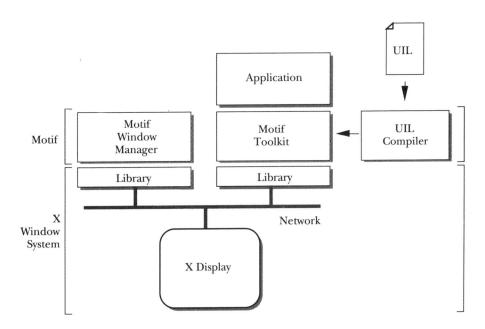

Figure 1.2: The main components of OSF/Motif. Applications built with the Motif toolkit use the facilities of the X Window System for input and output.

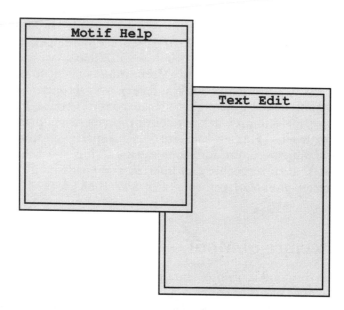

Figure 1.3: Overlapping windows of different applications. Both applications can use their windows as if they were fully visible. Drawing into invisible areas is ignored by X.

X Window System

As noted above, the X Window System is the base layer of Motif, and provides many desirable features. It is responsible for hiding machine-dependent differences as much as possible (although it cannot hide the fact that screens may have different resolutions or colour capabilities).

The X Window System allows multiple applications on different computers to be displayed in separate windows on the same screen. It coordinates the activities of the different applications that need not be aware of one another. The applications connect themselves to the display via some network service. Each application has one or more windows of its own, which may overlap those of others. Figure 1.3 shows such a situation.

However, the X Window System leaves the contents of the respective windows completely to the applications. A program can use some simple graphical primitives to draw into a window, but is free to fill the window as it likes. This makes it possible for environments with very different looks and feels to coexist. In particular, you can mix Motif applications (which have a distinctive appearance inside their windows) with all other X applications on the same screen, whatever the others look like.

Although the idea of graphical output across a network sounds astonishingly simple, a great deal of work is required to make it work reasonably quickly. The main problem is that a program cannot assume that it has direct access to the screen memory. Most of the optimization work has been (or must be) done by the X implementor, but you must be aware of the restrictions when you write your program. Luckily, in most cases Motif does the work for you.

Section 1.3 gives an introduction to the X Window System. Some other details are presented later in the book when needed in the context of Motif. If you plan to work more directly with the X Window System, however, you should definitely consult one of the books listed in Appendix B, because only a small amount of information can be given here.

Window Manager

Although an application can control what is going on inside its window, there are some functions which must be consistent for all applications (e.g. moving or resizing the different windows). Traditionally this was regarded as one of the tasks of a window system. To make the base window system independent of certain policy decisions, such as how to manage these windows, the X designers delegated these functions to a special application, the *window manager*.

For the X Window System the window manager is just another application, so you can substitute your favourite window manager for the default one or even write your own. Motif, too, provides a special window manager optimized for Motif applications. You can replace it if you like, but to achieve full optical and behavioural consistency you should refrain from doing so. X applications written with other toolkits run equally well with the Motif window manager. This is made possible by a set of conventions (known as the Inter-Client Communications Conventions—ICCC) to which the Motif window manager adheres.

The window manager not only handles moving and resizing, it also manages the stacking order of overlapping windows (see Figure 1.3)—you only have to click in a window to stack it on top and make it visible. To reduce screen clutter you can make every application main window into an *icon*, a small symbol representing the application (shown in Figure 1.1). The window manager also controls the *input focus*, which determines which application window receives the keyboard input.

Most of these functions are activated with the mouse in a region around every window called the *decoration* (see Figure 1.4). The decoration area belongs to the window manager, which directly receives notification of all mouse actions in this region.

You can resize the window by dragging the resize handles along its borders with the mouse; similarly you can move it by dragging the title bar. Three small buttons in the title bar activate the other functions, either directly or through a pull-down menu. The outlined area inside the borders is the window, as seen and controlled by the application.

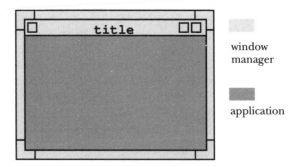

Figure 1.4: Screen areas controlled by the window manager. The inner part is controlled by the application. The window manager decoration consists of the eight resize handles and the title bar with three buttons.

Interface Toolkit

For the programmer the most relevant part of Motif is its toolkit, which implements a variety of interface objects. The Motif toolkit mainly constitutes the Application Programmers' Interface (API). Currently it is implemented as a C library.

The Motif toolkit works with interface objects which are called *widgets*. Typical widgets are push buttons, scroll bars or text entry fields. Widgets can be parameterized by attributes such as colour, size, font, border width, spacing, orientation and so on. Figure 1.5 shows some of the Motif widgets.

Primitive widgets as shown in Figure 1.5 can be grouped together by *composite* widgets. Composite widgets have facilities to lay out their components automatically.

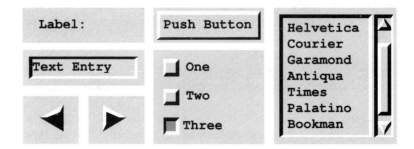

Figure 1.5: Typical Motif widgets. On the left you see a label, a text, and two arrow buttons. In the middle there is a push button above a group of toggle buttons. The last toggle button shows how a "depressed" state is simulated visually. On the right you see a scrollable selection list.

Figure 1.6: A simple menu constructed as a row of buttons. Note that buttons in a menu do not have individual shadows.

A menu, for example, can be constructed from simple buttons which are laid out in a column by a composite widget that is capable of row-column layout. The width of the menu and all the buttons is automatically calculated as the maximum width needed. Figure 1.6 shows such a menu.

The functionality of the Motif toolkit can be separated into functions applicable to all widgets, and functions needed to implement special widgets. The former are also known as the *X Toolkit Intrinsics* and are actually part of the standardized X Window System interface. There are other toolkits on the market which also use the Intrinsics.[1]

The distinction between the Intrinsics and the Motif widget set is difficult to understand at first. Section 1.4 explains the difference using an analogy, but it may not be clear until you have finished Chapter 2.

User Interface Language

A large part of a program using Motif consists of statements specifying the widget structure and several attributes. Most of these specifications do not influence the actual functionality of the program. For example, the way menu entries are labelled, ordered and arranged (except for code modifying this arrangement) is usually irrelevant to the program logic. The application code only needs to know that a menu entry exists somewhere that triggers function *xyz*.

Motif allows an application designer to specify these presentation details outside of his program (see Figure 1.7). The specifications are read in at runtime when the program starts, so they can be modified without recompiling or relinking. You may even use multiple specifications, e.g. for different countries or for experimentation.

---

[1]In Motif 1.0 the implementors have made some changes and additions to the Intrinsics library. In version 1.1 the original MIT implementation is used.

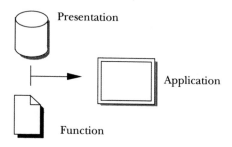

Figure 1.7: Dividing an application into function and presentation. The presentation details reside in a separate file that is used at run-time.

```
value
        c_selections : exported string_table ("Red", "Blue", "White", "Black");
        k_selections : exported 2;
object
        selections : XmList {
                arguments {
                        XmNvisibleItemCount = 4;
                        XmNitems = c_selections;
                }
                callbacks {
                        XmNcreateCallback  = procedure create_proc (k_selections);
                        XmNsingleSelectionCallback = procedure back (k_selections);
                }
        row : XmRowColumn {
                arguments {
                        XmNspacing = 4;
                }
                controls {
                        XmPushButton button {
                                arguments {
                                        XmNlabelString = k_button_label;
                                }
                                callbacks {
                                        XmNactivateCallback = procedure push_me (k_pb);
                                }
                        }
                }
        }
}
```

Figure 1.8: Section from a UIL specification. This program defines two constants and four widgets, with a label and a push button contained in a row-column manager.

The external specifications are described in the so-called *User Interface Language* (UIL) and are translated by the UIL compiler into an internal file format. Figure 1.8 contains a short section from a UIL program. The UIL will be described later, in Chapter 10.

Although you can choose whether or not to use the UIL support in your program, there are advantages in doing so. First of all your program will become clearer and smaller, because unnecessary presentation details are left out. However, you should document these omissions when necessary, so that someone reading your program knows that procedure *xyz* expects to be called from a menu.

Another advantage is that you can customize your program more easily and adapt it for different targets (novice/professional, different countries and languages). You can also use the UIL for fast prototyping (although this is not a simple trial-and-error process).

The disadvantage is that the connection between the two parts of the program is more difficult to maintain, because you always have to correlate two documents. Furthermore, most of the UIL features are also available through the resource database mechanism that is always present.

Style Guide

A user of several programs generally benefits from a high degree of consistency between these applications, because the amount of mental adaptation when switching is minimized. This is one reason why the Apple Macintosh user interface is rated for excellence.

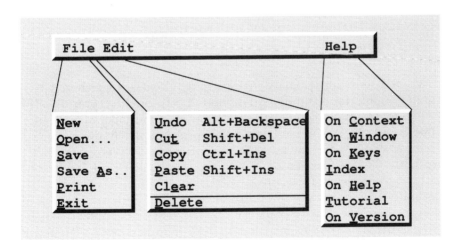

Figure 1.9: Some standard menus defined by the Motif style guide.

To achieve a similar quality, Motif defines a *style guide* which describes the preferred ways to design an application interface. Although a certain amount of consistency is normally ensured by using the toolkit, there are some guidelines which cannot be enforced by software and many (e.g. key bindings) which can be overriden.

Examples of such guidelines include some standard menu entries, which should be used in the same place in all applications that can use them. These are illustrated in Figure 1.9.

Some of the guidelines appear in the course of this book (especially in Chapter 10), but if you are actually designing a Motif application you should make yourself familiar with the style guide. Appendix B lists some other books you can use to gain background knowledge about interface design to understand why the style guide rules were chosen.

1.3 The X Window System

The X Window System was developed at MIT by project Athena. The design goal was to connect several different workstations in a network where graphical output could be sent transparently to any station. It soon became apparent that such a system would be of great public interest. With the help of external sponsors the academic prototype was turned into a system suitable as a basis for commercial implementations. The latest version, version 11, was designed with the help of several individuals outside project Athena.

Several companies have joined to form the X Consortium, where the future development of X is coordinated and where standards are defined to improve compatibility between different implementations.

Several design decisions differentiate the X Window System from other window systems. The most important goals and features are summarized below.

Network Transparency

As noted above, the primary goal was to develop a system where programs with graphical interfaces running on different hosts could be controlled from a single station. In a heterogeneous network environment there may be different machines, operating systems and networking protocols involved.

The X Window System uses the now often cited *client-server model* (see Figure 1.10). The display stations run a program which completely controls their respective screens. It accepts service requests from other programs and displays information in a window on the screen. Therefore it is called a *server*. The requesting programs are called the *clients*. They can reside on the same machine as the server (if this machine supports multi-tasking), or on any other host which can open a network connection to this machine.

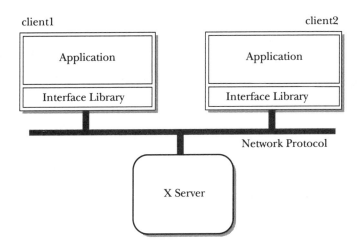

Figure 1.10: Client-server model and the X protocol. The client programs access the protocol through library functions. The requests are transmitted over the protocol connection to the X server.

Please do not confuse this usage of the words "client" and "server" with another common situation, where a server denotes a fully equipped machine offering storage and printing services for several smaller workstations. Usually the roles are the exact opposite: the small client machine is nearly always a server for X (because it has the screen) and the large disk server is often used to run memory-intensive X clients.

Client and server communicate via the *X protocol*, which defines what kinds of messages can be interchanged. The client issues a series of protocol requests that are transmitted to the server (e.g. to draw a string in some window). The transmission is asynchronous—the next request is sent without waiting for an acknowledgement of the previous one. Even while executing requests the server generates event messages for user actions (e.g. a mouse click in a certain window), which are sent to the respective client.

This asynchronous behaviour of the X Window System may surprise you if you are not aware of it. For example, since the client does not wait for a reply to a request, errors such as an invalid window ID must be reported as error events. Because of network latency the error notification arrives when the client has already issued a number of other requests, making it difficult to find the request responsible for the error.

The X protocol only requires that the connection between client and server is a reliable (i.e. no messages are lost), serial (the messages arrive in the order they are sent), and bidirectional byte stream. Such a stream can be implemented by inter-process communication primitives (if both client and server run on the same machine) or by popular network protocols such as TCP/IP and DECnet.

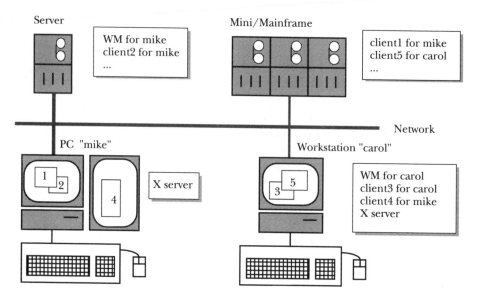

Figure 1.11: Multiple windows to multiple hosts. The table beside each system shows the processes running on it.

If a client program can open a connection to the X server on a machine, it may use the X services like any local program. Several programs on several machines may thus use a single display, because each program has its own window. Figure 1.11 illustrates such an environment. The X server distributes user events such as mouse clicks to the appropiate client. The destination usually depends on which window the mouse pointer is in.

Several different features of the X Window System are illustrated in Figure 1.11. First of all, it shows that even a PC can work as an X server. Because no multi-tasking is available on a PC, all applications as well as the window manager must run on another computer. In this example the applications visible on "mike" are distributed over all other machines.

A second feature is that one logical display may have more than one screen; this is often used in CAD applications where a lot of information has to be displayed in parallel.

The figure also shows that in a multi-tasking environment an application can run on the machine most suitable for the job. Numeric applications may need a floating-point accelerator. If the application is very disk-intensive, it should be run on a mainframe. Other reasons for choosing a specific host for execution may be the desire to balance the load on different machines, or the dependency on a program that has not yet been ported to other machines. All these applications are controlled from a single display.

Portability

Until all computers have equal capabilities, portability of software will always be an issue. Two different aspects are involved in porting X applications, namely the portability of the X Window System itself and the portability of application programs which use it for their interface. The more programs there are which use the X Window System the less important is the portability of the system itself compared with all the applications.

Portability of the X Window System really centres on two parts of the system: the library used on the client side and the server itself. The client's library (called Xlib) is written in C and is not difficult to port when the host has access to one of the common network protocols mentioned above (even mainframes have them these days). When the Xlib has been ported, a program can at least open a connection to another machine and route its output to this display (this would be sufficient for a mainframe).

The most difficult part to port is the X server itself, because it has to cope with any idiosyncracies of the display hardware and must be optimized for speed. Because the server has to hide specialities of the hardware as much as possible, it has to do some really complicated work. Implementing an optimized server is now often taken care of by the hardware manufacturer.

To make porting the server easier, the X designers have chosen to implement only simple graphic primitives on which more powerful libraries (such as GKS or PHIGS) can be built. Bearing in mind today's common hardware, the primitives mainly deal with bitmaps. In addition you can draw text, points, lines and arcs. Coordinates are specified in pixels, because geometric transformations are currently better handled by backend number crunchers.

The design of the primitives was also influenced by the problem of network bandwidth, i.e. sending a request with a large number of parameters requires too much time. As a solution most of the possible request parameters are already stored in the server and can be referenced by IDs. The resulting programming style is rather different from working directly with memory-mapped displays.

Another design decision your program has to deal with is the absence of a guaranteed display memory. Because there may be many different windows stacked on top of one another, storing the contents of all windows in the server can easily exceed the memory capacity of virtually all display workstations. Therefore every X application must be always be capable of refreshing the contents of its windows on demand, if, for example, it is uncovered by dragging another window away. To improve performance you can set hints to save the bitmap under a pop-up window ("save under") or to store the contents of a window ("backing store"); but these hints can be safely ignored by the server if it does not have enough memory available.

These decisions make it possible to design a simple terminal which understands the X protocol and works as a standalone X server. These *X terminals* may well replace the traditional ASCII terminal in the near future.

The X design ensures that parts of a program which are dependent on the display hardware are properly handled in the X server. Since the code for the user interface in a highly interactive application may easily account for more than a half of the total size, the X Window System solves a large part of your porting problems.

However, not all hardware dependencies can be hidden by the X server. One prominent example is the colour capability of the display hardware. If your application requires colour as part of its functionality (and not only as a discrimination aid), you have to decide whether and how this functionality can be implemented in monochrome.

Window Hierarchy

Traditionally, window systems are targeted at managing overlapping windows belonging to different applications. The number of these windows is usually fairly small (usually a few dozen for a large screen). X has extended the meaning of "window" to mean rectangular subparts which are regarded as full-featured windows—following the motto "windows are cheap" (although you will see in a later chapter that nothing is free). This can easily lead to every button being a separate window. Figure 1.12 illustrates such a situation.

Windows and subwindows (or *children*) are arranged in a hierarchical structure with each window having exactly one parent. Programmers usually call this a *tree*. The window hierarchy plays an important role in X and also in Motif, because the purpose of a window and its associated code depends on its position in the hierarchy.

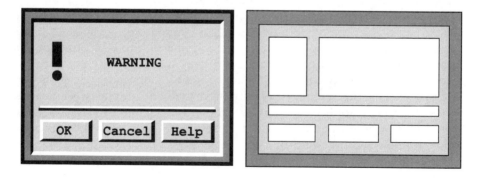

Figure 1.12: Children of a window. Their purpose is to partition the code so that a small piece of code is independently responsible for each window.

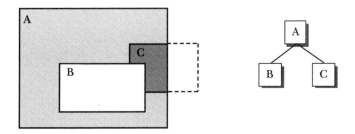

Figure 1.13: Clipping and hiding. On the right the window hierarchy is shown, with B and C being children of A. C is clipped by A and partly hidden by B. B and C hide parts of their parent.

A child window can never be visible outside its parent—otherwise the output of one application could not be restricted to the area of its topmost window. In computer graphics this operation is known as *clipping* (Figure 1.13). To be visible at all, a window must hide the contents of its parent underneath. A parent overlapping one of its children would be meaningless, because the child may not be visible outside its parent and is hidden inside it.

As a consequence, only siblings may overlap one another. Siblings are stacked in a strict order, i.e. if A overlaps a part of B, then B may not overlap another part of A because that would "twist" the sheets. The normal overlapping of main windows results from a root window covering the whole screen. All applications have a direct child of the root window as their main application window.

Extending window principles to a whole hierarchy has been very successful, partly because this enables the implementation to deal with only a small number of general structures whose correctness can be more easily checked. The main reason, though, is that it facilitates *object-oriented* design.

The term "object-oriented" is explained in more detail in the next chapter. It is a very important principle which allows large programs to be constructed from simple pieces with clear separation. For the window hierarchy this means that you can concentrate on programming one window at a time because the X Window System limits interaction with other windows (you have local coordinates inside your window, you cannot write outside the window, nobody writes into your window, you can move the window relative to its parent etc.).

You may even take somebody else's "pre-programmed" windows, set some suitable parameters for them, such as the colour you want, and let the system work. This is what you usually do with Motif. A more exact description follows in Chapter 2.

No Policy

Another design goal of the X Window System was to provide mechanism and not policy. This is an important reason for its success throughout the whole industry, because everyone can use X to create a particular corporate look.

There is no special "X look". Inside your windows you can draw what you want, while on the outside, the window manager, which may be substituted as desired, takes control. Motif applications perform much more consistently when working with the Motif window manager, but at the same time applications written with other toolkits may run on the same screen if necessary.

Motif has a characteristic look, and this is implemented by the toolkit described in the next section.

1.4 The Motif Toolkit

The toolkit of "pre-programmed windows" is the central feature of Motif. It supplies the base elements from which user interfaces can be built. The toolkit can be separated into three different layers, each supported by a separate library. The three layers fit within a larger multi-layer model of user interface programming as shown in Figure 1.14.

The lowest level in this model is the device protocol that talks to different hardware devices, in this case the X protocol. The X library of basic window systems functions, called Xlib, comes next. The Xlib is a portable interface layer which a programmer can safely use, but it is rather low-level and not very convenient to use.

The next three layers constitute the Motif toolkit. It is based on the *X Toolkit Intrinsics*, a standard library of routines to implement different interface objects called *widgets*. The Intrinsics are a part of X. The Motif widgets, the

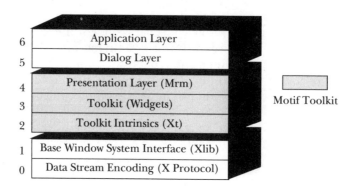

Figure 1.14: Layer model of user interface programming. Layers 2–4 constitute the Motif toolkit.

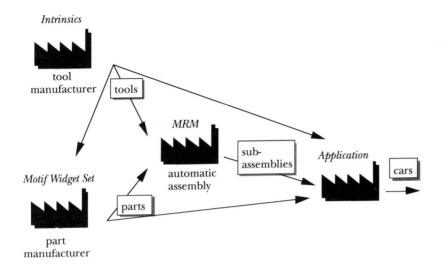

Figure 1.15: Manufacturing analogy of the Motif toolkit.

largest part of the toolkit, are built on top of the Intrinsics and define the actual types of objects available. The top layer of the Motif toolkit is the *Motif Resource Manager* (MRM), which allows widget descriptions to be read in at run-time. It constitutes the presentation layer because it allows the presentation details such as placement, fonts, colours etc. to be separated from the program functionality. The MRM is optional and only used in conjunction with the UIL.

The layer above the Motif toolkit deals with dialogs. The term "dialog" is used in a slightly different sense here from in the rest of the book, where a dialog denotes a temporarily appearing window. In this context, a dialog means a complete interaction sequence. In the dialog layer you should be able to describe interaction sequences in a high-level format. This layer is not currently addressed by Motif. At the top of the stack you find the application program.

It is not easy to understand the differences between the three layers of the Motif toolkit at this point. The differences can be made somewhat clearer by means of an analogy. The analogy is taken from the automobile industry and illustrated in Figure 1.15.

To manufacture cars a company buys parts and assembles them. In the same way you, as a programmer, take Motif widgets as parts and assemble an application program with them. The car company not only buys parts, but also manufactures some itself. In the same way you can create your own widgets if you want. The central layer of the toolkit can be compared to a manufacturer supplying parts (widgets) to the final assembly line (programmer).

In order to manufacture parts, the supplier needs machine tools. These are, in turn, supplied by another special manufacturer. This is analogous to the

Toolkit Intrinsics, which supply mechanisms to build widgets. The services of the tool manufacturer (the Intrinsics) can be used by the part manufacturer (the Motif toolkit) and the car manufacturer (the application programmer).

In the factory of the future the assembly lines will be far more flexible than today. They will be automatically constructed from the design input of the engineers. In the same way the Motif Resource Manager creates subassemblies of widgets, instructed by a textual description of the desired structure.

You should not take this analogy too far, however, because it is inaccurate concerning the details. But it may serve as a rough guideline until the details become clearer during the next chapters.

The three layers of the Motif toolkit will now be examined in a little more detail.

X Toolkit Intrinsics

The X Toolkit Intrinsics are a library of C routines on which a toolkit can be built. The interface of this library is standardized by the X Consortium as a part of the X Window System. Following the X design decision, the Intrinsics do not define any visible behaviour. Instead they define the routines with which the programmer can create and manipulate interface objects called *widgets*.

A large part of this book (Chapters 2 and 3) deals with widgets in general before the specific Motif widgets are discussed. As there are other toolkits built on the Intrinsics, this part of the book is not only relevant to Motif, but also to the X Window System in general.

If you have never come across it before, the concept of a widget as an active interface object will not be very meaningful. You will gain greater understanding in the next chapters, so please read on if you have difficulties during

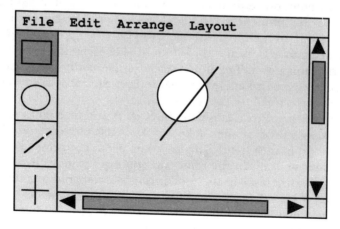

Figure 1.16a: Sample main window without the window manager decoration.

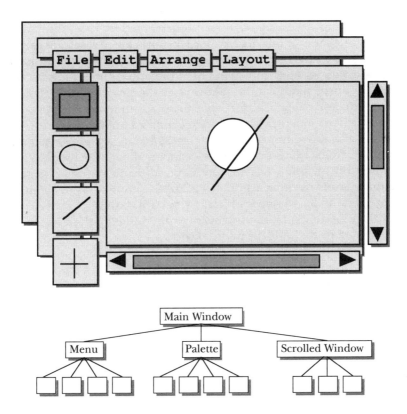

Figure 1.16b: Anatomy of the sample main window and the corresponding window hierarchy.

the first reading.

As already mentioned, X arranges its windows in a hierarchy. Figure 1.16 shows a typical application screen dissected into its window constituents and the resulting hierarchy. This is a simplified picture as there are actually more (invisible) windows involved.

Every window has some functionality associated with it. It has a specific size and location, specific contents, and reacts to user actions (the buttons can be pressed to pull down a menu, the scroll bars can be dragged to scroll the text, you can enter text into the text window etc.). A window combined with its functionality, represented by some code and some status information, is called a *widget.*

At the start of your program you specify which widgets to include. For instance, your program first creates a main window widget, inserts a menu bar widget, two scroll bar widgets and a text widget, then inserts three button widgets into the menu bar. Afterwards your program waits for any user actions to happen. The widgets know how to draw themselves; you only have to specify some attributes (e.g. the width of the scroll bars, the text to be displayed in the button or the thickness of the shadow border drawn around several elements).

There are actually a lot of parameters (called *resource fields*) which can be specified for a widget, most of which affect the appearance (colour, shadows, fonts etc.). Resource fields can be specified by the program at widget creation and also outside in a *resource database* consulted at run-time. The resource database is a powerful mechanism to customize compiled applications.

Widgets also know how to handle *events*. Events are generated by the X server as notifications that something has happened, e.g. the user has pressed a mouse button or a window has been uncovered. Events are always generated with respect to some window, e.g. the window the mouse was in when the button was pressed, or the window which has been uncovered. These events are automatically dispatched by the Intrinsics to the widget belonging to the window and handled by the widget's internal code.

Your application program is only notified when intervention is really necessary. For instance, the buttons in a menu bar pop up a menu in response to a button being pressed (a button press event) without your program being explicitly involved. Only when a menu choice is selected does the menu widget call one of the program's routines (using a *callback*) to trigger the execution of the application command.

Figure 1.17 shows a simplified diagram of a widget's interfaces to the outside world.

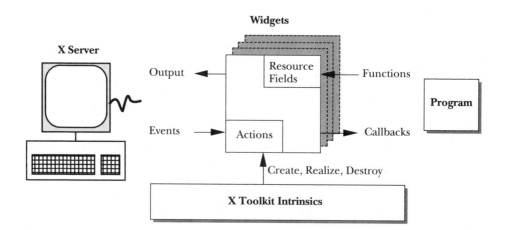

Figure 1.17: Simplified widget interfaces. A widget autonomously responds to events from the X server, triggering some internal actions. Actions may produce output to the window, changes in the internal state, and callbacks to the application. The application may intervene by setting resource fields and executing functions.

Motif Widget Set

Widgets of the same type are arranged into *classes* which share the same program code. For example, all buttons have the same code, but different attributes. The Motif widget set contains the code to implement several different classes of widgets.

The actual objects at run-time are called *instances* of a widget class. Each instance contains separate storage for its attributes, but shares the common code. For example, every button has a different string (to be displayed) associated with it. To be exact, it should always be specified whether a widget instance or a widget class is meant by the word "widget", although this will usually be clear from the context.

The widget classes are further classified in a *class hierarchy*. This is something very different from the window hierarchy! The purpose of the class hierarchy is to share common features between classes and not only between instances of a class. For example, Motif defines several classes of buttons (normal push buttons, buttons with submenus like the ones described above, toggle buttons etc.) which are all capable of displaying a text and drawing a border around it.

The attribute "label string" and the common code are defined in the superclass "label" of all buttons. The individual code for the button classes only has to define the special behaviour where the buttons are different. The attributes and the code are said to be *inherited* from the superclass.

Inheritance is a feature which defines an approach as object-oriented. It is a powerful mechanism for implementing larger programs, because it naturally organizes the code to facilitate debugging and maintenance. The inheritance mechanism between widget classes is rooted in the Intrinsics.

The functionality of the Motif widget classes is described in detail in Chapters 4–6. Figure 1.18 shows the complete class hierarchy of Motif but only gives you a general impression. To differentiate between class and widget hierarchy, class hierarchies are displayed from left to right, with a superclass to the left of its subclasses, while widget hierarchies use vertical orientation, with the parent on top of its children (as in Figure 1.16).

The Motif widget classes can be divided into three categories. *Simple widgets* (such as buttons) have no subparts and are the basic building blocks. *Composite widgets* such as the menu bar usually have other widgets as children. Most composite widgets' visual aspects are restricted to background and shadow borders. Instead they manage the layout (i.e. geometry in general) of their children. For example, the menu bar widget automatically places its buttons in a row with each button occupying the exact place it needs for the text. Therefore, you do not usually have to specify coordinates in Motif.

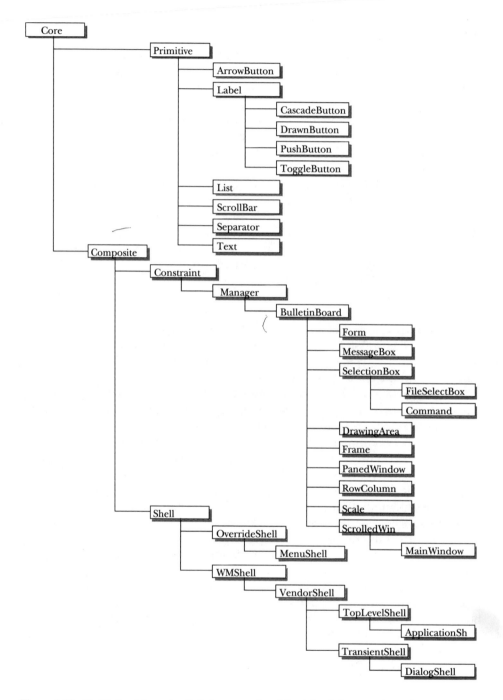

Figure 1.18: Motif class hierarchy. Subclasses, to the right, inherit features from their superclasses, to the left.

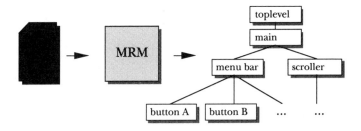

Figure 1.19: MRM operation. A UID file generated by the UIL compiler from an UIL document is read by the MRM to build a widget hierarchy.

Shell widgets are always invisible because they are always identical in size to their single child. The only purpose of shell widgets is to act as containers for other widgets. Shell widgets occupy the top positions in an application's window hierarchy and are the target of interactions with the window manager.

Motif Resource Manager

The functionality of an application program is to a certain degree independent of the widgets actually representing it. For example, a command invoked by a menu entry does not usually depend on the entry being in a certain menu and at a certain position or on the label of this entry.

Therefore it makes sense to define the widget hierarchy (the presentation aspects) outside the program. In Motif this is possible with the UIL. The compiled UIL specification is read in at program start-up to create the widgets.

Interpreting the external description file is the task of the *Motif Resource Manager* (MRM). You can choose whether you want to create the widgets at start-up or later on demand (if all widgets are not routinely used, e.g. some special dialogs or warnings). The MRM then calls the necessary Intrinsic routines to create the widgets with the parameters extracted from the UIL specification.

The compiled hierarchy description is contained in a user interface database (UID) file. The UID file may also contain symbolic constants whose values can be used by the application. On the other hand the UIL description may refer to symbolic constants that are defined by the application (such as the addresses of callback procedures). Before the hierarchy is created the application is responsible for defining these constants through the MRM (see Figure 1.19).

Chapter 2

Widget
Fundamentals

This chapter will give you a detailed introduction to the principles of the
X Toolkit Intrinsics. These are the mechanisms underlying all Motif widgets
(and other toolkits). They are not easy to comprehend, but once you are familiar with them you can apply them to all (current and future) widget classes.

Note that this chapter does not tell you about the actual programming
language calls used to invoke the mechanisms—there are simply too many
technical details and these would obscure the principles. If you want to start
coding now you should skim this chapter and then start with Chapter 3. You are
advised, though, to read this chapter before you study the official reference
manuals or start any larger task.

2.1 Widgets as Active Objects

This section deals with the object-oriented aspects of the X Toolkit
Intrinsics. If you are new to object-oriented programming you should read this
section carefully, as some new terminology is introduced. Furthermore, the
subject deserves at least a book of its own, so only basic principles which apply
to the toolkit are explained here.

Purists should note that there are many places in the Intrinsics where
object-oriented principles are violated, partly because of portability concerns
and C restrictions, and partly because of time constraints. Please bear in mind
that a suboptimal solution is infinitely better than no solution at all.

- Widgets are active objects.

This statement implies two different facts: first, a widget is an *object* (in the sense of object-oriented programming, to be explained below) and, second, it is *active*—it can handle events without program intervention.

The term *"object-oriented"* has many meanings (and of course many more definitions). It usually implies some form of private data and a mechanism for inheritance. The latter term was briefly explained in the previous chapter. The first term refers to the *principle of information hiding.*

Information hiding has nothing to do with computer security (i.e. stealing private data). In principle data belonging to one object should not be directly accessible from the outside, but only through a defined interface. In this way you create an *abstract data type*, which is a type of object with some defined functions, which are the only possible functions applicable to this type.

Class and Instance

As noted in Chapter 1, a *class* is a description of objects to which the same functions may be applied, but which may differ in the values of their private data items. An *instance* of a class is a single object created according to this description. The term class is comparable to a type in conventional programming languages; the analogue of an instance is a variable.

Throughout this chapter the push button class will be used as an example. Push button widgets simulate the behaviour of physical push buttons on the screen. If the mouse button is pressed inside the button window, the button will darken and the shadows around make it appear depressed. If the mouse button is released again, an application-specific action is started. The button may carry a string or a bitmap as a label. Figure 2.1 illustrates the two button states.

There may be many buttons in your interface, possibly each with a different size or label but all sharing a common set of features.

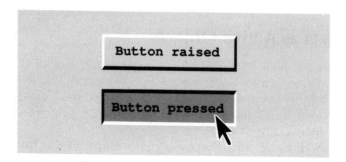

Figure 2.1: A push button in different states. The upper button shows the normal inactive state, while in the lower button the mouse button is pressed.

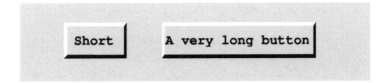

Figure 2.2: Buttons with automatic width calculation.

Every push button instance has a set of variables which influence the behaviour of this button. These are called *instance variables*, because they are separate for every instance. Examples of such variables are

- The string to be displayed in the button.

- The width of the shadow border in pixels.

- The colour of the button face.

- The width and length of the button rectangle.

Which instance variables are defined for an object is a property of its class. All buttons have the same instance variables, but their values are different for each button. For widgets, instance variables are called *resource fields*[1]. A widget's internal structure is comparable to a record in conventional programming languages.

Resource fields are the primary means to control the behaviour of widgets. As mentioned in the previous chapter they can also be set from outside the program through the resource database.

Information Hiding

Although the resource fields are internally declared as a record, you cannot access them directly in C (because of the principle of information hiding). Instead you must call a special function to read or write a value. The write function may execute some additional calculations and it can also disallow certain changes. Although this function has the same name for all widget classes its actual implementation depends on the class to which the widget belongs. In object-oriented terminology this function is called a *method* (see below).

For example, the width of a button usually depends on the string which is to be displayed in it. If you change the string, the width is automatically recalculated to enclose this string (see Figure 2.2). If the string and the width could be set directly in the record structure, you would have to maintain the consistency between the two values manually.

Internal variables also demonstrate how information hiding improves program modularity. Internal instance variables are derived from external ones

---

[1] Elsewhere they are also simply referred to as resources.

which are accessible as resource fields and are only stored for performance reasons.

For instance, a button needs *graphics contexts* for drawing. Graphics contexts are IDs of attribute bundles stored in the X server to reduce the number of parameters of primitive graphic requests. The parts of the graphics contexts like foreground and background colour, font and drawing mode are calculated from the externally accessible resource fields at button creation or whenever one of these resource fields changes.

Allowing only controlled access to the instance variables of an object is called the *principle of information hiding*. Its intention is to reduce the amount of possible interference between different objects (the amount of coupling) to make large tasks more manageable.

One advantage of information hiding is that the implementation of an object may be changed without invalidating all programs accessing this object. In Motif, performance is improved by a very clever way of sharing graphics contexts between different buttons because these are often the same[1]. Because you do not have direct access to the graphics context your programs are not affected by this change and can take immediate advantage of the improved performance.

Loose coupling between objects reduces programming errors. For example, if a program accesses an internal variable, the programmer might forget about this case and change its usage. Information hiding produces a much more concise definition of the interface because everything which is not explicitly allowed is forbidden.

The disadvantage of this principle is that it is usually less efficient than direct access, because each access must be checked and some sorts of optimization are not allowed. However, this is usually only noticeable when the interface has been badly designed. With a good interface the performance can be enhanced with all sorts of caching techniques which even a novice programmer can take advantage of. In most cases the improved stability is far more important than reduced performance, because a usable program is always better than a fast one which has bugs.

The principle of information hiding can be regarded as a new phase in the history of abstraction mechanisms for programming languages. This history is illustrated in Figure 2.3.

In the "dark ages", programs were "structured" by goto statements (also known as spaghetti code). The "advantages" of this approach should be sufficiently clear by now.

In the next phase procedures were used to define new commands on which, in turn, more abstract ones could be built. This is known as *procedure abstraction*.

---

[1]Motif 1.1 employs further clever methods of internal caching.

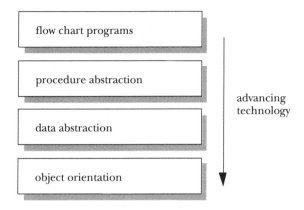

Figure 2.3: Phases of abstraction mechanisms in programming languages.

Information hiding belongs to the phase of data abstraction, where data are enclosed together with some functions to form a new entity called an *abstract data type* (ADT). This approach is taken by modern programming languages such as Ada and Modula-2.

You will now enter the next phase, where data abstraction is combined with inheritance. This is object-oriented programming.

Inheritance

The use of inheritance distinguishes object-oriented programming from programming with abstract data types. Inheritance is used in defining classes which have something in common with other classes.

In Motif not all features of push buttons are defined in the push button class itself. Instead there exists a class of labels, which you can view as unpressable buttons, i.e. they may have the same appearance but are insensitive to mouse clicks. Figure 2.4 shows such a label.

Labels and push buttons have many resource fields in common, e.g. the label string and the margin widths around the text. They also have some functionality in common, e.g. the code to draw the button or to resize it according to the text.

To share these facilities, push buttons are declared as a *subclass* of labels. A subclass inherits all the resource fields of its superclass and all its code. In addi-

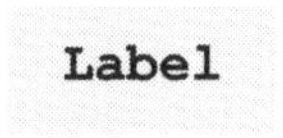

`Label`

Figure 2.4: A label widget displaying a text.

tion, it can define new resource fields and add code for new features. For example, push buttons define a new resource field for the colour the button shows if depressed (to enhance the shadow effect).

A subclass can also override some features of the superclass, i.e. redefine a procedure or change the default value of a resource field.

There are important advantages to this approach. Common features can be shared and are maintained in an appropriate place. The shorter code is better structured and can be controlled more easily. The code is split into separate units according to meaningful categories. This especially pays off in larger programming projects.

In theory it should also be easy to reuse code because a specialization of an existing class can be implemented with little effort as a subclass. If you need a special sort of button with an unusual behaviour you should be able to implement it easily as a button subclass. Regrettably, owing to the technical difficulties of implementing a usable inheritance mechanism in C, this is not so easy with the X Toolkit Intrinsics. There are many rules which you have to obey manually (e.g. writing special header files). You have to wait for an implementation of the Intrinsics in a real object-oriented language such as C++ to make this easier.

Methods

Instead of simply inheriting a procedure from its superclass, a class can also redefine this procedure. This results in a procedure whose implementation may differ according to the class of its argument.

The procedure for setting resource fields, called *SetValues*, is defined for all classes. Because every class has a different set of resource fields, the procedure must check different conditions and calculate different dependencies for each class. The implementation of the *SetValues* procedure function may thus vary from class to class depending on the class of the widget argument. Such a function or procedure is called a *method*.

Figure 2.5 demonstrates how to call a procedure that varies with the class of its argument.

A subclass may vary the implementation of a method of its superclass in different ways. If it inherits the method, the implementation is simply the same for widgets of both classes. For instance, if a subclass does not define any new resource fields the *SetValues* method can be inherited without modifications.

A subclass can also completely override the method of its superclass. This is meaningless for *SetValues* because the subclass inherits some resource fields which must be dealt with. Therefore the *SetValues* method is *chained* (a third possibility) for all superclasses, i.e. the corresponding procedure for every subclass is called in the sequence which handles the corresponding resource fields.

The same chaining effect can be achieved if the method in a subclass explicitly calls the method of the superclass at an appropriate moment.

method1 (object1, ...)   function (object1, ...)

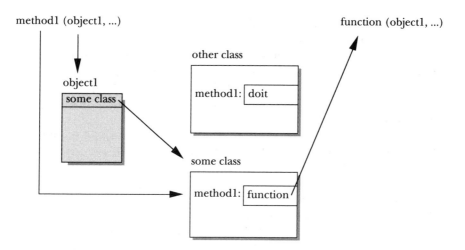

Figure 2.5: Method dispatching. The object used as the first parameter to a method points to its instance variables, where another pointer refers to the object's class. The class record contains pointers to all procedures available as method implementations. A certain method is defined as an offset into the class record. Depending on the contents of the class record the appropriate procedure will be called.

All these strategies are implemented in the X Toolkit Intrinsics by using procedure pointers. Every method a class supports has a pointer to its implementation. In this way inheritance simply means copying the pointer to the subclass. The pointer can be replaced by another one and chaining can be implemented by calling all pointers in the chain. A subclass can call the method of a superclass by calling the relevant pointer.

If a method is called from the outside, it looks up the pointer in the class definition of its argument and calls it. Therefore the overhead is tolerable.

Event Handling

The previous pages explained the meaning of "object-oriented" in the term "active object". In this term "active" means that widgets can not only be controlled by the program, but can also react autonomously to events from the X server.

There are a number of different event types signalling different situations. Each event is directed to a window. Every widget has an associated window, and events addressed to this window are handled by that widget.

As mentioned in Chapter 1, it is the responsibility of the X client to maintain the contents of its window. For that purpose the X server sends a message (an *Expose event*) to the client whenever a part of the window needs redrawing. The Expose event is automatically handled by the widget by calling an internal redraw procedure that redisplays the destroyed part of the window using X drawing primitives. As a result, maintaining the window contents requires no intervention by the application program.

Other events may cause an internal state change to the widget, i.e. some of the instance variables are changed in response to the event. For example, when the mouse button is pressed with the pointer inside a push button window, the button marks itself "armed". Without application intervention, the push button redraws itself "depressed".

If intervention is required, the application can be notified by means of a *callback*. A callback is a procedure that the application registers with the widget for it to be activated in a certain situation. For each supported callback a widget class defines a separate *callback list* where procedures may be registered.

For example, the push button widget class defines a callback list for button activation. The application registers a procedure in this callback list to be called when the user has pressed and released the mouse button inside the push button window (it is the primary purpose of a push button to trigger a command of the application). You can register more than one procedure in a callback list.

By default callback lists are empty. For example, the push button widget class defines an additional callback which is activated when the button changes to the armed state. Few applications will be interested in this situation; no notification occurs if the callback list remains empty.

2.2 Widgets as Windows

This section discusses the relation between widgets and X windows. Every widget has one corresponding X window. A window is a rectangular region on the screen used as a coordinate reference and clipping region for output as well as a reference for input.

Window Hierarchy

All windows on a screen are arranged in a hierarchy with a single root (see Figure 2.6). The root window covers the whole screen and usually only displays a background. It cannot be moved or resized.

The direct child windows of the root are called *top-level windows*. Every application must have one or more top-level windows. Top-level windows are controlled by the window manager. Inside the top-level windows an application creates child windows which are controlled by only that application. Child windows cannot influence other applications because all children are clipped by their parents (clipping was briefly mentioned in the previous chapter).

However, the previous description is oversimplified. To make room for the decoration, the window manager inserts windows of its own into the hierarchy

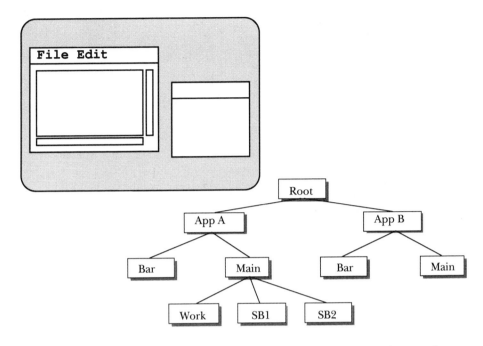

Figure 2.6: Window hierarchy. Here are two applications, whose top-level windows are direct children of the root window.

(between the root window and the application top-level windows). This process is called *reparenting* (see Figure 2.7).

After reparenting, top-level windows are no longer top-level. However, they continue to be called top-level windows because the window manager tries to make reparenting transparent to applications by intercepting configuration requests for the top-level windows and by executing them on the decoration window instead. The only noticeable difference should be that the window manager processing may take time and the application has to wait until the request is processed. This problem is taken care of by *shell widgets,* which are classes designed for top-level windows.

Except for a slight complication caused by pop-up windows (explained below), the widget hierarchy exactly mirrors the window hierarchy, i.e. composite widgets have a window which is the parent of all the child widgets' windows.

Window/Widget Classification

The different widget classes can be roughly classified by purpose according to their position in the window hierarchy (do not confuse the window

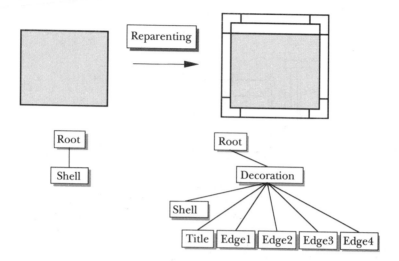

Figure 2.7: Reparenting. At the bottom the window hierarchies are shown. The shell window is the top-level window of an application as a direct child of the root window. The decoration window introduced between the shell and the root window has five children.

hierarchy among widget instances with the subclass hierarchy between widget classes—these are completely different things).

As already mentioned, top-level windows are maintained by *shell widgets.* Shell widgets have no display purpose but only serve as contacts for the window manager.

Shell widgets are actually a special kind of *composite widget,* with only one child widget. Composite widgets in general can have many children. They not only control the window surrounding their children, but perform additional manager tasks like geometric layout (discussed below).

The end points of the widget hierarchy are occupied by *primitive widgets,* which have no children and display most of the visible information. Figure 2.8 shows the role of the three widget categories in a typical application.

The main window of this application actually consists of two widgets, a composite widget and a shell. The shell is invisible because the composite window has the same size. Although this may be a "waste of windows" it is a good example of separating functionality in different widget classes. It is characteristic of shell widgets that they are always exactly hidden by their single child.

The menu bar is another composite window. It is an example of how a composite widget manages the geometry of its children. The button children of the menu bar are automatically positioned and adjusted to the same height. The application need not and cannot change the geometry of the buttons.

A composite widget can also manage composite children. For example, the main window widget always makes the menu bar the same width as itself,

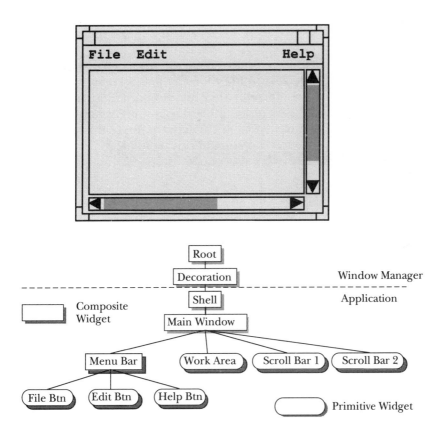

Figure 2.8: Role of widget classes in a main application window. The widget hierarchy for the window at the top is shown below it.

regardless of how the user resizes the window. A resizing process started by dragging the window borders is handed down from the window manager to the shell widget, which in turn resizes the main window widget to make both equal in size. The main window widget in turn resizes the menu bar appropriately. You will learn more about this geometry management process in Section 2.5.

The buttons inside the menu bar (called *cascade buttons* because they can activate a pull-down menu), the scroll bars and the text window are primitive widgets because they have no further components.

Shells and Pop-Up Windows

Shell widgets introduce the only situation where window and widget hierarchies do not coincide. Shell widgets possess independent top-level windows; therefore the window hierarchy is not a tree but a *forest*. Widgets, however, are forced into a single hierarchy. As a result an arbitrary parent may be chosen for a shell widget.

Shell widgets as children work differently from normal children. For instance, they do not participate in the geometry management process of their parent, which is not surprising since they are not contained in their parent. Shells are referred to as *pop-up children.* Because no management is required, even primitive widgets may have pop-up children. In future the term "children" will not include pop-up children unless explicitly mentioned.

Shell widgets can be further subdivided into three categories with different purposes:

- *Top-level shells* are the main windows of an application. An application can have multiple top-level shells.

- *Dialog shells* are used for top-level windows which normally exist only temporarily and depend on another application shell (typically dialog boxes).

- *Pop-up shells* are transient in nature. They are ignored by the window manager and are typically used for pop-up menus.

If the user presses the mouse button in one of the cascade buttons in a menu bar, a pull-down menu is displayed (see Figure 2.9). The pull-down menu pane is a separate top-level window because it is not guaranteed to fit in the main window if that is made very small. A menu which is mostly invisible owing to clipping would not be very useful.

The pull-down menu is an example of a *modal* pop-up widget, because you cannot do anything outside the menu until it is popped down when you release

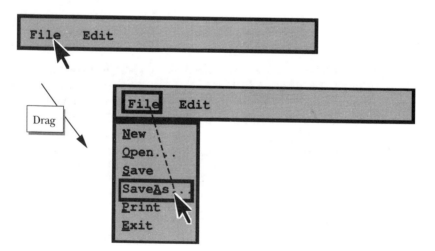

Figure 2.9: A pull-down menu activated by pressing the mouse button in a menu bar is traversable while the button is held down.

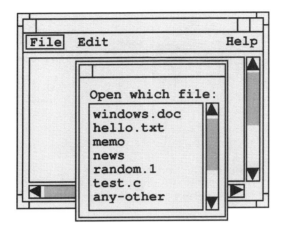

Figure 2.10: Application with a dialog. The dialog window is independently moveable and resizable.

the button. It also receives no decoration as this would not be useful. This functionality is achieved by enclosing the menu pane in a pop-up shell.

To illustrate the use of a dialog shell, imagine the user has chosen a menu entry requiring some parameter to be entered (see Figure 2.10). The dialog box is enclosed in a dialog shell, producing another top-level window.

The dialog shell also receives the window manager decoration. The dialog window can be moved or resized independently from the main window. The icon button from the decoration is missing because the dialog is always iconified together with the main window.

A dialog may have different modalities. It is frequently *application modal,* i.e. the main window is inactive until you have finished with the dialog. You can work with other applications during this time or iconify this application for later use. If the dialog is *system modal,* you cannot work with any other application until the dialog disappears. This should only be used in extreme situations which require exclusive attention (such as a disk failure). You will rarely use system modal dialogs in a normal application.

The dialog may also be *modeless,* i.e. you can also work with the main window while the dialog is visible. You should design your application this way, because a user may wish to scroll the contents of the main window until he can fill in a field in the dialog, for example. Although modeless operation is desirable, it is sometimes difficult to implement.

X Window Properties

Some properties of windows in X are independent of widgets. Remember that windows are a basic X mechanism and widgets are built on top of them. A

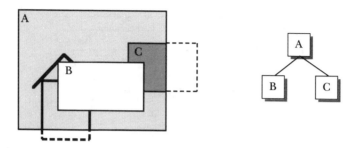

Figure 2.11: Clipping in a window. On the right you see the window hierarchy for the situation on the left. Drawing operations only affect visible parts of a window. The picture drawn into A does not overwrite B and does not extend past A's borders. The contents of C are clipped by A.

window has a number of attributes (such as size, location, background etc.). In order to minimize net traffic the attributes are contained in a structure resident in the X server and not in your application program. You only have an ID to refer to a window.

A window has two general properties regarding output: it clips its contents and serves as a relative coordinate system.

The clipping property has already been mentioned in the previous chapter. Clipping affects both drawing operations in the window and the visibility of any child windows. It is illustrated in Figure 2.11.

Clipping drawing operations simplifies programs because they do not have to check the current window size. A simple program can always draw the contents to the maximum size of the window, with X clipping this drawing to the current size and the area not covered by children.

Clipping of child windows can also be used to implement a scrolling facility. If the child is larger than its parent, the parent only serves as a clipping region because its contents will never be visible. The child can now be moved relative to the parent to display the desired area (Figure 2.12), requiring that the origin of a child can be moved to negative coordinates. Simple scrolled windows in Motif use this feature.

Drawing and origin coordinates are measured relative to the window's upper left corner (see Figure 2.13). Coordinates are counted in pixels because X assumes most displays have square pixels and delegates any other transformations to the clients. Relative coordinates facilitate writing independent drawing procedures for windows because it is not necessary to consider where the window has been moved.

The purpose of a window regarding input is to serve as a reference for dispatching events. X events are always addressed to a specific window—the one which should be most concerned with the event.

For example, if a mouse button is clicked, an event is sent to the window which is visible under the mouse position. Many other types of events may be

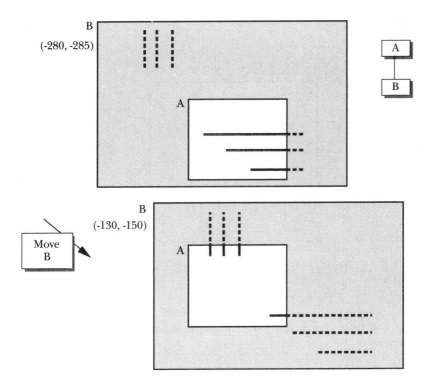

Figure 2.12: Scrolling by clipping. On the right you see that B is a child window of A. On the left you see the (negative) position of B relative to A. By moving B in this way any part of B can be scrolled into view.

generated—see Section 2.5 for details. Another example concerns enter/leave events which are generated when the mouse button crosses a window border. In this way a window can always stay informed regardless of whether the mouse is inside or not.

The events generated for a window are handled by the corresponding widget. A widget must explicitly request the types of events it wants to receive. If a widget is not interested in enter/leave events, the X server does not send them. Events not requested by a child window can be redirected inside the X server to the parent.

A window can be in two different states. When a window is created, the attributes structure is allocated inside the server and the corresponding ID is generated. Because this is a relatively time-consuming process, windows are often created at program start-up although they will only be displayed later (e.g. dialog windows). If a window already exists, it need only be *mapped,* which is much faster. A window can be *unmapped* again to disappear from the screen.

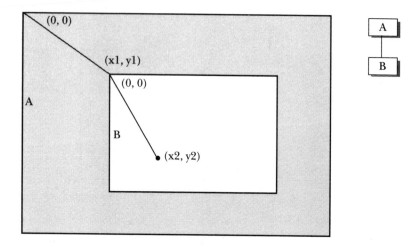

Figure 2.13: Relative coordinates. Positions in a window are measured in pixels relative to the upper left corner.

Mapping and unmapping are especially useful for pop-up menus to minimize pop-up latency.

Widget States

The picture becomes more complicated when widgets are considered. A widget has different states of its own in addition to the mapped/unmapped state of its window.

Usually, on widget creation the corresponding window is not immediately created at the same time. The window creation is delayed until the complete widget hierarchy is established because of the geometry management process.

The widget hierarchy must be created from top to bottom (i.e. from the top-level shell) because a widget must know its parent. Parentage cannot be changed later except by destroying the widget and creating an identical new one. On the other hand, a composite widget cannot determine its size before all children exist, because geometry management tries to maintain the smallest reasonable size enclosing all children.

If the window is created together with the widget (remember the window attributes reside in the server), its size would have to be changed several times during the geometry management process, i.e. each time a new child is created. This would cause excessive and completely unnecessary net traffic. To avoid such traffic, the windows are created after all sizes are determined.

A widget is said to be *realized* if the corresponding window has been created. In addition to the mapped/unmapped distinction the unrealized initial setting introduces a third widget state (see Figure 2.14).

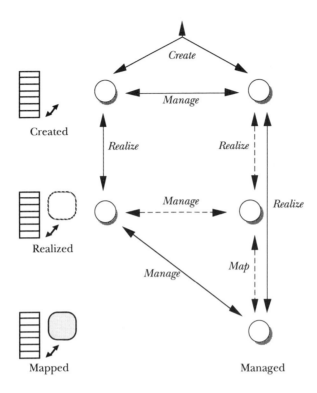

Figure 2.14: Widget states. The dashed variation is introduced when a widget is not mapped-when-managed. Only in this case can a widget separately map its own window.

To complicate this simple picture there is an additional state to consider. Usually composite widgets *manage* all their children. A managed child is considered in all geometry calculations.

Because widget creation is also a time-consuming process, the unmanaged state is used to make widgets temporarily invisible without destroying them. As mentioned above, a widget's window can also be unmapped to make it invisible, but as the widget is further included in geometry calculations, the space it occupied is not reused and leaves the parent's background visible.

Consider some buttons arranged in a column like a menu. If one of the widgets is unmanaged, the layout is recalculated and the box shrinks. If the widget's window is unmapped instead, the geometry is not recalculated and the button simply disappears (see Figure 2.15).

The managed state is also shown in Figure 2.14. The managed state is in principle independent of the others, but not all combinations are useful.

You usually want all your widgets to be managed and visible. To produce this situation follow these steps:

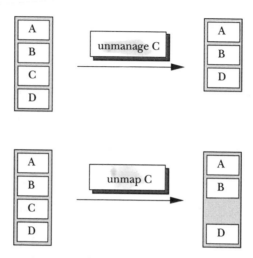

Figure 2.15: Making widgets invisible. If a widget is unmanaged, the visual place is reclaimed. In both cases the internal widget data structures remain intact.

- Create the widgets in the managed state so that geometry calculations are performed.
- Realize the top-level widget. This realizes all children down the tree. All widgets have a mapped-when-managed flag. If this flag is set the windows are also automatically mapped.

There are two cases where you need to change these steps. The first case applies when a widget is temporarily invisible. You either create and realize the widget and manage it later on demand, or create the widget in the managed state but with the mapped-when-managed flag reset and map the window later.

The second case is really an optimization. If a composite widget has many children and you create all children as managed, new geometry calculations take place every time a new child is created. In such a situation you first create all children unmanaged, then manage them (in one call) so that geometry calculations take place only once.

Gadgets

The widget creation phase described above usually takes place at program start-up. You may even create widgets which are only displayed later (such as menus and dialog boxes) to make them appear quickly if needed. Window and widget creation take some time because sizable structures must be allocated, initialized and maintained.

To help alleviate the problem Motif also has *gadgets*. Gadgets are widgets without a window. This sounds contradictory at first because a widget needs a window for many purposes. In the case of gadgets a part of the X server's work is assigned to the composite widget managing the gadgets. The total amount of work is reduced because the X server's operation is necessarily more general than the closer interaction between manager and gadget.

Substituting gadgets for widgets is especially efficient where many simple widgets are used, such as buttons in menus. To ease the transition, the Motif gadget classes mirror the functionality of their widget class counterparts as closely as possible. Motif only implements primitive gadgets, and not all primitive widget classes have a gadget equivalent. This prevents hierarchies of gadgets, which would be more difficult to handle. There is also no compelling reason to use manager gadgets, because primitive widgets normally account for the larger part of the number of widgets.

To handle gadgets correctly, all composite Motif widgets are prepared to dispatch events to their gadget children. Because gadgets have no windows, the X server sends events to their parent. The managing parent decides if the events were meant for a gadget (by calculating whether the event occurred inside that gadget) and notifies the respective gadget of it.

On the other hand gadgets have to respect the rectangle assigned to them because no automatic clipping is provided. Gadget clipping must therefore be implemented by appropiate programming.

There are some functions of the X Toolkit Intrinsics which will not work with gadgets because of the missing window. However, you can always use gadgets where their functionality is sufficient, as in menus and dialogs.

2.3 Resource Fields

This section on resource fields is one of the most important for you if you want to program with Motif, because you will spend a lot of time figuring out how to make the various widgets behave as desired. Nearly all of a widget's behaviour is determined by the values of its resource fields. (Note: in the rest of the book the term widget also includes gadgets if not explicitly stated otherwise.)

There are several methods for setting resource fields. One of the programmer's tasks is to decide which method works best for a given widget and field. Usually you have to use more or less all methods, so you have to learn them all.

As mentioned in the previous chapter, resource fields are externally visible instance variables, i.e. there is a one-to-one correspondence between externally visible and internal fields. But, according to the principle of information hiding, this could be implemented differently in the future so you should not rely on this fact.

Which resource fields exist for a widget is defined in the widget's class. A class inherits all the resource fields of its superclass, i.e. it contains all of them

and possibly defines more. The inheritance feature is also noticeable in the
Motif reference manual where only new resource fields are described in detail
for a widget class. Figure 2.16 lists all the resource fields of the label widget class
as an example.

The resource fields of a class are defined in a structure called a *resource list.*
Although you do not usually use this structure in your program, its contents are
an important part of the class interface. The contents of a resource list entry are
outlined in Figure 2.17.

The first part of an entry is the name of the resource field used to access
its value. The next part is a class name. However, this class name has nothing to
do with widget classes. It refers to an abstract class of fields. A class of resource
fields only exists through its name, which is mentioned by all associated fields.
For example there are several resource fields which mention the class name
Background, all of which denote some kind of background colour for different
regions. The class name specified in the resource list is only used to allow a
single resource specification to refer to a group of resource fields. For information on how to specify resources see below.

The next part of the entry is the name of a *resource type*, specifying the
value representation. The resource type is used for automatic conversion between string values and values of resource fields (also explained below).

The last two parts specify a default value the resource field uses as the
initial value when no other specification for this field is found. The default

Core class fields	Primitive class fields	Label class fields
XmNaccelerators	XmNbottomShadowColor	XmNaccelerator
XmNancestorSensitive	XmNbottomShadowPixmap	XmNacceleratorText
XmNbackground	XmNforeground	XmNalignment
XmNbackgroundPixmap	XmNhelpCallback	XmNfontList
XmNborderColor	XmNhighlightColor	XmNlabelInsensitivePixmap
XmNborderPixmap	XmNhighlightOnEnter	XmNlabelPixmap
XmNborderWidth	XmNhighlightPixmap	XmNlabelString
XmNcolormap	XmNhighlightThickness	XmNlabelType
XmNdepth	XmNshadowThickness	XmNmarginBottom
XmNdestroyCallback	XmNtopShadowColor	XmNmarginHeight
XmNheight	XmNtopShadowPixmap	XmNmarginLeft
XmNmappedWhenManaged	XmNtraversalOn	XmNmarginRight
XmNscreen	XmNunitType	XmNmarginTop
XmNsensitive	XmNuserData	XmNmarginWidth
XmNtranslations		XmNmnemonic
XmNwidth		XmNrecomputeSize
XmNx		XmNstringDirection
XmNy		

Figure 2.16: All resource fields of the label widget class. A number of fields are inherited from
the Core and Primitive classes.

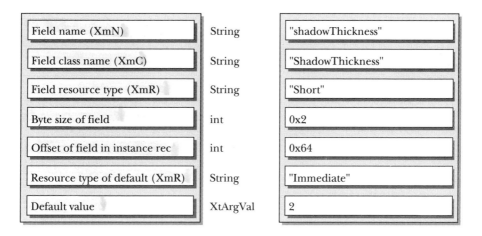

Field name (XmN)	String	"shadowThickness"
Field class name (XmC)	String	"ShadowThickness"
Field resource type (XmR)	String	"Short"
Byte size of field	int	0x2
Offset of field in instance rec	int	0x64
Resource type of default (XmR)	String	"Immediate"
Default value	XtArgVal	2

Figure 2.17: Format of a resource list entry, with an example entry on the right.

consists of a value and a resource type. If the type of the default value is different from the type of the field, an automatic conversion takes place.

Two further fields in the resource list entry specify an implementation-defined size and offset for the resource field. These fields are only used internally.

Access

The value of a resource field can only be accessed through a method, as direct access would violate the principle of information hiding. The two methods defined for this purpose (and, of course, for all widget classes) are *SetValues*, to set some resource values, and *GetValues*, to read them back.

Both methods take a widget (instance) and a parameter list of name/value pairs as arguments. The names in the parameter list denote the different fields you want to read or write, and the values are passed for writing or are returned when reading.

The *SetValues* method is under the control of the widget, i.e. the widget can decide which values are allowed. The widget may refuse to change a field and can calculate dependent values of internal or exported fields. It is possible for a value to remain unchanged although a new value was requested in the parameter list. The new value may also be a compromise between the old and the requested value. This most often happens with geometry values—if you specify a window size larger than the screen, the actual values will be adjusted to the maximum possible.

In some cases you receive warnings when specifying an invalid value; sometimes the request is simply ignored, although ideally this should not happen.

You must also take into account that fields may have been changed which were not specified in the argument list but were dependent on one of the arguments. Changing the displayed string of a label or button usually changes the button's size, too.

Changing the value of a resource field can trigger other reactions. Through geometry management the size of a parent widget may change in response to a change in the child. Changing a value may also cause repainting of the window. In some cases even a callback may be activated (see Section 2.4 for an explanation of callbacks).

Initialization

In contrast to local variables in most programming languages, all resource fields of a widget are initialized to a certain value when the widget is created. The initial values are acquired from three different sources according to the following priority list:

- Argument list of the creation procedure.

  The procedure for creating a widget also carries an argument list like *SetValues*. Values in this argument list override all other specifications.

- Resource database.

  All fields not explicitly mentioned in the program trigger a search for a value specification in the resource database. The resource database is a means of externally specifying resources for a program and is described in detail below.

- Internal default.

  Fields with no specified value are initialized to the internal default of the widget class, taken from the resource list. Some fields may have dynamically calculated defaults. For example, the shadow colours, which are needed to implement the so-called 3D-appearance, are automatically calculated to contrast correctly with the specified background colour.

As argument lists and defaults have already been described, only the resource database needs to be explained here.

Resource Database

As most of the resource fields in Motif deal with presentation aspects and thus are irrelevant to the program logic, they are better specified outside the program to make customization easier. A typical example concerns colour specifications, which are subject to personal preferences, environment dependencies (if each application has a different colour for recognition) or hardware differences (try light blue on a monochrome monitor).

Additionally, presentation specifications are usually similar for whole groups of widgets, e.g. "all buttons in this application shall have a three-pixel border shadow". To maintain consistency at all times, this requirement can be expressed in a single statement in the resource database.

The resource database may contain customization aspects for the following categories:

- User-specific (individual preferences).
- Display-specific (size and colour capabilities).
- Machine-specific (capacity limitations).

All these specifications are assembled from several different external files into an internal form at program start-up to form the resource database. The resource database resides in the program's address space (it is not a database on disk). The storage structure is optimized to allow fast access, because the database is queried for each resource field of each widget to be created. Although this sounds like a time-consuming operation, it is actually quite fast.

Resource Specification

The resource specifications to be compiled into the resource database are simply written as lines in a text file. Resource specifications are easily readable, but the powerful mechanism sometimes makes it difficult to understand the consequences of a combination of specifications..

The basic format of a resource entry is very simple: a resource field specification is followed by a value, separated by a colon. The resource field specification selects a resource field (or several) of one or more widgets. It is composed of three parts, the first two being optional:

- A program specifier, which restricts the validity of this line to one or more programs (if omitted, the line applies to all programs that have matching widgets).
- A widget specification, which identifies one or more widget instances.
- A field specification, which indicates a certain resource field.

This structure can be summarized in the following form (square brackets indicating optional elements):

[program-spec][widget-spec]field-name: value

The value is denoted as an unspecified sequence of characters until the end of the line and is automatically converted into its internal representation (see below).

Assuming your program is named "hello-world" and contains an application shell named "main" with a button named "pushme", you can set the width of the shadow border for this button to four pixels by using the following line:

hello-world.main.pushme.shadowThickness: 4

The names of your program and the widgets are specified in the program text and can be chosen arbitrarily. The name of the resource field is taken from the possible resource fields of the Motif widget classes.

The left hand side of this specification is called a complete *path*. Such a path can be illustrated using the widget tree of your application, augmented with the name of the program at the top and the names of all possible resource fields under each widget name. An abbreviated tree for the simple application with only a main shell and a button is illustrated in Figure 2.18.

If you collect the names on a straight route from the root (the program name) to any of the leaves and separate them with periods you get a full path. In this way you can uniquely address every widget and every field in your application. This is one of the reasons why a widget must have a fixed position in the hierarchy, otherwise it could not be addressed correctly from the outside.

If your program grows, it becomes more and more tedious to specify longer and longer path names. Therefore you can omit some widget names. This is indicated by an asterisk, replacing the period where names have been omitted. The following specification is equivalent to the one above:

hello-world*pushme.shadowThickness: 4

This is called *loose coupling* in contrast to *tight coupling* with a period. You can omit the widget names entirely, thus:

hello-world*shadowThickness: 4

This specification no longer only applies to a single widget; it addresses all widgets in your program which happen to have a resource field for the shadow thickness.

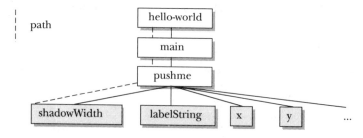

Figure 2.18: Augmented widget tree for the simple example. The resource fields of the first two widgets and most fields of the button are omitted.

If you omit even the program name, as in

*shadowThickness: 4

your specification affects all Motif programs (fortunately more specific entries can override this line; see below). Please note that you must have the name of a resource field at the end—otherwise it would not be clear which resource field to set (and you cannot set them all at once because they are not all integers).

Even if you specify a full path, you may address multiple widgets, because the widget names chosen in your program need not be unique. If you decide that *no one ever* needs to address a certain collection of widgets individually (e.g. buttons in a menu), they may all carry the same name. Naturally, identical widget names in different branches can be distinguished by their full path name.

Another way in which multiple widgets can be addressed is by means of *class names*. Each named component in the path name also has a class name. The class name of your program can be freely chosen like its name and is encoded in the program. The class names of the widgets are defined by Motif and are fixed for every different widget class. The class names of the resource fields are specified in the resource list in the widget class definition.

Class names are introduced to make possible the simple specification of resource fields for whole groups of objects of the same class. Because class names and instance names cannot be distinguished per se (because they are both strings), the convention that instance names start with a lowercase and class names with an uppercase letter has been established.

For example, to set the foreground colour of all invocations of the "xterm" program, you specify the following:

XTerm*foreground: blue

This works regardless of whether it was started under the name "myxterm" or any other. To set the word wrap of all text widgets in your program you write

myprogram*XmText.wordWrap: True

The class name "XmText" is defined by Motif ("Xm" is the prefix to most Motif-defined names). As you see in this example, you can freely mix class and instance names in one specification.

Usually your resource files contain more than one line. As a consequence you can easily write specifications that are in conflict for a certain widget. For example, without further rules it is not clear which shadow thickness to use for a main window given the following specification:

*shadowThickness: 4
myprogram*XmMainWindow.shadowThickness: 2

It is actually very useful to write such specifications because you may have a very general value (as in the first line) with exceptions—as in the second line which redefines the shadow thickness of all subwidgets of all main windows in "myprogram". To remove ambiguity from conflicting specifications some precedence rules have been established. The general principle is that more specific rules have priority over more general ones. The term "more specific" is defined by the following rules:

- A period is more specific than an asterisk. This rule is necessary because you can replace a period with an asterisk even if you do not omit any components, i.e. the asterisk may also stand for "nothing".

- Names are more specific than classes, i.e. a specification with the instance name overrides the same specification with the class name.

- Specifying a component is more specific than omitting it. This is the desired behaviour in the above example.

- Left components are more specific than right components. This is a somewhat arbitrary decision. It implies that specifications for all widgets of your program are more specific than specifications for all scroll bars of all programs.

Although these rules are not very difficult, they can cause some confusion, because, as you will see below, the resource database is merged from several different files. The files may contain conflicts that are not readily apparent.

Origin of Resource Database

Because there are different categories for which a program may be customized, there are multiple files from which the resource database is constructed. These files are then merged in a specific sequence into the resource database. In this process entries from one file may be overridden by entries from another.

The four main sources for the resource database are:

- The *application-specific* resource file should be delivered with an application, because it contains all the resource specifications not coded into the program. Normally it should not be changed by the user. The application defaults file resides in the public directory "/usr/lib/X11/app-defaults" by default. The name of the resource file in this directory is identical to the program class name specified in the program.

- The *user-specific* resource file contains customizations a user has made himself or herself. Accordingly it resides in his or her home directory with a name identical to the program class name. It can be relocated by setting the environment variable *XAPPLRESDIR*, to which the program class name is appended. For example, you could create a subdirectory "xresource" in your home directory (e.g. "/user/arthur"). By setting *XAPPLRESDIR* to "/user/arthur/xresource/" the "xterm" application would read the file "/user/arthur/xresource/XTerm" (please note the trailing slash in the value of *XAPPLRESDIR*—the program class name is appended without a delimiter).

- The *display-specific* resources are conveniently loaded into the X server by the *xrdb* program, so that every program can access them on its display connection. For compatibility with previous versions the display-specific resources may also reside in a file ".Xdefaults" in your home directory.

- The *host-specific* resource file is located in your home directory as the file ".Xdefaults-<hostname>".

Resource specifications can also be included directly or indirectly in the command line invoking a program—see the next chapter for details. Figure 2.19 summarizes the sources of the resource database.

resource database (*class, display, host*):

application specific
/usr/lib/X11/app-defaults/*class*

user specific
$XAPPLRESDIR*class*
($HOME/class)

display specific
xrdb-property (*display*)
($HOME/.Xdefaults)

host specific
$XENVIRONMENT
($HOME/.Xdefaults-*host*)

-xrm command
line option

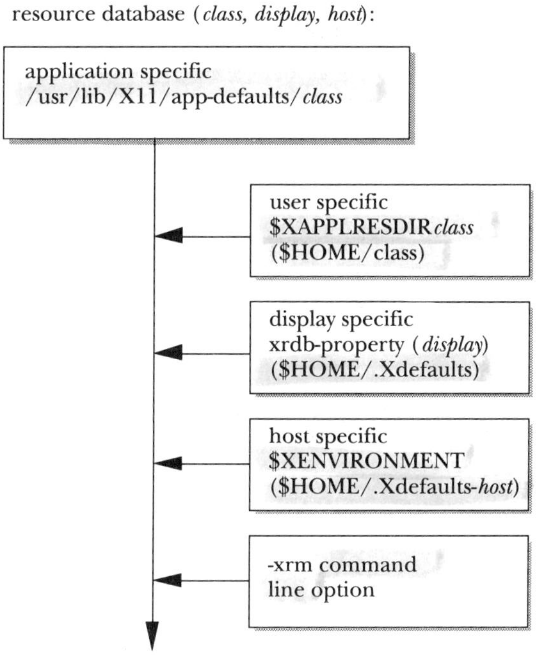

Figure 2.19: Sources of the resource database. Later sources override specifications in earlier ones.

2.4 Event Management

Like nearly all modern window systems, X is *event-driven*. This means that the flow of control is not primarily determined by the application. The program waits for user actions to occur (in a seemingly random fashion from the program's point of view) and reacts accordingly. Event-driven behaviour is necessary for highly interactive applications that provide many mouse-selectable choices simultaneously.

As was outlined in the first chapter, the X server generates *events* for whatever reasons it thinks appropriate. Events are dispatched to the corresponding widgets and handled accordingly. Figure 2.20 shows an overview of this part of a widget's interface.

The actions a widget executes in response to certain event types are not "hardwired", but can be dynamically specified. Translating events into actions is the task of the *translation manager*. The mapping between event types and actions is specified in a *translation table*, which is a resource field of every widget instance.

Actions are predefined internal procedures for a widget class. Actions determine the interactive behaviour of the widget. They can autonomously change the display and state of the widget, or they can notify the application program by means of a *callback*.

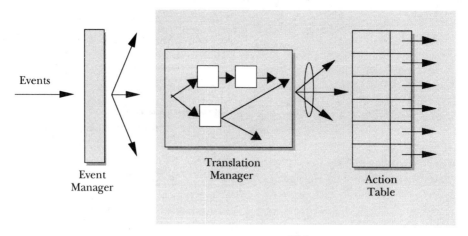

Widget **a**

Figure 2.20: Event handling part of widget interface. Events from the X server are dispatched by the event manager to the appropriate widget. Inside the widget the translation manager dynamically maps a sequence of events to a sequence of actions. Each widget class provides a table of possible actions implementing its interactive behaviour.

X Events

X generates several different types of events. Events may be directly initiated by a user action, they may be caused by another client's operation, or they may be an indirect consequence of another event. More than one event can be reported for a single occasion. For instance, moving a window may cause several *Expose* events for all the windows which are uncovered. Moving a window may even generate more than one event for a specific window, e.g. an Expose event and a VisibilityNotify event if the window was invisible before.

Because a large number of events can be generated, unwanted event types can be masked for a specific window. For example, a push button is usually not interested in the exact mouse movement. The *event mask* specifies which event types a client is interested in and is an attribute of a window. Although uninteresting events could equally well be ignored by the client, suppressing event generation helps to reduce the net traffic (remember, X has to operate across a network).

Events can also be propagated to parent windows if the child is not interested in them. You do not usually have to concern yourself with event masks, because they are taken care of by the translation manager.

Events are sent in a queue to the client program over one half of the communication channel the client has established to the server. The order in which they arrive is defined only for some rare cases where two events are generated together and where the order of these two events is specifically described. In all other cases events for different windows may be mixed at the X server's desire.

An event can be illustrated as a little packet carrying a type indicator (to see what you can expect inside) with a window ID as the address. The format of the contents depends on the event type. The window ID is used as a dispatching indicator.

An overview of the different event types now follows. Figure 2.21 contains a summary of the types. The discussion of event types is necessarily incomplete—for a complete description refer to the Xlib reference manual.

Keyboard Events

Events are generated when a key on the keyboard is pressed and when it is released. The event specifies a *key code*. A key code is an arbitrary number identifying a key on the keyboard. Even modifier keys such as Shift are reported with their key codes.

Because the key codes are clearly hardware-dependent, they are translated into *keysyms*, symbolic identifiers for key functions such as Enter, Delete, F1 etc. Keysym translation is performed in the client (by an Xlib function) to make programs possible that want to monitor the keyboard directly. The translation process is specified by a table resident in the server which is read by the clients. The keysym table can be changed by the user, but a change affects all clients simultaneously.

Keyboard	**Notification**	**Structure control**
KeyPress	ConfigureNotify	CirculateRequest
KeyRelease	CirculateNotify	ConfigureRequest
FocusIn	CreateNotify	MapRequest
FocusOut	DestroyNotify	ResizeRequest
	GravityNotify	

Pointer	MapNotify	**Client communication**
	MappingNotify	
ButtonPress	ReparentNotify	ClientMessage
ButtonRelease	UnmapNotify	PropertyNotify
MotionNotify	VisibilityNotify	SelectionClear
EnterNotify	KeymapNotify	SelectionNotify
LeaveNotify	ColormapNotify	SelectionRequest

Exposure

Expose
GraphicsExpose
NoExpose

Figure 2.21: Types of X events. The event types are divided into related groups.

Because it is not always desirable to report key events to the window the pointer is in, there can be a *focus window* to which key events are redirected. The focus window can be set by clients in collaboration with the window manager. A window can receive events when it receives the focus (FocusIn) or when it loses the focus (FocusOut). Focus events are used, for example, to display a blinking insertion cursor in a text entry field as long as this field has the focus.

Keyboard mapping and focus management are both built into the relevant Motif widgets, so that you need not deal with the details.

Pointer Events

Similar to keyboard events there are event types referring to the buttons located on the mouse (also called *pointer buttons*). As with the keyboard their number and their mapping to logical buttons 1...n are hardware-dependent and specified by a table in the server. Events are generated for pressing and releasing the buttons.

Events can also be generated when the pointer moves. The granularity of pointer movement reports is hardware-dependent and cannot be guaranteed. There is a trade-off between the frequency of reports and the resulting net traffic. Except for special cases like free-hand drawing programs the granularity is not critical, although the frequency is (otherwise a scroll bar does not move smoothly).

For every window a client can specify if it is interested in motion events at all or if it needs only rudimentary indications of pointer movement. Clients not satisfied with the default granularity can optionally request the detailed motion history. To reduce network traffic further, a client can also request motion events only to be sent while a button is pressed, because in a dragging operation motion events are only required while the button is pressed.

Most widgets are only interested in enter or leave events which are generated when the pointer crosses a window border.

Expose Events

In X it is the responsibility of the client to refresh the window contents whenever necessary. To notify the client, the X server generates an Expose event. The Expose event reports as additional information the exact rectangular region of the respective window which needs to be updated. To make the screen update appear smoother, the X server fills the exposed region with the window's background until the client reacts to the Expose event.

A special type of Expose event is generated when a client copies a bitmap inside the server, e.g. to scroll a window. Because parts of the windows may be overlapped by other windows, these parts of the bitmap cannot be copied without problems because their contents are not usually stored in the server. Therefore a GraphicsExpose event is generated for those regions to inform the client that it has to recompute these areas instead of simply copying them.

Notification Events

There are a number of situations in which a window should be notified of a certain action. For example, when a window is resized by its parent, it may receive a ConfigureNotify event. In the same way there are notification events for creating, destroying, mapping, and unmapping windows.

Notification events are of interest mainly because two different clients can operate on the same window. All they need to know is the window ID, which can always be found by searching the window tree from the root down.

Notification events also occur when some of the mapping tables inside the server change. These tables control the mapping to symbols for modifier keys, normal keys and mouse buttons. Other reasons for notification are reparenting (when the window manager inserts its decoration window into the hierarchy) and visibility changes (if a window is completely covered or uncovered).

Structure Control Events

A principle of X is that the window manager should stay out of the way as much as possible, i.e. a client should not depend on the special function of a window manager. To make this transparent for top-level windows—which are not really top-level windows because the window manager inserts its decoration window—certain requests on windows can be redirected to another client, in this case the window manager. The window manager is responsible for performing an action equivalent to the requested one.

Redirectable requests include those to circulate, configure, map and resize windows. Redirectable requests are sent as events to the window manager, which executes these requests on the decoration window.

The redirection feature is a source of possible programming errors. Usually, if you map a window and then draw into it, you can be sure that it is mapped when you draw into it because these requests are executed in sequence by the X server. If the map request is redirected, the server's task is finished when the redirecting event is generated. The window manager may then take an arbitrarily long time actually to map the window. In the meantime any drawing into the window gets lost.

Therefore the client has to wait for a MappingNotify event—or for the first Expose event—until he draws into the window.

Client Communication Events

X defines primitives for general client communication. A client may send arbitrary events to other clients which only pass through the X server. Client messages can be used to transfer application-specific data, but they have a fixed size like all events. Variable-length data can be stored in property lists associated with some window. Changes in a property list may generate a notification event for all interested clients.

Client messages and property lists are used to implement the X *selection* protocol, which in turn can be used to implement a clipboard. Client communication is the topic of Chapter 7.

Event Management Overview

Events arriving for one client process in the X event queue are dispatched by the *event manager* to the individual widgets. The *translation manager* then generates a sequence of actions from a sequence of events. The action names are mapped into call addresses by the action table. Figure 2.22 illustrates this process.

The event manager not only dispatches events to the translation manager. An application can register an *event handler,* specifying an event mask (i.e. which events this handler is for), a widget whose window serves as the event destination, and a procedure which handles the event. You can register multiple handlers for one widget.

A common handler registered for all widgets is the internal redraw procedure, which handles Expose events for the widget class. In addition to registering the widget ID in a hash table from which it can be looked up from the window ID, the event manager also builds the event mask for the widget's window, so that only events that have a corresponding handler are reported.

Although you can register your own event handlers in your program, you usually influence behaviour through the more comfortable translation manager. The translation manager is a special handler installed for every widget

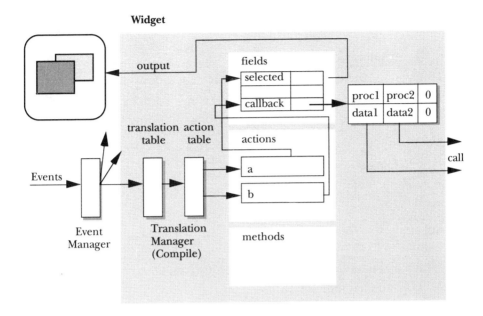

Figure 2.22: Event management. The translation table is compiled with the help of the action table. The translation manager uses the compiled table to determine when to call an action procedure. Actions may invoke callbacks, change fields, and trigger redrawing.

which interprets a compiled form of translation table. A *translation table* is a specification of how to map a sequence of events to a widget's actions (an example for an event sequence is the double click, which is a button press followed by a button release followed by a button press).

The translation table may reference actions of the widget class. Actions are procedures explicitly exported for use in the translation process. The action table defines the mapping between action names and procedure addresses necessary to compile translation tables.

Translations

The translation table is a resource field of every widget. You specify the translations in textual form which can be changed at run-time. After every change the specification is compiled into a more efficient internal table form.

Like any other resource field you can set the translation table at widget creation, by *SetValues,* or even through the resource database.

Because the translation specification may be large (e.g. for the text widget with a large number of different key combinations) you can choose to specify:

- That you want to replace all translations with a new set (*replace*).

- That you want to add some translation and possibly override previous translations if their left sides are equal (*override*).

- That you do not want to affect existing translations (*augment*).

To illustrate the event management process, the push button example is revisited here. The push button widget class has the following standard translation table:

<Btn1Down>:	*arm()*
<Btn1Up>:	*activate() disarm()*
<EnterWindow>:	*enter()*
<LeaveWindow>:	*leave()*
...	

Consider the following interaction sequence (Figure 2.23 contains a summary of this example):

1) Move the mouse pointer into the button window.

2) Press the left mouse button.

3) Move the mouse pointer out of the window (holding the button).

4) Move the mouse pointer into the window again (holding button).

5) Release the mouse button..

This sequence is handled by the Motif toolkit in the following way:

1) Moving the mouse pointer into the push button window generates an enter event. Because the push button has specified this event in the translation table, the event manager has set the appropriate bit in the event mask of the window, requesting enter events to be reported.

The event manager, triggered by the event arrival, calls the registered translation manager procedure, which checks the compiled table and looks for an entry for the event. It finds that the action *enter* should be called. During the compilation of the translation table at widget initialization, the name of this action has been looked up in the action table and replaced by its address in the compiled form.

The action *enter* is called, and checks if the button is armed, i.e. if the button has been pressed. At first the relevant flag has not been set, so this action does nothing.

2) Pressing the left mouse button generates a button press event with the left button specified. This event is dispatched to the translation manager procedure, too. The action *arm* is then called. This action sets a flag indicating that the button is armed, and redraws the button with the shadows exchanged and the face optionally filled with a darker colour to give the impression that the button was pressed into the screen surface.

If the programmer had registered a callback for this situation, the application could have been notified by this action, but this callback entry usually

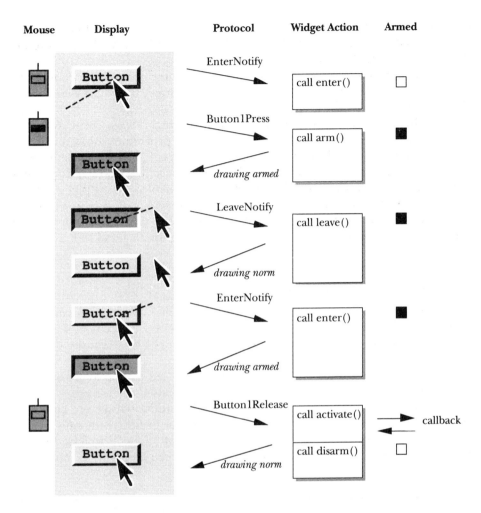

Figure 2.23: Example of event management. On the left you see the states of the display, the pointer, and the mouse button. In the middle the protocol traffic is described, and on the right the state and actions of the widget are shown.

remains empty. Consequently the action returns after having sent the drawing requests to the X server (it does not wait for completion as X is asynchronous).

3) Leaving the window again with the button pressed generates a leave event, causing the translation manager procedure to call the action *leave*. This action checks whether the button is armed and redraws the button in its normal shape because it is. The flag is not changed in case the pointer re-enters later.

Leaving a window with a button pressed automatically starts a *pointer grab* in the X server if not explicitly overridden. The grab causes most further events to be sent to the window that was left instead of being delivered normally. This continues until all mouse buttons are released. Grabbing is useful because the window needs to be informed when the mouse button is released again, even if this occurs outside the window.

4) Re-entering the window causes another enter event to be generated. The *enter* action this time finds the flag set and draws the depressed button shape again.

5) Releasing the mouse button causes a button release event to be generated by the X server. The translation manager procedure looks this up in the translation table and finds two actions to be executed in sequence: *activate* and *disarm*. The *activate* action triggers the activation callback, which usually has a registered application procedure, because you want to be notified that the button has been clicked. The registered procedure is called by the *activate* action. When the application processing is complete, the callback procedure returns and the second action is executed, resetting the flag and redrawing the button face in the normal state.

How to Specify Translations

Translations are specified as a sequence of lines. Every line contains a left hand side, which specifies an event sequence, followed by a colon. The right hand side consists of a sequence of actions to be executed when the event sequence on the left is generated.

The different event types are specified on the left side in angle brackets. Table 2-1 lists the denotations of the most frequently used event types.

Some event types such as key events require additional data to complete the event specification. It would not be very useful to have only one specification for different keys. Therefore the specification <Key> is followed by the name of a keysym. The list of all possible X keysyms can be found in the header

Generic event types	Abbreviations	Modifiers
<Key>	<Btn1Down>	Ctrl
<KeyUp>	<Btn1Up>	Shift
<BtnDown>	<Btn2Down>	Lock
<BtnUp>	<Btn2Up>	Meta
<Motion>	<Btn3Down>	Alt
<Enter>	<Btn3Up>	Button1
<Leave>	<BtnMotion>	Button2
<FocusIn>	<Btn1Motion>	Button3
<FocusOut>	<Btn2Motion>	
<Expose>	<Btn3Motion>	
<Map>		
<Unmap>		
<Reparent>		
<Message>		
<Mapping>		

Table 2-1: Frequently used event types in translation specifications.

file "/usr/include/X11/keysymdef.h" if you remove the *XK_* prefix from the definitions located there.

Key and button events may also be preceded by a modifier specification in order to invoke an action only when special modifier keys are pressed. The desired modifiers can be preceded by a tilde "~" to indicate negation.

Events in an event sequence are separated by a comma. Unless there is a possible specification for them, other events occuring between two specified events in a sequence are ignored.

A button event followed by a number in brackets denotes a repetition of this event, e.g. to specify a double click. It is equivalent to the respective expanded sequence.

Actions can take additional string parameters. The strings can be specified as constants inside the parameter brackets of the action specification of the right hand side.

If the actions defined by the widget classes are not sufficient, your application program can register its own additional actions which can then be specified in the translations of all widgets.

Action Interface

The actions of a widget class are for the interface side what the methods are for the application side. They represent the externally visible behaviour. Although they cannot be called directly by your application (without hacks) they are documented in the reference manual so that you can specify them in translations.

The actions are specific for a widget class. Which actions a widget class implements is recorded in the *action table* in the class definition. The action table contains the mapping between the action names as strings and the internal procedure addresses. Mapping is necessary because you can dynamically change the translations, thus requiring the name to be dynamically bound.

An action can have effects on all of the following: the display of the widget, the internal state and the values of resource fields, and the application program by means of callbacks.

The parameters which are supplied to an action routine are: the widget for which this action is called, the event record as sent from the X server with all necessary information about the event, and a list of constant strings which have been specified in the translations.

Callbacks

Callbacks are the main mechanism by which application functionality is bound to the interface. The direction of control flow is fundamentally different from the traditional way of programming where a program asks for input only when it needs it in the order of the computation. In contrast, Motif programs are always listening for input in the form of events and only call the application code when triggered by the user action.

Every widget class has several reasons for which callbacks may be invoked. For every reason there exists a resource field that contains a list of all registered callback procedures for these reasons. Because you have to specify pointers to the application program in this list, you cannot specify callbacks in a resource file (although nothing prevents you from doing so if you find a way to denote callbacks for your applications and write a converter which translates these denotations into callback lists).

For convenience, you do not normally use the *SetValues* method for adding callbacks, because there are more suitable methods which deal exclusively with callbacks.

The procedures registered in the callback list are called with three parameters: the calling widget, some data which are specific to this callback reason, and some data which the application itself has registered.

The reason-specific data are constant for all procedures in the callback list. They usually contain some indication of the reason, because you can register the same procedure for several callback reasons. In this case the procedure can determine the reason for which it was called. In addition, the reason-specific data contain the event record which triggered this callback.

The application-specific data are registered inside the callback list together with each procedure. They are often empty, but can be used to specify any additional parameters the procedure needs, depending on where it was registered. Therefore you can register the same procedure with several reasons, several different widgets, and even twice for the same widget and reason, and can always distinguish the different registrations. Figure 2.24 shows the structure of a callback list.

An example of programming with callbacks is a dialog box, which is a window that pops up in a certain condition and must be acknowledged by

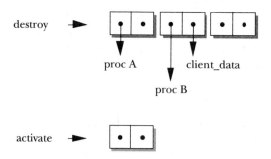

Figure 2.24: Callback lists for two different reasons. Each entry contains a pointer to a procedure and a pointer to application-specific data.

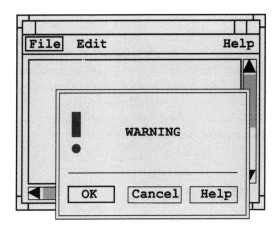

Figure 2.25: An error message as a dialog box. One of the buttons must be activated to make the dialog disappear.

clicking on one of the buttons inside the box. Error messages are typical examples (see Figure 2.25).

In traditional programming you would display the dialog box when the error is detected by the application. The application then waits for input about what the user wants and then proceeds accordingly.

In Motif you define two callback procedures, registered with the activation callbacks of the "OK" and "Cancel" buttons in the dialog box. When the error condition occurs, the dialog box is only mapped, so that the callbacks can be activated by the user. Widgets which cannot be activated owing to the error condition are made insensitive, so that their callbacks cannot be activated.

While the dialog box is visible, other parts of the application continue to respond to events. This is necessary for Expose events, because otherwise the contents of the application window would not be restored when moving the dialog.

The callback procedures attached to the two dialog buttons both unmap the dialog box and restore the global state of the application. The specific data concerning the error condition must be either globally accessible or indi- vidually registered with the two button callbacks when the dialog is mapped. In the latter case the callback routines have direct access to all necessary infor- mation.

You can view the callback reasons as a kind of event on a higher abstrac- tion level. In the same way as the X server sends events in a somewhat arbitrary sequence, a widget sends callbacks. There is one important distinction, how- ever. While events are asynchronous, i.e. the X server does not wait for a reaction, callbacks are implemented synchronously, because they are invoked by actions.

An action consists of a sequence of statements, some of which call callbacks. The implementation usually relies on the fact that this sequence is unaltered, i.e. all effects of a callback take place before the next statement is executed. Consider the example of the push button again. The button is disarmed after the *activate* callback has returned. Thus, the button stays visibly depressed until this action is complete. If the callbacks were asynchronous, this behaviour could not be enforced, so it would have been the task of the activation callback to disarm the button when appropiate.

2.5 Geometry Management

Geometry management is one of the features of both the X Toolkit Intrinsics and the Motif toolkit that require some forethought in order for you to achieve the desired effect. Using it pays off in the end.

Geometry management is based on two premisses:

- A top-level window can be arbitrarily resized by the user. The widgets in the widget hierarchy must reasonably adapt their individual geometries to the new situation.

- A window should appear in its optimum size for the first time. The optimum size, in which all information is visible, depends on the user preferences (such as font size).

Such behaviour is achieved by geometric negotiations between the widgets in the hierarchy. The programmer only gives hints about what strategy the widgets should use.

In this way the optimum geometry can always be dynamically calculated, independent of different font sizes, languages, screen sizes etc. For example, a box always tries to enclose all child widgets exactly if not prevented by its parent.

The variables affected by geometry management are size (width and height) and position (x and y coordinates). Theoretically, stacking order also belongs to this set, but it is very seldom used at present.

Principles

As indicated above, there are some principles guiding the process of geometry management. Geometry management is controlled by composite widgets. Composite widgets implement the decision process and actually perform the changes. The strategy used to determine the correct geometry is a specific feature of each composite widget class, and different widget classes have different management capabilities.

A basic principle of geometry management is that parents are in absolute control of their children. Only the parent widget can actually change the position and size of its children. The children have to accept unconditionally any geometry their parent calculates.

It is not always possible to display the complete contents of a window if it is reduced too much. Scaling facilities are not available in X. When the window is too small, the contents can be scrolled. If no special provisions are made, the contents of the window are simply clipped. You should ensure that at least the basic controls (e.g. buttons) remain accessible.

Although composite widgets autocratically determine the geometry of their children, they need to know their children's preferences in order to show a reasonable behaviour. For example, the preferred size of a push button exactly encloses the displayed string without wasting margin space. Composite widgets may query their children for their preferred geometry whenever a new decision is required.

When the state of a child has changed (e.g. a larger font is used), the child cannot set its new geometry itself. Instead, it has to issue a request to its parent. The parent widget then starts the geometry management process in order to decide whether the requested geometry is acceptable. If no objections are found the parent changes the child's geometry. Some examples of this process are presented in detail below.

Layout methods

There are different layout strategies suitable for different purposes. Accordingly, different strategies are available in different composite Motif widget classes. The most important strategies are outlined in this section.

The simplest and most inflexible strategy is to specify the geometry explicitly "by hand". That means that all positions and sizes of all child widgets are explicitly determined in either the program or a resource file. Specifying a fixed geometry is a somewhat "traditional" method used in most previous window systems. It may also be used in Motif, for example in dialog boxes (as shown in Figure 2.26).

A fixed geometry has the disadvantage that the layout cannot be changed if the dialog box is resized. The contents of the box can only be clipped, but this may render some important controls inaccessible. A fixed layout may be tolerable for non-resizable dialog boxes. However, fixed-size dialogs cannot be shrunk and put aside—it is important for modeless dialogs to keep the main window visible—and may not work on small screens.

Numerical coordinates can be more conveniently specified by an interactive design tool. Such a program allows you to position the individual elements on screen and to check the result visually. However, despite this "convenience" tool the layout remains valid only for a specific screen (because of different fonts and resolutions).

For regular structures, such as a column of buttons, the manual method soon becomes very tedious. Manual layout may in fact be impossible if the

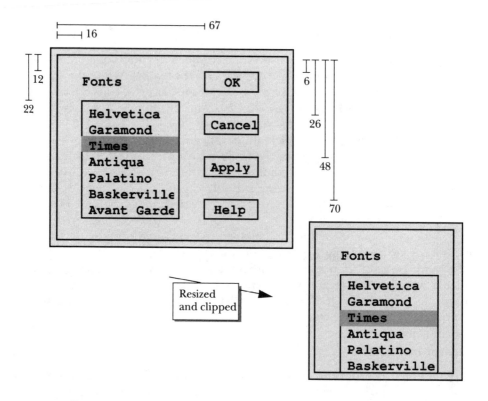

Figure 2.26: Manual layout in a dialog box. However, if the window is resized, parts of the window are clipped.

number of elements to position is not known in advance. In this case you can use a layout strategy that automatically maintains the regular structure by correctly aligning the children (see Figure 2.27).

A regular layout strategy can effectively use the available space by resizing all children accordingly. There are a number of parameters which can influence the exact placement, e.g. the number of columns, the amount of spacing between children, or whether different heights are allowed.

A regular layout strategy needs few parameters because there is a regularity to be exploited. For layout of arbitrary collections you must explicitly specify the contraints involved. An example of an arbitrary collection is a dialog box in general, where certain relations between widgets must be maintained.

For example, in Figure 2.28 the upper two widgets are attached to the respective sides of the box with a certain spacing. The lower widget is attached to the lower sides of the box and to one of the upper widgets. This setting results in stretching the lower widget when the box is resized. In the same way the upper left widget is attached to the upper right widget, so that the upper

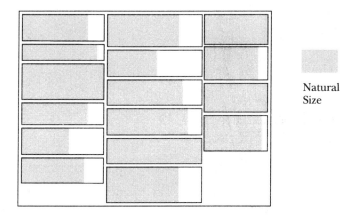

Figure 2.27: Row/column layout. The children are automatically aligned by the manager widget, using the preferred natural size as the required minimum. The parent must have control over the child geometry because the children do not know the layout strategy.

right widget remains at its initial size, while the upper left widget is stretched (or shrunk) to the new width.

Additional conditions such as these attachments are specified as *constraint resource fields* for each child. Constraint resource fields appear like normal resource fields to the outside, but are only allocated when the widget is inside a constraint widget. The child itself does not know about its constraint resource fields; these are only used by the parent to determine the geometry.

Although constraint-based layout is a very general and powerful method (and should be used if possible), specifying all connections is cumbersome at first. In addition it is not always easy to see whether the specified constraints really implement the desired behaviour.

If the constraints are already known for certain domains, the strategies can be directly built into specialized widget classes. For example, the layout of an application's main window consists of a menu bar of constant height at the top

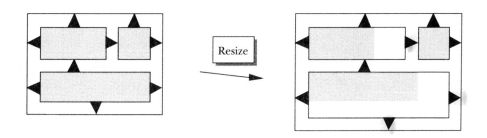

Figure 2.28: Constraint-based layout. The resize behaviour of the children is defined through attached constraints.

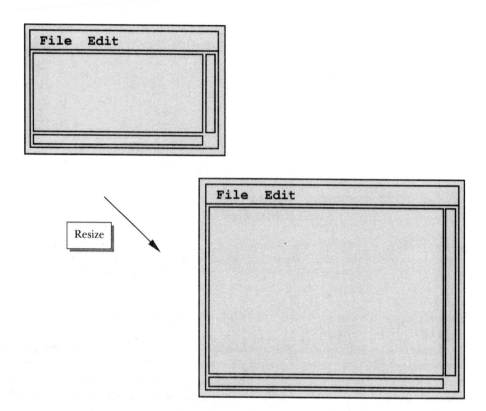

Figure 2.29: Layout of main window. The height of the menu bar remains constant and the work area grows or shrinks with the window.

which always spans the whole window, and a work area below, which takes up the rest of the space (see Figure 2.29).

Because the layout of the main window is similar for all applications, the main window widget implements the corresponding management strategy. The menu bar and the work area are children of the main window widget.

Triggering New Layout

Although the geometry management process is always performed by a composite widget for all its children, the process may be triggered by different sources.

User Intervention through Window Manager

The most drastic changes are triggered by resizing a window through the window manager by dragging the window borders of the window manager

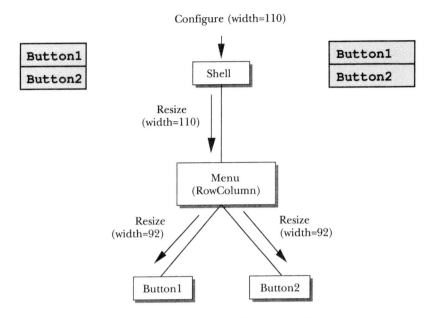

Figure 2.30: Geometry management triggered by the window manager. The resize operation is propagated through the widget hierarchy. Each composite widget uses its layout procedure to fit its children into the available space.

decoration. The window manager communicates this change to the top-level shell widget.

The window manager behaves like a kind of manager widget for the root window covering the screen background. As a consequence, top-level shells are treated like children of the window manager.

The shell widget propagates this change down to its single child. Further propagation through the widget hierarchy is straightforward and comes to an end when all primitive widgets have been resized correctly. All composite widgets have to execute their layout procedure to fit their children into the available space (see Figure 2.30).

Manage/Unmanage

The situation is more difficult when the set of managed children of a composite widget changes. In this case the whole layout must be recalculated.

To calculate the new optimum the composite widget normally first asks all children about their preferred sizes, although it is not obliged to do so. The query is necessary because the current size of the children may not be their preferred one—the preferred one may have been denied before and the optimum may have only just become possible. The composite widget then calculates its own optimum geometry (see Figure 2.31).

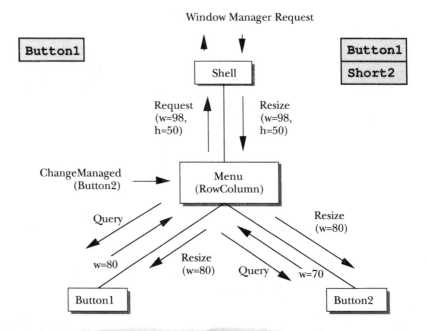

Figure 2.31: Geometry management triggered by managed set. The manager first recalculates its optimum geometry by querying its children. It then asks its parent to set the new size.

Because the composite widget is itself a child of another composite (for example a shell), it must first check if the new size will be allowed. Therefore it issues a request to its parent. In this case the parent is a shell that propagates the request to the window manager (because shells have few preferences of their own). If the window manager accepts the request, the resize operations trickle down from the window manager just as in the previous case.

The result is that the application window on screen resizes itself without user intervention. Self-resizing can be suppressed by setting a resource field of the shell to deny geometry requests at all times. The composite widget is then forced to live with its current size, squeezing more children into the same space.

If the requested geometry is not acceptable for the parent (e.g. it is too large) the parent may return a compromise (e.g. the largest size possible). The child then has a chance to decide whether it wants to accept the compromise (it then issues a second request with the compromise values), try another size (with a new request), or stay with the old size.

Changing Resource Fields (Primitive)

Changing a resource field in a primitive widget may change the geometry either explicitly (e.g. specifying width) or indirectly (specifying a different label string).

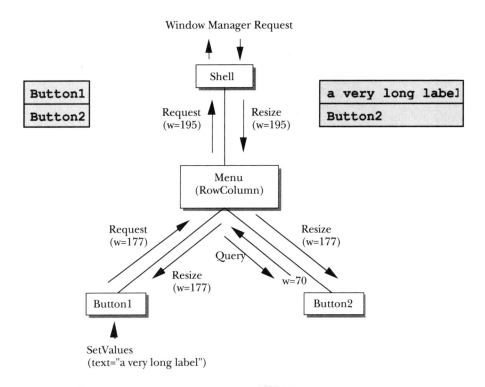

Figure 2.32: Geometry management triggered by primitive resource field.

Because the primitive widget cannot set its new size itself, it has to issue a request to its parent. The parent decides if the request can be fulfilled. As the parent is a child itself it has to send a request to its own parent for its own new size. Requests may be passed upwards until a shell widget is reached (one which has no parent widget). The shell then asks the window manager. If the requests are granted the new size is set from top to bottom (see Figure 2.32).

If any manager in the chain denies a request, the process also stops and a negative acknowledgement is passed back to the request-originating child.

Changing Resource Fields (Composite)

Changing resource fields in a composite widget may also start geometry calculations, for example because the desired spacing between children has been changed. Usually a complete layout is necessary. Although the reason is different, the subsequent process is identical to the one described above.

Chapter 3

Structure of a
Motif Program

This chapter describes the skeletal structure of a typical Motif program. A small sample program is developed which you can use as a template for developing your own programs. To understand the example, you should have some knowledge of C—but you need not be an expert, because advanced features will be explained where used.

3.1 Include Files

The C programming language uses *include files* to make external identifiers known to the compiler with their correct specification. Accordingly there are special header files for the Motif libraries.

There are two different classes of header files for Motif: those which are specific to the Motif widget library, and those which belong to the X Window System in general. The former usually reside in "/usr/include/Xm", the latter in the directory "/usr/include/X11". There may be good reasons, however, to place these header files in another location (your system administrator will know). In this case you should use the compiler's -I flag, e.g.

cc .... -I/vol/Motif/include ...

In a Motif program you have to include a general header ("Xm.h") and one header for every widget class used. You can of course include header files for classes you do not use; the only thing that suffers is the compiler, which has to read all the unnecessary definitions. The name of the header file for each class is included in the reference documentation for this class. The header part of the example program looks like this:

```
/* general Motif header */
#include <Xm/Xm.h>

/* headers for widget classes */
#include <X11/Shell.h>
#include <Xm/PushB.h>
```

In the example, only two widget classes are used, the application shell widget class and the push button widget class. The "Shell.h" file actually contains the definition for all shell widgets and is a standard part of X11.

The header files can in turn include other header files, so there are really some more files involved. In particular, the file "Xm.h" includes the necessary X11 files. Table 3-1 lists the names of all Motif include files you may need to specify (if you do not write your own widgets) together with an indication of which widget classes are covered by each file.

The complete code necessary for Motif programs is divided into four different libraries. The libraries are specified in the compile command in the following way, using the -l flag:

```
cc .... -lMrm -lXm -lXt -lX11 ...
```

The libraries must be listed in that order. The X11 library contains the Xlib code, the Xt library contains the X Toolkit Intrinsics, and the Xm library the Motif widget set. The Mrm library can be omitted if you do not use the UIL for your program.

The libraries normally reside in "/usr/lib" (under the names "libMrm.a", "libXm.a", "libXt.a" and "libX11.a"). Alternatively, you can use the -L flag, which works analogously to -I. The complete command to compile a simple Motif program like the example in this chapter looks like the following—if necessary, you can add the -I and -L flags.

```
cc -o demo demo.c -lXm -lXt -lX11
```

It seems a little premature to discuss the compiler flags for a program which hasn't even been described. The next sections will remedy that.

include file	class name	class pointer
Xm/Xm.h	\<all\>	\<all\>
\<no additional\>	"Composite"	compositeWidgetClass
	"Constraint"	constraintWidgetClass
	"Core"	widgetClass
	"XmGadget"	xmGadgetClass
	"XmManager"	xmManagerWidgetClass
	"XmPrimitive"	xmPrimitiveWidgetClass
X11/Shell.h	"ApplicationShell"	applicationShellWidgetClass
	"OverrideShell"	overrideShellWidgetClass
	"Shell"	shellWidgetClass
	"TopLevelShell"	topLevelShellWidgetClass
	"TransientShell"	transientShellWidgetClass
	"VendorShell"	vendorShellWidgetClass
	"WMShell"	wmShellWidgetClass
Xm/ArrowB.h	"XmArrowButton"	xmArrowButtonWidgetClass
Xm/ArrowBG.h	"XmArrowButtonGadget"	xmArrowButtonGadgetClass
Xm/BulletinB.h	"XmBulletinBoard"	xmBulletinBoardWidgetClass
Xm/CascadeB.h	"XmCascadeButton"	xmCascadeButtonWidgetClass
Xm/CascadeBG.h	"XmCascadeButtonGadget"	xmCascadeButtonGadgetClass
Xm/Command.h	"XmCommand"	xmCommandWidgetClass
Xm/DialogS.h	"XmDialogShell"	xmDialogShellWidgetClass
Xm/DrawingA.h	"XmDrawingArea"	xmDrawingAreaWidgetClass
Xm/DrawnB.h	"XmDrawnButton"	xmDrawnButtonWidgetClass
Xm/FileSB.h	"XmFileSelectionBox"	xmFileSelectionBoxWidgetClass
Xm/Form.h	"XmForm"	xmFormWidgetClass
Xm/Frame.h	"XmFrame"	xmFrameWidgetClass
Xm/Label.h	"XmLabel"	xmLabelWidgetClass
Xm/LabelG.h	"XmLabelGadget"	xmLabelGadgetClass
Xm/List.h	"XmList"	xmListWidgetClass
Xm/MainW.h	"XmMainWindow"	xmMainWindowWidgetClass
Xm/MenuShell.h	"XmMenuShell"	xmMenuShellWidgetClass
Xm/MessageB.h	"XmMessageBox"	xmMessageBoxWidgetClass
Xm/PanedW.h	"XmPanedWindow"	xmPanedWindowWidgetClass
Xm/PushB.h	"XmPushButton"	xmPushButtonWidgetClass
Xm/PushBG.h	"XmPushButtonGadget"	xmPushButtonGadgetClass
Xm/RowColumn.h	"XmRowColumn"	xmRowColumnWidgetClass
Xm/Scale.h	"XmScale"	xmScaleWidgetClass
Xm/ScrollBar.h	"XmScrollBar"	xmScrollBarWidgetClass
Xm/ScrolledW.h	"XmScrolledWindow"	xmScrolledWindowWidgetClass
Xm/SelectioB.h	"XmSelectionBox"	xmSelectionBoxWidgetClass
Xm/Separator.h	"XmSeparator"	xmSeparatorWidgetClass
Xm/SeparatoG.h	"XmSeparatorGadget"	xmSeparatorGadgetClass
Xm/Text.h	"XmText"	xmTextWidgetClass
Xm/ToggleB.h	"XmToggleButton"	xmToggleButtonWidgetClass
Xm/ToggleBG.h	"XmToggleButtonGadget"	xmToggleButtonGadgetClass

Table 3-1: Include files of all Motif classes.

3.2 Toolkit Initialization

Since the main procedures of most Motif programs are very similar you can use the example's main procedure as a template for your own programs. To facilitate re-use, it was written in a slightly more general way than is strictly necessary.

The skeleton structure of a Motif program's main procedure is shown in Figure 3.1. The first and last parts are more or less standard. The middle part contains the code to build the structure of the widget hierarchy and to link it with application code, and thus is application-dependent.

The initialization phase of a Motif program performs the following steps:

- Initialize toolkit.
- Open X display connection.
- Create resource database.
- Create top-level shell widget.

These steps will now be examined in detail.

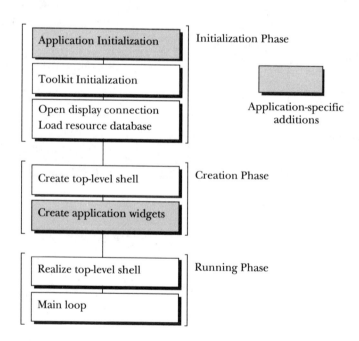

Figure 3.1: Skeleton of a Motif main procedure.

Initialization

To initialize the X Toolkit, the following statement is used:

XtToolkitInitialize();

This statement must precede all other calls to the X Toolkit or Motif widgets, but other initializations of the program can be placed before it.

Open Display

The next step is to open the network connection to the desired X server. The X server is best specified by the user—either by setting the DISPLAY environment variable or through the command line option *-display*—so there is no need to code a special value into the program. The connection is opened by the following call:

```
context = XtCreateApplicationContext();
display = XtOpenDisplay (
      context,      /* application context                        */
      NULL,         /* use DISPLAY from environment               */
      NULL,         /* use last of argv[0] as name                */
      PROGRAM_CLASS,
      NULL,         /* no additional command line options         */
      0,            /* ditto                                      */
      &argc,
      argv);        /* use and delete standard options            */
```

The first parameter should be an *application context.* An application context is a vehicle to allow multiple logical applications within a single physical program, but you usually need only one.

The second parameter is the display specification. If it is *NULL*, the display specification is taken from the command line or the environment variable (in that order).

Create Resource Database

The second purpose of *XtOpenDisplay* is to initialize the resource database. As mentioned in the previous chapter, the resource database is loaded into memory and later used to query values of resource fields which are not set by the program.

Every complete resource specification needs either the name or the class of the program at the beginning (see Section 2.4). These two are the third and fourth parameters to *XtOpenDisplay.* Specifying the application name as *NULL* gives the user further possibilities of parameterization. In this case the application name is taken from the command line (option *-name*) or from the last component of *argv[0]*, i.e. the name of the executable. The user can then write different resource specifications for the same program started in different ways.

For example, when started under the name *motif* by renaming the executable or by using the following command line

> *demo -name motif*

the demo program is no longer affected by resource definitions starting with "demo". A complete set of resource specifications can be kept in parallel for the "demo" and the "motif" invocations.

The program's class name should be constant and coded into the program. In the example it is defined using a preprocessor definition:

> *#define PROGRAM_CLASS "Demo1"*

As stated in the previous chapter, a class name should start with an uppercase letter.

In addition to the display specification, there are a number of standard command line options which are recognized by *XtOpenDisplay*. To make this possible you have to pass the command line in the last two parameters. All recognized options are removed from the command line—therefore both parameters must be given as an address.

If you want to define your own options which can be processed in the same way, you can supply an option descriptor table as arguments number 5 and 6. In the example, these parameters are set to *NULL/0*. Details of this mechanism can be found in the X Toolkit Intrinsics manual.

Any other options specific to your application (if any) can be processed by examining the remaining command line.

The most important task after calling *XtOpenDisplay* is to check the result. The result is a pointer to the toolkit internal display record, declared at the beginning of the main procedure as

> *Display   *display;*

If the display connection could not be established, the value returned is *NULL*. There are various reasons why this can happen:

- The user has not specified a display (no environment variable and no command line argument).
- The display specification is wrong.
- There is no X server running on the specified machine.

- • The host on which the program is running is not authorized to connect to the X server (use the X command *xhost* to grant access rights).

When the display cannot be opened your program should report an error (no error dialog is available without connection to the X server). The procedure *XtErrorMsg* allows for customization of error messages via the resource mechanism:

```
if (display == NULL)            /* necessary !                    */
        XtErrorMsg (
            NErrCannotOpen, TErrMain,   /* resource name      */
            ERROR_CLASS,                /* resource class     */
            "cannot open display",      /* default message    */
            NULL, NULL);                /* parameters         */
```

The error messages are taken from the error database, which is similar to the resource database. The error database has not been mentioned yet, but will not be further discussed here (you can find out about its customization in the Intrinsics manual). For a demo program it is sufficient to specify a default message to be used when no error database is present.

To prepare the program for future customization, the specific error message gets an identifying name and a class. The name is concatenated from two strings, in this case *NErrCannotOpen* (denoting the general kind of error condition) and *TErrMain* (specifying the place where the error occurred). All these strings are introduced by preprocessor definitions. The set of definitions will be enlarged in a real application and may be put into a separate header file.

```
#define ERROR_CLASS        "Demo1Error"

#define NErrCannotOpen     "cannotOpen"
#define TErrMain               "Main"
```

Create Application Shell

Every application has to create a top-level shell widget serving as a root for the widget tree and all resource specifications. There is a special procedure to create the top-level shell because it has no parent widget (although it has a parent window, namely the root window).

```
XtSetArg (args[0], XmNallowShellResize, True);
toplevel = XtAppCreateShell (
            NULL,                 /* use same program name   */
            PROGRAM_CLASS,    /* repeat class param       */
            applicationShellWidgetClass,
            display,
            args, 1);                 /* argument list            x*/
```

The first two parameters are a repetition of the application name and class, specified exactly as in *XtOpenDisplay*. The next parameter specifies the widget class. The identifier *applicationShellWidgetClass* is defined in "Shell.h" as a pointer to the class record of the application shell class (but you should not access the class record directly). The symbolic names for other classes can be found in Table 3-1. Although you may use other shell classes for your top-level shell, this is discouraged.

Because no parent widget can be given, you have to pass the display variable to determine the root window to be used for this application. The last two arguments specify an argument list to supply initial values for some resource fields of the new widget. The argument list is created in the statement beginning with *XtSetArg*. Because argument lists are a common mechanism for several different procedures, their creation is explained below.

3.3 Widget Creation

Creation Phase

After the top-level shell has been created, all other widgets are created as subtrees of this shell. In programs with only a few widgets, the simplest approach is to create all widgets at start-up, even the dialog boxes which are not displayed immediately (they are popped up on demand). For large applications with many widgets, this may introduce a significant start-up delay. In this case parts of the widget tree can be created when they are needed.

The different procedures to create widgets are described in the next section. To factor out a considerable amount of detail involved in creating the many widgets, it is advisable to remove this creation from the main procedure, as in the example:

> *CreateMainWindow (toplevel);*

Only the parent top-level widget is required as a parameter for building the widget tree.

Creation Procedures

There are three possible ways to create a widget, namely:

- Creating an unmanaged widget with *XtCreateWidget*.
- Creating a managed widget with *XtCreateManagedWidget*.
- Using one of the Motif convenience functions.

The first method is seldom used. In most cases the Motif convenience functions are simple wrappers around a call of *XtCreateWidget*. Some convenience functions create two widgets at once, but only one is returned as the result. In this case you have to be aware that another widget is present, too. A slight inconvenience with the Motif convenience functions is that two of the parameters are in exactly the opposite order to those for *XtCreateManagedWidget*.

The second method is therefore the preferred one to start with. The parameters required for *XtCreateManagedWidget* are:

- The *name* of the widget, which you can choose freely. Conventionally, though, it should start with a lowercase letter. The purpose of the name is to allow external resource specifications (see Section 2.3).

- The *class identifier*, which should be regarded as opaque. It is implemented as a pointer to the class record of the widget class. The identifiers for the different classes can be found in Table 3-1. The class also determines the class name to be used in resource specifications.

- The *parent widget*. Every widget must have a parent. Specifying the parent during creation also implies that the widget hierarchy is built strictly top-down.

- The *argument list*, which specifies program-determined resource field values for this widget. How to create an argument list is explained below.

- The *argument count*. Because C has no built-in list data type, the number of list elements must be passed separately.

An example call to create a simple push button widget named "button" is as follows:

```
button = XtCreateManagedWidget (
        "button",
        xmPushButtonWidgetClass,
        parent,
        args, 1);
```

To create additional top-level windows for an application (e.g. dialog boxes) you have to use a different call. This is explained in Chapter 7, where shell widgets are discussed in detail.

Specifying Argument Lists

Usually most of the widget creation code is concerned with building argument lists, because the resource fields play such an important role for widgets. Each Motif widget class has several powerful options and must be carefully parameterized to achieve the desired behaviour.

An argument list is represented in C as an array declared in the following way:

Arg   args[NUM_ARGS];

The array size must be greater than the maximum number of arguments used in one call. Usually a value for *NUM_ARGS* of around 10 will be sufficient.

Every element of the array is a name-value pair, where the name determines the resource field to be addressed. The names of all resource fields are defined in the Motif header file—to allow simple misspellings to be caught by the compiler. The symbolic names are constructed from the "real name" (i.e. what you would specify in a resource file) by adding the prefix *XmN*. "Xm" is the general Motif prefix, where "N" denotes a resource name. Remember that the identifiers are case sensitive.

There are a number of different ways to fill the array with parameters. The simplest way is to assign name and value separately:

args[0].name = XmNallowShellResize;
args[0].value = (XtArgVal) True;

The value must be cast to the type *XtArgVal,* because values of different types may be assigned. The most common types are *Boolean, int, String* (respectively pointers or opaque pointer types in general)—all these fit into a long word. Obviously, the separate assignment is very tedious for multiple arguments. The macro *XtSetArg* can be used as an abbreviation. The following statement is expanded by the C preprocessor to the same two statements as above:

XtSetArg (args[0], XmNallowShellResize, True);

During program development you frequently add or remove arguments. In this case you have to adjust all array indices, so that no "holes" are left in the list, and the total number of arguments must also be changed manually. Therefore it is sometimes more convenient to introduce an index variable which counts the elements at run-time:

an = 0;
XtSetArg (args[an], XmNallowShellResize, True); an++;
XtSetArg (args[an], XmNtitle, "Demo"); an++;

The final value of the counter can then be used as the number of elements in the argument list. Please note that the index cannot be auto-incremented in the macro call, because it would be expanded twice and thus would be incremented twice. Using this method you can add or remove arguments without further changes to other lines—at the expense of an additional declaration and some additional statements.

Which of the last two methods you prefer is mostly a matter of taste and the way you develop your application.

There is yet another way to create argument lists. You can implement all needed argument lists as statically initialized arrays, e.g.

```
static Arg args[] = {
        {XmNallowShellResize, (XtArgVal) True},
        {XmNtitle, (XtArgVal) "Demo"}
};
```

The number of parameters can be properly calculated at compile time using the macro *XtNumber,* provided the array is declared with indefinite size, e.g.

```
..., args, XtNumber (args), ...
```

If some of the value arguments must be calculated at run-time, they can be initialized to a dummy value. The real value is then assigned using the first method described above.

Declaring argument lists statically has a serious drawback: you have to invent a sensible name for each argument list (and you need many argument lists, even in a medium-size program). Furthermore, it is not easy to trace the correspondence between a list declaration and the call where it is used.

To avoid these difficulties, the second method is used in this book because it is the easiest to read. You can use and mix the other methods in your program, of course, if this is more convenient for you.

Realizing Widgets

After all the widgets have been created as managed, the next step is to realize all these widgets in order to create their windows and calculate the initial geometry. Because most widget classes have the *mapped-when-managed* flag set by default, they are mapped and thus displayed on the screen. This process is invoked by a single call to realize the top-level widget:

```
XtRealizeWidget (toplevel);
```

XtRealizeWidget realizes all the child widgets of the top-level shell before the top-level shell itself. If the children have children themselves, these are realized first. In this way the whole widget hierarchy is realized from bottom to top.

There are two situations where you do not want child widgets to be mapped:

- Some child widgets should not be visible until later. You can either create the widget unmanaged and manage it later, or reset the *mapped-*

when-managed flag and map it later. The differences between these two possibilities were explained in the previous chapter.

- Pop-up windows must only be visible when needed. Because this is a common requirement, pop-up widgets are constructed with special shell widget classes and are handled differently in several respects. You will learn about the special characteristics of shell widgets in the next chapters.

Actually, after the widgets have been realized, they are displayed with only their background (colour or bitmap pattern) at first. The window contents are drawn later in response to an Expose event. Therefore the next task of the program is to process events, whether they are generated by the X server or by user actions.

3.4 The Main Loop

The Main Event Loop

The preferred way of handling events in an X program is to enter an endless loop that waits for events to be handled. Processing a single event should not take too long, because other events may be coming in in the mean-time. Keeping processing time short ensures that every user action has an instant response. This is important because even short delays have a noticeable impact on the user's perception of direct manipulation operations (such as dragging with the mouse).

The X Toolkit Intrinsics have a prefabricated main loop to handle events, because all events are dispatched to the widgets. It is invoked with the following line:

XtAppMainLoop (context);

Registering Callbacks

Callback procedures, which implement the application-specific event processing, have to be registered with a widget. The registered procedures are called at a time determined by the widget's semantics. Every callback reason is implemented as a resource field and has a name. To invoke a callback when the button widget is pressed, the following line in the sample program adds a callback procedure to the (initially empty) list of callbacks for the reason *XmNactivateCallback*:

XtAddCallback (button, XmNactivateCallback, PressMe, NULL);

When the button is activated (signalled by a button release event) the widget calls the procedure *PressMe*, which implements the application-specific response.

You can install more than one callback procedure for a single callback reason by adding it to the list. On activation, all procedures in the list are called in sequence. Remember that the callback is registered with only one widget, not with all push buttons. You can register different callback procedures with other push buttons. For example, in a menu every button has a different purpose and may use a different callback procedure.

You can also register the same procedure with different callbacks of different widgets, because the callback procedure can adjust its behaviour by looking at its parameters (see below).

Callback lists may be empty, and this is their default value. In fact, most callback lists will remain empty because there are far more callback reasons available than your program is usually interested in.

Callback Parameters

Because they are handled by common routines, all callback procedures have the same parameters, as in the following header:

```
static void PressMe (widget, client_data, call_data)
     Widget                  widget;
     caddr_t                 client_data;
     XmAnyCallbackStruct *call_data;
```

The first parameter is always the widget the procedure was registered for, allowing you to examine the resource fields of the calling widget and to change them if appropriate.

The next two parameters are pointers. The second pointer refers to a structure specific to the callback reason, e.g. every activation callback of every push button passes a reference to an *XmAnyCallbackStruct*. The structure used by a callback is described in the reference documentation (see Appendix B) and also in the following chapters. The first pointer simply returns the value you registered with *XtAddCallback*, in this case *NULL*. By using these *client_data* you can specify additional private parameters.

The parameters allow you to choose between the following possibilities to structure your callback code:

- You can register a different callback procedure for every widget and every reason. Then you do not need to examine the parameters.

- You can register a common procedure for a group of widgets, which adjusts its behaviour according to the parameter values. In the simplest case the procedure may switch depending on the calling widget; this is a poor but sometimes necessary substitute for using different callback procedures. A common procedure is especially useful if there is common code around the switch.

Accessing Resource Fields

In a callback procedure you often need additional information, such as the values of some of the resource fields of the affected widget. You can retrieve resource field values with *XtGetValues*. *XtGetValues* takes an argument list as a parameter, so you can read multiple values in one call.

The argument list mechanism is slightly complicated by the fact that the values are not returned in the value field of an argument list entry. Instead you have to supply a pointer in the value field to indicate where the real value will be stored. *XtGetValues* is used in the example program to read the foreground and background colours of the push button in the callback procedure. The following code stores the two colour specifications (of type *Pixel*) into the variables *fg* and *bg*:

```
Pixel       fg, bg;
Arg         args[NUM_ARGS];

XtSetArg (args[0], XmNforeground, &fg);
XtSetArg (args[1], XmNbackground, &bg);
XtGetValues (widget, args, 2);
```

New values can be set in the same way using *XtSetValues*. Here the values are passed directly in the argument list, similar to *XtCreateManagedWidget*.

```
XtSetArg (args[0], XmNbackground, fg);
XtSetArg (args[1], XmNforeground, bg);
XtSetValues (widget, args, 2);
```

The described callback procedure has the effect of inverting the button face when activated by switching the foreground and background colours.

Program Exit

There are two common methods of leaving your program once it has entered the application main loop. The first possibility is to define a callback which executes an *exit* call.

You can change the example program so that pressing the button exits the program by substituting the following callback:

```
static void PressMe (widget, client_data, call_data)
      Widget                    widget;
      caddr_t                   client_data;
      XmAnyCallbackStruct  *call_data;
{
      exit (0);
}
```

In simple cases such as this example the Motif window manager's close function is sufficient. It is executed by double-clicking on the window menu button in the upper left corner of the window manager decoration. The default reaction to the close command is to exit the application.

3.5 The Complete Example

The example program is now complete. You can use it as a starting point for further improvements. It demonstrates the most important techniques used to create a Motif application.

The use of an *XmString* variable to set the text for the button face, and the corresponding call *XmStringLtoRCreate*, are not explained in this chapter. The XmString mechanism is a replacement for normal strings used generally in Motif and is explained in the next chapter.

```
/* general Motif header */
#include <Xm/Xm.h>

/* headers for widget classes */
#include <X11/Shell.h>
#include <Xm/PushB.h>

/* global definitions */
#define    PROGRAM_CLASS    "Demo1"
#define    ERROR_CLASS      "Demo1Error"

#define    NUM_ARGS         10

/* error definitions */
#define    NErrCannotOpen           "cannotOpen"
#define    TErrMain                 "Main"

/* forward declarations */
static void PressMe();
```

```
/****************** create the widget hierarchy *******************/

static void CreateMainWindow (parent)
      Widget       parent;
{
      Widget       button;
      Arg          args[NUM_ARGS];
      XmString     face;

      face = XmStringLtoRCreate ("PressMe",
                                 XmSTRING_DEFAULT_CHARSET);
      XtSetArg (args[0], XmNlabelString, face);
      button = XtCreateManagedWidget (
            "button",
            xmPushButtonWidgetClass,
            parent,
            args, 1);
      XmStringFree (face);

      XtAddCallback (button, XmNactivateCallback, PressMe, NULL);
}


/******************** callback procedure ********************/

static void PressMe (widget, client_data, call_data)
      Widget                widget;
      caddr_t               client_data;
      XmAnyCallbackStruct   *call_data;
{
      Pixel      fg, bg;
      Arg        args[NUM_ARGS];

      XtSetArg (args[0], XmNforeground, &fg);
      XtSetArg (args[1], XmNbackground, &bg);
      XtGetValues (widget, args, 2);

      XtSetArg (args[0], XmNbackground, fg);
      XtSetArg (args[1], XmNforeground, bg);
      XtSetValues (widget, args, 2);
}


/******************** main procedure ********************/

void main (argc, argv)
      unsigned int     argc;
      char             **argv;
```

```
{
    Display              *display;
    XtAppContext         context;
    Arg                  args[NUM_ARGS];
    Widget               toplevel;

    /* initialize toolkit */
    XtToolkitInitialize();
    context = XtCreateApplicationContext();
    display = XtOpenDisplay (
        context,              /* application context               */
        NULL,                 /* use DISPLAY from environment      */
        NULL,                 /* use last of argv[0] as name       */
        PROGRAM_CLASS,
        NULL,                 /* no additional command line options */
        0,                    /* ditto                             */
        &argc,
        argv);                /* use and delete standard options   */

    if (display == NULL)                         /* necessary !       */
        XtErrorMsg (
            NErrCannotOpen, TErrMain,     /* resource name     */
            ERROR_CLASS,                  /* resource class    */
            "cannot open display",        /* default message   */
            NULL, NULL);                  /* parameters        */

    /* create application shell */
    XtSetArg (args[0], XmNallowShellResize, True);
    toplevel = XtAppCreateShell (
        NULL,                    /* use same program name     */
        PROGRAM_CLASS,           /* repeat class param        */
        applicationShellWidgetClass,
        display,
        args, 1);                /* argument list             */

    /* create main window */
    CreateMainWindow (toplevel);

    /* start loop */
    XtRealizeWidget (toplevel);
    XtAppMainLoop (context);
}
```

Part
Two

Functionality

Chapter 4

Some
Primitive Widgets

4.1 Class Hierarchy

After a long discussion of widgets in general you will want to know what widget classes Motif has to offer. The predefined widget classes of the Motif toolkit determine the functionality normally available for building applications without defining new widget classes.

Figure 4.1 shows the basic superclasses. The remaining Motif widget classes fall into one of three different categories:

- *Primitive* widgets, which have no children.

- *Manager* widgets, which may have other composite or primitive widgets as children.

- *Shell* widgets, which implement the functionality of top-level windows and have exactly one child (usually a composite widget).

In the description of the widget classes in the next chapters a task-oriented classification is used, because in practice a set of widgets from different categories is needed for a specific task. In this part of the book the widget classes are presented in the following order:

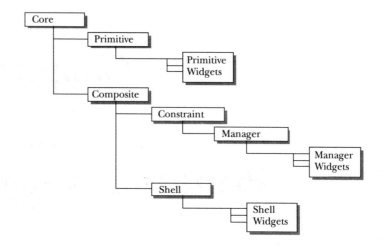

Figure 4.1: General widget classes of the Motif class hierarchy. Remember that the class hierarchy has nothing to do with the composition hierarchy between widget instances.

- This chapter introduces some primitive widgets which are widely used in different contexts. These include labels, buttons, text fields and scroll bars. They serve as simple examples for some generally used resource fields and mechanisms.

- The menu system is explained in the first part of Chapter 5, because its classes are used in a highly standardized manner. The different types of menus are constructed from normal buttons and row-column manager widgets. There are only a few possible parameterizations that you need to know (provided you do not want to achieve highly non-standard behaviour).

- The main window of an application can also be easily constructed with some specialized widget classes. These are explained in the second part of Chapter 5.

- The layout of control areas is a more difficult topic, especially if a flexible geometry is desired. Chapter 6 introduces some more primitive widget classes for individual control elements, and manager widget classes to group them together. Geometry management is especially important in this case, because a fixed-size layout should generally be avoided.

- Dialog boxes are the topic of the second part of Chapter 6. Widget classes for common dialogs such as errors and warnings are discussed, as well as the dialog shell widget class, which you can use to construct general pop-up windows.

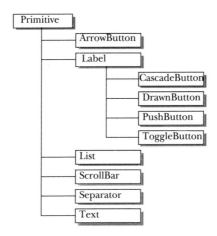

Figure 4.2: Primitive class hierarchy.

Some Motif widget classes combine different functions; their personality can be changed through resource fields. For example, the row-column widget can operate in five different modes, each one using one or two resource fields exclusively dedicated to this mode. The different functions are built into a single class for purely technical reasons. However, the discussion of such classes that follows is separated according to the different roles where appropriate.

As mentioned above, primitive widgets have no children. They are the simplest building blocks of an application interface. The hierarchy of the primitive widget classes is shown in Figure 4.2.

The *Primitive* widget class implements common features as a superclass of the primitive Motif widgets. It is only used by widget writers. All primitive widget classes inherit the common resource fields, so the meaning of these resource fields is of considerable importance. In this book these resource fields are explained taking a usable widget class (i.e. a subclass) as an example.

4.2 The Label Widget

The label class has a dual purpose. It is intended to display simple strings or pictures (see Figure 4.3), but is also a superclass of the different button classes. Inheriting the label features makes sense because buttons must also display a string or picture as their identification.

Because the label class is used as a superclass, some of its resource fields are useful only in subclasses. For example, menu buttons may have a mnemonic abbreviation. The mnemonic character is underlined in the string appearing as

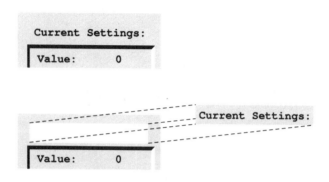

Figure 4.3: Typical label widget.

the menu selection. The label class has a resource field *XmNmnemonic* which specifies this character, although only buttons in menus use this feature.

Mnemonics are implemented in the label class for technical reasons. Underlining the respective character must be performed in the drawing routine of the button class. If underlining had not been provided by the label class, the buttons would not be able to inherit the drawing routine—which is quite long given the different possibilities described below. So providing part of the functionality in a superclass is really a mechanism for avoiding duplicate work for the toolkit as a whole.

Geometry

There are a number of resource fields which determine the geometry of labels, as outlined in Figure 4.4 and summarized in Table 4-1.

You should note that, although there are shadow borders around the label in Figure 4.4, label widgets cannot display shadows. The relevant resources are defined in the label widget class for use in the button subclasses (see the next section), but the shadow thickness is always reduced to 0 for label widgets. The shadows are included here to give a complete overview of the geometry resources.

You should generally leave the position and size of label windows alone, because they are either set to the preferred size of the label (if the parent allows it) or are determined by the geometry management strategy of the parent. In the latter case you can only change the geometry through parameterization of the parent.

The label widget calculates its preferred size from the size of the label text, taking the resource fields described in Figure 4.4 into account. The size of the text is calculated automatically from the string you specify (see below for details

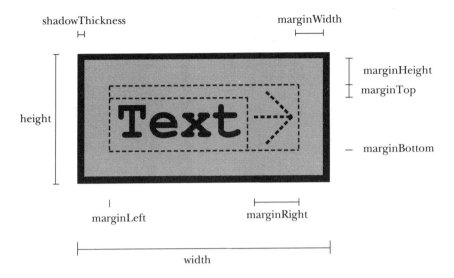

Figure 4.4: Anatomy of a label. The resource fields for all the dimensions are defined by the label class, but some are only useful in subclasses.

of how to specify the string) and the specified font (which is usually determined by the end user). The other resource fields have reasonable default values.

If you *must* set the geometry explicitly, you can set any of the *XmNx*, *XmNy*, *XmNwidth* or *XmNheight* resource fields with *XtSetValues*. You must be prepared, however, for these values not to be accepted if they interfere with the parent's geometry management.

To enhance portability, you should use *resolution-independent* specifications when you specify the geometry explicitly. All geometry resources are measured in screen pixels by default (this is the normal X strategy). If anyone uses this specification on a screen with a different resolution or a non-square aspect ratio the relations will be distorted. Motif, however, allows you to specify these resource fields in other units.

The resource field *XmNunitType* determines which units to use for this particular widget (millimetres, inches, or printers' points). The resolution dependent field values are internally converted to pixels according to screen characteristics.

You can also scale geometric specifications with the font used by specifying the unit type *Xm100TH_FONT_UNITS*. In this way you can, for example, create a margin which is relative to the font size the user chooses (e.g. in his default resource file).

There are six resource fields controlling the margins around the label's contents. Only two of them are normally of interest—*XmNmarginWidth* and

XmNx	Position	X coordinate relative to parent window
XmNy	Position	Y coordinate relative to parent window
XmNwidth	Dimension	Width of complete window
XmNheight	Dimension	Height of complete window
XmNunitType	enum	Unit of geometry values *XmPIXELS Xm100TH_MILLIMETERS Xm1000TH_INCHES Xm100TH_POINTS Xm100TH_FONT_UNITS*
XmNshadowThickness	short	Width of shadow
XmNmarginWidth	short	General margin width
XmNmarginHeight	short	General margin height
XmNmarginTop	short	Additional top margin
XmNmarginBottom	short	Additional bottom margin
XmNmarginLeft	short	Additional left margin
XmNmarginRight	short	Additional right margin
XmNalignment	enum	Alignment of text/graphic *XmALIGNMENT_BEGINNING XmALIGNMENT_END XmALIGNMENT_CENTER*

Table 4-1: Geometry resource fields of the label class. The middle column defines the type of the field. *Enum* is a meta notation for enumeration values, whose possible values are described in the right column.

XmNmarginHeight. They are used to tune the visual appearance of the label or button.

The margin specifications will not always be strictly obeyed, as they are only used to determine the preferred geometry. For example, in a menu all the buttons are adjusted to the same width, thus increasing the right margin of smaller buttons (Figure 4.5). The individual preferences of the buttons are overridden by the parent to standardize the appearance of the menu. Nevertheless the margin specification has an influence, because the widest button determines the overall width of the menu, so enlarging its margin width will enlarge the width of the menu.

The other four margin resource fields are used in subclasses of the label class to reserve space for additional graphics (see, for example, the arrow shown in Figure 4.4, which is used to indicate a cascading menu, or the toggle indicator of a toggle button). As they should not be changed by the programmer their default value is 0.

If the button is resized larger than its default, the text (or pixmap) may be positioned differently within the space left by the margins. Depending on the resource field *XmNalignment*, it is either centred or aligned to the left or the right.

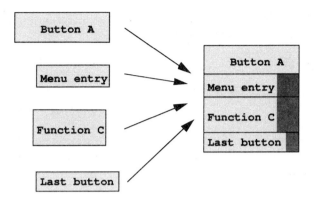

Figure 4.5: Adjusting button margins in a menu.

Both *XmNalignment* and *XmNunitType* are examples of enumerated re-source fields[1]. Their possible values are restricted to predefined constants. In a C program, these constants are defined in the Motif header files. Enumeration constants always start with "Xm", followed by an uppercase identifier, possibly with underscores. If you want to specify such a value in a resource file, a simple convention is used to determine the denotations of possible values.

In resource files the "Xm" prefix should be removed, and the case of the other letters is ignored. For example the following specification requests a *XmNalignment* value of *XmALIGNMENT_CENTER*:

*XmLabel*alignment: alignment_center*

Using XmStrings

The label widget can display either a text string or a graphical image described by an X pixmap. This property is inherited by the subclasses, i.e. you can create graphical buttons in Motif. Both methods require some preparation to specify what will be displayed.

Motif does not use ordinary C strings for labels. You have to create an *XmString* object from the string instead. This is a major burden for simple programs, but Motif was created to make applications more portable and this is the price to pay for internationalization. XmStrings have the ability to mix different character sets and writing directions in one text structure. This ability is required to display foreign-language text.

XmStrings are further discussed in Chapter 10. Here you will only learn how to create XmStrings and how to get rid of them when they are no longer

---

[1]Enumerated fields are usually defined as *unsigned char*.

needed. A variable of type *XmString* is a pointer to a hidden structure and is instantiated with the following program fragment:

> *XmString   s;*

> *s = XmStringCreateLtoR ("an example C string",*
> *   XmSTRING_DEFAULT_CHARSET);*

This call creates an XmString with the writing direction from left to right and the default character set. If you set the resource field *XmNlabelString* to this value (see the example program in the previous chapter), the string *"an example C string"* is displayed.

The XmString is copied into an internal area by the label widget. Therefore you can free the storage associated with the string by calling *XmStringFree* after *XtCreateManagedWidget* or *XtSetValues* are finished.

> *XmStringFree (s);*

If you want to use the C string hidden inside the XmString, e.g. for comparison, you can extract it with the call:

> *char   *string;*

> *XmStringGetLtoR (s, XmSTRING_DEFAULT_CHARSET, &string);*

Make sure that the character set specified is identical to the one the string was created with—otherwise you will not get anything useful back. *XmStringGetLtoR* allocates memory for the string returned. You can free it using *XtFree* when the string is no longer needed.

Because an XmString may contain segments in different character sets, there must be a font specification for every character set used (imagine some Hebrew segments in an English text—you need a normal and a Hebrew font). Therefore, fonts are specified using the resource field *XmNfontList* (listed in Table 4-2) This field accepts pairs of character set/font combinations. As long as you only use the default character set you can treat this resource field like a normal font resource, i.e. you only name one font which is automatically paired with the default character set.

Fonts should generally be specified in resource files, because they are very dependent on the display resolution and the user preferences. Without further

| XmNlabelString | XmString | String to display in label |
| XmNfontList | XmFontList | Font(s) to use for string |

Table 4-2: Label string resource fields.

knowledge you are unable to set the font via *XtSetValues* at this moment. You cannot simply use a string because only strings from the resource database are automatically converted. Instead you have to create an *XmFontList* object. Since you should avoid that, an explanation is omitted here.

Using Pixmaps

Using bitmaps for a label or button face also requires some additional knowledge. First you have to understand the terminology. A *bitmap* is a two-dimensional array of bits, as used on monochrome displays. A *pixmap* is a generalization where the bits are replaced with *pixels* which use multiple bits to indicate more than two values (as on a colour screen). The pixels can be regarded as a third dimension of the array (normally called the z-axis). Therefore a bitmap is a special case of a pixmap.

You can use pixmaps as a simple means of enhancing your application's interface with graphical pictures and icons (Figure 4.6). In the next section you will see that you can also create graphical buttons, as in the palettes of a graphics editor, because this feature is inherited by the button classes.

To prepare a label for accepting a pixmap you have to set the resource field *XmNlabelType* to *XmPIXMAP* (the default is *XmSTRING*). You also have to specify a pixmap for the *XmNlabelPixmap* resource field. A pixmap is specified as an opaque type *Pixmap*, which internally identifies an X server resource. To obtain a *Pixmap* value, the image data must be sent to the X server and must also be registered. There are two ways of achieving this, namely:

- Using the resource mechanism to convert a pre-installed image or a bitmap file automatically.

- Including a bitmap file in the program, and creating a pixmap from it.

There are a number of pre-installed images, which can be chosen by simply specifying their name in a resource file. These are most useful for background and shadowing effects on monochrome screens, as you can see from

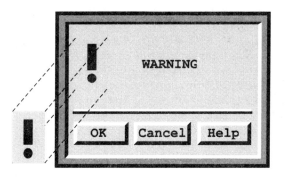

Figure 4.6: Label with pixmap used to display an icon in a dialog box.

Default symbols:	
default_xm_error	error message symbol
default_xm_information	information message symbol
default_xm_question	question message symbol
default_xm_warning	warning message symbol
default_xm_working	working message symbol
Pattern pixmaps:	
background	solid background colour
25_foreground	pattern with 25% foreground colour
50_foreground	pattern with 50% foreground colour
75_foreground	pattern with 75% foreground colour
horizontal	pattern with horizontal lines
vertical	pattern with vertical lines
slant_right	pattern with -45 degree lines
slant_left	pattern with 45 degree lines

Table 4-3: Pre-installed pixmaps.

Table 4-3. You have to create any useful icon images yourself. For this purpose you can use the X11 utility *bitmap*, an interactive editor which produces a text file as result.

If you specify the name of such a file in a resource file, the resource mechanism does the dirty work for you and reads in the bitmap files at run-time. You can either use an absolute path name (i.e. one starting with a slash and enumerating all directories from the top) or a relative one, which is searched in the path set by the environment variable *XBMLANGPATH*.

A bitmap file has a format suitable for direct inclusion into a C program, as in the following example:

```
#define folder_width 32
#define folder_height 32
#define folder_x_hot -1
#define folder_y_hot -1
static char folder_bits[] = {
  0x55, 0x55, 0x55, 0x55, 0xaa, 0xaa, 0xaa, 0xaa, 0x55, 0x55, 0x55, 0x55,
  0xaa, 0xaa, 0xaa, 0xaa, 0x55, 0x55, 0x55, 0x55, 0xaa, 0xaa, 0xaa, 0xaa,
  0xf5, 0xff, 0xff, 0x55, 0xfa, 0xff, 0xff, 0xaa, 0xfd, 0xff, 0x7f, 0x54,
  0x0a, 0x00, 0x80, 0xa8, 0x0d, 0x00, 0x00, 0x51, 0x0a, 0x00, 0x00, 0xba,
  0x0d, 0x00, 0x00, 0x5c, 0x0a, 0x00, 0x00, 0xbc, 0x0d, 0x00, 0x00, 0x5c,
  0x0a, 0x00, 0x00, 0xbc, 0x0d, 0x00, 0x00, 0x5c, 0x0a, 0x00, 0x00, 0xbc,
  0x0d, 0x00, 0x00, 0x5c, 0x0a, 0x00, 0x00, 0xbc, 0x0d, 0x00, 0x00, 0x5c,
  0x0a, 0x00, 0x00, 0xbc, 0x0d, 0x00, 0x00, 0x5c, 0xfa, 0xff, 0xff, 0xaf,
  0x55, 0x55, 0x55, 0x55, 0xaa, 0xaa, 0xaa, 0xaa, 0x55, 0x55, 0x55, 0x55,
  0xaa, 0xaa, 0xaa, 0xaa, 0x55, 0x55, 0x55, 0x55, 0xaa, 0xaa, 0xaa, 0xaa,
  0x55, 0x55, 0x55, 0x55, 0xaa, 0xaa, 0xaa, 0xaa};
```

XmNlabelPixmap	Pixmap	To display as face
XmNlabelType	enum	If text or pixmap
		XmSTRING
		XmPIXMAP

Table 4-4: Pixmap resource fields of the label class.

This declaration effectively creates a static bit array in the program's memory image that must be converted to a server-resident pixmap before it can be used by the label widget. The conversion, which involves transferring the bitmap information to the X server, is performed by the following call:

```
#include "folder.bm"
/* defines folder_bits, folder_width, folder_height */

Pixmap pix;

/* this only works on monochrome screens, i.e. depth of window = 1 */
pix = XCreateBitmapFromData (display, DefaultRootWindow (display),
                folder_bits, folder_width, folder_height);
```

The first two parameters specify the display connection (returned from *XtOpenDisplay*) and an arbitrary window which indicates the screen. The other parameters specify the bitmap in memory. If successful, the call returns the identification of the pixmap, otherwise it returns *None* (e.g. if there is not enough memory available to the X server).

The bitmap format used for label images has one important limitation: it can only express two colours. In contrast, pixmaps may contain as many different colours as the number of bits in a pixel allows. However, no directly supported format currently exists with this capability.

To use a bitmap on a colour screen, you must specify the two colours that will be used for the pixmap (e.g. the bitmap may be displayed in yellow on blue). A different call is required to generate a general pixmap, and somehow you also have to obtain the two colours. Usually you take the foreground and background colours from a widget, so the most frequent usage looks like the following:

```
#include "folder.bm"
/* defines folder_bits, folder_width, folder_height */

Pixmap      pix;
Pixel       foreground, background;
Widget      label_widget;
Arg         args[2];
```

```
label_widget = XtCreateManagedWidget (...);
XtSetArg (args[0], XmNforeground, &foreground);
XtSetArg (args[1], XmNbackground, &background);
XtGetValues (label_widget, args, 2);


pix = XCreatePixmapFromBitmapData (display, DefaultRootWindow (display),
            /* you cannot use XtWindow (label_widget) before XtRealize */
            folder_bits, folder_width, folder_height,
            foreground, background,
                DefaultDepthOfScreen (DefaultScreen (display)));
XtSetArg (args[0], XmNlabelPixmap, pix);
XtSetArg (args[1], XmNlabelType, XmPIXMAP);
XtSetValues (label_widget, args, 2);
```

4.3 Button Widgets

Together with scroll bars, buttons are the most important Motif classes. They are universally used, and most application commands are triggered by button activation. Because they are relatively simple they also serve as a good example of the concept of widgets as active objects.

Motif features the following different button classes (see also Figure 4.7), of which all except the arrow buttons are direct subclasses of the label class:

- Push buttons, which are labels that can be depressed.
- Toggle buttons, which can toggle between two states.
- Arrow buttons, which are push buttons with an arrow face.
- Drawn buttons, which have a callback to draw the contents.
- Cascade buttons, which are push buttons that activate pop-up menus.

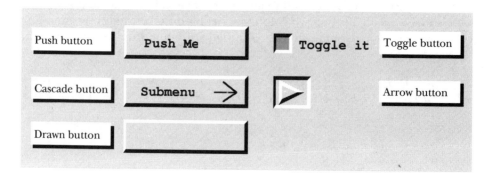

Figure 4.7: Appearance of different button classes.

Figure 4.8: Push buttons in a dialog window.

Only the first three classes will be explained here, because the others have a rather special purpose. Cascade buttons are used in conjunction with menus and thus belong to the topic of Chapter 5. Drawn buttons are used to implement application specific functionality. They are explained in Chapter 9.

A push button differs from a label in its ability to be "depressed" by pressing the (first) mouse button while the pointer is inside the button's window. Activating the button (i.e. pressing and releasing the mouse button) invokes a callback to trigger an application command.

Push buttons are used in practically all applications (see Figure 4.8). Even menu entries are push buttons at heart, although their appearance is slightly different (see Figure 4.9). The depressed state of the button is graphically simulated by appropriate shadowing around the button (see overleaf for details).

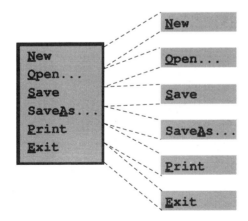

Figure 4.9: Push buttons in a menu pane. A push button in a menu only has shadows during menu traversal.

3D Appearance

The shadow borders around the push buttons are responsible for the now famous "3D look". Although this is certainly not 3D, somehow the button looks raised in one state and depressed in the other (see Figure 4.10).

The shadow effect is created by simulating a light source coming from the upper left corner. Anything raised on a surface thus lighted will have the left and upper borders brighter and the right and lower borders darker than the surface. If it is depressed, the intensities are simply switched. In addition, the interior may be somewhat darker in that state, because it receives less reflected light.

All these conditions can be conveniently simulated on a colour or grey-scale display (because at least three different shades are required). Surprisingly (since the light source could just as easily be in the lower right corner), there is usually little doubt which is the depressed state. Apparently we are more accustomed to light coming from above.

The shadow effect is simple to implement in colour, whereas its realization on monochrome screens is very difficult. Shades of grey must be simulated by bitmap patterns of different overall intensity (using the pre-installed bitmaps). To maximize the effect, the general background should be a medium grey pattern, but unfortunately, text is nearly illegible on this background in normal font sizes because the characters diffuse too much. Therefore the defaults for monochrome screens are adjusted for maximum legibility and not maximum shadowing effect.

If you want to start fiddling with the shadow effects on a monochrome screen, you can use the resource fields described in Table 4-5 (for every widget which supports shadow borders).

Although you can create your own bitmap patterns as described above, there is really no need to use any others but the built-in ones. The pattern resource fields are clearly hardware-dependent—you would not use patterns on a

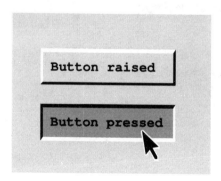

Figure 4.10: Two states of a push button simulated by switching shadows and darkening the depressed button.

XmNbackgroundPixmap	Pixmap	Background pattern of the window
XmNtopShadowPixmap	Pixmap	Pattern for top and left shadows
XmNbottomShadowPixmap	Pixmap	Pattern for bottom and right shadows

Table 4-5: Resource fields for pattern pixmaps.

colour screen—so they should only be set in a resource file, not by the application.

Dynamic Defaults

Just as there are problems with monochrome displays, life isn't too easy with a colour display. If you want to have different windows in different colours (that's what you bought that expensive colour display for), the shadows must be set to the same colour as the window background but in a different shade (lighter or darker). Therefore you have to specify not only the background colour of a window, but the shadow colours as well. The colour resources for primitive widgets are described in Table 4-6.

XmNbackground	Pixel	Background colour
XmNforeground	Pixel	Foreground colour
XmNtopShadowColor	Pixel	Colour for top and left shadows
XmNbottomShadowColor	Pixel	Colour for bottom and right shadows

Table 4-6: Colour resource fields for primitive widgets.

To make the interior of a button slightly darker when depressed, an additional colour is necessary. The *XmNarmColor* is only used if the corresponding flag *XmNfillOnArm* is set—which is the default setting.

Fortunately Motif provides a built-in dynamic default mechanism to determine appropriate values for colour and pattern resource fields depending on the screen characteristics and the specified background. You only have to specify the colour and pattern resource fields if you want to achieve special effects.

The dynamic default mechanism works as follows, depending on whether the screen is monochrome or not. On a monochrome screen the appropriate pixmap patterns are set to their monochrome defaults, so the colour fields can only assume two possible values.

On a colour (or grey-scale) display, the pattern resource fields are not

| XmNfillOnArm | Boolean | True uses arm colour |
| XmNarmColor | Pixel | Colour when button depressed |

Table 4-7: Additional colour resource fields for push buttons.

used (i.e. are set to *NULL*) and the shadow and arm colours are calculated from the window's background colour. The shades are calculated by multiplying the RGB values (i.e. the intensities of the red, green, and blue guns of the tube) by a certain amount.

As a result, you only have to specify the background colour (preferably in a resource file) to create pleasing effects. However, the process does not work as well with saturated colours (i.e. colours where at least one of the three guns is at maximum intensity).

You should watch out for another problem with colours. Usually your display can only show a small number of colours simultaneously, although you can choose from a much larger palette (e.g. 256 from 16 million). This is a hardware-related restriction and it manifests itself in the form of colour maps (a table having say 256 possible entries, each entry indicating the real colour value as one of the 16 million). You only have to deal with colour maps if you are using direct X calls through the Xlib.

However, if you use a large number of different colours, the number of simultaneously available colours is quickly used up (i.e. the colour map becomes full). Motif contributes somewhat to the problem because the shadows need two or three additional colours per different background. The problem becomes apparent when an application needs a large number of different colours itself, for example when displaying a colour picture.

An application needing more colours than fit in the free part of the colour map can only resort to allocating its own colour map, i.e. requesting its own set of colours. Only one of the two colour maps can be active at one time, therefore only one of the applications is displayed in true colours (the others go "Technicolor"). To avoid this effect you should use as few colours as possible. If you want to know more about X and colour, study one of the better books on Xlib programming listed in Appendix B, since the topic is too complicated to explain it here.

Callback Reasons

The whole business about shadows and colours is certainly very attractive. Nevertheless the purpose of push buttons is to invoke application procedures and not to be flashy.

You already know the activation callback invoked when "pressing" the button widget. However, there is more than one situation an application might want to be informed of, i.e. there are more callback reasons for a button than simple activation. To understand the other callbacks, the different states of a push button must first be analysed more closely.

The button is "armed" if the mouse button is pressed with the mouse pointer inside the button. For as long as the mouse button stays pressed and the mouse pointer is inside the button, the button is displayed in a depressed state. Leaving the button window while holding the mouse button down re-creates the normal appearance, but the button stays armed as long as the mouse button is held.

The button is "disarmed" when the mouse button is released. However, the button is only activated when the mouse button is released *inside* the window. In this case the activation callback is executed.

To support further interaction techniques, callbacks are also executed when the button is armed and disarmed. They can be used, for example, to implement a "Run" button keeping some process running while the button is depressed (i.e. armed), and stopping when the button is disarmed. Activation has no meaning in this case, so the activation callback list will remain empty.

The state transitions for the push button and the respective callback reasons are summarized in Figure 4.11. All three callback reasons are implemented as callback lists and are named resource fields.

The procedure *XtAddCallback*, as shown in the example in the previous chapter, will associate a callback procedure with any of the three lists. In the variable *call_data* a pointer to a structure called *XmAnyCallbackStruct* is passed. This structure is defined as follows:

```
typedef struct {
        int         reason;
        XEvent      *event;
} XmAnyCallbackStruct;
```

The *XmAnyCallbackStruct* is something like the minimal structure all Motif callbacks pass as *call_data* (other structures used for other callbacks have more members). The *reason* field is useful if you register the same procedure for different callback reasons to differentiate between those callback reasons in a code segment somewhere deep inside your procedure. The reason constants for

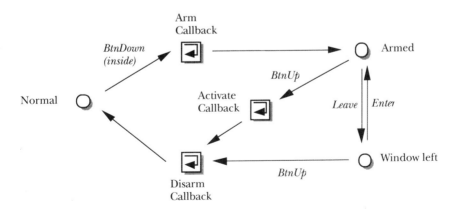

Figure 4.11: State transitions of a push button. During some transitions callbacks may be activated.

XmNactivateCallback	Callback	When button released inside
XmNarmCallback	Callback	When button pressed inside
XmNdisarmCallback	Callback	When button released

Table 4-8: Push button callback reasons.

the three push button callbacks are:

> *XmCR_ACTIVATE*
> *XmCR_ARM*
> *XmCR_DISARM*

Toggle Buttons

The second type of buttons to be discussed in this chapter are the toggle buttons. A push button reverts to its inactive state whenever it is disarmed. The armed state is only temporary. In contrast, the toggle button switches between two permanent states when activated. The term "activation" means pressing and releasing the mouse button inside the widget's window, just as for push buttons.

The toggle button supports three different strategies to represent the two toggle states visually:

- *Default* configuration. A permanent toggle indicator with two states (in and out) is shown; there are no shadows around the border.

- *Menu* configuration. The toggle indicator is only displayed when the toggle is set; there are no shadow borders.

- *Palette* behaviour. No indicator is shown; only the border shadows are toggled.

In its default configuration the toggle button displays a small shadowed indicator area in addition to the button face. Because the shadows around the indicator already have a 3D appearance, there are no shadows around the window. Examples of the default appearance are shown in Figure 4.12.

As you can see in this figure, there are two types of indicators, a square-shaped and a diamond-shaped one. They are used to differentiate between one-of-many and n-of-many selections when multiple toggle buttons are arranged in a group (see Figure 4.13).

The responsibility for implementing the different behaviours is distributed between several widgets. A single toggle button can only control its own behaviour and no other toggle buttons in the group. Therefore the toggle button widget only defines the visual appearance of the indicator. The n-of-many behaviour needs no additional provisions, because the toggle buttons are independent objects. The one-of-many behaviour—i.e. switching the previous

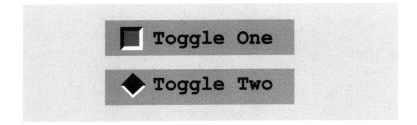

Figure 4.12: Default appearance of toggle buttons.

toggle off when another is switched on—is achieved by a manager widget, the *radio box* (discussed later in this chapter).

To select one of the two possible indicator types you use the resource field *XmNindicatorType*.

In the menu variation of the toggle button (the second case of visual appearance as outlined above) the indicator disappears when the button is in the unselected state. This configuration is selected by the resource field *XmNvisibleWhenOff*, which is automatically switched to *False* when a toggle button appears inside a menu. Figure 4.14 shows examples of this version.

The third variation, the palette behaviour, is achieved by setting the resource field *XmNindicatorOn* to *False*. In this case the indicator totally disappears (see Figure 4.15). The different states of the button are indicated by the shadows around the widget. To see the shadows you have to set the field *XmNshadowThickness* to something greater than zero (0 is the toggle button default).

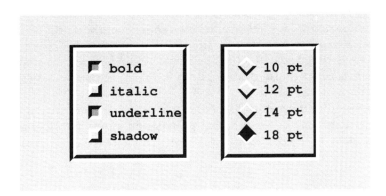

Figure 4.13: Two toggle button groups. The left group represents an n-of-many, the right one a one-of-many selection.

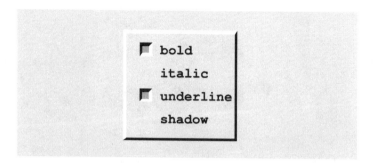

Figure 4.14: Toggle buttons inside a menu. The indicator only appears when the toggle is on.

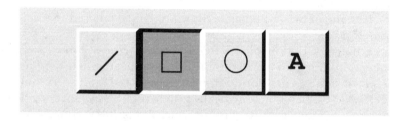

Figure 4.15: Toggle buttons in a palette.

In all cases, whether the indicator is present or not, the selected state of the button is indicated by the shadows going into the surface (depressed).

Just like the resource fields *XmNfillOnArm* and *XmNfillColor* for push buttons there are equivalent fields *XmNfillOnSelect* and *XmNselectColor* for toggle buttons. They control the background colour of the indicator area in the selected state[1].

The two different states of a toggle button are recorded in the value of the resource field *XmNset*. This field can be used to read and write the state.

To be alerted to any state changes performed by the user, the toggle button defines the *XmNvalueChangedCallback*, whose task is similar to the *XmNactivateCallback* of push buttons. Both callbacks are triggered by the same user behaviour.

Conveniently, the callbacks of the toggle button pass a pointer to the following structure as *call_data*, which provides an additional field to indicate the current state of the toggle:

---

[1]In Motif 1.0 the selected colour does not apply to the whole button face if the indicator is switched off.

XmNindicatorType	enum	Appearance of indicator XmN_OF_MANY XmONE_OF_MANY
XmNvisibleWhenOff	Boolean	True=indicator always visible
XmNindicatorOn	Boolean	False=indicator never visible
XmNfillOnSelect	Boolean	True uses select colour in indicator
XmNselectColor	Pixel	Colour of indicator in select state

Table 4-9: Indicator-related resource fields for toggle buttons.

```
typedef struct {
        int         reason;
        XEvent      *event;
        Boolean     set;
} XmToggleButtonCallbackStruct;
```

If the state toggled, the new value is reported because the callback is executed after switching.

Another way to change the state of a toggle button is to use the procedure *XmToggleButtonSetState*. This procedure is roughly equivalent to *XtSetValues* on the *XmNset* field, but as a third parameter you can specify whether to execute the *XmNvalueChangedCallback* if the state changes.

```
Boolean     new_state = True;
Boolean     exec_callback = True;

XmToggleButtonSetState (toggle_button_widget, new_state, exec_callback);
```

Triggering the callback from the application itself is useful because it allows you to isolate the response to state changes in one place, namely the callback procedure. Use of this procedure is also recommended when the toggle button is part of a radio box, because the dependencies between the toggle buttons are maintained by callbacks. The behaviour of toggle buttons in a radio box is discussed later.

Being able to set the toggle state from the application program implies that toggle buttons can also be used to display some information which is not changeable by the user. You have two possibilities to prevent user interference. The first one is to set the toggle button to an insensitive state:

```
XtSetSensitive (toggle_button_widget, False);
```

Insensitive means that the button does not react to any keyboard or mouse events. The insensitive state is normally used for buttons that are not available for use at that moment, but which remain in place to aid the user in spatial memorization.

Figure 4.16: An insensitive button compared with a sensitive one.

Unfortunately the label's drawing routine, inherited by all buttons, greys out any label text in the insensitive state (Figure 4.16), which is not very useful for state-displaying toggle buttons. If you want the text to appear with normal intensity, you have to resort to the second method.

User interaction for any widget class is also inhibited by setting the *XmNtranslation* resource field to an empty translation table (remember, the translation table defines the mapping between events and actions). An empty translation table causes no action ever to be called. No button or key events are recognized by the widget.

Clearing the translation table is accomplished most easily with the following entry in an application defaults resource file (replace the widget specification with a correct one for your application):

    your_app*your_widget*translations: #replace

Buttons with Pixmaps

Providing a label widget with a pixmap face is rather simple, as there is only one pixmap to specify. Buttons have additional states, which are difficult, if not impossible, to draw automatically when only one pixmap is provided. A text button may be greyed out by overlaying the text with a tiling pattern pixmap. Tiling would render most pixmaps unrecognizable, therefore a second pixmap should be used to indicate the insensitive state of a pixmap button.

In the armed state a text button is filled with a darker colour. Darkening is difficult to achieve with pixmaps because they may contain more than two different colours. A third pixmap is needed to represent the armed state.

Additional resource fields have been implemented for buttons to specify appropriate pixmaps for these states. For the insensitive state the resource field is called *XmNlabelInsensitivePixmap* (although the insensitive state is not very useful for labels—but it is defined in the label class to be inherited by subclasses). The push button class defines a resource field *XmNarmPixmap* to distinguish the armed state. The three states of a push button are illustrated in Figure 4.17.

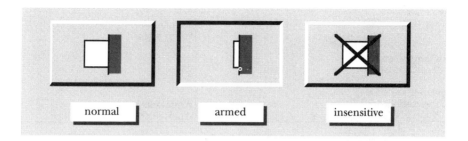

Figure 4.17: Using different pixmaps for different push button states.

Toggle buttons need one more pixmap. Whereas push buttons cannot be armed while insensitive, toggle buttons can be in either the set or the unset state when insensitive (see Figure 4.18). All the pixmap resource fields are summarized in Table 4-10.

Arrow Buttons

The arrow button widget features the same behaviour as a push button. The only difference is that the button face is predefined as an arrow. You may wonder why a special class was defined for this purpose. The reason is that the shadows are not drawn in the rectangular form of the window, but around the arrow. Therefore a special shadow drawing routine is necessary.

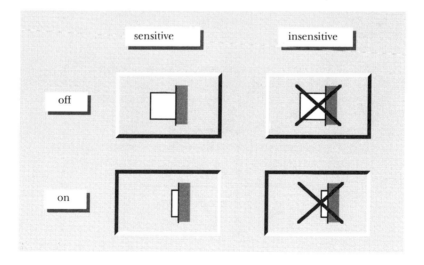

Figure 4.18: Using different pixmaps for different toggle button states.

Label class		
XmNlabelPixmap	Pixmap	Normal face
XmNlabelInsensitivePixmap	Pixmap	When insensitive
Push button class		
XmNarmPixmap	Pixmap	When armed
Toggle button class		
XmNselectPixmap	Pixmap	When selected and sensitive
XmNselectInsensitivePixmap	Pixmap	When selected and insensitive

Table 4-10: Pixmap resource fields of button classes.

Because the arrow button does not have a text or pixmap to display, it is not defined as a subclass of the label class, but only inherits general features of the Motif primitive widgets. Owing to the specialized nature of this class, there are also fewer resource fields to consider.

In addition to the three callback reasons for push buttons explained above (the arrow button has the same state transitions as the push button), the arrow button class defines only one new field as described in Table 4-11. Figure 4.19 shows an arrow button in each of the four orientations.

XmNarrowDirection	enum	Pointing direction
		XmARROW_UP
		XmARROW_DOWN
		XmARROW_LEFT
		XmARROW_RIGHT

Table 4-11: Special arrow button resource field.

4.4 The Text Widget

Even in a graphical and mouse-driven environment you have to enter

Figure 4.19: Orientations of arrow buttons.

some information via the keyboard. The text widget is designed for this task. (Please note: "the text widget" really means "the text widget class" or "all instances of the text widget class".)

The text widget allows the usual editing functions to be performed on the text entered. It also supports the selection of text with the mouse to delete, copy or move it. The text widget comes in two variants:

- *Single line text,* mainly used as a text entry field in dialog boxes. The text can be of any length (you can set a maximum) and may be scrolled with the cursor keys if it is longer than the visible size.

- *Multi-line text,* to be used like a small text editor. A multi-line text is nearly always used in conjunction with a scroll bar, because the contents may be unlimited. Scrolling aspects are discussed in Section 5.6 on scrolled windows.

Examples of the two types of text widgets are shown in Figure 4.20. Both types are implemented by the same widget class because they share most of their code. You have already seen another example of different personalities in one widget class: the text/pixmap modes of labels and buttons.

User Interface

Because of the editing functionality the text widget needs a larger number of interactive functions than buttons; most of these are activated through the keyboard. Divided into suitable groups, they will be discussed below.

If a text widget accepts input, it shows a blinking *insertion cursor* to indicate where typed characters will go. The cursor position can be changed either by clicking with the left mouse button at the new location or by moving it with the cursor keys. In addition, the right and left cursor keys move the cursor to the end or beginning of the line respectively if pressed simultaneously with the Ctrl modifier key.

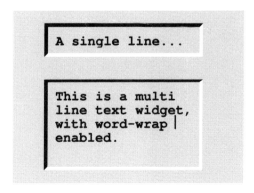

Figure 4.20: Examples of text widgets.

<Btn1>:	set cursor
<Key>Left:	back one character
<Key>Right:	forward one character
<Key>Up:	previous line (only multi-line)
<Key>Down:	next line (only multi-line)
Ctrl<Key>Left:	back one word
Ctrl<Key>Right:	forward one word

Table 4-12: Cursor movement functions. The specification on the left follows the syntax for defining the left-hand sides of translations.

Pressing a character key inserts the respective character at the cursor location and advances the cursor. Deleting characters may be performed with the Backspace or Delete keys, which, depending on your keyboard, delete the character to the right or the left of the cursor (see below for how to change that). Used together with the Shift modifier, they delete a whole word.

In addition to these rather conventional and primitive editing functions, the text widget allows the user to select a continuous portion of the text. A selected part can be moved, copied or deleted. Two classes of functions concern selections: those that allow for the specification of a selection, and those that operate on the current selection.

The selection can be established with either the mouse or the cursor keys. The simplest method is to click-drag with the mouse, i.e. move to the starting point of the new selection, press the mouse button, and move the pointer to the end of the selection. While the pointer is moving, the selection grows or shrinks accordingly. Releasing the mouse button then establishes the selection.

Another method is multiple clicking. A single click (i.e. press–release) of the left mouse button moves the insertion cursor. Further clicks within a short timeframe select a region around this location: a double click marks a word, a triple click selects the whole line, and four clicks in rapid succession select the whole text.

Using the keyboard, you can create a selection range by using the Shift modifier key together with the left and right cursor keys to extend the current selection in the direction of the respective cursor key. The selection can also be extended to a new position with the first mouse button in conjunction with Shift.

<Key>:	insert this character
<Key>BackSpace:	delete previous character
Shift<Key>BackSpace:	delete previous word
<Key>Delete:	delete next character
Shift<Key>Delete:	delete next word

Table 4-13: Insertion and deletion functions. The mapping of BackSpace and Delete depends on your keyboard, but can be changed by overriding translations.

<Btn1Down><Btn1Move><Btn1Up>:	mark selection
<Btn1>(2):	select word
<Btn1>(3):	select line
<Btn1>(4):	select all
Shift<Key>Left:	extend selection to the left
Shift<Key>Right:	extend selection to the right
Shift<Btn1>:	extend selection to position
<Btn3>:	copy selection to position
Ctrl<Btn3>:	move selection to position

Table 4-14: Selection commands. Multiple consecutive events on the left specify that these events must occur in sequence for the action to be taken. The numbers in brackets are a shorthand for a fixed number of repetitions with a short delay.

The selected text can be deleted by simply overwriting it—this is called the *pending delete* mode. When writing the first character, the current selection disappears and the new character appears in that place.

You can copy the selection by clicking with the right mouse button in the new location. Combined with the Ctrl modifier, the selection is moved rather than being copied.

Note that there may only be one selection on the whole screen, irrespective of the number of different applications. The selection is globally stored in the X server under the name PRIMARY. (The last sentence is an oversimplification—the real complexity of the mechanism is revealed in Chapter 7.) Therefore you can even transfer the selection value between text widgets of different applications.

The PRIMARY selection is not to be confused with the *clipboard* (the clipboard will also be explained in Chapter 7). Whereas the PRIMARY selection is something visibly marked in some window, the clipboard is a background storage which is normally invisible.

The final set of commands for the text widget concerns *keyboard traversal,* a mechanism to move the input focus by using the keyboard. Only one window (widget) on the screen can have the input focus. This is the window which receives all keyboard events. Normally you set the focus using the mouse, i.e. either by clicking into the appropriate window or by moving the mouse pointer into the window (either of these focus models can be selected through resource fields—see Section 6.5).

In a dialog box with multiple text widgets, which are usually filled one after the other, it is very convenient to move the focus between these fields without your hands leaving the keyboard. The focus transfer is accomplished using the Tab key. Further details of the keyboard traversal mechanism are given in Section 6.4.

| <Key>Tab: | to next tab group (only single-line) |
| Shift<Key>Tab: | to previous tab group |

Table 4-15: Traversal commands. Tab groups are the units of focus (normally text widgets).

Value Access

The most important function of a text widget from a programmer's point of view is accessing the string value. The value is available under the resource field name *XmNvalue*. Please note that the value is a simple C string and not of type *XmString*. Therefore you can set it in the following way:

> *XtSetArg (args[0], XmNvalue, "Initial text widget value");*
> *XtSetValues (text_widget, args, 1);*

You could also use this argument list when creating a text widget. The corresponding case of reading the value is only slightly more complicated. You have to define a string variable in which a pointer to the current value can be stored. The address of the string variable must be placed in the argument list:

> *String   result;*
>
> *XtSetArg (args[0], XmNvalue, &result);*
> *XtGetValues (text_widget, args, 1);*
> *printf (result)...*

The effect of this call is that the address of the internally stored string is copied into *result*. Therefore you must take care not to overwrite the string, because it is needed internally by the text widget. If you want to use the string for other purposes, you should copy it (Figure 4.21).

In contrast, the string is automatically copied to the internal location when you set the value. If the string is not constant (as it is in the example above), and you do not use it further, you should free the memory associated with it after calling *XtSetValues* or *XtCreateManagedWidget* (using *XtFree*—see the example below).

This asymmetrical behaviour between setting and reading is caused by the definition of *XtGetValues*. The code in the widget cannot interfere with the argument copying of *XtGetValues*. However, an internal hook is defined for *XtSet-Values* where extra processing can be done. *XtGetValues* does not know the type of field it must copy. It only knows its fixed length, which is coded into the widget. As a result, no dynamical structures can be copied, only pointers to them.

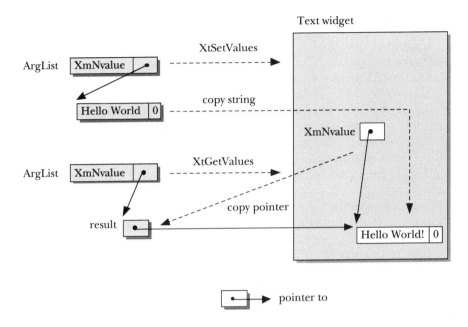

Figure 4.21: Setting and getting strings (and other dynamic structures). *XtSetValues* copies the value referenced in the argument list to an internal location. *XtGetValues* returns an address that points to the internal value.

A more symmetrical pair of routines is specially designed for accessing the text widget's value:

String   result;

XmTextSetString (text_widget, "Another sample text.");
result = XmTextGetString (text_widget);
...
XtFree (result);

With these routines the string is copied in both cases. That means that storage is dynamically allocated for the result of *XmTextGetString,* which should be freed when no longer needed with *XtFree.*

XmNvalue	String	Current value of text

Table 4-16: Value resource field of the text widget.

Geometry Resources

In the default setting of the text widget you can enter a single line of text of nearly unlimited length. The text widget itself, however, must have a finite width to fit on the screen. If the length of the entered string exceeds this width, it can be scrolled with the cursor keys. Although the width of the text widget is solely controlled by its parent widget (see the discussion on geometry management in Chapter 2), you can specify a preference using the resource field *XmNcolumns*. This number measures the width in font spaces. The resulting size is relative to the font size. The preferred width of the text widget is in most cases respected by the parent. A similar field *XmNrows* exists for multi-line texts.

You can specify the font for the text widget using the resource *XmNfontList*. Only the font for the default character set is used, however, because the text widget does not support XmStrings. A font list is used instead of a single font to make font specification for Motif applications uniform.

If your application requires a maximum number of characters for a string, you can specify *XmNmaxLength*. Any user attempt to make the entered string longer than this value is rejected by the text widget. Be careful not to set a longer value from your program. Programmatic accesses are not checked, and a longer string may thoroughly confuse the text widget (or at least the user).

If you want the text widget to display as much of its contents as is allowed by the geometry-managing parent instead of scrolling its contents, you should set *XmNresizeWidth* to *True* (and *XmNresizeHeight* in a multi-line text).

These flags do not inhibit resizing by the parent (the parent has total control over the geometry of children). Instead they determine whether the widget itself shall request a new geometry when the value is changed. If *XmNresizeWidth* is *False*, the text widget will always stay at its initial width (determined by *XmNcolumns*) if not resized by the parent (see Figure 4.22).

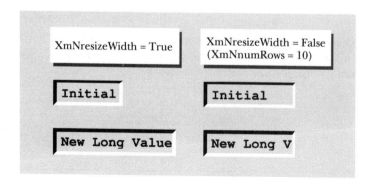

Figure 4.22: Effect of *XmNresizeWidth* (provided parent allows it).

XmNcolumns	short	Default width in font spaces
XmNrows	short	Default height in font heights
XmNmaxLength	int	Max length of user entered text
XmNresizeWidth	Boolean	Resize to show all
XmNresizeHeight	Boolean	Resize to show all (if multi-line)
XmNfontList	XmFontList	Font to be used
XmNmarginWidth	short	Margins around text
XmNmarginHeight	short	

Table 4-17: Geometry resource fields of the text widget.

Two other resource fields affecting the geometry are *XmNmarginWidth* and *XmNmarginHeight*. These determine the space between the text and the enclosing shadow. (Note: the shadow around the text can be controlled in the same way as was described for the label widget.)

Behaviour Resources

The position where the next typed character will go is marked by a blinking insertion cursor. The cursor can be switched off by setting the field *XmNcursorPositionVisible* to *False*, and the blinking frequency can be controlled with *XmNblinkRate*. The position of the character following the insertion cursor (starting from 0) is reflected by the resource field *XmNcursorPosition*. You can change this position if you want to implement special key functions (such as jumping to the next space).

If the cursor is moved by the application to a position outside the currently visible range, the text should scroll to make the cursor position visible again. You can inhibit that behaviour by setting *XmNautoShowCursorPosition* to *False*. Another way to deal with such situations is to scroll explicitly by changing the resource field *XmNtopCharacter*, which denotes the first character to appear in the text window. This resource field, however, will not work when *XmNresizeWidth* is set, because then the widget always tries to make the whole text visible.

You have already seen that the text widget can be used to display either single-line or multi-line text. This behaviour is controlled by the resource field *XmNeditMode*, which defaults to the single-line mode. A further mode is introduced by *XmNeditable*, which enables the editing functions. A non-editable widget is different from an insensitive one, because an insensitive widget does not react to any keyboard or mouse events, while the non-editable text at least

XmNcursorPosition	XmTextPosition	Cursor before (0...)
XmNautoShowCursorPosition	Boolean	Scroll cursor into view
XmNblinkRate	int	On time of cursor in ms
XmNcursorPositionVisible	Boolean	If cursor is displayed
XmNtopCharacter (in 1.0: XmNtopPosition)	XmTextPosition	Start before (0...)

Table 4-18: Cursor resource fields of the text widget.

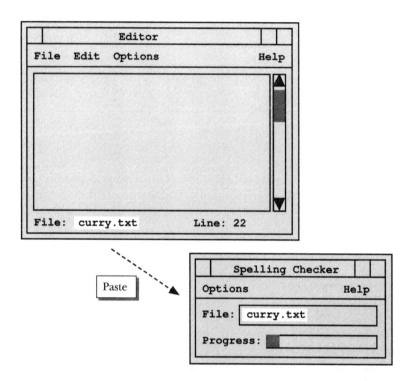

Figure 4.23: Example of where a text that is selectable but not editable is useful. The selected value in the upper window has been pasted into the text widget of another application that owns the lower window.

allows selections and scrolling.

The ability to allow selections makes it sometimes preferable to use the text widget when a label widget would otherwise be appropriate. (Remember that you can quite easily change the label text to display information.) A label is most useful if the displayed texts belong to a fixed and limited set. If the texts are generated by your program and contain user specific information, the user may profit from the ability to select parts to use elsewhere.

As an example, imagine the user has to specify a file name as a parameter for some useful little utility, say a spelling checker (see Figure 4.23). If the file to be checked is already open in the editor (which usually displays the file name somewhere), it would be most convenient if the user could just select this file name from the editor window and insert it into the text widget in the parameter dialog window of the utility. You could object that it is the utility's job—it should provide a file navigation tool instead of the primitive text entry field (such as the file selection box widget as explained in Chapter 6). But why should a user even navigate to locate a file he has already found? Therefore,

XmNeditMode	enum	Single or multi line
		XmSINGLE_LINE_EDIT
		XmMULTI_LINE_EDIT
XmNeditable	Boolean	May be modified
XmNwordWrap	Boolean	Perform word wrap (multi-line)

Table 4-19: Mode resource fields of the text widget.

providing reusable information in a non-editable text widget is an easily implemented and useful feature.

Another mode of the text widget is controlled by *XmNwordWrap*, which makes sense only in a multi-line text. A nice feature of this is that even program-set text is automatically wrapped. Wrapping takes place at the current size of the window and not at the position specified by *XmNcolumns*. Therefore the wrapping changes when the window is resized. This may introduce undesired effects if the text widget is partially clipped, for example when the text is in a scrolled window.

Text Callbacks

Now it is time to explore the different callback reasons supported by the text widget. There are some simpler callbacks which only pass the usual callback data (namely a reason and the corresponding X event), and some callbacks that pass more information in their *call_data* structure.

The most important callback is the *XmNactivateCallback*, which is activated whenever the return key is pressed in a single-line widget. To use this callback in a multi-line widget you yourself must bind the *activate* action to an event of your choice—see below for how to change translations. You can use this call-back to initiate any actions when the user has finished entering a value.

If your application needs direct notification of value changes without waiting for the return key, it can use the *XmNvalueChangedCallback*. Whenever the text is changed—e.g. on every typed character—any dependencies can be updated to reflect the new value. A possible application is name completion, i.e. if there is only one possible value left which matches the incomplete entered text, the program can complete the user's entry.

The last of the three simple callbacks is the *XmNfocusCallback*. This call-back is executed whenever the text widget gets the focus, i.e. when the user clicks or tabs into it. This callback can be used to switch the environment to reflect which text is currently edited.

One (perhaps not very brilliant) example is a row of text widgets, each of which specifies the exact position of a tab stop (see Figure 4.24). At the same time the tab stops are displayed on a ruler. The program can always highlight the position that is just being edited by virtue of the *XmNfocusCallback*.

The other three text widget callbacks are more complicated for two reasons. First, they expect a response from the application about whether some

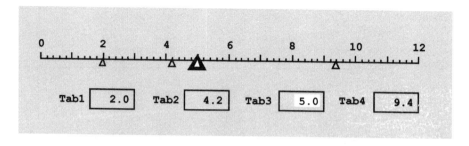

Figure 4.24: Focus callback example. A tab stop marker is highlighted when the text containing its position gets the focus.

action is to be executed by the text widget or not. Second, they have to provide some additional data necessary for decision making.

Passing information from the application back to the calling widget is an exceptional case. However, it is easily implemented by treating the *call_data* structure as writable and letting the widget analyse its contents after the callback procedures have been executed.

The *XmNlosingFocusCallback* is called when the text widget is about to lose the focus. The *call_data* argument to the callback routines is a pointer to a structure which contains a flag *doit*. This flag can be set to *False* by a callback procedure to make the text widget keep the focus (although losing the focus cannot be prevented in all cases).

The flag is initially *True*, so if you do not change it or if no callback routine is registered, the focus will be lost.

A pointer to the same structure is passed as *call_data* for all three callback reasons:

```
typedef struct {
        int                 reason;      /* XmCR_LOSING_FOCUS            */
                                         /* XmCR_MODIFYING_TEXT_VALUE */
                                         /* XmCR_MOVING_INSERT_CURSOR */
        XEvent              *event;
        Boolean             doit;
        XmTextPosition      currInsert,
                            newInsert;
        XmTextPosition      startPos,    /* not if MOVING_INSERT_CURSOR */
                            endPos;
        XmTextBlock         text;        /* only if MODIFYING_TEXT_VALUE */
} XmTextVerifyCallbackStruct;
```

Not all members of the structure contain valid information for all reasons. When losing focus, all text positions are valid, but they are equal and of no special interest.

XmNactivateCallback	Callback	<Return> in single-line
XmNvalueChangedCallback	Callback	If value changed
XmNfocusCallback	Callback	When text gets focus
XmNlosingFocusCallback	Callback	When text loses focus
XmNmodifyVerifyCallback	Callback	Use to check changes
XmNmotionVerifyCallback	Callback	Use to check position changes

Table 4-20: Callbacks of the text widget.

The next callback *XmNmotionVerifyCallback* uses the two fields *currInsert* and *newInsert* to let your callback routine decide whether the cursor position may be changed.

The last two fields of the callback structure are only used by *XmNmodify-VerifyCallback*, which is called to check the validity of text entry. It can be used to implement direct checking of text fields in form entry. The new text about to be entered (normally only one character except when copying or moving) is passed in the following structure:

```
typedef struct {
    char            *ptr;
    int             length;
    XmTextFormat    format;     /* FMT8BIT                          */
                                /* FMT16BIT                         */
} XmTextBlockRec, *XmtextBlock;
```

To check fields in a form, all you have to do is to write a modify-verify callback routine which checks the validity of the new value. Because the new value of the text widget does not yet exist, you often have to create it yourself and check this value. For example, in checking for a valid number, because the validity of a decimal point depends on its position you cannot simply reject its insertion without looking at the new value.

To build the preliminary new value, you must first read the current value with *XtGetValues* (or the convenience function *XmTextGetString*) and then apply the change. If the change is an insertion, both *startPos* and *endPos* equal *currPos*. Otherwise the indicated string part must be replaced with the new value in the text block. It might be a good idea to carry around a duplicate of the text value to avoid reading it every time, because you are informed of all changes.

Customizing Translations

Although the text widget already supports a rich functionality, it can be customized through additional translations. As the text widget has many keyboard functions, there is a natural desire to customize the key bindings for compatibility with older products or user preferences. How to achieve this is described in this section.

As you read in Chapter 2, translations are a resource field of every widget in which a mapping between events and corresponding actions is specified. In particular, this mapping can be changed at run-time by an entry in a resource file.

Text translations can be changed in two ways which differ only in their handling of an already existing translation for the same event. Existing translations can be overriden. The keywords *#override* and *#augment* at the start of the translation specification indicate the relevant mode. A third possibility is to replace all existing translations of the widget, but then you would lose the large number of default translations for the text widget.

A translation specification consists of an event specification part and the desired actions. The actions must exist and be registered, otherwise they will not be found at run-time. If you want to change the translations, you must either use existing actions, possibly attaching them to different keys or buttons, or register your own.

An example of the use of existing actions[1] is to bind the activate callback to a key in a multi-line text. The action to invoke this callback is simply called *activate*. If you want to connect this action to the function key F5, you can use the following lines in a resource file:

> **name_of_the_text_widget*translations:*   *#override* \
>   *\<Key>F5:*   *activate ()*

A second example of this kind of enhancement is the "help" callback, which is present in nearly all widgets, but is not bound to any key (the Motif style guide recommends F1). To connect this callback for a certain widget class, you specify something like the following:

> **XmText*translations:*   *#augment* \
>   *\<Key>F1:*   *help ()*

One snag to watch out for is that, given both of the above specifications, only one of them will have effect. That is a consequence of the fact that two different specifications for the same resource field and the same widget are treated as a conflict, although they can reasonably be merged in this case. Two separate translation specifications for one widget can be especially confusing if they reside in two different resource files (one in the application default file and one in the user default file, for example). As a solution you have to combine both specifications into one translation table.

An additional peculiarity is associated with the translations of text widgets. The translations are different for single-line and multi-line text widgets. The set of different translations is internally installed on creation, depending on

---

[1]The 1.0 documentation regrettably omitted a specification of which actions exist for a widget class. They can usually only be guessed from the default translations.

XmNeditMode, i.e. *after* values from the resource database have been obtained. The translations can therefore not be overridden in a resource file, only with *XtSetValues* in the application code.

   If no suitable action exists you can register your own actions at the start of your program, which can then be used in all translations. The only difference to the internal actions is that yours are valid for all widget classes, while the internal ones are specific to the particular widget class. Internal actions (such as *activate*) can also have the same name in different classes, while application-registered ones should be unique.

   The registration is performed by *XtAppAddActions* before the first widget that may use them is created (but after *XtToolkitInitialize*).

```
XtActionsRec action_table = {
        { "MyAction1",   (XtActionProc)MyAction1},
        { "MyAction2",   (XtActionProc)MyAction2}
};
...
XtToolkitInitialize ();
XtAppAddActions (context, action_table, XtNumber(action_table));
...
```

   The following is a silly but simple example for a self-defined action which decreases the cursor position by one character. It should only be used in the translations of a text widget, otherwise its function is undefined:

```
void MyAction1 (w, event, params, no)
        Widget      w;
        XEvent      *event;
        String      *params;   /* not referenced here   */
        Cardinal    *no;
{
        int         current = 0;     /* initialize if accidently used with other   */
                                     /* classes where no value is returned         */
        Arg         args[1];

        XtSetArg (args[0], XmNcursorPosition, &current);
        XtGetValues (w, args, 1);
        if (current > 0) {
                XtSetValues (args[0], XmNcursorPosition, current - 1);
                XtSetValues (w, args, 1);
        }
}
```

   If you have problems with text entry because some keys do not generate the character they are supposed to, it may be the fault of the keyboard mapping inside the X server. The tables which reside there are used by practically all X client programs for translating a *keycode* (which is an arbitrary number for a certain physical key of the keyboard) into a *keysym* (which is a symbol in a certain character set). The identifiers F1 and F5 used above are keysyms. Which keycode produces these symbols depends entirely on your keyboard.

The list of defined keysyms can be found in the file "keysymdef.h", which usually resides in the directory "/usr/include/X11". If you want to change the keyboard mapping, you can use the program *xmodmap*. However, this will affect all X clients, even those not using Motif, and you should only make modifications when the same problem also occurs in other programs.

4.5 The Scroll Bar Widget

After buttons and the text widget, the scroll bar represents a third major class of primitve widget. It is a rather specialized, but commonly used, widget.

The scroll bar is most often used as a part of a scrolled window, which provides the scrolling mechanism and an appropriate geometry management for a scrollable area. But even when using a scrolled window you need at least a general knowledge about the scroll bar operation.

The scroll bar is the first widget you have encountered that has a draggable part. Dragging means that an object on the screen can be moved by pressing the mouse button and then moving the mouse pointer. The draggable part of the scroll bar is the slider, which can be seen in Figure 4.25. The slider follows the mouse pointer while the mouse button is down—but only within the bounds of the scroll bar.

Dragging the slider is not the only way to perform a scrolling operation. There are four different areas in the scroll bar, and the reactions of each part to mouse events are different:

- The *slider* has already been discussed. It can be dragged from one end of the enclosing area to the other.

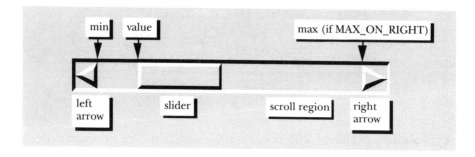

Figure 4.25: Anatomy of a scroll bar.

- The *scroll region* is the area over which the slider can be moved. Clicking in this area initiates movement in page increments (see below for how you can configure what one page means). If the button click occurs above (or to the left) of the slider, the slider moves one page up (or left); on the other side of the slider it moves in the opposite direction.

- The *up (or left) arrow* works like an arrow button. Clicking into this area initiates an upward (or left) movement of one unit.

- The *down (or right) arrow* moves the slider in the opposite direction to its cousin.

Clicking into the arrows while holding down the Shift modifier moves the slider to the respective end of the scroll bar. A continuous scrolling is started if the mouse button is held down in the scroll region or one of the arrows. Continuous scrolling occurs in the relevant units (page or single), thus providing two different scrolling speeds.

Although the scroll bar could have been implemented as a composite widget with the above mentioned parts, it really is a primitive widget because it is frequently used with the same configuration and is timing-critical to give instant feedback.

Scroll Bar Configuration

As mentioned above, the scroll bar operates with configurable units. The units can be chosen by the programmer. The scroll bar always reports movement in terms of these units, so you need not convert pixel values. This is especially useful when the scroll bar is resized (e.g. if the user resizes the main window), and the number of pixels between the minimum and maximum slider positions is changed. The scroll bar automatically handles the necessary adjustments of the conversion procedure.

After having selected the appropriate units specific to your application you must configure the scroll bar by specifying the minimum and maximum values to be reported at the end points. You also have to specify the size of the slider, because according to the Motif style guide it should be proportional to the visible part of the scrolled area. The last parameters to configure are the numbers of units to be used for single steps and for page scrolling.

XmNminimum	int	Minimum value reported
XmNmaximum	int	Maximum value reported
XmNsliderSize	int	Unit length of slider
XmNincrement	int	Unit increment for single step
XmNpageIncrement	int	Unit increment for page scrolling
XmNvalue	int	Current value of slider position

Table 4-21: Configuration resource fields of the scroll bar widget. All values are measured in application-defined units.

line n-14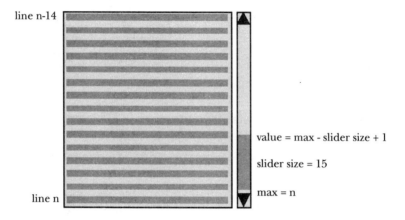

line n

value = max - slider size + 1

slider size = 15

max = n

Figure 4.26: Scroll bar configuration with no empty space at the end.

The resource field *XmNvalue* reflects the current position of the slider and is specified as the unit value corresponding to the beginning of the slider. In other words, the maximum value which can be reported is *XmNmaximum-XmNsliderSize+1*. This is consistent with the assumption that the value reported specifies the top of the data displayed in the visible area.

Consider for example a text editor. The value reported is the number of the first line to be displayed in the window. The slider size is the number of lines visible in the window. When the number of lines is taken as the maximum scroll bar value the text cannot be scrolled further if the last line of text appears at the bottom of the window. This configuration is illustrated in Figure 4.26.

If, however, you want to configure the editor to enable the user to scroll

line n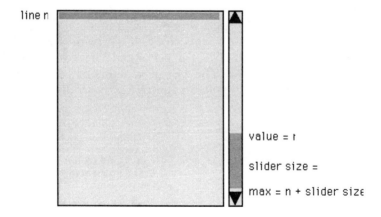

value = r

slider size =

max = n + slider size

Figure 4.27: Scroll bar configuration with empty space after the last line.

XmNinitialDelay	int	Delay before continuous scroll in ms
XmNrepeatDelay	int	Time between repeated steps in ms
XmNorientation	enum	Orientation of scroll bar
		XmVERTICAL
		XmHORIZONTAL
XmNprocessingDirection	enum	Where min and max are located
		XmMAX_ON_TOP
		XmMAX_ON_BOTTOM
		XmMAX_ON_LEFT
		XmMAX_ON_RIGHT
XmNshowArrows	Boolean	If arrows present

Table 4-22: Further configuration resource fields of the scroll bar.

further until only the last line is visible, you have to increase the maximum value by *XmNsliderSize-1*. This is shown in Figure 4.27.

There are further configuration options for the scroll bar. You can specify the delay and speed of continuous scrolling, using *XmNinitialDelay* and *XmNrepeatDelay*. One important parameter not mentioned yet is the orientation (horizontal or vertical). You can also specify which end of the scroll bar shall represent the maximum and which the minimum value, using the resource field *XmNprocessingDirection*. A final possibility is to leave out the arrows if you do not require the single-stepping facility.

The geometry of the scroll bar is determined by the parent, because the length should match the length of the scrollable region. The width has a reasonable default to make all scroll bars appear with a uniform width.

Callbacks

The main purpose of the scroll bar is to inform the application of any scrolling actions the user performs. There are a variety of different callbacks to which procedures can be connected. All scroll bar callbacks return a pointer to the following structure as *call_data*:

```
typedef struct {
        int             reason;     /*XmCR_VALUE_CHANGED        */
                                    /* XmCR_DRAG                */
                        /* XmCR_INCREMENT,   XmCR_DECREMENT */
                        /* XmCR_PAGE_INCREMENT              */
                        /* XmCR_PAGE_DECREMENT              */
                        /* XmCR_TO_TOP,      XmCR_TO_BOTTOM*/
        XEvent          *event;
        int             value;
        int             pixel;      /* only when TO_TOP or TO_BOTTOM*/
} XmScrollBarCallbackStruct;
```

XmNincrementCallback	Callback	When single increment
XmNpageIncrementCallback	Callback	When page increment
XmNdecrementCallback	Callback	When single decrement
XmNpageDecrementCallback	Callback	When page decrement
XmNtoTopCallback	Callback	Shift-click on top arrow
XmNtoBottomCallback	Callback	Shift-click on bottom arrow
XmNdragCallback	Callback	Continuously when dragged
XmNvalueChangedCallback	Callback	When increment or decrement

Table 4-23: Scroll bar callback reasons.

The most interesting part of this structure is the new value to which the slider has been moved. The different callback reasons correspond closely to the different user actions. They are summarized in Table 4-23.

If you do not have special requirements, you can leave the decrement and increment callbacks unconnected and use the *XmNvalueChangedCallback* instead, which is called when the respective increment or decrement callback list is empty. The *XmNvalueChangedCallback* is usually sufficient, because you need only one routine to handle the new value.

The *XmNvalueChangedCallback* is also executed when the user has finished dragging, so you nearly always need to handle it. Connecting only the *XmNvalueChangedCallback* means that the scrolling response to dragging the slider occurs only once after the mouse button is released. If you want instant feedback while dragging you must use the *XmNdragCallback*. These two callbacks should fulfill most of your needs.

The *XmNtoTopCallback* and *XmNtoBottomCallback* are something of a speciality, because they do not reposition the slider as the other callbacks do. If you want to implement these functions, you have to set the new slider position in the callback procedure.

A convenient way of setting the scroll bar position from another program component (for example if you want to scroll something automatically into view) is the routine *XmScrollBarSetValues*:

> *XmScrollBarSetValues (scroll_bar_widget, new_value, slider_size, increment,*
> *page_increment, true_if_callback);*

If the flag *true_if_callback* is set, the *XmNvalueChangedCallback* will be called as if the user had moved the slider. If not, the routine works as a somewhat more convenient way of performing a complex *XtSetValues*.

Chapter 5

The Application's Main Window

In addition to the primitive widgets of Motif described in the previous chapter you need two more groups of composite widget classes to assemble a basic repertoire of useful widgets for a complete application. In this chapter menus and the standard main window components are presented. These are suitable as starting points for most larger applications.

5.1 Menu Overview

Motif offers a variety of different menu types. These are presented together because they are all different combinations of the same elements. The different types are:

- The *menu bar*, which is a row of menu titles at the top of the main window. Clicking into a title activates the underlying pull-down menu.

- *Pull-down menus*, which are are columns of menu selections that appear underneath the menu bar on the activation of a menu bar entry. Because a menu entry can be activated by dragging into the menu, the menu is called "pull-down".

- *Cascading menus.* Certain menu entries in a pull-down menu can activate another menu, which appears to the right of this entry. This is really a pull-down menu positioned differently. Cascading menus can be nested to arbitrary depth (but few users will like that).

137

- *Pop-up menus* are menu panes activated by clicking on arbitrary screen regions. There are only minor differences compared with pull-down menus. Pop-up menus can also have submenus.

- *Option menus* consist of a combination of the option menu itself and a pull-down menu. The option menu reflects the current value from a short list of choices. On activation of the option menu the choices appear in the pane, allowing the user to select a new value.

All these systems are built from basically only three different components, albeit very flexible ones:

- *Menu entries,* which are buttons of different kinds, as described in the previous chapter. In addition, there is one special button class which is capable of activating a menu pane. All entries in a menu bar and cascading entries, as well as the option menu value, are called *cascade buttons.*

- *Panes.* All combinations of buttons are special varieties of the general row-column manager class. The row-column widget provides the geometry management for the entries in the desired orientation and is capable of handling the interaction required for the different menu types.

- *Menu shells* are necessary because the pop-up panes are not contained inside their parent widget. The menu shells are barely noticeable if you use the convenience routines provided.

Figure 5.1 shows a complete menu cascade, built from a menu bar with cascade buttons, a pull-down menu with different button entries, and a cascaded menu. The whole hierarchy can be traversed with the mouse button depressed, highlighting the respective menu entry with a shadow. A menu selection is activated when the mouse button is released inside a button widget.

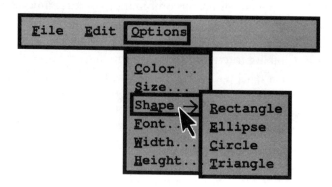

Figure 5.1: Menu cascade.

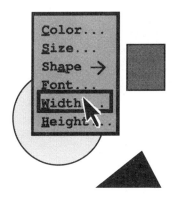

Figure 5.2: Pop-up menu.

If the mouse button is released outside the menu, no entry is activated and the complete cascade disappears.

A pop-up menu consists of a single pane that appears on clicking into an application-defined region. In fact, the activation of a pop-up menu must be programmed explicitly, so the activation reason may be almost anything (see Figure 5.2).

The option menu uses a menu pane, too. The option menu itself consists of two parts: a label on the left, indicating the type of value represented, and a value field on the right, showing the current value. The accompanying menu pane, showing all possible values, is activated by pressing the mouse button in the value field. The current value is positioned exactly over the value field of the option menu. The other possible selections extend above and below (see Figure 5.3).

It is recommended that you use the Motif convenience functions to create menus, not only because their usage is highly standardized, but because they provide additional functionality as well (such as shared menu shells).

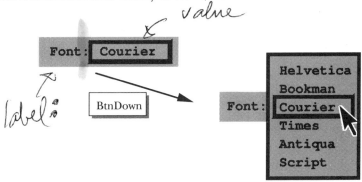

Figure 5.3: Option menu.

5.2 Pull-Down Menus

The first menu type to be discussed will be the pull-down menu, because it is used in nearly every program. The pull-down menu system starts from a menu bar, which contains the headers for all submenus. In the next section you will see how to connect the menu bar to an application window; in this section it is simply discussed in isolation.

The menu bar consists of a row-column manager widget containing several cascade button widgets for the headers. The row-column widget ensures that all the headers are properly aligned and arranged one after the other in their natural width. The geometry management features of the row-column widget are discussed in Section 6.2; in menus the reasonable default values are usually sufficient.

The cascade buttons in the menu bar are similar to push buttons, except that they do not normally display a shadow (but this is the case for all buttons in menus). The shadow only appears when the button is armed, when it appears raised and not depressed. While it is armed, a cascade button pops up its associated menu pane. The menu pane is positioned according to the type of menu the cascade button resides in. If the cascade button is inside a menu bar, the menu pane is positioned underneath.

One of the cascade buttons in the menu bar may be treated differently, because the Motif style guide defines a help menu which is always positioned on the far right of the menu bar, regardless of how much space is free in the bar (see Figure 5.4).

A menu bar is created with the convenience function *XmCreateMenuBar*, which creates a row-column widget of type *XmMENU_BAR*.

```
Widget     bar, parent;
Arg        args[];              /* your argument list */
int        num_args = 0;


...                             /*parent must be created before */
bar = XmCreateMenuBar (parent, "bar1", args, num_args);
XtManageChild (bar);
```

You can add the necessary cascade buttons by creating them as children of the menu bar. Provided they are created in the managed state, the cascade buttons are automatically arranged in a row in the sequence in which they were

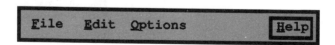

Figure 5.4: Menu bar with help button.

XmNmenuHelpWidget	Widget	Cascade button to rightmost position

Table 5-1: Menu bar specific resource field.

added. Usually it is more convenient to create the menu pane before the corresponding cascade button, because the cascade button must know its associated pane.

Note that the widget-creating Motif convenience functions create them unmanaged. The widgets must be explicitly managed with *XtManageChild.*

When you have created all the cascade buttons and want to designate one as the header for the help menu, you must set the *XmNmenuHelpWidget* resource field of the menu bar to the widget ID of this button:

> *Widget   help_casc;*
>
> *XtSetArg (args[0], XmNmenuHelpWidget, help_casc);*
> *XtSetValues (bar, args, 1);*

The buttons will be rearranged if necessary, moving the help button to the right.

Menu Panes

A menu pane appears when a cascade button is activated (provided the widget ID of the pane is known to the button). A menu pane is built as a row-column of menu entries, but because the pane may exceed the bounds of the main window, a *shell widget* is needed as the parent of the row-column. The shell widget provides the top-level window necessary to position the pane as desired relative to the main window.

However, a menu pane does not need the machinery normally associated with a top-level window, such as the decoration and the ability to move and resize it. Therefore a special kind of shell widget is used, which sets a property called *override redirect* to inhibit any window manager interference. This shell class is called *XmMenuShell.*

A menu shell is created automatically by the appropriate convenience functions. The immediate child of the shell is a row-column widget operating as a pull-down menu pane. The children of the pane are the menu entries. Entries are mainly push buttons, which execute the corresponding menu function when activated using their *XmNactivateCallback* list.

Pull-down menu panes may be created as follows:

> *Widget   pane;*   *parent of PD is Menubar*
>
> *pane = XmCreatePulldownMenu (bar, "panel", args, num_args);*
> *XtManageChild (pane);*

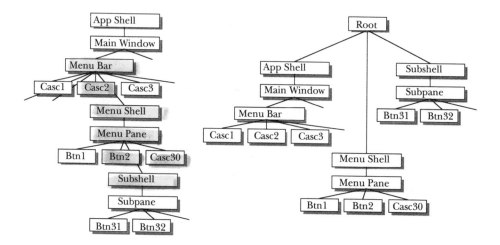

Figure 5.5: Widget and window hierarchies of menu cascade. The widget hierarchy is shown on the left. On the right the corresponding window hierarchy shows that all shells are independent children of the root window.

For the menu system to operate properly the parent of the pane must be the menu bar. Being the parent of the menu pane does not mean that the menu bar reserves space in the same way as for a normal child, because there is a shell in between, and shell children are handled differently by manager widgets (see Figure 5.5).

The push buttons may be created normally as children of the pane. When the pane has been created, its widget ID can be used in the argument list when creating the cascade button. This creation cycle is illustrated in Figure 5.6.

Cascade Buttons

Cascade buttons are best created after their corresponding pane, because the widget ID of their corresponding menu pane must be registered in the resource field *XmNsubMenuId*. In a menu bar, cascade buttons are used to pull down a menu. They can also be used to create cascading menus.

In the latter case a cascade button is created as a child of a menu pane. When it is activated, another menu is shown to the right. This cascade can be nested to arbitrary depth.

The creation sequence of cascading menus (shown in Figure 5.7) is similar to the normal case, except that a submenu is created instead of a push button. The submenu consists of a menu pane (as a child of the previous pane) and a cascade button.

Cascade buttons are similar to push buttons in many respects. Most of the similarities stem from the fact that they are both label subclasses. Therefore all of the label features, such as pixmap faces, can be used for cascade buttons.

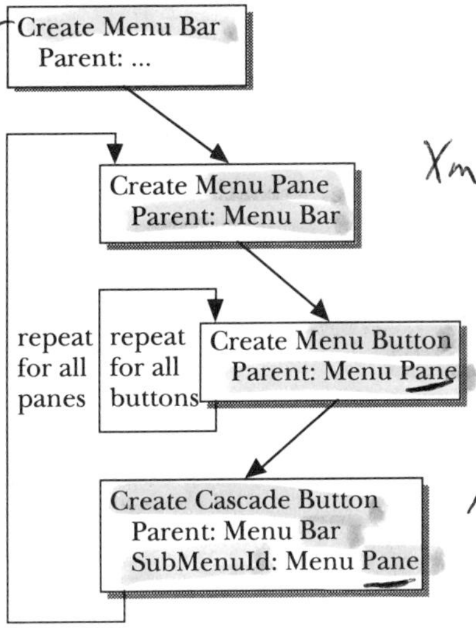

XmCreateMenuBar

Create Menu Bar
Parent: ...

XmCreate PulldownMenu

Create Menu Pane
Parent: Menu Bar

repeat for all panes | repeat for all buttons

Create Menu Button
Parent: Menu Pane

*PB, TB, CascadeB,
(label, separator)*

Create Cascade Button
Parent: Menu Bar
SubMenuId: Menu Pane

label in Menubar

Figure 5.6: Menu creation sequence for a single level of menu panes under a menu bar.

The difference between cascade and push buttons is that for the cascade buttons the activation callback is substituted by an automatic pop-up procedure which activates the pane specified by the resource field *XmNsubMenuId*. Except in a menu bar, the cascade button is visually distinguished by a cascade indicator to the right of the label.

When used in a cascading menu, there is a delay between arming the cascade button and popping up the submenu, in order to prevent unnecessary flashing when quickly traversing a menu. This delay is configurable. Table 5-2 shows the resource fields of the cascade button, which should be self-explanatory.

Menu Callbacks

The purpose of menus is to serve as a space-saving construction to execute application functions, and this is accomplished by connecting callbacks to the buttons in the menu panes. The *XmNactivateCallback* of the push button can be used for this purpose as usual.

XmNsubMenuID	Widget	ID of menu pane to pop up
XmNmappingDelay	int	Time in ms
XmNcascadePixmap	Pixmap	To use as cascading indicator
XmNcascadingCallback	Callback	Before pane is popped up

Table 5-2: Cascade button resource fields.

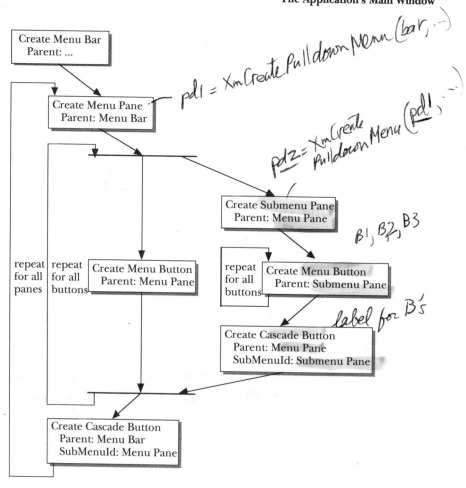

Figure 5.7: Menu creation with submenus. *multi level cascades*

An alternative method is to connect a callback to the menu pane, which is activated whenever an *XmNactivateCallback* is executed from one of the pane's buttons. If there is some common code for all the callbacks this method is the preferred one.

The callback reason for this purpose is the *XmNentryCallback* of the row-column widget. Whenever this list contains a registered procedure, all registered *XmNactivateCallbacks* for buttons in this pane are redirected. A pointer to the following structure is returned as *call_data*, which contains all the data of the original callback:

```
typedef struct {
    int         reason;     /* XmCR_ACTIVATE          */
```

```
                              /* XmCR_MAP                           */
                              /* XmCR_UNMAP                         */
   XEvent      *event;
   Widget      widget;        /* following only when ACTIVATE       */
   char        *data;
   char        *callbackstruct;
} XmRowColumnCallbackStruct;
```

The widget, client data and callback structure of the original callback are all recorded as members of this structure. These fields are only valid if reported by the *XmNentryCallback*, because two more callback reasons of the row-column widget use the same structure.

It is important that a correctly constructed menu system should grey out currently inapplicable entries by making those buttons insensitive, using the procedure *XtSetSensitive*. You should not simply ignore inapplicable entries or produce error messages. You can choose between two alternative methods of defining the sensitivity.

The first method always sets the sensitivity of the menu entry whenever a part of the application's internal state that affects this entry changes, even if the menu pane is currently invisible. The important disadvantage of this method is that it severely restricts dialog independence, i.e. the ability to change the interface without changing the application-specific code. All relevant state changing functions have to know the widget IDs of the menu entries which could be affected by that state change. Adding new menu functions is a mess, because numerous locations must be changed to get the right sensitivity. Moreover it is difficult to trace the conditions under which the entry is insensitive, and easy to forget one transition.

The second and preferred method is to check all entries before the menu is popped up. In this case, all checks are localized and clearly belong to the interface functionality. However, in order to minimize the pop-up delay the checks should not be too costly to implement. A compromise is to define some flags in the application state with a clear, application-specific meaning, which can easily be checked at pop-up time.

The *XmNmapCallback* of the row-column widget can be used for this sensitivity check. It is called before the pane is displayed. It can also be used to change the command labels, if necessary, e.g. for an appropriately named "undo" command ("undo draw", "undo delete" etc.). In a similar fashion, the *XmNunmapCallback* is called after the pane has disappeared.

XmNentryCallback	Callback	When button activated
XmNmapCallback	Callback	Before pane mapped
XmNunmapCallback	Callback	After pane unmapped

Table 5-3: Menu pane (= row-column) callback reasons.

5.3 Menu Entries

This section discusses the possible child classes of a menu pane (see Table 5-4). You have already read about push buttons, which serve as normal menu entries, and cascade buttons.

In general, children of menu panes may have a different appearance and behaviour from in other environments. Examples are the shadows of push buttons and the cascade indicator, which is invisible in menu bars. The behaviour may be subtly different—entering a push button in a menu with the mouse button pressed arms this button while such a traversal does not work with isolated buttons. Usually this need not concern you, because the programming interface is the same.

Whereas buttons are active components in a menu, i.e. they trigger application procedures, there may also be passive components. To draw a separating line between groups of menu entries is the purpose of the separator widget class.

To insert a separating line between buttons, you only have to create a separator after the buttons of the preceding button group:

```
...              /* create push button group before separator    */
XtCreateManagedWidget ("sep1", xmSeparatorWidgetClass,
                         pane, args, num_args);
...              /* create push button group after separator      */
```

The separator always provides a horizontal line of the appropiate width. The separator widget is further discussed in Section 6.3.

You can also use a label widget in a menu pane, e.g. as a title. However, you should employ a visually distinct font or a similar measure, otherwise the user may mistake it for a menu entry.

Toggle buttons are a third class of button that can be used in menus. However, the toggle indicator is only displayed when switched on (see Section 4.3). All button and label classes can also be used with pixmap faces.

Accelerators and Mnemonics

In addition to traversal with the mouse, menus can also be operated from the keyboard. *Accelerators* are the simplest mechanism to execute a menu func-

| Push button |
| Cascade button |
| Toggle button |
| Label |
| Separator |

Table 5-4: Possible child classes of menu panes.

tion without displaying that menu. The callback from the menu entry is executed directly if the accelerator key combination is typed on the keyboard.

There is a complication associated with such a mechanism in an X environment. Normally a widget only executes callbacks after having received an event. However, it cannot receive key events while the window is not mapped (as is the case when the menu pane is not popped up). Furthermore, it does not have the keyboard focus.

Therefore a collaborative effort of different widgets is required to propagate the keyboard event to the right button. This is accomplished by installing an event handler in the top-level window and all its children which forwards the event to the menu bar. The menu bar identifies the correct menu entry and calls the right callback (see Figure 5.8).

Because the normal translation mechanism is also an event handler, the propagation of accelerator keys to the menu bar is independent of the translations of the individual widgets. Therefore, where an accelerator for a menu entry is valid, it cannot be overridden by translations of widgets (i.e. in the complete main window).

An accelerator for a menu entry is specified by using the resource field *XmNaccelerator*, which is already defined in the label class, but only works with buttons. This resource field is a string which contains the left hand side for a translation specification, such as:

XtSetArg (args[0], XmNaccelerator, "Alt<Key>F5:");
XtSetArg (args[1], XmNacceleratorText, <make-an-XmString-out-of "Alt+F5">);

The accompanying resource field *XmNacceleratorText* provides a visual representation to be displayed to the right of the button label. Simply specifying the accelerator and using the button in a menu automatically performs the installation for you. You can even set these fields in a resource file.

There is a second mechanism used to operate menus from the keyboard. *Mnemonics* are single characters from the label of a menu entry. If a pull-down menu system is switched into keyboard traversal mode—using the default F10 accelerator, for example—pressing one of the mnemonic characters of this menu activates the corresponding button, which in turn may post another menu.

Mnemonics have the advantage that they need not be unique across all menu entries. Activating a command by its mnemonics requires a sequence of keys to be pressed (following the menu cascade) instead of a single combi-

XmNaccelerator	String	Accelerator event specification
XmNacceleratorText	XmString	Text to display as accelerator
XmNmnemonic	char	Mnemonic to underline

Table 5-5: Label resource fields for use in menu entries.

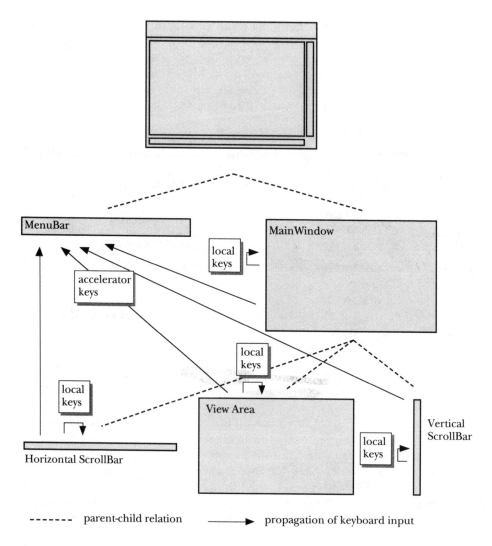

- - - - - - parent-child relation   ▶ propagation of keyboard input

Figure 5.8: Accelerator propagation.

nation. Mnemonics can be defined in the resource field *XmNmnemonic*, which is
a single character (you must use single quotes):

    XtSetArg (args[2], XmNmnemonic, 'k');

    The mnemonic character must occur in the exact case in the label string
of the button, since the first occurrence is underlined by the label's drawing

XmNmenuAccelerator	String	Accelerator to post menu
XmNmnemonic	char	Mnemonic for option menu
XmNwhichButton	enum	Button to activate menu
		Button1
		Button2
		Button3

Table 5-6: Button and key specifications of row-column widgets.

procedure. Otherwise the user has no clue as to what the mnemonic is. You can see examples of mnemonics in Figures 5.1 and 5.2.

The previously discussed resource fields all concerned individual menu entries. Whole menu panes also have button and key related resource fields. The accelerator used to activate a menu for keyboard traversal, which defaults to F10 for menu bars, is specified by *XmNmenuAccelerator*. Option menus also have a mnemonic. Finally, the mouse button used to operate the menu pane can be customized (see Table 5-6).

Gadgets

Even a program that is only moderately large may have a large number of menu entries. Since all menu entries have an associated X window, the number of windows is equally large. All these windows reside as structures in the X server, although they are normally unmapped. Creating all these windows may have a significant impact on the start-up time of an application.

As a performance enhancement, *gadgets* were devised which have no X window but rely on their manager parent for event dispatching etc. They can be used as a direct replacement for their corresponding widget cousins in most cases and are especially useful for menus.

The following widget classes have corresponding gadget classes: labels, push buttons, toggle buttons, arrow buttons, cascade buttons, and separators. To use a gadget instead of a widget, you have to substitute an *xm..GadgetClass* for the corresponding *xm..WidgetClass* in the call to *XtCreate(Managed)Widget*.

5.4 Option Menus

An option menu is built from two row-column widgets: a pull-down menu pane and the option menu itself (see Figure 5.3). The option menu contains two gadgets, which are created by the following convenience function:

Widget   option;

option = XmCreateOptionMenu (parent, "option", args, num_args);

XmNlabelString	XmString	String of left label gadget
XmNmenuHistory	Widget	Currently selected widget
XmNmnemonic	char	Mnemonic of label
XmNsubMenuld	Widget	ID of sub pane (a pull-down menu)

Table 5-7: Row-column resource fields specific to the option menu.

These gadgets are a label and a cascade button. The label indicates the purpose of the option menu and the cascade button the current value. The label string of the label gadget can be set directly as a resource field of the option menu.

The option menu is similar to a cascade button in many respects—only a changeable value must be handled additionally. Therefore the option menu duplicates some resource fields of the cascade button. Like the cascade button, the menu pane should be created before the option menu; the menu pane should have the same parent as the option menu.

The current value of the option menu is managed by the resource field *XmNmenuHistory*, which contains the ID of the currently selected widget from the menu pane. By setting this field you can change the currently displayed value.

Any value changes are reported via the *XmNentryCallback* of the option menu (which is a row-column widget). *XmNmenuHistory* indicates the newly selected button.

5.5 Pop-Up Menus

A pull-down menu pane as discussed in the previous sections is always pulled down automatically by some kind of cascade button. A pop-up menu, however, may be displayed as a reaction to any application-defined event, and thus must be popped up explicitly.

The simplest way is to specify a menu accelerator for the pop-up menu pane. However, then the menu can only be activated from the keyboard.

Alternatively you can use a callback procedure (nearly any callback will do) to display the menu. The Motif-specific shell classes (menu shells and also dialog shells, which are discussed later) use a different convention for pop-up from the X Toolkit Intrinsics. They appear when their child is managed. The following code will post a pop-up menu:

XtManageChild (pane);

This way was chosen because, in Motif, multiple panes can share the same shell widget. Normally shells have only one child. But if only one of several

panes is visible at one time, these panes can be children of the same shell and
be managed when they are needed.

One problem remains. You have to position the menu pane so that it
appears where the mouse cursor is. If you have no special requirements, you
should use the following:

```
XmMenuPosition (pane, event);
XtManageChild (pane);
```

The event can be obtained from most *call_data* structures. Only the mouse
position is used from the event structure. If you want to position the menu
differently, you have to set the coordinates (*XmNgeometry* or *XmNx* and *XmNy*) of
the menu shell yourself.

Alternatively, if you want to pop up a menu through an event specification
in a translation table, you can write a suitable action procedure. The mechanism has already been described in Section 5.4. A general version of the
necessary action procedure is shown below. It requires the widget name of the
menu pane to pop up to be passed as a parameter.

```
static void MotifMenuPopup (w, event, params, noparams)    args?   Code wrong?
        Widget     w;
        XEvent     event;
        String     *params;
        Cardinal   *noparams;
{
        Widget     popup;
        Widget     parent;

        if (noparams == 0) return;          /* no name given */  ?
        parent = XtParent (popup);

        /* get to top-level widget */
        while (XtParent (parent) != NULL) parent = XtParent (parent);
        popup = XtNameToWidget (params[0], parent);

        if (popup == NULL) return;          /* not found */
        XmMenuPosition (popup, event);
        XtManageChild (popup);
}

XtActionsRec actionsTable[] = {
        {"MotifMenuPopup", (XtActionProc) MotifMenuPopup}
};

/* don't forget to register this action table at program initialization */
```

A translation for a widget can then be specified as follows, using the action to pop up a menu in response to pressing the function key F5:

```
*editor_view.translations:     #override  \
            <Key>F5:           MotifMenuPopup ("property-menu")
```

5.6 The Main Window

Until now only primitive widgets and isolated widget compositions have been described. The main window is the place where the individual pieces are combined into a complete application window.

A typical main window of a Motif application has the following parts, some of which are optional:

- *Menu bar.* The menu bar occupies a line at the top of the main window (inside the window manager decoration, of course). It is always stretched to the width of the window and possibly wrapped if the entries do not fit onto one line.

- *Command area.* This area is used to display messages or to enter commands. It is placed underneath the menu bar and has the same width. The command area is seldom used.

- *Scrolled window.* The space left under the first two parts is occupied by the scrolled window with optional scroll bars. The scrolled window itself is only a container for other parts and does not appear as a separate object to the user.

- *Work window.* Application-specific contents occupy this area. If scroll bars are used, this area is clipped and can be scrolled, otherwise it simply occupies the rest of the main window.

- *Scroll bars.* They are optionally used to scroll the contents of the work window. They can be individually switched off.

A main window with all parts in place is shown in Figure 5.9. The partitioning of the main window is managed by the main window widget. The subparts (menu bar, command area, work window, scroll bars) are children of the main window widget. The primary task of the main window widget is to manage the geometry of its subparts.

The main window recognizes its subparts by a special mechanism. In contrast to a row-column widget, all of the main window's subparts are handled differently, depending on the role they play. The main window itself detects common configurations. For instance, when a menu bar is created as a child of the main window, it is automatically registered as the menu bar child. However, a text widget could equally well serve as the command or work area.

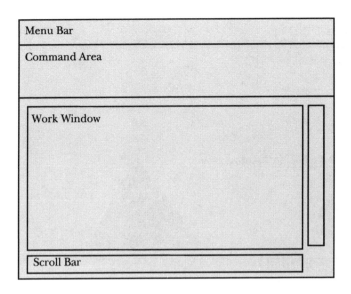

Figure 5.9: Anatomy of a main window.

You should therefore mark the role of the children explicitly. The main window provides a resource field for every subpart that accepts a widget ID for the corresponding part. However, the simplest method is to use the following convenience function, which sets all subparts at once:

XmMainWindowSetAreas (main_window_widget, menu_bar, command_window, horizontal_scrollbar, vertical_scrollbar, work_area);

Naturally, you must first create all the subwidgets before calling this procedure, otherwise you would not have the widget IDs. All parts are optional and can be specified as *NULL* if not used. Because the main window shares most of its functionality with the scrolled window widget, some of its aspects are discussed in the next section.

The specific layout of the main window does not fit all applications. At least three common cases can be identified:

- *Graphics view.* The work area contains a viewing area which is drawn in an application-specific way using fundamental Xlib operations (see Figure 5.10). Application-defined views are used when widget functionality is not sufficient, such as for graphic editors. The work area is occupied by a *drawing area* widget, otherwise the main window is used unchanged. Chapter 9 describes how to implement custom views using the drawing area widget.

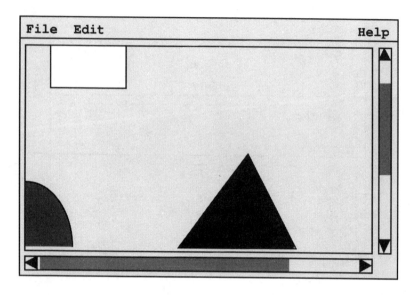

Figure 5.10: Main window with graphics view.

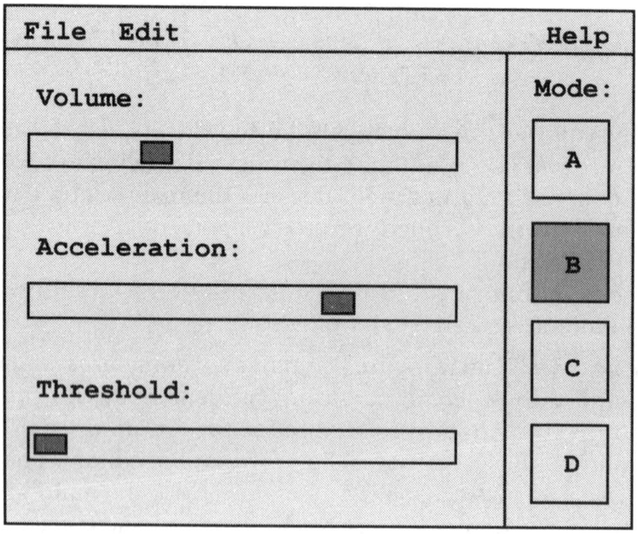

Figure 5.11: Main window with fixed control panel.

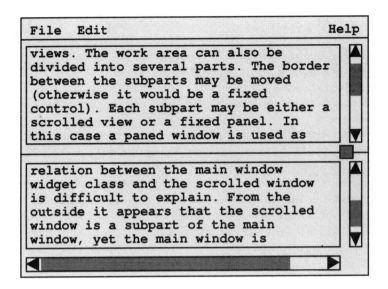

Figure 5.12: Main window with subpanes.

- *Control section.* The main window consists of a control panel with a fixed set of controls (see Figure 5.11), often employed in simpler applications. Only the menu bar is used from the main window. A *form* widget (for customizable layout) with several subparts is used as the work area. The scroll bars are omitted; therefore the work area part fills the whole scrolled window area. Chapter 6 discusses the construction of control areas.

- *Divided views.* The work area can also be divided into several parts (see Figure 5.12). The border between the subparts may be moved (otherwise it would be a fixed control). Each subpart may be either a scrolled view or a fixed panel. A *paned window* widget implements the division of the work area; children of the paned window may be either scrolled windows or form widgets. The paned window is described in Section 5.7.

Scrolled Windows

The relation between the main window widget class and the scrolled window is difficult to explain. From the outside it appears that the scrolled window is a subpart of the main window, yet the main window is actually a subclass of the scrolled window. This contradiction is a misunderstanding of the two relations involved.

One class being a subclass of another means only that the subclass may inherit the behaviour and structure of the superclass, and may add more. That means that, if a subclass inherits all the features of its superclass unchanged and only adds functionality, the superclass functionality can be regarded as a subpart of the extended functionality. This relation is in most cases not as obvious as this, because subclasses often substantially change the behaviour of their superclass.

The difference between a scrolled window and a main window is that the main window provides two more areas at the top. Otherwise they are identical in their scrolled part.

The scrolled window can operate with different policies concerning how the scroll bars are managed. One fundamental distinction is whether scrolling is automatic or not. This mode is controlled by the resource field *XmNscrollingPolicy*. Automatic scrolling uses the X clipping mechanism to move the work area behind a clipping window (see Figure 2.12). Automatic scrolling works with all X windows, although it may be inefficient if the window is always repainted as a whole, and it will definitely break down when the work area reaches the size limit of an X window (at 32Kx32K pixels). However, it does not require any additional work on the programmer's part.

For automatic scrolling a *clipping window* is created with the visible size of the work area, while the work area may be much larger. If the clipping window is larger than the work area, the background of the clipping window will appear in the regions not covered by the work area.

If the scrolling policy is *XmAUTOMATIC*, the scroll bars are created automatically by the scrolled window, and appropriate callbacks are connected to move the work area's window behind the clipping window. You can add your own procedures to the scroll bar callbacks to be informed of the scrolling (they are added to the list of internally installed callbacks). The widget IDs of the scroll bars are made accessible in the resource fields *XmNverticalScrollBar* and *XmNhorizontalScrollBar*.

The other possibility is to use application-defined scrolling (which is the default). In this case, the scroll bar widgets must be created explicitly and any scrolling callbacks must be defined and implemented by the application. The resource field *XmNscrollingPolicy* must be set at widget creation and cannot be changed later.

If you do not create any scroll bars when using the application-defined scrolling policy, the work area occupies the whole scrolled window. This behaviour is useful for a main window if an unscrolled form or paned window widget below the menu bar is desired.

If the scrolling policy is *XmAUTOMATIC*, the scroll bars may be dynamically managed depending on the size of the work area if the resource field *XmNscrollBarDisplayPolicy* is set to *XmAS_NEEDED*. As shown in Figure 5.13, the respective scroll bars only appear if the size of the work area exceeds the clipping region in this dimension. The effect can be observed noticeably when

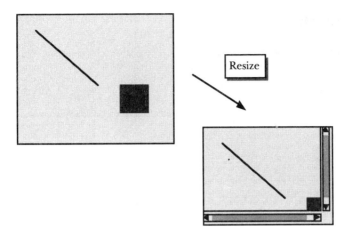

Figure 5.13: Dynamic scroll bars.

resizing the scrolled window. The other possibility (*XmSTATIC*) forces the scroll bars to be displayed all the time, even if there is nothing to scroll. The slider size will be adjusted to the relative size of the viewable region in both cases.

Under the automatic scrolling policy the size of the scrolled window is decoupled from the size of the work area. Resizing the scrolled window does not resize the work area, but only the clipping window. Resize requests originating from children of the work area (e.g. label text changed to a longer string) will only resize the work area and will not influence the size of the scrolled window.

However, decoupling the size is not always useful when the scrolling policy is *XmAPPLICATION_DEFINED*. In this case the application usually implements scrolling by displaying only the relevant subpart of the underlying data in the work area. That means that the work area has the same size as the clipping window. If the scrolled window is resized, the work area should also be resized accordingly, so that exactly that area can be used for drawing by the application. This is achieved by setting the resource field *XmNvisualPolicy* to *XmVARIABLE*. A side effect is that a resize request from the work area will resize the scrolled window, if possible.

XmNscrollingPolicy	XmNvisualPolicy	XmNscrollBarDisplayPolicy
application-defined	variable	->static
application-defined	constant	->static
automatic	->constant	static
automatic	->constant	as-needed

Table 5-8: The four different scrolled window policy configurations. The arrow indicates that the field is forced to that value.

XmNscrollingPolicy	enum	If scrolling interaction is automatic *XmAPPLICATION_DEFINED* *XmAUTOMATIC*
XmNscrollBarDisplayPolicy	enum	If scroll bars are always displayed *XmSTATIC* *XmAS_NEEDED*
XmNvisualPolicy	enum	If the work area resizes with widget *XmCONSTANT* *XmVARIABLE*

Table 5-9: Policy resource fields of scrolled windows.

Because of the internally enforced dependencies between these three policy resource fields, there are only four possible combinations, which are summarized in Table 5-8.

If you want to scroll the scrolled window from your program, e.g. to implement auto-scrolling, you can use the procedure *XmScrollBarSetValues* (as described in Section 4.5), setting the parameter flag so that the scroll bar executes a callback[1]. Auto-scrolling means that the user can drag an object in the work area to a new place which is currently not visible. When dragging the mouse slightly outside the window the work area is scrolled in the opposite direction to bring the desired part into view.

As usual, there are a number of resource fields which control the geometry and appearance of the scrolled window. The sides on which to place the scroll bars can be configured. The margins have been named differently for scrolled windows and main windows, so that you can easily differentiate between the two in your resource files. The main window also has the ability to display separators between the upper parts and the scrolled part.

The subparts of the scrolled window can all be accessed through resource fields (this is important when they are created automatically). As noted above, all application-created child widgets should be identified through a call to *XmScrolledWindowSetAreas* or *XmMainWindowSetAreas*:

> *XmScrolledWindowSetAreas (scrolled_window_widget,*
> *horizontal_scrollbar, vertical_scrollbar, work_area);*

> *XmMainWindowSetAreas (main_window_widget, menu_bar, command_window,*
> *horizontal_scrollbar, vertical_scrollbar, work_area);*

---

[1]This does not work in Motif 1.0, because the value-changed callback is not connected internally.

XmNscrollBarPlacement	enum	Which sides the bars are on
		XmTOP_LEFT
		XmBOTTOM_LEFT
		XmTOP_RIGHT
		XmBOTTOM_RIGHT
XmNspacing	Dimension	Distance to scroll bars
XmNscrolledWindowMarginWidth	Dimension	Outer margin
XmNscrolledWindowMarginHeight	Dimension	
Main window only:		
XmNmainWindowMarginWidth	Dimension	Outer margin, overrides above
XmNmainWindowMarginHeight	Dimension	
XmNshowSeparator	Boolean	Show separating lines

Table 5-10: Geometry resource fields of scrolled windows.

Other Scrolled Widgets

Two widget classes are specially prepared to work in combination with a scrolled window: the text widget and the list widget. The text widget has already been described; its multi-line variant often needs scrolling if the number of lines exceeds the available space. The list widget, which presents a number of textual choices to the user, will be described in Section 6.3.

For both widget classes there exists a convenience function to create a scrolled window together with a child of the respective class. The effect of this convenience function is that all relevant parameters of the scrolled window are set to guarantee the optimal cooperation of the widget combination.

In this widget combination the scrolling policy of the scrolled window is left to the default value *XmAPPLICATION_DEFINED*. This does not mean, however, that the application has to create the scroll bars. Instead they are created by the child widget.

The interesting consequence of this is that the convenience functions are equivalent to simply creating a text or list widget as a child of a scrolled window. Both widget classes detect the identity of their parent and take the necessary measures, i.e. create the scroll bars and connect appropriate callbacks.

Scrolled window:		
XmNworkWindow	Widget	Work area widget
XmNhorizontalScrollBar	Widget	One scroll bar
XmNverticalScrollBar	Widget	The other
XmNclipWindow	Window	Clipping area if *XmCONSTANT*
Main window only:		
XmNmenuBar	Widget	The menu bar
XmNcommandWindow	Widget	Optional command window

Table 5-11: IDs of main window subparts.

You can observe the difference between automatic and child-controlled scrolling by creating the scrolled window with automatic scrolling policy. In this case the child respects the parent's setting, so scrolling occurs in pixel units, not by lines, and without any knowledge of the window's contents.

Because the text and list widgets already influence their scrolled window parents, both widget classes have resource fields to control some aspects of scrolling. These fields are only used with a scrolled window parent and are otherwise ignored. In this section only the text case will be discussed. The scrolled variant of the list widget follows in Section 6.3.

Scrolled Text

A scrolled text is created using the following convenience function:

Widget scrolled_text;

scrolled_text = XmCreateScrolledText (parent_widget, "widget-name",
*   args, num_args);*
XtManageChild (scrolled_text);

This procedure implicitly creates a scrolled window as the parent of the text with the following settings:

XmNscrollingPolicy:	*XmAPPLICATION_DEFINED*
XmNvisualPolicy:	*XmVARIABLE*
XmNscrollBarDisplayPolicy:	*XmSTATIC*
name:	*"widget-name" + "SW"*

It is important to be aware of the additional widget created between the parent and the text. The convenience function can only return one of these two. The ID of the text widget is returned because it is easier to find the parent of the child than the other way round.

As mentioned above, you can also create the same combination by creating the scrolled window and the text widget separately. Since the above settings are the defaults, you can even omit the argument list for the scrolled window.

The text widget has four resource fields which control the appearance of the scrolled text. The presence of a scroll bar can be individually switched off for both directions using the *XmNscrollHorizontal* and *XmNscrollVertical* flags.

XmNscrollHorizontal	Boolean	If horizontal scroll bar present
XmNscrollVertical	Boolean	If vertical scroll bar present
XmNscrollTopSide	Boolean	If horizontal scroll bar placed on top
XmNscrollLeftSide	Boolean	If vertical scroll bar placed to the left

Table 5-12: Scrolled text resource fields.

Naturally, vertical scrolling is meaningless for single-line text, thus the flag *XmNscrollVertical* is forced to *False* in this case.

You can also control the position of the scroll bars with *XmNscrollTopSide* and *XmNscrollLeftSide*. These resource fields translate into appropriate settings for the *XmNscrollBarPlacement* of the scrolled window.

5.7 Paned Windows

As mentioned above, an application's main window may have several areas, which can be independently resized by the user. This is a possible configuration if an application presents multiple views and you want to avoid using multiple windows. A window subdivision can be achieved with the paned window widget.

The paned window is a composite widget which arranges all its children with moveable separators in between. Moving a separator resizes the two adjacent child widgets. Such a window is shown in Figure 5.14.

The separator can be moved by dragging a small rectangle, called the *sash*. As usual, the geometry (width and spacing) of the paned window can be configured with several resource fields. In addition, you can specify whether the separator line shall be visible or not. Table 5-13 shows these resource fields.

The field *XmNrefigureMode* specifies whether the paned window recalculates the optimum size for the whole window when one pane is resized. Otherwise, the sizes of the other panes remain at their previous settings.

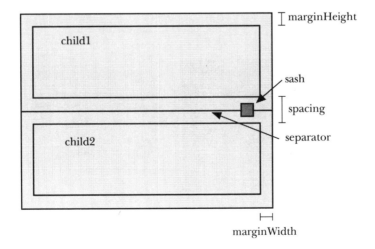

Figure 5.14: Paned window.

XmNmarginHeight XmNmarginWidth XmNspacing XmNseparatorOn XmNrefigureMode	short short int Boolean Boolean	Margin around children Distance between panes If separator line between panes If new layout when paned window changes

Table 5-13: Geometry resource fields of paned windows.

XmNsashHeight XmNsashWidth XmNsashShadowThickness XmNsashIndent	Dimension Dimension int int	Size of sash rectangle Shadow of sash Distance of sash from left border (from the right if negative)

Table 5-14: Geometry resource fields of the sash.

The sash itself is really a child widget (as are the separators), but the sash widget class is not useful outside the paned window. The important geometry resources of the sash can be controlled by resource fields of the paned window, which are shown in Table 5-14 and Figure 5.15.

Constraint Resource Fields

There are some parameters of the paned window which can be specified on a pane-by-pane basis. For example, the maximum and minimum heights to which a user can size a pane are individually controllable for each pane. The X Intrinsics provide an elegant mechanism for this kind of resource field.

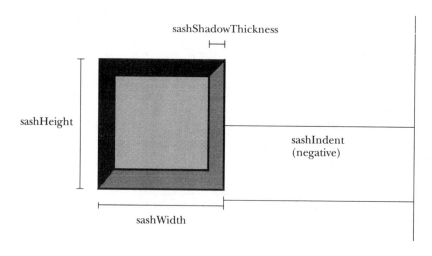

Figure 5.15 Sash geometry.

XmNallowResize	Boolean	If pane may resize itself
XmNskipAdjust	Boolean	If pane is skipped in indirect resizing
XmNpaneMaximum (XmNmaximum in 1.0)	int	Max size of this pane
XmNpaneMinimum (XmNminimum in 1.0)	int	Min size of this pane

Table 5-15: Constraint resource fields for paned window children.

All composite widgets which are also *constraint* widgets can define additional resource fields for their children. These *constraint resource fields* can be accessed like ordinary resource fields of the children, but the children are not aware of them. The contents of these fields are managed by the parent.

If, for example, a button is installed as a child of the paned window, you can set the resource fields *XmNpaneMinimum* and *XmNpaneMaximum* which are not normally defined for push buttons. The individual minimum and maximum values of each different push button are stored as extensions of the push button widget, but the values are only used by the paned window parent.

Constraint resource fields are only defined for direct children of the constraint widget. If the child is a composite widget, the grandchildren are not affected by the constraint fields (but may have other constraint fields if their parent is yet another constraint widget).

Constraint widgets are one of the places where you have to be careful with the scrolled window's convenience functions. If a scrolled text is created with a paned window as its parent, the contraint resource values cannot be specified in the argument list of the convenience function, since these arguments are only fed to the text, which is a grandchild of the paned window. Instead you must either create the two components separately, using two different argument lists, or set the constraint values later (via *XtSetValues*) to the *XtParent* of the text.

In addition to the size limits for user initiated resizing, there are two more constraint resource fields for geometry management.

The field *XmNallowResize* controls whether the child may request a new size. If this flag is *False*, the size of a pane can only be changed by ancestors in the widget hierarchy but not when the child's resource fields change.

The field *XmNskipAdjust* controls whether a pane is resized when the user moves the sash with the Ctrl or Shift modifier down. When using these modifiers other panes than the two adjacent to the sash are affected. Panes with *XmNskipAdjust* set are *moved*, compressing or expanding the next available of the other panes instead. To observe the effect you need at least three panes. Using Shift or Ctrl determines in which direction the next available pane is searched. If this pane reaches minimum or maximum size, the next pane in this direction is used. The process stops when no resizable pane is found even after the search has wrapped around and started from the other end.

Panes with *XmNskipAdjust* set are also ignored when the whole paned window is resized, i.e. instead of the last pane another pane may be selected for resizing.

5.8 Top-Level Shells

One other piece is essential before you can construct a complete application from the widgets discussed so far. As you already know, a composite widget may not stand alone. At the top of the widget hierarchy there must be a shell widget. You also know the menu shell as one type of shell widget, but it will not work as the shell for a main window.

For the main shell of an application another shell class must be used. It is called the *application shell* class, which you have already encountered in the example in Chapter 3.

If you want to create more than one window for your application (please note that window here means top-level window), you have to use a superclass called *top-level shell*. There must be exactly one application shell per program, but multiple top-level shells are allowed. Because you create the application shell automatically if you follow the program skeleton in Chapter 3, this section is really about multiple top-level windows.

The top-level shell class should only be used for secondary windows which are independent so that closing and iconizing them separately makes sense. Otherwise they are subordinate to another window and are regarded as temporary dialog windows (the associated dialog shell is discussed in Section 6.5).

Because shells (except for the application shell) are children of the root window, they are created differently from other widgets. You have to use the following call:

Widget   shell;

shell = XtCreatePopupShell ("shell-name", topLevelShellWidgetClass,
*   parent_widget, args, num_args);*

Menu shells (and dialog shells, as you will see) are popped up by managing their child. To display a top-level shell you have to use a different call. The reason is that the top-level shell class is a part of the Intrinsics, which do not use shared shells. The necessary call is:

XtPopup (top_level_shell_widget, XtGrabNone);

You can ignore the "grab" argument, which is intended for other shell types. To pop it down, you can use a similar call:

XtPopdown (shell);

There are quite a number of resource fields which influence the shell's behaviour. Most of them control the interaction with the window manager—which is not surprising, since this is the shell's task. These resource fields are described in Chapter 7. Only the most important two will be mentioned here.

The first one sets the title in the window's decoration. If *XmNtitle* is not specified, the name of the shell widget is used as the title. However, you usually want to include the name of the current document or some other description as the title. Please note that the title is specified as a string and not an XmString.

The second resource field is important for the geometry management process. If *XmNallowShellResize* is not set, all resize requests from the child widget will be denied. This is similar to the *XmNallowResize* constraint resource field of the paned window. *XmNallowShellResize* is *False* by default, so the complete window stays at its initial size regardless of any geometry changes in the children.

This resource field does not inhibit resizing the windows through the window manager. In fact, resizing through the window manager can only be inhibited through the window manager itself, because the shell has to obey the resizing. Shells can therefore be considered as children of the window manager as far as geometry management is concerned.

| XmNtitle | String | Title to appear in decoration |
| XmNallowShellResize | Boolean | If shell may resize itself |

Table 5-16: Important top-level shell resource fields.

Chapter 6

Layout
and Dialogs

6.1 Control Areas

Chapter 5 dealt with specialized widget classes for special purposes (the menu system and the main window structure). Although these classes can be parameterized in many ways, their composition is already dictated by their function. For style guide conformance, all these widgets should look and feel the same in every application.

This chapter describes widgets needed to construct control areas. In a control area different widgets are combined into application-specific structures. In contrast to the widgets mentioned in the previous chapter the composition is determined by the application. You have already encountered most primitive widgets used as the basic elements of control areas, but the challenge is to arrange these elements with proper consideration for geometry management.

A typical control area is shown in Figure 6.1. Control areas are used for the following purposes:

- To ascertain additional *parameters* for a menu command. In this case the control area is embedded in a dialog shell.

- To display and edit *properties* of some application-defined object, such as a paragraph in a text or a circle in a graphic editor. The control area can be a subpart of a main window or a separate dialog.

- To display the state of the application (*control panel*).

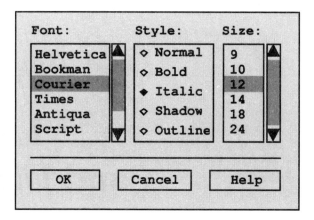

Figure 6.1: Typical control area.

6.2 Geometry Managers

This section first discusses the row-column and the form widgets, which have geometry management as their primary purpose. Their presence is only visible through the placement of their children. Afterwards more basic widget classes are described, which are used as elements.

The Row-Column Widget Class

You have already encountered the row-column widget as a menu pane in the menu system. The basic function of the row-column, however, is to arrange its children in a column format. The additional menu functionality would have been better introduced in a subclass.

The personality a row-column widget assumes is determined at creation time by the resource field *XmNrowColumnType*. The default is *XmWORK_AREA*, but it can also be set to one of the menu types.

The behaviour of the row-column widget in the menu modes has already been discussed, therefore this section concentrates on normal behaviour. Most of the options described here are also valid for menus.

The default behaviour of a row-column widget is to arrange all children in a column. If *XmNorientation* is changed to *XmHORIZONTAL*, the children are laid out in a row. The sequence in which the children are arranged is determined by the sequence of child creation.

The children are packed *tight* by default, i.e. their heights are left untouched, but the width is aligned to the maximum width of all children (or the

XmNrowColumnType	enum	Subtype to create *XmWORK_AREA* *XmMENU_BAR* *XmMENU_PULLDOWN* *XmMENU_POPUP* *XmMENU_OPTION*

Table 6-1: Type resource field of the row-column widget.

height, when in horizontal orientation). The spacing between the children and the row-column borders is controlled as usual with the fields *XmNmarginWidth*, *XmNmarginHeight* and *XmNspacing*. The default tight-packing layout is shown in Figure 6.2.

   In the default mode the row-column widget first tries to expand vertically before a new column is started. If you create the row-column directly as the child of a shell, the window may end up being longer than the screen if many children are added (because the window manager only limits the shell size to twice the screen size, unless otherwise instructed). A new column is only added when it is impossible to expand further in this direction.

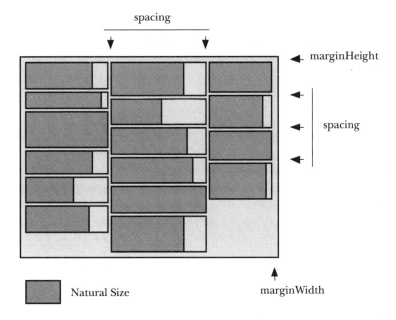

Figure 6.2: Tight-packing layout. The columns are aligned to their individual maximum widths. A new column is only started when no vertical growth is possible, i.e. when the row-column is constrained somehow by its parent.

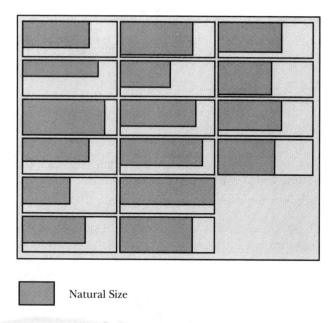

Natural Size

Figure 6.3: Column packing layout. All children are sized equally. The number of rows is calculated from the number of columns requested.

If you want to add a large number of children and want to have multiple columns, you have to restrict the size of the row-column through its parent widget, e.g. by configuring the window manager for a smaller maximum size, by restricting the maximum shell size (see Chapter 8), or by including the row-column in something like the paned window.

Further columns are aligned independently. Their widths do not depend on the widths of other columns, while the individual heights of the children are left alone.

An alternative layout strategy is *column* packing, where all children are sized identically, specified by setting *XmNpacking* to *XmPACK_COLUMN* (see Figure 6.3). In this mode you can also specify the number of columns you want, using *XmNnumColumns*. *XmNnumColumns* will set the number of rows in horizontal orientation, just as rows and columns are interchanged in the description of the layout method.

It is currently impossible to align the children horizontally and vertically without making all children equal sized. This would be useful for a dialog showing a number of text fields with label prompts. The labels and text fields must be aligned vertically, but the two columns need not be equal sized. Every label must be aligned with its text field, but not all rows need to be of equal height.

XmNorientation	enum	Which is major dimension *XmVERTICAL* *XmHORIZONTAL*
XmNpacking	enum	How to squeeze children together *XmPACK_TIGHT* *XmPACK_COLUMN* *XmPACK_NONE*
XmNnumColumns	short	Columns/rows if *XmPACK_COLUMN*
XmNadjustLast	Boolean	Extend last column/row to edge
XmNmarginHeight	Dimension	Margin between edge and children
XmNmarginWidth	Dimension	
XmNspacing	Dimension	Space between children
XmNadjustMargin	Boolean	Force column/row margins of label children (and subclasses) equal
XmNisAligned	Boolean	Force common alignment for labels
XmNentryAlignment	enum	Common alignment for labels *XmALIGNMENT_BEGINNING* *XmALIGNMENT_CENTER* *XmALIGNMENT_END*
XmNresizeHeight	Boolean	If row-column requests new geometry
XmNresizeWidth	Boolean	when itself or its children change

Table 6-2: Geometry resource fields of the row-column widget.

A third packing option, *XmPACK_NONE*, is available which leaves all row-column children alone. In this mode you have to set the size and location of the children yourself, creating a kind of drawing board. The row-column widget simply tries to grow large enough to enclose all children.

The widget classes of row-column children are completely arbitrary, because geometry management can be performed with any widget. However, the row-column is most useful with primitive widgets, and there are some resource fields which specially influence label subclasses.

The alignment of entries (meaning the alignment of the label inside the child) can be forced to the same value. Equally, the inner margins of label subclasses (left and right margins if the row-column is vertically oriented) can be adjusted to their respective maximum values.

Similar to other composite widgets the row-column defines resource fields to specify whether geometry requests from children are propagated. You can specify individually whether the row-column may resize itself either horizontally or vertically if children are added, removed or changed.

Radio Box

The row-column widget can also operate as a *radio box*. A radio box is a group of toggle buttons, of which at most one button may be on (see Figure 6.4). If another button is set, the previously set button is toggled back—just like the mechanical button assembly found in older radios.

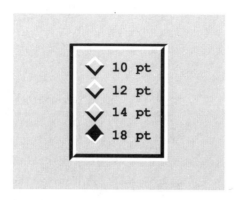

Figure 6.4: Example of a radio box.

To make the toggle behaviour visible to the user, toggle buttons in a radio box have a diamond-shaped toggle indicator instead of the normal square. However, the diamond-shaped indicator is not used by the toggle buttons in a radio box automatically: you have to request the different indicator explicitly when creating the individual buttons. The radio box behaviour is achieved by setting the resource field *XmNradioBehaviour* of the row-column parent of the toggle buttons.

If you want to ensure that exactly one of the toggles is always switched on, you can set the flag *XmNradioAlwaysOne*. In this case, the currently active toggle cannot be switched off without selecting another. You have to be careful in your program because switching toggles by the application is not checked (you can delete, unmanage, or switch the toggles at will). Moreover, one of the toggles must already be set when the radio box is created.

Switching the toggles is reported by the *XmNentryCallback*, which has already been described in the menu section.

As an additional aid you can let the row-column widget check that only one class of children is allowed. Checking is achieved with the resource fields *XmNisHomogeneous* (which switches the checks on) and *XmNentryClass* (which specifies the class to check against).

XmNradioBehaviour	Boolean	If only one toggle shall be active
XmNradioAlwaysOne	Boolean	Disallow switching the last toggle off
XmNentryCallback	Callback	Common callback for buttons
XmNisHomogeneous	Boolean	Only allow one class for children
XmNentryClass	WidgetClass	Class if *XmNisHomogeneous*

Table 6-3: Behaviour resource fields of the row-column widget.

The Form Widget

The form widget is the second general layout manager. It is the most powerful (and the most complicated).

Just like the paned window described in Section 5.7, the form uses constraint resource fields to specify alignment relations for its children. In contrast to the paned window, the form widget defines a rather large set of constraint resource fields, because all four sides of a widget can be handled differently.

The alignment of the child widgets is specified as *attachments* of different kinds (flexible or fixed) to different objects (other widgets, sides of the form widget, positions in the form).

Each side of every child can either be left alone, or it can be kept at a fixed distance from some other part (this is a directed dependence as you will see below), or it may be pinned to some relative position in the form widget.

The form widget supports the following different types of attachment, which can individually be chosen for each side of a child:

- *None.* The side is left floating and its location is determined by the preferred size of the child. This means that the widget may grow or shrink in this direction by its own preference if only one of the pair of opposite sides is attached; the unattached side moves as required.

- *Form.* The side is attached to the same side of the form with a fixed distance specified by an offset field. The attachment is directed, meaning that the widget moves if the side of the form moves, but not the other way round.

- *Opposite Form.* The side is absolutely attached to the other side of the form. This type of attachment is rarely used.

- *Widget.* The side is attached to the opposite side of another widget, which must also be a direct child of the form. This attachment is also directed, i.e. a widget cannot influence the other widget it is attached to.

- *Opposite Widget.* The side is attached to the same side of another widget. Please note that the meaning of "opposite" is reversed with widgets compared with attachments to the form sides.

- *Position.* The side is attached to a relative position in the form. The behaviour in this case can be illustrated by nailing the side to a specified point in the form. Imagine the form being made of rubber, such that the nail point stays at a certain relative position when the form resizes. The nail position is specified by giving the ratio of the relative distances to the form sides.

- *Self.* The side is attached to its initial relative position in the form. *Self* attachment is similar to *Position* attachment, except that the relative

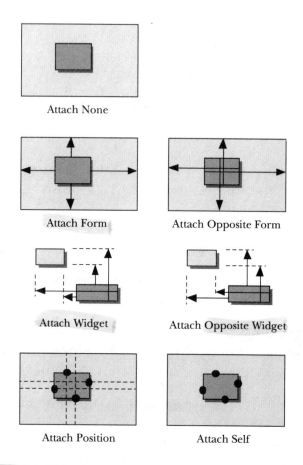

Figure 6.5: Different attachment types that can be used for children in a form widget. The attachment can be specified individually for each side of a child.

position is determined by the absolute position of this side at the time of the child creation. This is useful when you do not know the size of a child (e.g. a label in different languages).

The different attachments and their analogies are illustrated in Figure 6.5. Because most attachments need an additional specification (e.g. the widget to connect to), there are four constraint resource fields for every side:

- *Attachment.* Specifies one of the above attachments. The valid constants to use are shown in Table 6-4.

- *Offset.* The distance when using absolute attachments. Used for the attachment types *XmATTACH_FORM, XmATTACH_OPPOSITE_FORM, XmATTACH_WIDGET,* and *XmATTACH_OPPOSITE_WIDGET.*

XmNtopAttachment	enum	Attachment of top side
XmNbottomAttachment	enum	Attachment of bottom side
XmNleftAttachment	enum	Attachment of left side
XmNrightAttachment	enum	Attachment of right side
		XmATTACH_NONE
		XmATTACH_FORM
		XmATTACH_OPPOSITE_FORM
		XmATTACH_WIDGET
		XmATTACH_OPPOSITE_WIDGET
		XmATTACH_POSITION
		XmATTACH_SELF
XmNtopOffset	int	Offset to top attachment
XmNbottomOffset	int	Offset to bottom attachment
XmNleftOffset	int	Offset to left attachment
XmNrightOffset	int	Offset to right attachment
XmNtopPosition	int	Relative position of top side
XmNbottomPosition	int	Relative position of bottom side
XmNleftPosition	int	Relative position of left side
XmNrightPosition	int	Relative position of right side
XmNtopWidget	Widget	Attached widget of top side
XmNbottomWidget	Widget	Attached widget of bottom side
XmNleftWidget	Widget	Attached widget of left side
XmNrightWidget	Widget	Attached widget of right side
XmNresizable	Boolean	If form can resize this child

Table 6-4: Form constraint resource fields.

- *Position.* The relative position used for *XmATTACH_POSITION* and *XmATTACH_SELF*. It is specified as the nominator of a ratio. The denominator is specified as a resource field of the form.

- *Widget.* The ID of the widget this child is connected to when using *XmATTACH_WIDGET* and *XmATTACH_OPPOSITE_WIDGET*. The widget must be a direct child of the form.

The names of the resource fields to use are enumerated in Table 6-4. The four fields are repeated for all four sides of a child widget of the form. Additionally, you can specify whether a child may be resized by the form. If not, you can possibly save some attachment specifications.

At least one side of a child in each direction should be attached, otherwise the position of the widget would not be properly defined. The form widget attaches the left and upper sides of a widget by default (see below), so you must override this default explicitly with *XmNONE* if you want only the bottom and right sides attached, for example.

Form Example

To provide a better understanding the form widget is now illustrated with an example.

In this example a window is to be laid out in a tiled format, with three subwindows in a row and another below (see Figure 6.6). Arbitrary classes can

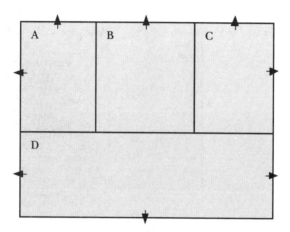

Figure 6.6: Form widget example. The picture shows the desired layout. The arrows indicate the necessary attachments to the form sides to make the subwindows resize with the form.

be used for the child widgets, because all widgets must accept any size their parent determines.

It is obvious that some sides must be connected to the form borders to make the subwidgets resize with the form. The top sides of widgets A, B, and C, the left sides of A and D, the right sides of C and D, and the bottom side of D are affected. Every side automatically chooses the appropriate form border to attach to if the attachment is set to *XmFORM*. Because no spacing is desired, all offset resource fields are left at their default value of 0.

Now you have to decide in which way the added or subtracted space of a resize operation is distributed. First the horizontal direction will be examined. There are several ways of distributing the space:

Localized Distribution. All the space may be absorbed by one of the widgets, the others keeping their preferred size (see Figure 6.7). A widget keeps its preferred size if only one side is attached and the other is left alone (*XmATTACH_NONE*). The widget which serves as a space buffer has both sides attached. The attachments are to either the neighbour widget or the form.

Therefore if the middle widget is the buffer, it is attached to the left and right widgets, and the outer widgets are attached to the form. As a result the sides of the middle widget are dragged or pushed by the unattached sides of the outer two. Unattached means that the side itself is not attached to a position (i.e. it is a free variable), but other sides may be attached to it (and be dependent on it).

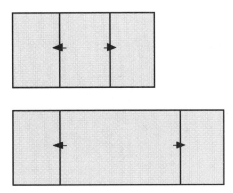

Figure 6.7: One widget serving as a space buffer.

To give a physical analogy to this behaviour, imagine that widgets with two sides attached are made of rubber, while the other ones are solid (with respect to one direction).

Even Distribution. The space may be distributed proportionally between the widgets (see Figure 6.8). In this case the middle sides must be attached to a relative position in the form. You should attach only one of two coinciding sides to the relative position in the form widget and make the other one dependent on it (*XmATTACH_WIDGET*). This ensures that the exact value of the relative position is set only once, and you can later define a spacing between the two.

The disadvantage of relative positions is that you must know the approximate relative sizes of the subwidgets to set appropriate relative positions, because the preferred size is not taken into account. Alternatively you can attach

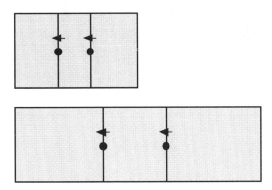

Figure 6.8: Relative distribution of space. The right-hand sides of two widgets are attached to relative positions in the form, while the left-hand sides coinciding with those positions are attached by reference to avoid specifying the same position twice.

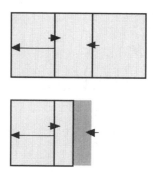

Figure 6.9: Absolute division of space. Parts of the window may be clipped if made too small.

the sides to their initial positions. Then the form calculates the initial sizes and arranges the relative positions in the ratio of the preferred sizes[1]. In this case you must attach one widget side with *XmATTACH_WIDGET*, because an initial position for two opposite sides of one widget is meaningless.

Absolute Positions. – Some sides may be set to absolute positions by attaching them to the form sides with a fixed offset (see Figure 6.9). However, a good design avoids encoding fixed values in the program, because the widget sizes may be different in different program versions as a result of different texts and fonts.

With absolute positions (and with localized distribution when the buffering space is exhausted) it may be possible that parts of a child are clipped if the form is very small, because there is no way to reposition the child without breaking the constraints.

If you want to combine some of these methods, for example to size widget A absolutely and have B and C share the *remaining* space equally, you may have to use another form as a child of the form, because the form has no notion of relative positions between some arbitrary points, but only between the form sides (see Figure 6.10). The spacing in Figure 6.10 has only been introduced for clarification—you can attach the widgets directly with no spacing as shown in the examples above.

The principles shown for the horizontal direction can also be applied to vertical divisions of the form. In the example, depending on whether the upper or the lower part is variable, either the bottom sides of A, B and C can be attached to D, or the top side of D can be attached to the bottom of the tallest window of A, B and C. One resulting case is shown in Figure 6.11.

---

[1]In 1.0 the form widget does not calculate its preferred size correctly. This defeats some of the advantages of geometry management. The symptom is that the form is very small on start-up, but may be resized correctly. As a remedy you can set a suitable geometry for the nearest shell ancestor. However, this geometry may not be correct if the user chooses a larger font.

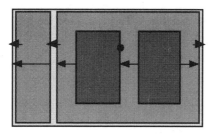

Figure 6.10: Form as a child of another form.

The vertical subdivision in this example requires that the largest of the upper widgets is chosen as a leader to which the others are attached. However, the largest widget may not be known in advance. If you want to align the upper three widgets to their maximum, you have to enclose them in another form widget, using the ability of the form to set its size to the maximum height.

In Figure 6.11 B and C are attached to D, which in turn is attached to A. Another possibility is to align A, B, and C directly, which would be necessary if D didn't exist. Figure 6.12 shows a situation where the widgets are aligned on their left sides (the same can be applied to all sides). Alignment can be achieved by connecting one side with the attachment *XmOPPOSITE_WIDGET*. Because attachments work only in one dimension, a left side may be attached to another left side which is above or below it.

By specifying an offset other than 0, one widget may be indented relative to the other. By aligning the left and right sides to the first widget in a column you can achieve a row-column-like effect. The difference is, however, that the

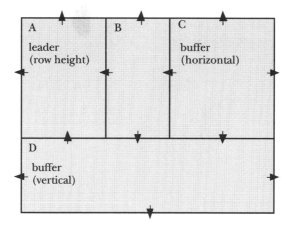

Figure 6.11: Complete constraint example.

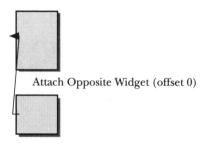

Figure 6.12: Vertical alignment by attaching with *XmOPPOSITE_WIDGET*.

preferred width of a row-column is calculated as the maximum of all child widths, while in the form the first widget acts as a leader and determines the width.

The *XmN...Widget* resource fields can be specified in a resource file by using the name of the referenced widget.[1] The name must be unique and only direct children of the form can be referenced in this way.

Form Resources

The few resource fields of the form itself determine the defaults for various constraint fields. The default attachment for the left and top sides of children is either *XmFORM* or *XmSELF*. The latter is assumed when *XmNrubberPositioning* is set. The default attachment for a direction takes effect if no attachments are specified for two opposite sides of a widget. If you omit the attachments you must at least specify an appropriate offset (if *XmFORM*) or position (if *XmSELF*), otherwise all children end up overlapping in the upper left corner.

If you want to leave a uniform spacing between the child widgets, you can set the default offset for horizontal or vertical distances instead of specifying all offsets individually. One field you also need to specify if you use relative positions is the *XmNfractionBase* already mentioned.

XmNrubberPositioning	Boolean	If default attachment is *XmSELF* (else *XmFORM*) for top and left
XmNfractionBase	int	Base for relative positions
XmNhorizontalSpacing	int	Default offset for left and right
XmNverticalSpacing	int	Default offset for top and bottom

Table 6-5: General form resource fields.

---

[1] In 1.0 the necessary resource converter is missing.

Figure 6.13: A list widget.

6.3 Further Control Area Elements

The List Widget

The list widget is used to select one or more strings from an arbitrary number of items (see Figure 6.13). The list widget is a primitive widget, because the selectable parts are internally managed strings and not child widgets.

The strings which can be selected are stored internally as an array of XmStrings. They can be accessed via the pair of resource fields *XmNitems* and *XmNitemCount*. The count is necessary because the lists can be defined with any size large enough to hold the entries, just like argument lists, and the count specifies the number of occupied entries. To construct an item list, similar methods to that for argument lists can be used.

The item list is of type *XmStringTable*, a synonym for *XmString**. Just like string resources the list is copied on *XtSetValues*, so you can free the item list afterwards if you allocated it dynamically.

In general any subset of the list items may be selected at one time (depending on the selection policy, only a single selection may be allowed). The selected subset can be accessed via a similar pair of fields, *XmNselectedItems* and *XmNselectedItemCount*. The identification of items is achieved by comparing their values, so an item list should not contain the same string twice.

As usual, the list widget provides resource fields for margins and the spacing between items (although it is not a manager widget). Like the label

XmNitems	XmStringTable	All items in list
XmNitemCount	int	Number of items in *XmNitems*
XmNselectedItems	XmStringTable	All selected items
XmNselectedItemCount	int	Length of *XmNselectedItems*

Table 6-6: Content resource fields of the list widget.

XmNlistMarginWidth	Dimension	Margins between items and border
XmNlistMarginHeight	Dimension	
XmNlistSpacing	short	Space between items
XmNfontList	XmFontList	Font for the items
XmNstringDirection	enum	Writing direction
		XmSTRING_DIRECTION_L_TO_R
		XmSTRING_DIRECTION_R_TO_L

Table 6-7: Geometry resource fields of the list widget.

widget, it has to define a font and a string direction for the XmStrings. The geometry resource fields are described in Table 6-7.

The list widget has several different policies to control how items can be selected. You can choose from the following policies depending on your application's needs:

- *Single Selection.* Only one of the items may be selected at a time. In this case the list works along similar lines to a radio box.

- *Multiple Selection.* All items can be individually selected and deselected by clicking on them. In this mode the list works like a group of toggle buttons.

- *Extended Selection.* Items can be selected in a similar way to a sequence of characters in a text widget. Pressing the button and moving the mouse selects a range of items. In contrast to the text widget, multiple ranges may be selected if the Ctrl modifier is used.

- *Browse Selection.* This is a single selection mode which works like the traversal of a menu pane. While the mouse button is down, traversed items are selected and unselected as the mouse pointer moves through them. Compared with single selection the advantage is that additional feedback can be generated while traversing items (e.g. a quick flashing of what would happen if the traversed item were be selected).

The desired policy is specified in the resource field *XmNselectionPolicy*. An additional field *XmNautomaticSelection* determines whether callbacks are invoked while browsing, or if callbacks are only delivered when a selection is committed by raising the mouse button. *XmNautomaticSelection* is only effective for extended and browse selection.

List Callbacks

A different callback reason is provided for each policy. The respective callback is usually executed when a new selection is committed by releasing the mouse button. This process is simple in the single, browse and multiple selection modes, because only one item is affected by those actions.

XmNselectionPolicy	enum	Operating policy
		    XmSINGLE_SELECT
		    XmMULTIPLE_SELECT
		    XmEXTENDED_SELECT
		    XmBROWSE_SELECT

XmNautomaticSelection	Boolean	Callback even when button down
XmNdoubleClickInterval	int	Time in ms

Table 6-8: Policy resource fields of the list widget.

The affected item is reported in the structure pointed to by *call_data* in all list callbacks. The structure has the following definition:

```
typedef struct {
    int         reason;            /* XmCR_SINGLE_SELECT      */
                                   /* XmCR_MULTIPLE_SELECT    */
                                   /* XmCR_EXTENDED_SELECT    */
                                   /* XmCR_BROWSE_SELECT      */
                                   /* XmCR_DEFAULT_ACTION     */

    XEvent      *event;
    XmString    item;
    int         item_length;
    int         item_position;
    XmString    *selected_items;   /* only when MULTIPLE_SELECT*/
    int         selected_item_count; /* or EXTENDED_SELECT      */
    int         selection_type;    /* only when EXTENDED_SELECT*/
                                   /* XmINITIAL               */
                                   /* XmMODIFICATION          */
                                   /* XmADDITION              */
} XmListCallbackStruct;
```

For single and browse selection modes the item itself is sufficient because any other previously selected items will have been unselected when the callback occurs. Therefore only this item is reported with its length and its position in the item list as convenience information. Please note that positions start from 1, in contrast to the C usage of arrays starting with 0.

For the multiple selection callback the list of currently selected items is reported, saving an explicit query for this value. All XmString values in the callback structure are allocated and de-allocated by the list widget. You must copy them if you want to use them after the callback terminates.

The most complicated mode is extended selection. The extended selection callback also reports whether the cause of the callback was a new initial selection (selecting a range of items without modifier keys deselects all previous ranges), a modification of an existing range (with the Shift key), or the addition of a new range (with the Ctrl key).

XmNsingleSelectionCallback	Callback	Invoked when the corresponding
XmNmultipleSelectionCallback	Callback	policy is in effect
XmNextendedSelectionCallback	Callback	
XmNbrowseSelectionCallback	Callback	
XmNdefaultActionCallback	Callback	On double click

Table 6-9: List callbacks.

When the automatic selection mode is in effect, callbacks are reported on button press and when a new item is traversed, but not on the final button release.

The *XmNdefaultActionCallback* is called when any list item is double-clicked. As a side effect the item is selected (this will have been reported by the first click of the series).

Scrolled List

The list widget includes special support for being installed as the child of a scrolled window. In this case it uses an additional set of resource fields to control the behaviour of the scrolled window. The additional resource fields are present if the list is not inside a scrolled window, but they have no effect. The text widget has a similar feature which was discussed in Section 5.6. How to create widget combinations with a scrolled window was also explained in that section.

The most important field is the *XmNlistSizePolicy*. It controls the width of the list inside the scrolled window. If the policy is *XmCONSTANT*, the width will stay constant even if longer items are added later. The default policy is *XmVARIABLE*. In this case a horizontal scroll bar never appears and long items are cut off if the list is not allowed to grow sufficiently. A compromise is used with *XmRESIZE_IF_POSSIBLE*: the horizontal scroll bar only appears when the list cannot grow sufficiently.

A related resource field is the scroll bar display policy. If *XmSTATIC*, scroll bars always appear (except for variable list size policy, when there is no horizontal bar). If *XmAS_NEEDED*, the scroll bars appear when there is

XmNhorizontalScrollBar	Widget	ID of scroll bar
XmNverticalScrollBar	Widget	
XmNlistSizePolicy	enum	How the list resizes itself
		XmCONSTANT
		XmVARIABLE
		XmRESIZE_IF_POSSIBLE
XmNscrollBarDisplayPolicy	enum	Whether permanent scroll bars
		XmSTATIC
		XmAS_NEEDED
XmNvisibleItemCount	int	Value for initial height

Table 6-10: Scrolled list resource fields.

something to scroll.

The height of the visible area (the clip window) is indirectly determined by *XmNvisibleItemCount*, which sets the number of items that should fit in this area.

The Scale Widget

The scale widget shares many similarities with the scroll bar (in fact it is implemented with a scroll bar as a subpart). In contrast to the list widget, which looks like a composite widget but isn't, the scale looks like a primitive widget, but is really a composite one.

The scale widget may be used to display a value from a fixed range, which may also be changed by the user (see Figure 6.14).

There are quite a number of resource fields needed to configure the operation of the scale, as summarized in Table 6-11. Just like the scroll bar the scale automatically translates pixels to application-relevant values. You can specify a maximum and a minimum value for the scale, and the current value is translated to a corresponding slider position.

The scale has the additional ability to display the current value as a number beneath the slider. Because the value is specified as an integer, you may instruct the scale to insert a decimal point at a specified position if you want to display fractional values.

A further part of the scale is the title string, whose value and font can be set through the scale, but which is really a label gadget child.

Four resource fields are propagated to the scroll bar child. They set the orientation, the processing direction, and the size of the slider. The slider width also determines the width of the scrolling region. The length of the scrolling region is always equal to the size of the scale widget.

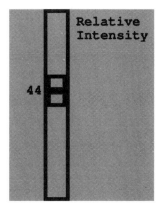

Figure 6.14: Typical scale widget.

XmNminimum	int	Min value
XmNmaximum	int	Max value
XmNvalue	int	Scale value
XmNshowValue	Boolean	Display value at slider
XmNdecimalPoints	short	Decimal points of displayed value
XmNtitleString	XmString	Title for scale
XmNfontList	XmFontList	Font for title
XmNorientation	enum	Scale direction *XmVERTICAL* *XmHORIZONTAL*
XmNprocessingDirection	enum	Which side is max *XmMAX_ON_TOP* *XmMAX_ON_BOTTOM* *XmMAX_ON_LEFT* *XmMAX_ON_RIGHT*
XmNscaleHeight	Dimension	Size of slider area
XmNscaleWidth	Dimension	

Table 6-11: Scale resource fields.

The scale widget creates three standard children: the scroll bar (without arrows), the title, and the value label. The title is positioned in the upper right corner. Any further children you create are used as labels for the scale (see Figure 6.15). Further children may be of any widget class, but labels are the most useful.

The labels are equally spread out over the length of the scale. If you want to position labels at specified locations, you must use a form widget as parent of the scale and create the labels as children of the form with specified relative positions. The relative positions ensure that the whole construction can be resized correctly. This kind of set-up is illustrated in Figure 6.16.

The two most important scroll bar callbacks also appear as callbacks of the scale. Normally you want to use the *XmNvalueChangedCallback*, which is called whenever the user has dragged the slider to a new position. If additional feedback in addition to displaying the current value is required while dragging the slider, you can use the *XmNdragCallback*. The drag callback is especially useful if the scale does not directly represent a numerical value, but for example something like a colour. The equivalent of the current scale position can then be displayed in another widget as feedback.

Figure 6.15: Horizontal scale with labels.

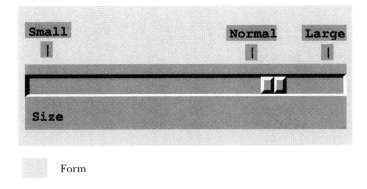

Form

Figure 6.16: Scale with positioned labels in a form. The labels and separators that form the scale marks are children of the form as well as the scale.

Just like the scroll bar, the scale passes a pointer to a structure with its callbacks which also contains the current value.

```
typedef struct {
        int         reason;     /* XmCR_VALUE_CHANGED        */
                                /* XmCR_DRAG                 */
        XEvent      *event;
        int         value;
} XmScaleCallbackStruct;
```

Separators

In the previous sections two categories of widgets for control areas were discussed: simple widgets which serve as control elements, and composite geometry managers which lay them out for correct resizing. What is missing are elements to decorate a control area (*separators*) and for visual grouping of subareas (*frames*).

You have already encountered the separator widget. Its single purpose is to maintain a straight line in various styles. It does not merely draw the line, but as a widget can naturally participate in the geometry management process to maintain the correct length all the times.

In Section 5.3 the separator widget in a menu was only used in its default configuration, a single horizontal line. You can also change the orientation with

| XmNvalueChangedCallback | Callback | If slider moved |
| XmNdragCallback | Callback | While dragging |

Table 6-12: Scale callback resource fields.

Figure 6.17: Etched separator line.

XmNorientation. The line style is selected with the field *XmNseparatorType.* In addition to the conventional single, double, and dashed lines, the separator can also draw "etched" lines, which use two different shadow colours drawn side by side. Depending on which colour is used for which side, the appearance is either "etched in" or "etched out", just like the normal shadow effects (see Figure 6.17).

As a final resource field *XmNmargin* determines the space between the line ends and the widget's border. It does not influence the height of a horizontal separator or the width of a vertical one, the preferred size makes the separator so thin that the line is just visible. The separator length is determined by the parent, because the separator has no notion of the necessary length, and you should avoid setting the geometry explicitly.

Frames

The frame widget class is used to surround a group of widgets with a shadow border, because row-column and form widgets cannot display shadows in their normal modes (the row-column can, but only as a menu). In addition, the frame widget can also display etched lines, while most other widgets are only capable of simple shadows (see Figure 6.18).

XmNorientation	enum	Orientation of line *XmHORIZONTAL* *XmVERTICAL*
XmNseparatorType	enum	Type of drawn line *XmNO_LINE* *XmSINGLE_LINE* *XmDOUBLE_LINE* *XmSINGLE_DASHED_LINE* *XmDOUBLE_DASHED_LINE* *XmSHADOW_ETCHED_IN* *XmSHADOW_ETCHED_OUT*
XmNmargin	short	Space between line end and border

Table 6-13: Separator resource fields.

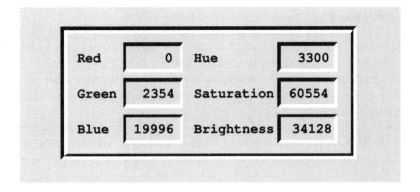

Figure 6.18: Frame around a widget group.

If you want to surround a group of widgets with a shadow, you have to create the controlling manager widget as a child of a frame. As with shells, a frame widget only accepts a single child.

Shadow type and shadow thickness can be set as resource fields of the frame. Remember that although the shadow thickness is already defined in the *manager* class, the superclass of all composite Motif widgets, not all manager widgets implement the shadow drawing.

The frame widget must have exactly one child of an arbitrary class. In geometry negotiations the frame widget passes through all requests in both directions, always adapting the child correctly to its own size.

If you want to group some widgets in a control area, such as a radio box, you should use etched lines for the frame. The individual elements of a control group must be controlled by a manager widget, because the frame widget may have only one child. You can instruct the frame to leave margins between the shadow and its child.

XmNshadowType	enum	Type of shadow *XmSHADOW_IN* *XmSHADOW_OUT* *XmSHADOW_ETCHED_IN* *XmSHADOW_ETCHED_OUT*
XmNshadowThickness	short	Inherited from manager class
XmNmarginWidth	short	Margin between border and child
XmNmarginHeight	short	

Table 6-14: Frame resource fields.

6.4 Traversal

The widget philosophy is based on the fact that each widget may be viewed in isolation because the tasks of a single widget are clearly defined. Isolated operation is adequate when the interface is operated with the mouse, because it is usually very clear which widget is addressed by a user operation (determined by the window hierarchy in the X server).

However, the situation is more difficult when keyboard input is taken into account. In the section on the text widget you have already seen that it is possible to transfer the input focus (by "tabbing") from one widget to another, which may be in a completely different position in the widget hierarchy. This process requires cooperation between several widgets.

Focus Management

In X only a single window on the screen may have the input focus, i.e. may receive KeyPress and KeyRelease events. There are two modes in which the focus window can be determined:

- *Follow-Pointer.* In this mode the window where the mouse pointer resides has the input focus.

- *Explicit.* The focus must be explicitly transferred from one window to another, either by clicking with the mouse into the new window, or by a key command in the old window.

The focus policy may be different in different sub-hierarchies. For example the follow-pointer policy is most useful with large windows, because you do not have to position the pointer too exactly. Therefore it is common practice to use the follow-pointer mode between top-level windows and have the explicit focus policy inside. The focus policy between top-level widgets is determined by the window manager, while the policy inside is controlled by a resource field in the shell widget.

The focus policy inside top-level windows defaults to explicit, because it usually does not make sense to require the pointer to be in the text widget for text entry, for example, if there is only one text widget inside a top-level window.

Usually focus is only important for text widgets, as the other widgets are mainly controlled with the mouse. Text widgets indicate (by blinking the insertion cursor) that they have the focus.

Tab Groups

Normally the focus can be transferred to a text widget by clicking into it. To continue text entry in another text widget it is often inconvenient to switch between mouse and keyboard. "Tabbing" the focus between text widgets inside one top-level window is an alternative method.

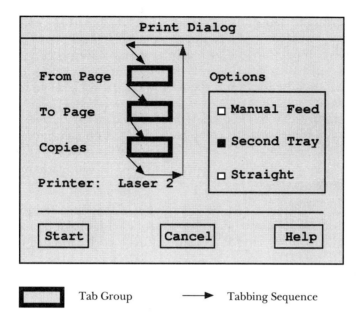

Figure 6.19: Text widgets in a dialog box defined as tab groups.

For tabbing to work, the participating text widgets must be defined as *tab groups*. All tab groups are collected under their next shell parent, regardless of how deep the tab groups are located in the widget hierarchy.

You may wonder why the text widgets are defined as *groups*, although they are only primitive widgets. This naming was chosen because composite widgets can also be defined as tab groups for the keyboard traversal mechanism explained below.

Tab groups are ordered in the sequence in which they were declared as tab groups. Tabbing works by following this sequence forwards or backwards to the next or the previous tab group (see Figure 6.19).

There are considerable differences in the handling of tab groups between version 1.0 and version 1.1 of Motif. Fortunately, although the 1.1 model is cleaner, compatibility with the 1.0 version has been retained.

A widget is declared as a tab group with the following call. In version 1.0, this should be called at least for all text widgets after creation:

XmAddTabGroup (widget_which_will_form_a_tab_group);

In version 1.1 the resource field *XmNnavigationType* for all widgets controls whether this widget is automatically added as a tab group on creation. This resource field has reasonable default values for the different widget classes. You do not have to add tab groups explicitly in 1.1, and the *XmAddTabGroup* procedure may be removed in a future version.

When a shell pops up, the first tab group automatically gets the focus and the user can start typing right away. If no tab group is explicitly defined in 1.0, the whole shell has the focus and the user must first click into a text widget to transfer the focus.

A tab group will only be considered for focus transfer when it is able to accept the focus. If the widget is completely invisible, unmanaged or insensitive, it is skipped.

Keyboard Traversal

In Motif all widgets can be completely controlled via the keyboard through a mechanism known as *keyboard traversal*. Keyboard traversal requires that every widget may acquire the input focus and complicates the focus process.

In keyboard traversal mode a *location cursor* is drawn around the widget that can currently be controlled from the keyboard. The appearance of the location cursor may vary depending on the highlighted widget. The location

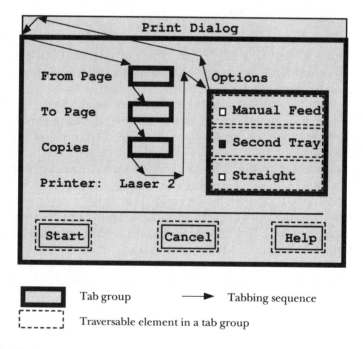

Figure 6.20: Keyboard traversal. The complete dialog and the button group are also tab groups that become accessible when keyboard traversal is enabled. The cursor keys are used to move the location cursor between traversable elements of a composite tab group.

cursor can be moved with the arrow keys or by tabbing. The arrow keys move the location cursor within a tab group; the Tab key moves it to another tab group.

The widget highlighted by the location cursor has the focus and can now be controlled by key commands. For example, buttons can be activated with the space bar or the Return key. The normal translation mechanism determines the keyboard behaviour of a widget.

For example, in Figure 6.20 the window contains five tab groups. When the window first appears, the whole dialog as the first tab group acquires the focus. The dialog contains three traversable elements, namely the three buttons at the bottom. All other elements are themselves tab groups. Using the arrow keys the location cursor can be moved between the three buttons, while the space bar activates the currently highlighted button. By repeated tabbing the focus can be transferred to the toggle group which also contains individually traversable elements.

Figure 6.20 shows that tab groups may be nested. The whole dialog is a tab group that also contains other tab groups as children. Traversal inside a tab group only regards primitive children which are not themselves tab groups.

The keyboard traversal mechanism is optional. Every widget that has to participate must have its resource field *XmNtraversal* set. *XmNtraversal* should only be set in a resource file so that the user may switch it off. Only labels and separators do not need to be traversable, as well as scroll bars in scrolled windows (because the scrolled window itself manages keyboard scrolling). In Motif 1.0 you can use the following lines in your application defaults file to enable traversal to take place:

traversalOn:	*True*
XmLabel.traversalOn:	*False*
XmSeparator.traversalOn:	*False*
XmScrolledWindow.XmScrollBar.traversalOn:	*False*

These are the default values in 1.1. You can inhibit keyboard traversal by setting *XmNtraversalOn* generally to *False*.

In 1.1 all necessary tab groups are usually created automatically. In 1.0 you have to create these tab groups yourself if you want to support the keyboard traversal mechanism. If traversal is switched off by the user, tab groups without texts are not accessible any more because they cannot accept the focus. Therefore they are skipped and only text widgets work as before (because they always have traversal switched on).

Direct shell children should always be declared as tab groups to be the first to acquire the focus. The following widget classes should always be defined as tab groups: text, list, scroll bar, scale, main window, scrolled window, and drawing area. These classes define a different behaviour for the arrow keys dependent on their own substructure. For example, individual items of a list may be highlighted by the location cursor and the location cursor may be moved as usual with the arrow keys. Therefore it does not make sense to include a list in another tab group.

The row-column widget should be a tab group when it contains buttons. The widget classes for dialogs (discussed in the next section) should also be tab groups if they contain buttons at the bottom.

6.5 Dialogs

Although the previous section mentioned that control areas can be used as dialog windows, there is again an appropriate shell widget missing. This section will cover the dialog shell widget and some prefabricated widgets for common dialog situations.

Dialog Shell

The dialog shell is the third most important shell type in Motif (after the menu shell and the top-level shell). The difference between a dialog shell and a normal top-level shell is that a dialog window is subordinate to some other window and may not be iconified separately. In contrast to a pop-up menu window it receives window manager decorations and can be resized.

Just like menu shells a dialog shell is popped up by managing its child (because it is a Motif-specific shell type).

The dialog shell has no special resource fields of its own; it only flags its window differently for the window manager to construct the right amount of decoration. More on shells in general can be found in Chapter 7.

Bulletin Board

The bulletin board is a widget class specially built to be a child of the dialog shell. It has some resource fields appropriate for dialogs which are translated into the general shell resource fields of the dialog shell. The bulletin board resources have the advantage that they are considerably easier to specify.

The bulletin board is mainly used as a parent class for some more specific dialog widgets and has only minimal geometry management features.

The resource field *XmNdialogStyle* controls the modality of the dialog. The modality determines whether the user may work with other windows while the dialog is visible. For example, if you display an important error message which the user must acknowledge before the program can continue its work, all interaction with the normal application window must be inhibited. This is an *application modal* dialog, because other applications continue to work normally.

XmNdialogStyle	enum	Modality of dialog *XmDIALOG_SYSTEM_MODAL* *XmDIALOG_APPLICATION_MODAL* *XmDIALOG_MODELESS* *XmDIALOG_WORK_AREA*
XmNdialogTitle	XmString	Shell title for decoration
XmNnoResize	Boolean	Exclude resize handles around shell
XmNdefaultPosition	Boolean	If centred around parent of shell
XmNmapCallback	Callback	Before mapped
XmNunmapCallback	Callback	After unmapped

Table 6-15: Bulletin board resource fields handled by dialog shell parent.

Although you should avoid it, you can also specify a *system modal* dialog, which inhibits all system interaction, even with other applications.

If possible, you should use a *modeless* dialog. In a modeless style your program must be prepared to handle interactions in its main window while the dialog is shown. Making a dialog modeless creates the most natural situation for the user, but often requires some program restructuring compared with traditional programming methods.

If the bulletin board is not a child of a dialog shell, the dialog style should be *XmDIALOG_WORK_AREA.*

You can specify the title of the dialog window directly through the bulletin board's *XmNdialogTitle* field. If the dialog need not be resizable by the user, *XmNnoResize* instructs the window manager to exclude the resize handles around the window. Normally the dialog appears centred on top of the next higher shell. If you switch centring off by resetting *XmNdefaultPosition* you are responsible for setting a position yourself before the dialog is popped up.

Actions such as positioning a dialog can be conveniently located in a *XmNmapCallback* routine which is called before the dialog appears. Like the rowcolumn, the bulletin board also has a *XmNunmapCallback.*

The bulletin board is mainly used as a supporting superclass for other dialog classes. Therefore it performs only a minimal geometry management. All children must specify their own positions: the bulletin board only checks

XmNallowOverlap	Boolean	If children may overlap
XmNmarginHeight	short	Margin between children and border
XmNmarginWidth	short	
XmNresizePolicy	enum	If may resize itself *XmRESIZE_NONE* *XmRESIZE_GROW* *XmRESIZE_ANY*
XmNshadowType	enum	Shadow around the bulletin board *XmSHADOW_IN* *XmSHADOW_OUT* *XmSHADOW_ETCHED_IN* *XmSHADOW_ETCHED_OUT*

Table 6-16: Geometry and visual resource fields of the bulletin board.

| XmNdefaultButton | Widget | Button to activate on \<Return\> |
| XmNcancelButton | Widget | Only for subclasses |

Table 6-17: Special children of the bulletin board. They are not created by the bulletin board.

whether they overlap if requested by *XmNallowOverlap*. The bulletin board also tries to enclose all children.

XmNresizePolicy specifies whether the bulletin board tries to resize itself if required by a changing child. Furthermore the bulletin board is capable of shadow drawing.

For use in subclasses the bulletin board defines two standard buttons, whose IDs are available as resource fields. However, the bulletin board does not create the buttons itself. If a button is installed as the *XmNdefaultButton,* an accelerator is used to activate this button when the Return key is pressed in the bulletin board.

The Return accelerator of the bulletin board is a common source of mistakes because translations for the Return key are overridden in all children. This feature is inherited by subclasses such as the form widget.

Because dialogs generally use some common primitive widgets, the bulletin board provides resource fields that are propagated to children of certain classes. Three default font lists can be specified (one each for buttons, texts, and label widgets) that override the individual settings for bulletin board children of one of these classes. Text children also get a common writing direction, and can also have an additional set of translations.

The *XmNtextTranslations* can be used to re-install the Return key behaviour of single-line text by specifying the following resource entry:

```
*XmBulletinBoard.textTranslations:    #override  \
    <Key>Return:    activate()
```

As a convenience, *XmNautoUnmanage* instructs the bulletin board to be unmanaged if any of the predefined buttons is activated. This will cause the dialog window to disappear if the bulletin board is used in a dialog shell.

XmNbuttonFontList	XmFontList	Fonts for button children
XmNlabelFontList	XmFontList	Fonts for label children
XmNtextFontList	XmFontList	Fonts for text children
XmNstringDirection	enum	Used for text children XmSTRING_DIRECTION_L_TO_R XmSTRING_DIRECTION_R_TO_L
XmNtextTranslations	XtTranslations	Used for text children
XmNautoUnmanage	Boolean	Add callback to buttons to unmanage dialog

Table 6-18: Bulletin board resource fields propagated to children.

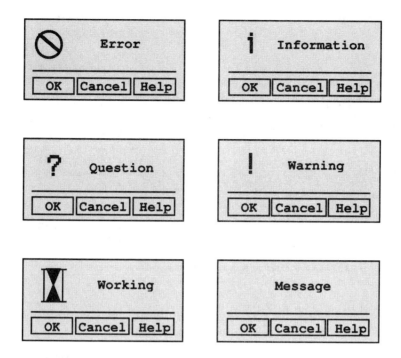

Figure 6.21: Message boxes with different standard symbols.

Messages

The simplest subclass of the bulletin board is the message box, which displays a message together with a symbol characterizing the type of message. It allows different reactions through a choice of buttons.

The *XmNdialogType* field determines which graphical symbol is used to characterize the message. This symbol can also be overriden by a custom pixmap.

The message itself is specified as an XmString. It may contain multiple lines. Line breaks are inserted when the "\n" construct is encountered in a C string during conversion. Its alignment may be controlled by *XmNmessage-Alignment.* Both the pixmap and the message are automatically created label gadget children of the message box, so these resource fields are passed on to the respective gadget.

The message box uses three buttons, which are also automatically created as gadget children: OK, Cancel and Help. The text of each button can be individually customized. One of the buttons may be selected as the default button (to be activated when the user presses the Return key). The default button is visually distinguished by an additional shadow around it.

XmNdialogType	enum	Type of dialog symbol
		    XmDIALOG_ERROR
		    XmDIALOG_INFORMATION
		    XmDIALOG_MESSAGE
		    XmDIALOG_QUESTION
		    XmDIALOG_WARNING
		    XmDIALOG_WORKING

XmNsymbolPixmap	Pixmap	Use instead of default symbol
XmNmessageString	XmString	Message to appear

XmNmessageAlignment	enum	Alignment of message
		    XmALIGNMENT_BEGINNING
		    XmALIGNMENT_CENTER
		    XmALIGNMENT_END

XmNokLabelString	XmString	Label for OK button
XmNcancelLabelString	XmString	Label for Cancel button
XmNhelpLabelString	XmString	Label for Help button

XmNdefaultButtonType	enum	Which button is marked as default
		    XmDIALOG_CANCEL_BUTTON
		    XmDIALOG_OK_BUTTON
		    XmDIALOG_HELP_BUTTON

Table 6-19: Message box appearance resource fields.

All the subparts of the message box can be accessed as individual widgets. You can request the widget IDs of the subparts with

> *child_widget = XmMessageBoxGetChild (message_box_widget, child_type);*
>   */* child type :*
>   *XmDIALOG_CANCEL_BUTTON*
>   *XmDIALOG_DEFAULT_BUTTON*
>   *XmDIALOG_HELP_BUTTON*
>   *XmDIALOG_OK_BUTTON*
>   *XmDIALOG_MESSAGE_LABEL*
>   *XmDIALOG_SEPARATOR*
>   *XmDIALOG_SYMBOL_LABEL*
>   */**

If you do not want any of these elements to appear, you can manually un-manage this child widget after creation of the message box.

The message box widget defines three callbacks (see Table 6.20). The callbacks are connected as activation callbacks of the three buttons.

XmNokCallback	Callback	OK button activated
XmNcancelCallback	Callback	Cancel button activated
XmNhelpCallback	Callback	Like other primitive and manager widgets

Table 6-20: Message box callbacks.

Waiting for Confirmation

Because of the nature of the X Toolkit Intrinsics it is not easy to construct subroutines which display a message and wait for a reaction. The reason is that the program cannot simply wait for a user reaction, but must at least handle Expose events (otherwise the message would not even appear). The waiting subroutine, however, is already called out of handling some event, such as a menu selection. Therefore a recursive event loop would be necessary— handling events within event handling.

Such a subroutine would be complicated by the fact that events for widgets outside the dialog box must be processed. For example, a part of the main window may be obscured and then re-exposed by another application. The resulting Expose events must be processed, otherwise the screen region will not be updated until the user has reacted to the message!

A feasible solution is to change your program structure to avoid such cases. Where you previously wrote

> *...(first part of callback routine)*
> *PostMessage;*
> *WaitForAnswer;*
>
> *if (ok)*
> *...(ok-part of callback routine)*
> *else*
> *...(cancel-part of callback routine)*

you now set callbacks, save vital information as *client_data,* and return to the main loop:

> *...(first part of callback routine)*
> *AddCallback (OK_button, OK_handler, &vital_record);*
> *AddCallback (Cancel_button, Cancel_handler, &vital_record);*
> *PostMessage;*
> *return;*
> *...*
>
> *OK_handler:*
> *...(ok-part of callback routine)*
>
> *Cancel_handler:*
> *...(cancel-part of callback routine)*

Restructuring a program in this way is difficult when the error message occurs deeply nested. It can be argued, however, that errors are better not handled at the deeper levels, because it is most likely that a large part of the remaining routine will be skipped when the user cancels the function.

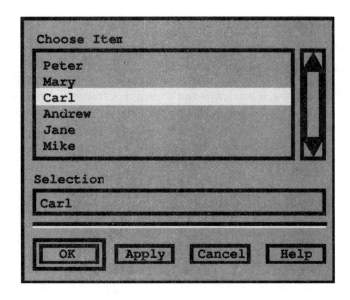

Figure 6.22: Selection box with all parts managed.

Selection Box

The second subclass of the bulletin board to be discussed in this chapter is the selection box. A selection box consists of a scrolled list of selectable items, a text entry field for manual selection, and up to four buttons.

The meaning of the three standard buttons (OK, Cancel, and Help) used in other dialogs is obvious. The fourth button is the optional Apply button, which can be used to activate a process that does not finish the dialog, such as applying the user's selection, but allowing new selections afterwards. The Apply button is used in the file selection box, a subclass of the selection box.

XmNlistLabelString	XmString	String above list
XmNselectionLabelString	XmString	String above text field
XmNapplyLabelString	XmString	String for Apply button
XmNokLabelString	XmString	String for OK button
XmNcancelLabelString	XmString	String for Cancel button
XmNhelpLabelString	XmString	String for Help button
XmNlistVisibleItemCount	int	Lines to display in list
XmNtextColumns	int	Default width of text field
XmNminimizeButtons	Boolean	Inhibit forcing equal size

Table 6-21: Appearance resource fields of the selection box.

XmNlistItems	XmStringList	Selectable items
XmNlistItemCount	int	Items in list
XmNtextString	XmString	Contents of text entry field

Table 6-22: Value resource fields of the selection box.

In common with the message box, the strings of the buttons and labels can be set as resource fields of the selection box. The preferred sizes of the list and the text field are also directly available. Normally all buttons are forced to the same size. This can be switched off, e.g. when one very long button label is used.

The values of the selection list and the text field can be directly accessed as resources of the selection box. They can be handled like the corresponding list and text resource fields (all these subparts of the selection box are again automatically created child widgets).

In common with the message box, the selection box can have different dialog types. These are:

- *Selection.* This is the default type when the selection box is enclosed in a dialog shell. All subparts are present except for the Apply button.

- *Prompt.* In this case the list with its label is unmanaged, allowing only keyboard entry of a selection.

- *Work area.* This is the default if the selection box is not a child of a dialog shell. All standard children are managed. They can be individually unmanaged as desired.

The selection box defines callbacks for all four buttons. In addition, the selection box can check whether a selection typed into the text field occurs in the list. If *XmNmustMatch* is set, a mismatch executes the *XmNnoMatchCallback* instead of the *XmNokCallback*.

The structure returned with each callback reports the currently selected value in addition to the normal information.

typedef struct {

XmNdialogType	enum	Type of selection box
		  XmDIALOG_SELECTION
		  XmDIALOG_PROMPT
		  XmDIALOG_WORK_AREA

XmNmustMatch	Boolean	Check if entry exists
XmNapplyCallback	Callback	Apply button activated
XmNokCallback	Callback	OK button activated
XmNcancelCallback	Callback	Cancel button activated
XmNhelpCallback	Callback	Help button activated
XmNnoMatchCallback	Callback	OK and no match

Table 6-23: Behaviour resource fields of the selection box.

```
   int         reason:      /* XmCR_OK                  */
                            /* XmCR_APPLY               */
                            /* XmCR_NO_MATCH            */
                            /* XmCR_CANCEL              */
                            /* XmCR_HELP                */
   XEvent      *event;
   XmString    value;
   int         length;
} XmSelectionBoxCallbackStruct;
```

In common with the message box a procedure is provided to request the widget IDs of the individual children. It is called *XmSelectionBoxGetChild.* If you do not want some subpart to appear, you can request the ID and unmanage that child. Possible child designations are:

XmDIALOG_LIST_LABEL
XmDIALOG_LIST
XmDIALOG_SELECTION_LABEL
XmDIALOG_TEXT
XmDIALOG_SEPARATOR
XmDIALOG_WORK_AREA
XmDIALOG_APPLY_BUTTON
XmDIALOG_CANCEL_BUTTON
XmDIALOG_HELP_BUTTON
XmDIALOG_OK_BUTTON
XmDIALOG_DEFAULT_BUTTON

Unmanaging children of the selection box can be used to produce a general dialog box which supports the geometry of the typical dialog buttons. Specifying the behaviour and geometry of buttons in a dialog is not easy if you have to use general manager widgets like the form. You can use the selection box buttons if you unmanage the rest of the box and insert a form widget with your own dialog layout instead.

You should start with a prompt dialog because it contains the smallest number of unnecessary children. After unmanaging the selection label and text only the buttons remain. The selection box accepts one arbitrary *work area* child that is positioned above the buttons. This place will be occupied by creating a form widget as a child of the selection box.

File Selection Box

The file selection box is an even more specialized widget class. It is constructed as a subclass of the selection box.

The file selection box uses a directory mask to construct a list of filenames. The user can select one of these or type in the name directly. The directory mask is an additional text entry field with a label and is handled like the text

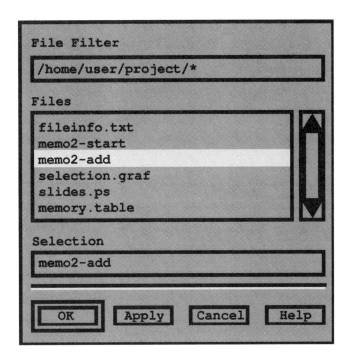

Figure 6.23: File selection box.

entry field already present in the selection box. The contents of the text entry field are accessible under a different, more specific resource name.

For specific requirements the procedure for searching for filenames can be overriden (and thus you can search for anything which is application-specific). The search procedure is called with two arguments, the widget and a pointer to the following callback structure:

```
typedef struct {
        int        reason;
        XEvent     *event;
        XmString   value;
        int        length;
        XmString   mask;
```

XmNdirMask	XmString	Mask for files listed
XmNdirSpec	XmString	Current selection field
XmNfilterLabelString	XmString	Prompt for directory mask
XmNfileSearchProc	XtProc	For special requirements
XmNlistUpdated	Boolean	Set after fileSearchProc

Table 6-24: File selection box resource fields.

int   mask_length;
} XmFileSelectionBoxCallbackStruct;

It is the responsibility of the search procedure to fill *XmNlistItems, XmNlist-ItemsCount, XmNdirSpec,* and *XmNlistUpdated.* The last field is required to signal the end of the search. The *XmNdirSpec* should be filled with a valid entry of the list (or the empty string).

If the application itself creates files (or other searchable objects), it can trigger a new search procedure by using the procedure *XmFileSelectionDoSearch.* This ensures that the file selection is always up to date.

XmString   dir_mask;

/ dir_mask may be NULL if current mask of widget will be used */*
XmFileSelectionDoSearch (file_selection_box_widget, dir_mask);

The Command Widget

The command widget also has a rather specialized functionality. It is used for command entry through the keyboard, with the additional aid of a command history from which items can be reused. The command widget automatically creates two children, a text widget for entry and a scrolled list widget for the history.

The command widget is a composite widget, but may have only one additional child. All other children are predefined and created as necessary. The additional child is inserted between the history and the command.

The resource fields of the command widget mostly propagate their values

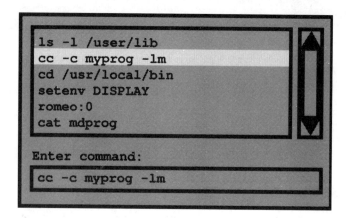

Figure 6.24: Command widget.

XmNpromptString	XmString	Prompt for command
XmNcommand	XmString	Value of command entry text widget
XmNhistoryMaxItems	int	Max stored history
XmNhistoryVisibleItemCount	int	Size of visible history region
XmNhistoryItems	XmStringTable	All stored history items
XmNhistoryItemCount	int	Current number of items

Table 6-25: Command resource fields.

to the appropriate child widgets. The value of the text widget (the currently entered command) can be accessed via a resource field in the same way as for a text widget, but as an XmString.

The limit of stored history items can be specified. The number of visible items is used to determine the size of the command widget. The history itself is implemented by a list widget. You do not usually need to manipulate the history explicitly, but you can access its value directly as an array of XmStrings.

The command widget defines two callbacks. Like the *XmNvalueChanged-Callback* of the text widget, the *XmNcommandChangedCallback* is executed whenever the current command is changed. The *XmNcommandEnteredCallback* is executed whenever a command is to be executed, i.e. after pressing the Return key or double-clicking an item in the history.

Both callbacks pass a pointer to the following structure as *call_data*, which contains the current command value and its length.

```
typedef struct {
        int         reason;     /* XmCR_COMMAND_ENTERED      */
                                /* XmCR_COMMAND_CHANGED      */
        XEvent     *event;
        XmString   value;
        int         length;
} XmCommandCallbackStruct;
```

The procedure *XmCommandError* is available to display an error message in the history section temporarily. The message is overwritten when the next command is entered.

XmCommandError (command_widget, error_as_XmString);

XmNcommandChangedCallback	Callback	If command value changed
XmNcommandEnteredCallback	Callback	If return or double-click

Table 6-26: Command callback resource fields.

Chapter 7

Inter-Client Communication

The design of the X Window System ensures that multiple clients can use the same display simultaneously. Although they operate in parallel, they do not necessarily cooperate. There are two situations where applications need additional information about other clients:

- The window manager is a client that coordinates the other applications. The more the window manager knows about the other clients, the better the management policy can be adapted to the individual programs.

- When there are multiple applications on the same screen, a natural desire arises to exchange data between these programs. This requires some kind of standardized exchange protocol that can be used by nearly all programs.

These areas are discussed in the following two sections. Successful cooperation between all kinds of applications requires some standardization. The basic X protocol only defines mechanisms for communications. All further rules are contained in the Inter-Client Communications Conventions Manual (ICCCM).

The rules in the ICCCM should ideally be followed by all applications and thus be integrated into every toolkit. However, the rules evolve over time as new methods of communication are developed. As a result, implementations always lag some time behind in support of these rules. Fortunately Motif supports the ICCCM rather well, so there is seldom a need to resort to basic Xlib programming to correct deficiencies.

7.1 Window Manager Interfacing

The relationship between the window manager and the client programs is in some respects similar to the relation between parent and child widget. The window manager controls the position and size of the application windows, and just like child widgets applications can make geometry requests and express their preferences.

However, more information is passed from the application to the window manager. For example, the window titles and icon names can be set by the application. The decoration around windows is different if the window is a transient dialog and not a normal top-level window.

Information is also passed in the other direction. For example, the "Close" selection in the window menu may be passed as a callback function to the application, allowing the application to confirm this action or to save files on request.

Because the task of the window manager is clearly defined (whereas its management policy is not), the minimum amount of information passed is defined by the ICCCM. Window managers obeying these rules are advertised as ICCCM-compliant. Window managers adhering to this standard should be interchangeable without drastic effects on the applications.

The ICCCM only defines a minimal set of conventions, so Motif is allowed to use more features. These extensions need both the Motif window manager and a Motif application to take effect; they are ignored for other combinations. The nature of the conventions is explained in the following section.

For communication, X applications can only rely on the facilities of X. For example, the window manager and the client may run on completely different systems with incompatible architectures. If both connect to a simple X terminal they may have no other communication path (which is rare nowadays but nevertheless possible).

Therefore, one client cannot directly call another without going through the X server. There are two principal ways in which clients can communicate via X:

- Clients can attach arbitrary *properties* to their windows to be read by other clients. In fact, a client can attach properties to any window because every client has access to all other windows of the X display (provided it is allowed to connect to this X server).

- Clients can send *events* to other clients. However, to avoid disturbing the other client, events should only be sent when the other client is expressly capable of handling this kind of event by flagging a property.

Communication through events is used when a direct response is required. Most of the information, however, is passed through properties. In fact, the communication protocols discussed in this chapter rely on a carefully selected mixture of both methods.

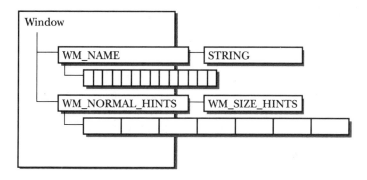

Figure 7.1: Window properties. A window property has a name and a type expressed as atoms, a format (8, 16, or 32) and a value as a sequence of format-sized elements.

Setting Window Manager Hints

The largest amount of information transferred between client and window manager is used for expressing the client's wishes, e.g. concerning window position or title text. Clients can only give *hints*. The window manager may ignore them if they are in conflict with window manager policy; they may even be inapplicable because the window manager does not support that particular feature.

The hints are stored as properties of the respective top-level window. *Properties* are a general mechanism to attach arbitrary information to an X window. Each property is identified by a unique name (e.g. *WM_NAME*). A property is like an attribute of the window. For instance, *WM_NAME* of window A has a clearly defined value that may be different from *WM_NAME* of window B.

Because the name of a property is needed for every value access, it is stored in the X server. The identifying number of the string, called an *atom*, is sufficient for access. Every client receives the same atom for the same string, so atoms can be exchanged between clients.

A number of atoms are predefined by the ICCCM, mainly for some standard properties. However, atoms are also used for other communication purposes, as you will see in the next section. Atoms defined by Motif start with "_MOTIF" to avoid name clashes. You can freely define your own atoms if you want (start them with two underscores).

The value of a property may be a list of either 8-bit, 16-bit, or 32-bit words (this *format* designation is exploited by the X server to swap the bytes of a 32-bit value between different machine architectures correctly). A property also has a *type*, which is an atom denoting the kind of value stored in the property (e.g. *STRING* or *WINDOW*).

WM_NAME	String for title area
WM_ICON_NAME	String to use for icon
WM_NORMAL_HINTS	Size-related hints
	(min/max, increment, apsect-ratio)
WM_HINTS	Further hints for icon and input
WM_CLASS	Name and class for wm resource
	specifications
WM_TRANSIENT_FOR	The window a dialog belongs to
WM_PROTOCOLS	Advertise understood protocols here
WM_COLORMAP_WINDOWS	List of windows with private colormaps
WM_STATE	The wm stores the window state here

Table 7-1: ICCCM window properties.

You do not have to access the predefined properties with low-level Xlib routines directly because there are convenience functions for this purpose. The main purpose of the shell widget classes is to make these values easily accessible. Nevertheless you should be aware that all hints are merely conventions from the ICCCM—X only supplies the basic mechanism, namely atoms and properties.

To give you an impression of the contents of these hints, the ICCCM-defined and Motif-defined properties for top-level windows are summarized in Tables 7-1 and 7-2. The format and contents of these hints are not discussed here further as they can be more conveniently set as resource fields of a shell widget.

7.2 Shell Widgets

The most important Motif shell widget classes were briefly discussed in the previous chapters. Their primary purpose is to control any top-level windows an application needs. As such, they are the primary target for interaction with the window manager. In geometry negotiations shells are responsible for passing window manager operations to their children and for negotiating child requests with the window manager.

Shell widgets set all the necessary properties of their window to provide hints to the window manager. The information is extracted from corresponding resource fields of the shell widget to make setting the hints easy for the programmer. These resource fields will be discussed below.

_MOTIF_WM_HINTS	Hints for decorations, modality,
	and functions
_MOTIF_WM_MENU	Custom window menu entries
_MOTIF_WM_MESSAGES	Applicable client messages from wm

Table 7-2: Motif window properties.

Three different types of shell widgets are used in Motif: top-level shells (including application shells), dialog shells, and menu shells. They differ mainly in the amount of decoration they receive from the window manager.

Top-level shells are fully decorated (unless otherwise instructed). They can be iconified separately. If an application has multiple top-level shells, the user cannot normally distinguish between top-level windows of the same application and windows of another process instance of the same application. Therefore it is an implementation decision whether multiple top-level windows are implemented by one application process or by multiple processes.

Application shells differ from top-level shells only in one additonal hint they set (remember that there may be only one application shell per application process). The additional hint contains the command line that can be used to restart this application. A *session manager* program may employ this information to shut down all running applications in their current state and restart them later. In this way application shells can be distinguished from other top-level windows in a program.

A dialog shell is subordinate to a top-level window. If it is modeless it may stay on the screen for an arbitrarily long time, but it is always iconified together with its top-level window. Therefore a dialog window automatically receives a slightly reduced decoration without minimize and maximize buttons.

The menu shell is only used for *spring-loaded* pop-up windows, i.e. windows which pop up on a button-press or key-press and disappear when the button or key is released. Menu shells override any window manager interaction, so they receive no decoration and cannot be moved or resized by the user.

There are a number of further shell classes in Motif, arranged in the class hierarchy shown in Figure 7.2. These classes mostly serve as common super-classes and are not used directly. For example, the top-level shell and the dialog shell share a number of hints for the window manager. These are implemented

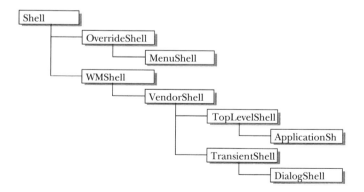

Figure 7.2: Hierarchy of Motif shell classes.

as resource fields of the class window manager shell.

Most of the shell classes are defined by the X Toolkit Intrinsics. Specific functionality for the Motif window manager is implemented in the vendor shell class. Menu shell and dialog shell are Motif-specific classes.

Menu Shell

As the menu shell class resides high in the class hierarchy, it has only the basic shell resource fields. Both the override shell and the menu shell do not define additional resource fields, but only vary the general shell functionality slightly. The resource fields of the shell widget class described in the following also apply to the other shell classes as they are inherited.

The resource field *XmNallowShellResize* has already been mentioned. It controls whether geometry requests of the shell's child are passed to the window manager or are directly denied. *XmNallowShellResize* has no influence on resize operations initiated by the user and performed by the window manager.

An initial geometry for the shell can be specified in *XmNgeometry*, but should only be set in a defaults file. The command line option *-geometry* also provides a value for this field. The geometry specification is a string of the form "<width>x<height>±<x>±<y>"—exactly the format used on the command line.

If the resource field *XmNoverrideRedirect* is set, the window manager ignores the shell. You do not set this flag directly because the override shell sets it by default. This default is also inherited by the menu shell.

In common with the special case of the *XmNmapCallback* and *XmNunmap-Callback* in the row-column and bulletin board widget classes, the shell class defines the more general callback reasons *XmNpopupCallback* and *XmNpopdown-Callback*.

A final flag, *XmNsaveUnder*, instructs the X server to save the contents underneath the top-level window to restore the screen quickly when the window is popped down. Normally Expose events would be generated, requiring the client owning the underlying window to redraw the contents. However, the save-under flag is only a hint and can be ignored if the X server runs out of memory.

As mentioned above, the menu shell widget does not define new resource fields, but the default values for *XmNallowShellResize*, *XmNoverrideRedirect*, and *XmNsaveUnder* are changed to *True*.

XmNallowShellResize	Boolean	If accepts resize requests from child
XmNgeometry	String	User-specified shell geometry
XmNoverrideRedirect	Boolean	If window manager is to be ignored
XmNpopupCallback	Callback	Called on *XtPopup*
XmNpopdownCallback	Callback	Called on *XtPopdown*
XmNsaveUnder	Boolean	If bits underneath should be saved

Table 7-3: Important shell resource fields.

General Window Manager Resource Fields

All shell classes that interact with the window manager are subclasses of the window manager shell widget class. This class defines resource fields which are translated into window manager hints as required by the ICCCM.

Remember that these resource fields only give hints, which need not be obeyed. Depending on the window manager you use, the interpretation of the values may be slightly different.

A shell may specify its appearance when it is made into an icon. You can either set an *XmNiconPixmap* or use a separate *XmNiconWindow*. If you use a separate window, this window is mapped and unmapped by the window manager as required. You only have to draw into the window by handling Expose events. However, you cannot receive input through this icon window.

The icon pixmap should be one bit deep, i.e. a bitmap. The window manager will choose appropriate foreground and background colours. If you want to use general pixmaps in your own colours you should display them in an application-controlled window.

In *XmNinitialState* you specify whether the window first appears as an icon or in the normal state.

A second set of resource fields controls the resize behaviour of the shell. A minimum and a maximum size of the window can be specified. You can also specify a minimum and a maximum aspect ratio for the window. If both ratios are equal, the window will always resize proportionately.

When the window contains information in a fixed grid you can also specify the increment for resizing. This hint is used in the terminal emulator *xterm*, for example. The increments start from the minimum size.

You already know the resource field *XmNtitle* to set a title for the window manager decoration.

XmNiconPixmap	Pixmap	Pixmap to use as icon image
XmNiconWindow	Window	Window to use as icon
XmNinitialState	enum	Whether started iconic or not
		NormalState
		IconicState
XmNminWidth	int	Desired minimum size
XmNminHeight	int	
XmNmaxWidth	int	Desired maximum height
XmNmaxHeight	int	
XmNminAspectX	int	Minimum aspect ratio
XmNminAspectY	int	
XmNmaxAspectX	int	Maximum aspect ratio
XmNmaxAspectY	int	
XmNwidthInc	int	Incremental width resize
XmNheightInc	int	Incremental height resize
XmNtitle	String	String to use as title

Table 7-4: Important window manager shell resource fields.

Motif-Specific Shell Resource Fields

The resource fields which are only useful for communication with the
Motif window manager are defined in the class vendor shell. These resource
fields can be used in top-level shells and dialog shells by inheritance.

The first two resource fields are bit fields containing flags denoting the
presence or absence of individual elements. The flag bits are available as
constants declared in the include file "mwm.h". All these constants begin with
"MWM_".

With *XmNmwmDecorations* you can control the amount of decoration a
window receives. The top-level shell and the dialog shell set reasonable defaults
for this field. If you need different decorations you can individually control
border, resize handles, title bar, system menu button, minimize button, and
maximize button. However, some dependences exist. For example, the system
menu button requires the title, and the resize handles always include the
borders.

If you include the bit *MWM_DECOR_ALL* the other specified bits are
excluded from the complete set of decorations (this is a kind of minus sign).
You have to be aware that the decorations can also be configured by the user,
through resource specifications for the window manager. In this case, the program cannot add decorations that the window manager configuration has already removed.

A similar resource field is *XmNmwmFunctions*. It specifies which functions
of the window menu are to be present. The remarks of the last paragraph also
apply to this field.

The resource field *XmNmwmInputMode* controls the modality of the window, which is maintained by the window manager. In Motif version 1.0 modal
dialogs rely exclusively on the Motif window manager, so using another window
manager will render all dialogs modeless.

With the resource field *XmNmwmMenu* you can add additional entries for
the window menu. This resource field is a string with a number of items separated by a newline ("\n"). Each item has the format

> *Label   [mnemonic]   [accelerator]   function*

Label, mnemonic, and accelerator are similar to other Motif menus. The
function designates one of the predefined window manager functions. The
most important ones are *f.exec* (to execute a shell command) and *f.send_msg* (to
send a message to the application). Application messages are discussed in
Section 7.3.

If the label is preceded by "@" it is used as the path specification for a bitmap file, producing an iconic menu entry. The following is an example for a
menu specification:

> *"@/usr/local/install/bitmaps/printer"   f.exec "lpr /tmp/.output100" \n*
> *"Stay Up"   _S   Alt<Key>F2   f.send_msg 2*

XmNmwmDecorations	int	Flags which decorations to include
		   MWM_DECOR_ALL
		   MWM_DECOR_BORDER
		   MWM_DECOR_RESIZEH
		   MWM_DECOR_TITLE
		   MWM_DECOR_SYSTEM
		   MWM_DECOR_MINIMIZE
		   MWM_DECOR_MAXIMIZE

XmNmwmFunctions	int	Flags which functions to include in
		the window menu
		   MWM_FUNC_ALL
		   MWM_FUNC_RESIZE
		   MWM_FUNC_MOVE
		   MWM_FUNC_MINIMIZE
		   MWM_FUNC_MAXIMIZE
		   MWM_FUNC_CLOSE

XmNmwmInputMode	enum	Modality of the window
		   MWM_INPUT_MODELESS
		   *MWM_INPUT_*
		      APPLICATION_MODAL
		   MWM_INPUT_SYSTEM_MODAL

XmNmwmMenu	String	Additional entries for window menu

XmNkeyboardFocusPolicy	enum	Focus policy for this window
		   XmEXPLICIT
		   XmPOINTER

XmNdeleteResponse	enum	How to react to Close function
		   XmDESTROY
		   XmUNMAP
		   XmDO_NOTHING

XmNshellUnitType	enum	Units for shell geometry resources
		   XmPIXELS
		   Xm100TH_MILLIMETERS
		   Xm1000TH_INCHES
		   Xm100TH_POINTS
		   Xm100TH_FONT_UNITS

Table 7-5: Vendor shell resource fields.

XmNiconName	String	String to use as icon title
XmNiconic	False	If to start as icon

Table 7-6: Top-level shell resource fields.

Changing State of Top-Level Windows

Top-level windows may be in one of three different states: normal, iconic, and withdrawn. Two different X windows are involved, the shell's window and the icon (the icon window may be created by the application or the window manager). Only one of these two windows will be visible at one time; the other one will be unmapped. If the top-level window is in the withdrawn state, both windows are unmapped.

Transitions between the withdrawn state and the other two are initiated by the application. Transitions between the normal and the iconic state are usually performed by the window manager on a user request, but may also be caused by the program. This section describes how to initiate the state transitions in your application.

The top-level window is in the withdrawn state when the shell widget is initially created. It will leave this state when calling *XtPopup* or *XtManageChild* (depending on the shell class). Whether it reaches the normal state is controlled by *XmNiconic*.

This transition is reversed by *XtPopdown* or *XtUnmanageChild* (or possibly by an implicit reaction to a Close operation or button activation in a dialog). The window again enters the withdrawn state, but continues to exist (in contrast to *XtDestroyWidget*).

To iconify a window from the normal state you have to send the window manager a client message with a specific format described in the ICCCM. The reverse case is simpler: you only map the window again using *XtMapWidget*. Support for this state transition has been added in Motif 1.1. In Motif 1.1 you can cause the transition by setting *XmNiconic* to the desired value.

The current state of the window (whether normal or iconic) as chosen by the user is more difficult to obtain. There is no way to request the state information directly, nor is it reflected in the value of *XmNiconic*. If you have set *XmNiconic* to *False* and the user iconifies the window, *XmNiconic* does not change. The only way to obtain the state is permanently to monitor the user's operation by asking the X server for MapNotify and UnmapNotify events on the shell's window. How to install such an event handler is described in Chapter 9.

Some problems with accessing top-level windows are introduced by window manager reparenting and you sometimes have to take care. For example, if you want to raise a shell window on the top of the stack, you can use the Xlib function *XRaiseWindow*.

XRaiseWindow (XtDisplay (shell), XtWindow (shell));

This will make the window the topmost among its siblings. If, however, the window manager has added a parent window for decoration purposes, the other top-level windows you see on the screen are no longer siblings of the reparented window. The request would only raise the window among the decoration.

Fortunately the window manager can circumvent the problem by instructing the X server not to perform this operation but instead to send a message to the window manager. This request is called *substructure redirect.* The window manager is then responsible for performing the operation as it was intended, i.e. raising the decoration window among the other top-level windows.

This redirection causes a delay that depends on how fast the window manager is able to respond. In any case you cannot count on the fact that the next X request you send will see the window raised, because the X server may continue processing events while the redirected message is on the way to the window manager.

7.3 Window Manager Protocols

Most of the control information from the window manager to an application is passed by directly manipulating the top-level window inside the X server. The application is indirectly informed of these changes through events. However, some requests cannot be communicated through this channel because they were not anticipated in the design of the general window structure.

An example is the Close entry in the window menu. X only provides an operation to cut the client's connection, exemplified in a little utility program suitably called *xkill*. To enable a reaction from the application, the window manager has to send a message with less drastic consequences.

X provides *client messages* as a general mechanism for this kind of communication. Client messages are directed to a window and delivered to the owner of this window as events. If you send a client message to the root window it will be received by the window manager; sending to another top-level window will reach the corresponding application.

Because reception of client message events cannot be inhibited, you should avoid sending events to clients which are not prepared to handle them. Although most applications simply ignore uninteresting events, unsolicited messages may conflict with applications requiring tight control over their incoming event queue.

Clients prepared to receive certain client messages advertise their ability by setting commonly defined properties of their top-level windows. The contents of these properties signal which messages the application wants to receive.

For window manager interaction the property *WM_PROTOCOLS* is defined by the ICCCM. This property is a list of atoms, each atom indicating a certain kind of window manager protocol the client wishes to participate in.

The protocol for the Close operation in the window menu is identified by the atom *WM_DELETE_WINDOW*. The *WM_DELETE_WINDOW* protocol is advertised by the Motif shell classes. The protocol message from the window manager is handled by the shell, reacting as indicated by *XmNdeleteResponse*.

As mentioned above, you have to handle that message yourself if you need a more complicated reaction than the shell's built-in ones. Handling the protocol message is not as difficult as it sounds, because Motif provides a protocol manager which transforms the incoming message into a simple callback.

The application callback is registered using the following call, adding a callback to the already existing list (which contains the callback notifying the shell internally):

```
#include <X11/Protocols.h>

Atom       xa_wm_delete_window =
                 XmInternAtom (display, "WM_DELETE_WINDOW", True);
caddr_t    client_data = NULL;

XmAddWMProtocolCallback (shell, xa_wm_delete_window,
                 CallbackProc, client_data);
```

Another predefined window manager protocol is *WM_SAVE_YOURSELF*. It is a checkpoint facility, i.e. the application must save all state information, update the command line hint *WM_COMMAND*, and then wait for the next event or death. The purpose of this protocol is to allow a session manager program to shut down all applications in an orderly manner and get the necessary information about how to restart them later in exactly that state. A more detailed description is found in the ICCCM.

If you want to support this protocol, you have to add another callback for the new protocol:

> *Atom   xa_wm_save_yourself =*
> *XmInternAtom (display, "WM_SAVE_YOURSELF", False);*
> *caddr_t   client_data = NULL;*

> *XmAddWMProtocolCallback (shell, xa_wm_save_yourself,*
> *CallbackProc, client_data);*

The last parameter of *XmInternAtom* specifies whether the desired atom must already exist; in this case it probably doesn't. Adding the callback will also add the protocol atom to the *WM_PROTOCOLS* property.

There is another set of protocols specific to the Motif window manager to be used with the *f.send_msg* window manager function. These messages are identified by numbers, and your application indicates through the property *_MOTIF_WM_MESSAGES* which messages it wants to receive. As a consequence, messages which are currently not understood by the application but which are defined as menu entries are greyed out in the menu.

For example, the following line defines an additional window menu entry suitable for the resource field *XmNmwmMenu*:

> *"Hello   f.send_msg 2"*

To receive this message your application must first signal that it is willing to participate in Motif window manager messages in general by including the atom *_MOTIF_WM_MESSAGES* in the *WM_PROTOCOLS* property. No callback procedure is associated with the general protocol; its atom must only be listed using the procedure *XmAddProtocols*.

> *Atom   xa_motif_wm_messages =*
> *XmInternAtom (display, "_MOTIF_WM_MESSAGES", False),*
> *xa_wm_protocols =*
> *XmInternAtom (display, "WM_PROTOCOLS", True),*

errors ?

> *XmAddProtocols (shell, xa_wm_protocols, &xa_motif_wm_messages, 1);*

XmAddProtocols allows you to add more than one protocol at a time; therefore a one-element list is passed as parameter. The next step is to install a callback for this protocol and message number 2:

> *caddr_t   client_data = NULL;*

XmAddProtocolCallback (shell, xa_motif_wm_messages, (Atom) 2,
CallbackProc, client_data);

XmAddProtocolCallback takes two atoms as parameters. The first atom specifies the property to be used for advertising and the second specifies the atom to be included in the property. The procedure *XmAddWMProtocolCallback* is a convenience macro which automatically supplies the *WM_PROTOCOLS* atom as the first atom parameter.

The second atom parameter in this example is not really an atom. The window manager uses numbers to identify the messages, and internally an atom is no more than a number; therefore the number is simply cast to the *Atom* type.

To indicate that the message is temporarily not understood, the application has to remove the atom from the property. It is not necessary to remove the complete callback for this purpose; instead you can simply deactivate the protocol. Deactivation removes the atom, but leaves the callback information intact. The protocol can later be simply reactivated. There are two procedures for this purpose:

XmDeactivateProtocol (shell, xa_motif_wm_messages, (Atom) 2);
...
XmActivateProtocol (shell, xa_motif_wm_messages, (Atom) 2);

Window manager message callbacks together with custom menu entries can be used to implement application-specific entries in the window menu. However, this feature should be used sparingly to avoid cluttering the system menu and confusing the user.

Example: Letting Dialogs Stay Up

A possible application for client-defined window menu entries is to implement a command that makes a modeless dialog box stay on the screen even if the OK button has been activated. This is useful, for example, for an "Open" dialog when the user wants to open multiple files in close succession. If the dialog stays on screen, the user does not have to wait for it to appear and the selection dialog will be in exactly the previous state.

However, in most situations the user wants the dialog to disappear after selecting a new file. To allow both situations, the window menu will contain a new entry "Stay Up". Selecting this entry inhibits the default behaviour of automatic unmapping of the dialog, except that the Cancel button will remove the dialog as usual.

The additional menu entry is defined on creation of the dialog. A message box is taken here as an example. You will probably integrate the following code into the creation of the dialog box, but it will be defined as a procedure here. The example code will only work on message and selection dialogs. However, the solution can easily be transferred to custom dialogs. The example requires that *XmNautoUnmanage* is *False*.

```
#define    STAY_UP        "\"Stay Up\"      f.send_msg 4417"
#define    XA_STAY_UP     (Atom)4417

void MakeDialogStayUp (message_box)
      Widget      message_box;
{
      Atom        xa_motif_wm_messages =
                        XmInternAtom (XtDisplay (message_box),
                                "_MOTIF_WM_MESSAGES", False),
                  xa_wm_protocols =
                        XmInternAtom (XtDisplay (message_box),
                                "WM_PROTOCOLS", True);
      Widget      shell = XtParent (message_box);
      Arg         args[1];

      XtSetArg (args[0], XmNmwmMenu, STAY_UP);
      XtSetValues (shell, args, 1);

      XtAddCallback (message_box, XmNokCallback, DoUnmanage, NULL);
      XtAddCallback (message_box, XmNcancelCallback, DoUnmanage, NULL);
      XmAddProtocols (shell, xa_wm_protocols, &xa_motif_wm_messages, 1);
      XmAddProtocolCallback (shell, xa_motif_wm_messages, XA_STAY_UP,
                        StayUp, (caddr_t)message_box);
}

void DoUnmanage (message_box, client_data, call_data)
      Widget      message_box;
      caddr_t     client_data, call_data;
{
      XtUnmanageChild (message_box);
}
```

The code follows the pattern described above. A new menu entry is defined in the resource field *XmNmwmMenu*, which will send a message with number 4417. A protocol callback is defined for this message, which will automatically activate the protocol. When the dialog is first popped up, the new entry in the window menu is selectable.

The protocol callback will activate the procedure *StayUp*. The message box widget is passed as *client_data* because the callback will only pass the shell's ID. *StayUp* first removes the *DoUnmanage* callback for the OK button.

The next step is to deactivate the protocol message, because it will be meaningless while the dialog stays on screen. The menu entry is greyed out as a consequence, so the new state is clearly recognizable.

Finally, a second callback is installed for the Cancel button that will re-activate the protocol when the message box is unmapped.

```
void StayUp (w, client_data, call_data)
      Widget      w;
      caddr_t     client_data, call_data;
{
      Widget      message_box = (Widget) client_data,
                  shell = XtParent (message_box);
      Atom        xa_motif_wm_messages =
                        XmInternAtom (XtDisplay (message_box),
                                    "_MOTIF_WM_MESSAGES", False);

      XtRemoveCallback (message_box, XmNokCallback, DoUnmanage, NULL);

      XmDeactivateProtocol (shell, xa_motif_wm_messages, XA_STAY_UP);
      XtAddCallback (message_box, XmNcancelCallback,
                  ReactivateEntry, NULL);

}
```

The callback procedure *ReactivateEntry* reinstalls the *DoUnmanage* callback for the OK button after unmanaging the dialog. The protocol is then activated again for the next time. At last the callback removes itself from the callback list to restore the original state.

```
void ReactivateEntry (message_box, client_data, call_data)
      Widget      message_box;
      caddr_t     client_data, call_data;
{
      Widget      shell = XtParent (message_box);
      Atom        xa_motif_wm_messages =
                  XmInternAtom (XtDisplay (message_box),
                              "_MOTIF_WM_MESSAGES", False);

      XtAddCallback (message_box, XmNokCallback, DoUnmanage, NULL);

      XmActivateProtocol (shell, xa_motif_wm_messages, XA_STAY_UP);
      XtRemoveCallback (message_box, XmNcancelCallback,
                  ReactivateEntry, client_data);
}
```

In a real application you must also consider the Close menu entry, which serves as an equivalent of the Cancel button for dialogs. You can extend the example for this case by also setting *XmNdeleteResponse* appropriately and by adding or removing *ReactivateEntry* as an additional protocol callback for the *WM_DELETE_WINDOW* protocol. You will find the extension together with the complete example in Appendix C.

7.4 Client Communications

The basic mechanisms used for window manager protocols can also be used for communication between different clients, starting from the principle that one client advertises its willingness to use a certain protocol by setting a property on its top-level window. Another client may read this property and send appropriate client message events.

In addition, clients can instruct the X server to be notified when a property of another window changes. In this way protocols consisting of multiple steps can easily be realized. For example, to transfer data between two clients the following method can be used.

The source client advertises the availability of data through a property. A target client requests the data by sending a client message. The source client responds by writing the first data segment into some other property (the two clients must agree on the property and the window they will use—the window may belong to either client).

Both clients instruct the X server to be notified when the property changes. The target client is notified when a new segment has been written and the source client notices when the property has been read and emptied. This

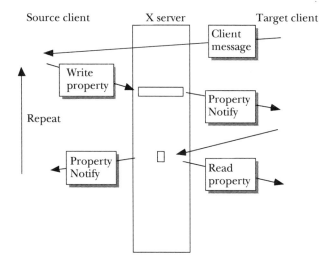

Figure 7.3: Incremental data transfer through window properties.

process continues until an empty segment is passed (see Figure 7.3).

Communication through the X server should mainly be used for screen-related information (such as the *selection* mechanism described below) or short information, because the process is not optimized for throughput (usually the X server has other things to do). However, sometimes the communicating clients have no other communication mechanism in common.

The general mechanism is not described further here, because it must be implemented with Xlib primitives and is seldom necessary. In most cases you can use the selection mechanism that is supported by the X Toolkit Intrinsics. The basic selection mechanism and the special Motif support for a clipboard are described in this section.

Selections

As the name implies, selections have something to do with selected objects on the screen. The purpose of selections is to allow any client access to the value of a selected object to enable data exchange between applications.

Selections are supported by a special mechanism in the X server. There is only one selection at any time. The X server controls who owns a selection. If a new object is selected by a client, the previous selected object loses the selection ownership. Therefore if you select a piece of text in one window and then click on a list entry in a window of another application, the highlighting of the text disappears at the same time as the list entry is selected.

Because a single selection does not fulfill all needs, X allows an arbitrary

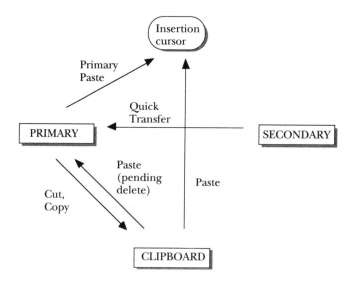

Figure 7.4: Relation between the three ICCCM selections and the insertion cursor position.

number of different selections with different purposes. Selections are identified by atoms. Three selections are defined in the ICCCM and are used in Motif: *PRIMARY, SECONDARY,* and *CLIPBOARD.*

The *PRIMARY* selection is used for any data the user normally selects on the screen. The selected region is highlighted permanently. There may be only one such selection on the screen.

The *CLIPBOARD* selection does not usually appear on the screen; it represents a kind of background storage. The *CLIPBOARD* selection is involved in the operations known as Cut & Paste. Data is transferred between the primary selection and the clipboard. The following operations can be distinguished:

- *Copy.* The contents of the primary selection are copied to the clipboard without destroying the primary selection.

- *Cut.* The contents of the primary selection are transferred to the clipboard and the primary selection is deleted.

- *Paste.* The contents of the clipboard are copied and inserted at the current position of the insertion cursor. The exact semantics may vary depending on the application. For example, some graphic editors have no notion of an insertion cursor. Applications that have no separate insertion cursor from the primary selection delete the primary selection and place the clipboard contents at this position.

- *Delete.* The primary selection is deleted and the space it occupied is reclaimed (like deleting a text selection). The clipboard is left untouched.

- *Clear.* The primary selection is deleted, but its space is occupied by white space or background. Depending on its semantics an application supports either Clear or Delete.

Although Cut & Paste is the simplest way to transfer data between applications, it is a two-step process and thus time-consuming for repeated operations. For experienced users there are faster ways to transfer data.

The *Primary Paste* mechanism allows you to copy the primary selection to the location of the insertion cursor. A single mouse-click at the destination location is sufficient to transfer the contents of the primary selection to the new location. Because the primary selection is globally accessible for all clients of the X server, this will also work without problems between different applications.

In some cases there is a still faster way. For example, if you want to assemble a text section from different parts of other texts (this is a common operation when editing programs or shell commands), the Primary Paste mechanism forces you to switch between selecting the desired fragment as PRIMARY and clicking into the same target location for every part transferred.

In the *Quick Transfer* mechanism the target position is identified by the primary selection, i.e. you select the target location only once. You then quickly select the parts to be copied with a modifier key one after the other. The quick-selected parts are transferred immediately when the selection operation is terminated by releasing the mouse button, and the primary selection is replaced. If you do not want to replace anything, the insertion cursor may be regarded as an empty primary selection.

Quick Transfer requires that the quick selection does not disturb the primary selection, therefore the *SECONDARY* selection is used. By using an X selection the Quick Transfer may also work across different applications.

Acquiring the Selection Value

Usually you do not have to program with selections because the necessary functionality is built into the respective widget classes, for instance the text widget. You do need the functionality if you build your own work area, e.g. for a graphic editor. The programming interfaces are therefore discussed briefly in this chapter. For exact information see the Toolkit Intrinsics reference manual and the ICCCM.

If you want to obtain the current selection value, regardless of whether the selection is owned by another widget of your application or by a different application, you can use the procedure *XtGetSelectionValue*. *XtGetSelectionValue* has the following parameters, which require a more detailed explanation:

- *Widget.* A widget parameter is necessary because the selection owner must have a window to respond to—there is no other way to identify the requestor. As a result, the widget should already be realized when this call is issued. Only the widget's window ID is used.

- *Selection.* This is an atom to identify the selection whose value is requested. The three predefined selections can be identified by the constants *XA_PRIMARY*, *XA_SECONDARY*, or *XA_CLIPBOARD*.

- *Target.* The target is an atom specifying what kind of information is requested about the selection. Life is too complicated for a single value to be sufficient for a selection. The selected value may be delivered in different formats (e.g. text or graphics), but there may also be different aspects of the selection. For example, one program may be interested in the textual value of a selection, another may need the beginning and ending locations if both operate on the same file. Further examples of targets are described below.

- *Callback.* Acquiring the selection value may take time. If *XtGetSelectionValue* were to wait for a response, all event processing would be blocked during this time. Therefore a callback procedure is activated some time later out of the main event loop when a notification arrives from the selection owner. If your own application is the selection owner, however, the callback is called before *XtGetSelectionValue* returns.

- *Client data.* As usual you can register some application-specific information to use in the callback.

- *Timestamp.* A timestamp is necessary because the connection to the X server may have noticeable delays. For example, suppose the user selects Paste in one document and then Cut in another. If the first client's connection is delayed for some reason, the Cut request may arrive earlier in the X server. This would mean that the wrong value was pasted.

  If a timestamp is included, the new selection owner of the clipboard is able to see that the request was really for the previous clipboard value. With a timestamp the operation can at least be refused if the previous value cannot be obtained.

  Timestamps are included in keyboard, button, motion, crossing and property notification events as the member *time* in the event structure. Usually a keyboard or button event triggers the selection request. In Motif version 1.1 you can obtain the last processed timestamp using the procedure *XtLastTimestampProcessed* with a display as parameter. In Motif 1.0 you have to extract the timestamp from the event structure passed in the callback structure.

An event handler is installed by *XtGetSelectionValue* to assemble the incoming selection, which may arrive in pieces through an incremental transfer process, later. When the value is complete the callback procedure is called with the following parameters:

```
Widget          w;
caddr_t         client_data;
Atom            *selection;
Atom            *type;
caddr_t         value;
unsigned long   *length;
int             *format;
```

The widget and client data parameters are similar to other callbacks. Also reported is the selection whose value was obtained. The other four parameters describe the value of the selection.

The *type* atom describes the kind of data structure the selection value is represented in (e.g. *STRING* or *INTEGER*). You do not usually need this information, because most of the predefined targets imply a certain representation—in fact, some clients simply set the type equal to the target.

The format value is either 8, 16, or 32. This designation is necessary to transfer data to a machine with a different byte order. A side effect is that you cannot mix 8-bit and 32-bit values in one selection or property as is possible in a

C structure—the selection must always be composed of equal-sized elements. The length is reported in these units, not in bytes.

A *NULL* value and zero length are returned when the selection owner does not support the target or when the selection owner has changed in the meantime. A type of *XT_CONVERT_FAIL* is returned when no response has been received in the timeout interval.

If you require the selection value in multiple targets (e.g. the text *and* the beginning and ending positions), you cannot simply call *XtGetSelectionValue* repeatedly because selection ownership may change between calls. Instead you must use the procedure *XtGetSelectionValues*, which requires a list of atoms as a parameter. The procedure uses an atomic *MULTIPLE* request to the selection owner.

For each target the callback procedure is called exactly once. Therefore the *client_data* parameter is also a list of pointers, each pointer being passed to one callback invocation.

Selection Ownership

The characteristic feature of the selection mechanism is that the selection value is not stored in a publicly accessible location. Selections are always owned by a client who is responsible for supplying the value to other requesting clients. If the selection value is never requested, it need not even be generated.

If the user selects something in a window, the application must assert ownership of the selection by calling *XtOwnSelection*. In addition to a widget and the selection atom you have to pass a timestamp as a parameter. Again the timestamp is obtained from the event that triggered the selection. As mentioned above, the timestamp is required because it is possible that two clients assert selection ownership in quick succession, but the requests arrive in reverse order in the X server.

If a client is claiming selection ownership and another request with a later timestamp has already arrived, the assertion instantly fails. In this case *XtOwnSelection* returns *False*. Otherwise it returns *True* and installs three procedures as callbacks for the responsibilities of the selection owner.

The first procedure is called to convert the selection into the requested target, the second procedure is called when the selection owner changes, and the last procedure optionally informs the owner that the requestor has received the value.

The last procedure is necessary if the conversion procedure allocates storage for the selection value that it wants to reuse later. The allocated storage must be maintained until the complete value has been transferred, because the transfer process may require some time and is performed behind the scenes. If the last procedure is specified as *NULL*, the X Toolkit Intrinsics simply free the storage for the converted value when the transfer is complete.

The second procedure is called when another client acquires ownership of the selection. A client cannot prevent the loss of the selection. Any visual feedback of selection ownership must be removed in the second callback procedure.

The most important callback procedure is the first one. It is called whenever another client requests the selection value. The owner passes a pointer to the converted value to the Intrinsics and returns *True* if it is able to supply the requested target, otherwise it returns *False*. When programming this procedure you have to decide what targets you want to support.

If your program wants to give up the selection on its own, it may call *XtDisownSelection*, for example if the window containing the selection is closed. If you delete the selection, e.g. by a Cut operation, you can decide whether you want to retain an empty selection or whether you want to give it up.

Targets

A necessary precondition of a working selection mechanism is that the clients not only agree about the selections, but also about the targets and their representations. A lot of targets are briefly mentioned in the ICCCM, and this list will grow over time. The most important targets will be sketched here.

There are three classes of targets, which differ in their general purpose and not only in contents:

- *Functional targets* are a kind of meta information and are used to extend the functionality of the selection mechanism.

- *Value targets* specify the selection value in a format that is widely understood among different clients for data exchange.

- *Identifying targets* refer to some common entity such as a file where the real value may be obtained. Identifying targets require that the clients have some other communication channel.

The most important functional target is *TARGETS*. Every selection owner must support this target and return a list of target atoms he supports. In this way other clients can get an overview of which targets they may request.

This and other functional targets are listed in Table 7-7. The second column in this table indicates the atom the owner should return as type. All types except strings consist of 32-bit values, so their format is 32.

A second target is *MULTIPLE*, which is used to request multiple targets simultaneously. A *MULTIPLE* request is handled automatically by the X Toolkit Intrinsics, but you have to include this target in the list of targets your program supports.

The *MULTIPLE* request also needs input parameters. The property which normally contains the returned selection value contains a list of atom pairs in this case. Each pair contains a target and a property where this target's value is to be stored.

TARGETS	ATOM	List of valid target atoms
MULTIPLE	ATOM_PAIR	Return multiple targets
TIMESTAMP	INTEGER	Timestamp of acquisition
DELETE		Delete selection
INSERT_SELECTION		Insert other selection

Table 7-7: Functional targets.

This list of atom pairs demonstrates the difference between format and type. The format is 32, meaning that the property contains a number of 32-bit values. The type *ATOM_PAIR* indicates that two numbers are always paired. But even nonsense in the type field would not change the contents or representation of the value; it is only a hint.

The target *TIMESTAMP* returns the time when the selection ownership was obtained. The ICCCM requires that every selection owner responds to these three targets. The Intrinsics take care of *MULTIPLE*, but you have to implement the other two. Remember that you must include all three in the list of supported targets.

Two other targets are defined that do not deliver a return value. *DELETE* returns a zero-length value if the selection can be and has been deleted. The target *INSERT_SELECTION* requests the selection owner to insert another selection in place of the current one. This target is used by Quick Transfer to insert the contents of the *SECONDARY* selection in place of the *PRIMARY* selection.

The value targets really deliver data in a form that can be used by the requesting client. The most important target is *STRING*, which specifies the ISO Latin 1 encoding plus the two special codes *TAB* and *NEWLINE*. The target *TEXT* is similar, but the owner may return the value in any encoding it likes. For *ODIF* you have to consult some additional documentation.

If you do not want to transfer all the data at once, you can first query the *LENGTH* target which gives the number of bytes the value occupies. The *LIST_LENGTH* target gives the number of disjoint parts in the selection. For

STRING	STRING	ISO Latin 1 (+TAB+NEWLINE)
TEXT	...	in owner's encoding
ODIF	...	ISO Office Document Interchange
LIST_LENGTH	INTEGER	number of disjoint parts
LENGTH	INTEGER	length of selection in bytes
PIXMAP	DRAWABLE	Pixmap ID
BITMAP	BITMAP	Bitmap ID
FOREGROUND	PIXEL	Foreground pixel value
BACKGROUND	PIXEL	Background pixel value
COLORMAP	COLORMAP	Colormap ID

Table 7-8: Value targets. An ellipsis for the type indicates that the owner may use any encoding in its return.

HOST_NAME	...	Name of host
OWNER_OS	...	Name of operating system
USER	...	Name of user running owner
CLASS	...	Application class
NAME	...	Application name
FILE_NAME	...	Full path name
CHARACTER_POSITION	SPAN	Start and ending
LINE_NUMBER	SPAN	Start and ending
COLUMN_NUMBER	SPAN	Start and ending

Table 7-9: Identifying targets.

example, if you select a number of entries in a list and want to copy them, they can be treated as disjoint parts and are separated by null characters in the *STRING* value.

Graphical data can currently only be exchanged as bitmaps or pixmaps using the targets *PIXMAP* and *BITMAP*. Because not all attributes of pixmaps can be obtained from the X server, you should also support the targets *FORE-GROUND, BACKGROUND* and *COLORMAP* if you support pixmaps.

If two clients both run on the same machine or have a common file system, there is no need to transfer the data through the X server. The clients can agree to look in a certain file at a certain position for the selection value. The targets listed in Table 7-9 are used to inquire about whether the two can share a file and to identify the part of the file.

The textual targets all return an owner-specific encoding. The type *SPAN* indicates that the representation consists of cardinal pairs. The size of the pairs is determined by the format, and there may be any number of pairs, e.g. if the selection is discontinuous.

For example, if the format is 16 the selection value consists of pairs of 16-bit unsigned integers, and there are half as many pairs as the length parameter indicates (there should be as many as the *LIST_LENGTH* target specifies).

7.5 The Clipboard

Although you can access the clipboard selection using the selection support procedures defined in the X Toolkit Intrinsics, Motif provides a support library for the clipboard which has an extended functionality. The Motif clipboard allows you to store the clipboard value in a common place where it can be directly accessed by all Motif clients, but remains compatible with the selection mechanism.

The Motif mechanism is more suited to the clipboard semantics, because the program can really store away the value. The selection mechanism requires that the owner of the clipboard selection is always ready to answer requests. If the owner program exits, the clipboard value is lost. This poses no problem for the primary or secondary selections, because they naturally disappear when a client exits.

To be accessible by all Motif clients, the clipboard value can only be stored in two places: in the X server itself or in a special clipboard client. Motif currently uses the first approach.

Storing the value as a property in the X server has the following advantages and disadvantages:

- The value is directly accessible by all (Motif) clients and lives as long as the X server itself. Only two processes (X server and requestor) are involved in either a Cut or a Paste operation, thus possibly improving performance on small machines.

- The memory requirements in the X server pose serious problems if the X server runs on a limited machine (a PC or X terminal). Server memory is no problem if client and server run on a workstation, because the value would have to be stored in either client or server space anyway.

In the future Motif may be enhanced by a separate clipboard client. The following points apply to this mechanism:

- The clipboard client would have fewer storage problems, because it may even store the value in a file. The clipboard client can also be used to display the current value of the clipboard.

- More bandwidth is needed because the selection value must always be transferred to the clipboard client. Data transfer involves three processes (requesting client, X server and clipboard client).

- The user may forget to start the clipboard client.

Perhaps a clever combination of both approaches will provide the optimal solution. However, a future implementation should not change the programming interfaces described in this section.

Clipboard Structure

Just as there are different targets for selections, the clipboard value is stored in different representations. These are called *formats* in Motif, but do not confuse them with the format of a property (8, 16, or 32, called the *format length* in Motif). In fact, to be compatible with other clients using the clipboard selection, the formats correspond exactly to targets.

All the predefined targets of the ICCCM (see the tables above for a large subset) are understood by the clipboard routines. If you want to use an application-specific format, it has to be registered. Registering formats avoids misunderstandings between clients (two clients cannot register the same format

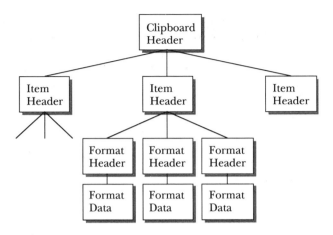

Figure 7.5: Structure of the clipboard.

with different specifications) and also keeps the argument lists shorter as only the format name is required.

A useful feature of the Motif clipboard is that there may be more than one *item* stored. An item is a completely different value, for example the previous clipboard value before a Cut operation. Normally one additional item is kept, to allow undoing a Cut operation by restoring the previous clipboard value. The clipboard structure is shown in Figure 7.5. A third item in this figure is under construction and will replace the current item when complete.

Because the clipboard represents a shared data structure, simultaneous accesses from different clients have to be coordinated. The Motif clipboard uses *locks* for this purpose. An application locks the clipboard while executing a state-changing operation to prevent other clients from seeing an inconsistent intermediate clipboard state.

Locking is known in the database world. If two programs read a record at the same time and then want to update it, one of the updates will be lost. Therefore one client must complete the update before the other may even read the record. This is achieved by both clients first trying to lock the record before they read it. One of the clients will fail until the other has finished.

However, a faulty client may never release the lock (there is always an endless loop waiting for you) and blocks all other clients in endless re-tries. A "good" client should detect this situation and inform the user to take some counter measures against the offending client.

From the list of targets in the previous section you see that most formats will have fairly short values. Therefore it is not too inefficient to store these values in the clipboard all the time even if they are never needed. The value targets, however, may be arbitrarily large, and it is often a good idea not to copy the selection value until it is really needed.

A long value is advertised as being copied by name, in effect using the same idea as the selection mechanism. There are some differences, though. You can mix formats by value (the short ones) with targets by name for the same selection item. When a value is first requested by name, its value is stored to satisfy further requests directly.

To be compatible with the clipboard selection your program becomes the owner of the clipboard selection if you copy data to the Motif clipboard. The event handler for this purpose is installed automatically and its activation is transparent, as requests can be answered using the data stored in the clipboard. Only requests from non-Motif clients need to be processed in any case, as Motif clients access the clipboard data directly.

Copying to the Clipboard

Copying data to the clipboard is a four step process:

- *Start copy.* Open the clipboard and register the necessary owner information. Some temporary space is allocated for the following process.

- *Register formats.* Register all formats not defined in the ICCCM.

- *Copy formats.* Copy the data in each format you support. Copy either by name, as one value, or as a sequence of values.

- *End copy.* Either commit the copy process, or cancel the whole transaction.

The transaction is started by the procedure *XmClipboardStartCopy*. The parameters are a display and a window used to identify the selection owner. They should always be the same for one application, because the clipboard routines use this information to detect whether the clipboard owner is a different application. These parameters can be obtained by calls to *XtDisplay* and *XtWindow*, respectively, using your top-level application shell (which must be realized).

```
Widget      toplevel;
XmString    clip_label;
Time timestamp;
long        item_id;
int         result;
```

```
result = XmClipboardStartCopy (XtDisplay (toplevel), XtWindow (toplevel),
            clip_label, timestamp, toplevel, ByNameCallback, &item_id);
```

A third parameter is an XmString to be used as an identifying label in the window of a clipboard client (such as the application name). The fourth parameter is a timestamp obtained from the triggering event.

A widget ID and a callback procedure are the fifth and sixth parameters. They are only needed when you copy data by name. The widget is only used as a place where a callback can be installed. The widget is not used for any other purpose, so you can also use the application shell here.

The return value from *XmClipboardStartCopy* may be either *ClipboardSuccess* or *ClipboardLocked*. If the clipboard is locked, you should re-try the operation until the clipboard is unlocked again. To avoid blocking infinitely if another client does not release the lock, you should use an upper bound for the re-tries, such as in the following example:

```
#define     RETRY_COUNT       1000
int         retries, result;

retries = RETRY_COUNT;
do
      if (retries- <= 0) XtErrorMsg (...);
      result = XmClipboardStartCopy(...);
while (result != Clipboardlocked);
```

A new format is registered with *XmClipboardRegisterFormat*. You have to specify a format name and a format length. The procedure may return *ClipboardSuccess*, *ClipboardFail* (if you try to redefine an existing format), or *ClipboardBadFormat* (if the length is not 8, 16, or 32, or the name is empty).

```
String            format_name;
unsigned long     format_length;

result = XmClipboardRegisterFormat (XtDisplay (toplevel),
                  format_name, format_length);
```

Afterwards the format definition is also valid for other clients. All the formats of the ICCCM are pre-registered.

As mentioned above, copying to the clipboard may occur in two variants: by value or by name. In both cases *XmClipboardCopy* is used. *XmClipboardCopy* needs the item ID returned by *XmClipboardStartCopy* as well as the format name to select the format to be written. When copying by value, a buffer and its byte-length are passed.

```
String            format_name;
char              *buffer;
unsigned long     buffer_length;


result = XmClipboardCopy (XtDisplay (toplevel), XtWindow (toplevel), item_id,
                  format_name, buffer, buffer_length, 0, NULL);
```

If the format is 16 or 32, the buffer length is two or four times the length you would have to specify for the selection mechanism described in the previous section.

The format value is not copied directly to the clipboard. It is assembled in temporary space so that you are able to cancel the process. If the value is composed of multiple pieces, you can use multiple calls to *XmClipboardCopy* with the same item ID and format name. The later calls simply append the value.

To pass the value by name, you specify the buffer as *NULL*. To identify this item/format combination in a later callback, a unique ID is generated.

int   data_id;

result = XmClipboardCopy (XtDisplay (toplevel), XtWindow (toplevel), item_id, format_name, NULL, 0, 0, &data_id);

The callback function registered by *XmClipboardStartCopy* will be called with this data ID when the value is requested for the first time. It is not allowed to call *XmClipboardCopy* multiple times for the same format if you copy by name. Instead you may copy the value piecewise in the callback procedure, if necessary.

The second-to-last parameter, specified as 0 in the examples, can be used to associate a private integer with the value. However, this mechanism is not compatible with the clipboard selection, because clients not using the Motif clipboard cannot access this value. This parameter should therefore be used with caution. Using an additional format is the better way to communicate additional information.

XmClipboardCopy may return *ClipboardSuccess* or *ClipboardLocked*. It should be used with re-tries as described above.

After repeating the above step for each format you support, the data are finally transferred to the clipboard by *XmClipboardEndCopy*.

result = XmClipboardEndCopy (XtDisplay (toplevel), XtWindow (toplevel), item_id);

Alternatively, you can use *XmClipboardCancelCopy* to forget the new values and leave the clipboard in its previous state.

result = XmClipboardCancelCopy (XtDisplay (toplevel), XtWindow (toplevel), item_id);

If data are copied by name, the application must support a callback procedure to respond to value inquiries. The callback procedure transfers the requested value to the clipboard using *XmClipboardCopyByName*.

```
void ByNameCallback (widget, data_id, private, reason)
      Widget       widget;
      int          *data_id;
      int          *private;
      int          *reason;
{
      int                result;
      char               *buffer;
      unsigned long      buffer_length;

      switch (*reason) {
            case XmCR_CLIPBOARD_DATA_REQUEST:
...
                  result = XmClipboardCopyByName (XtDisplay (toplevel),
                              XtWindow (toplevel),
                              *data_id,
                              buffer, buffer_length, *private_id);

...
            case XmCR_CLIPBOARD_DATA_DELETE:
...           /* no longer needed, free any buffers */

      }
}
```

If you call *XmClipboardCopyByName* multiple times to append data to the format in pieces, you have to lock the entire transaction to prevent intermediate accesses of other clients, because the data are transferred directly to the clipboard. You can use the following two procedures for this purpose:

```
result = XmClipboardLock (XtDisplay (toplevel), XtWindow (toplevel));
...
result = XmClipboardUnlock (XtDisplay (toplevel), XtWindow (toplevel));
```

Locking is not necessary when you respond to the callback with only a single call to *XmClipboardCopyByName*. The callback procedure may also be invoked with a reason field of *XmCR_CLIPBOARD_DATA_DELETE* when the clipboard item is permanently deleted and no further callback is expected. The callback should free any data structures temporarily allocated for that value.

Formats copied by name are no longer accessible to other clients when the owning client terminates. Therefore any client should check on termination whether there are any outstanding items copied by name. These can then either be supplied by value or be discarded from the list of supported formats.

The procedure *XmClipboardInquirePendingItems* returns a list of such items for a specified format. The list contains the data IDs that were returned by *XmClipboardCopy*.

```
XmClipboardPendingList       item_list, item_ptr;
unsigned long                count, i;

...XmClipboardLock(...)...
result = XmClipboardInquirePendingItems (
           XtDisplay (toplevel), XtWindow (toplevel),
           format_name, &item_list, &item_count);
item_prt = item_list;
for (i = 0; i < count; i++) {
        /* copy or withdraw */
        ..., item_ptr->DataId, ...
        item_ptr++;
}
XtFree (item_list);
...XmClipboardUnlock (...) ...
```

The application may use *XmClipboardCopyByName* to transfer the data to the clipboard before exiting, or may remove this format using the procedure *XmClipboardWithdrawFormat*.

```
result = XmClipboardWithdrawFormat (XtDisplay (toplevel), XtWindow (toplevel),
           data_id);
```

The whole process from inquiry to saving or removing the formats should be locked to prevent interference from other clients.

Retrieving from the Clipboard

The retrieval process works like the copy process. The transfer section is embraced by the two procedures *XmClipboardStartRetrieve* and *XmClipboard-EndRetrieve*. These lock the clipboard and ensure that no other clients change the clipboard in the meantime. The bracketing procedures may be omitted if you only want to retrieve a single format.

```
result = XmClipboardStartRetrieve (XtDisplay (toplevel), XtWindow (toplevel),
           timestamp);
...
result = XmClipboardEndRetrieve (XtDisplay (toplevel), XtWindow (toplevel),
```

A value in a specific format is read with *XmClipboardRetrieve*. This procedure requires a pre-allocated buffer large enough to hold the value. Allocating a buffer is no problem if you know the length in advance (as is the case with fixed-length formats such as *LENGTH*). In general you must either ascertain the length beforehand, or allocate a large buffer and count on being notified if it is not large enough. The former solution uses the procedure *XmClipboardInquireLength*.

```
unsigned long    length;
char             *buffer;
unsigned long    num_bytes;
int              private_id;
```

```
...XmClipboardLock (...) ...
result = XmClipboardInquireLength (XtDisplay (toplevel), XtWindow (toplevel),
         format_name, &length);
buffer = XtMalloc (length);
result = XmClipboardRetrieve (XtDisplay (toplevel), XtWindow (toplevel),
         format_name, buffer, length, &num_bytes, &private_id);
...XmClipboardUnlock (...) ...
```

The return value *ClipboardTruncate* is used to signal that the buffer was too small. The return value *ClipboardNoData* indicates that there is no data in this format (because the previous owner has exited or withdrawn the format).

One final problem remains. According to the style guide, the Paste command should appear in a menu. Menu entries should be made insensitive when they cannot be selected. For the Paste command you have to check whether there is data in the clipboard in a format your application understands.

For this purpose you can use the procedure *XmClipboardInquireCount*, which will give you the number of formats for the current clipboard item. If no clipboard item exists, it returns *ClipboardNoData*. When there are formats, you have to ascertain the names of the individual formats with *XmClipboard-InquireFormat*. Because you do not know the length of the format names in advance, the previous call to *XmClipboardInquireCount* reports the maximum length of all format names so that you can allocate a buffer accordingly.

```
int      count, i;
int      max_format_name_length;
int      name_length;
char     *name_buffer;
```

```
...XmClipboardLock (...) ...
result = XmClipboardInquireCount (XtDisplay (toplevel), XtWindow (toplevel),
         &count, &max_format_name_length);
name_buffer = XtMalloc (max_format_name_length);
```

```
for (i=0; i < count; i++) {
     result = XmClipboardInquireFormat (
              XtDisplay (toplevel), XtWindow (toplevel),
              i, name_buffer, max_format_name_length, &name_length);
     /* check if 'name_buffer' supported */
     ...
}
XtFree (name_buffer);
```

...XmClipboardUnlock (...) ...

If your application is only interested in one format, you can ascertain that format directly using *XmClipboardInquireLength.* All these checks should be included in a pop-up callback of the menu. However, the sensitivity of the menu item may suddenly become incorrect if another application changes the clipboard while the menu is on the screen. Therefore you must always be prepared if clipboard operations fail, even if they are checked before.

Part Three

Programming

Chapter 8

A Sample Program

This chapter contains the description of a larger example program. The complete code and necessary support files are in Appendix D. The program also serves as a convenient online reference for all the Motif widget classes.

This example is included here to give you an impression of a typical Motif program. It is useful as a demonstration of most of the techniques and constructs described in this book. It also serves as a case study of program design and proper resource usage. This topic will be covered in Chapter 10.

8.1 Overview

Purpose

The purpose of this example program (called *motifhelp*) is to serve as an online reference for the Motif classes. It uses the information contained in the online manual pages provided with Motif, but presents it in finer detail.

For each resource field, the description is presented individually to focus the information on the fields. You can quickly select the resource field you need—much quicker than by calling the UNIX *man* command or by searching in the manual.

You can also search for specific fields using a fragment of the name, and you can traverse the Motif class hierarchy to see the inheritance relations.

The information presented is extracted from the manual pages, using some preprocessing shell scripts (which, by the way, strip the formatting information that is not needed). You will find these scripts in the appendix. If you do not have access to the manual page files, a sample input file is included to test the program and to demonstrate the file structure.

This program is useful as a Motif example because most of the program code is concerned with the user interface. The code to read in the information is rather trivial.

Program Structure

The program is divided into two parts. One part is responsible for loading and maintaining the textual information to be presented. This part is reasonably independent from the user interface design and can thus be treated in isolation. The other part is the code for the actual user interface.

A separation like this is advantageous in nearly all cases. Usually the underlying functionality of the program can be specified and fixed quite early in the program design process, so the interface between the two parts does not change too much during the development. In contrast, the user interface usually keeps changing till the last stage. Similarly, the implementation of the underlying functionality changes, owing to performance optimizations.

Having a clear separation and a stable interface between the two parts ensures greater modularity. Two different teams can work on the different parts, and changes on either side do not propagate through the whole program.

In this example, the two parts of the program are contained in two different files, "motifhelp.c" for the interface and "helpbuf.c" for the data access layer—see Figure 8.1. For common definitions both files share an include file ("motifhelp.h"). Because the interface layer issues requests to the data access

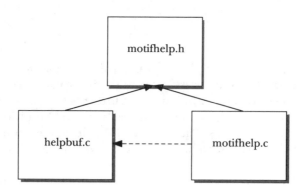

Figure 8.1: File structure of sample program.

layer, but not the other way round, the include file also contains the definitions for the exported procedures of the data access layer.

8.2 Data Access Layer

The code for the data access layer is not discussed here for two reasons. First, it is not relevant to the purposes of this book. And second, it is neither very elegant nor optimized—see so for yourself by looking at the appendix.

Only the exported procedure definitions are important for the understanding of the interface code. They are discussed in this section.

File Location

The information to be displayed resides in files in a certain directory. The files are constructed by processing the Motif manual pages through a shell script listed in the appendix. The program expects to find the preprocessed input files in a specific directory. They are searched either in the current directory or in a directory specified with *SetHelpDir*.

SetHelpDir ("/home/andy/motifhelp/");

The directory should be set before any other calls are made (because other calls may initiate the loading process). In the example program the parameter can be provided either by a command line option or a resource file entry.

The directory name must be followed by a trailing slash, because the filename to be loaded is simply appended to this string to create the correct path name.

Class Hierarchy

The help information is naturally centred around the Motif widget classes. There is one file per class, because there is also one manual page file per class. When information about this class is requested, the corresponding file is read and part of it filled into a memory resident structure.

Each structure for a class represents a node in the Motif class tree. Therefore the structures are connected with pointers to form a tree that allows up and down traversal.

The tree structure is initialized from the file "motifhelp.classes". This file contains the names of all Motif classes and their hierarchical ordering. On program start this file is read and used to build the tree (see Figure 8.2). All further procedures assume the presence of the tree, although not all fields need to be filled.

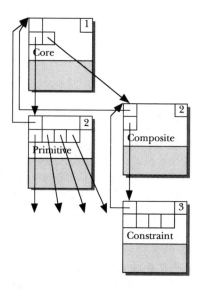

Figure 8.2: Internal data structures that mirror the Motif class tree.

There are two procedures which use this information and thus ensure that the tree is built. *GetClassNames* returns the list of all class names, sorted alphabetically, as a further reference showing which classes are present.

> *XmString   *name_array;*
> *int   no_class_names;*
>
> *name_array = GetClassNames (&no_class_names);*

The second procedure, *RootClass*, returns the root structure of the class tree. You can access the whole tree by starting from this node. The contents of a node are explained below.

> *ClassDoc   *root_node;*
>
> *root_node = RootClass ();*

As mentioned above, both procedures read "motifhelp.classes" if necessary.

Node Structure

Every node of the class tree is described by the following C structure:

```
typedef struct _classDoc {
    String          name;
    XmString        xm_name;
    struct _classDoc *super;
    struct _classDoc *subs[MAX_SUBCLASSES];
    int             no_subs;
    int             level;
    Boolean         file_read;
    int             no_res;
    String          res_name[MAX_RESOURCES],
                    res_text[MAX_RESOURCES];
    XmString        res_string[MAX_RESOURCES],
                    res_class[MAX_RESOURCES],
                    res_type[MAX_RESOURCES],
                    res_default[MAX_RESOURCES];
    int             res_access[MAX_RESOURCES],
                    res_range[MAX_RESOURCES];
    int             sections;
} ClassDoc;
```

This structure consists of two parts. The first part, including *file_read*, is filled on program initialization when the class hierarchy is read. The other parts, describing the resource fields of this class, are filled on demand from the corresponding class file.

The first part contains the name of the class, both as an ordinary C string and as an XmString, to facilitate usage with Motif. The next fields are pointers to the superclass and to all subclasses to allow traversal of the tree. The level in the hierarchy is also contained in the structure, starting from 1 for the root class and increasing by 1 for each level.

The field *file_read* is initially *False*, indicating that the following fields are not initialized. These fields are arrays containing the decomposed information about the individual resource fields of this widget class. The number of entries used in each array is given by *no_res*, which is the number of resource fields this widget class defines in addition to those of its superclasses.

The name of each resource field is included both as a string and as an XmString. The field *res_text* contains the multi-line description of this field. Resource class name, resource type, and default value are given as XmStrings. These values are taken from the resource field tables in the manual pages.

The *access* value denotes through individual flag bits whether the resource field may be set on creation, may be modified, and may be read. The *range* value indicates whether this resource field is special, is a constraint field, or is a field that is only valid for the scrolled widget variant. This value is taken from the header of additional resource field tables (for instance, there exists a table for "Scrolled Text Resource Fields" in addition to the normal "XmText Resource Fields").

The field *sections* contains flags indicating which of the general sections are present for the manual page of this class (e.g. "Description", "Behaviour", etc.). The text of these sections is only read into a temporary buffer when needed.

The fields for the node of a class where *file_read* is *False* may be read in by *FillHelpInfo*.

> *ClassDoc   *node;*

> *FillHelpInfo (node);*

Calling this procedure more than once is simply ignored because *file_read* is set to *True* (even if the file was not found in the previous call).

Section Information

The text of one of the general sections can be read into a buffer by using *ReadSection*. The parameter must be the number of a section (numbered from 1, also available as constants defined in "motifhelp.h").

> *String   buffer;*

> *buffer = ReadSection (CALLBACK_SEC);*

You should only call this procedure when the flags in the node structure for this class indicate that the requested section is indeed present in this file.

There is also a procedure *ReadLongSection* which takes explicit names for (1) the file to read and (2) the desired section in this file. This procedure is used to read in help information from the file "motifhelp.help".

Searching

You can search the class tree for either specific class names or fragments of a resource field name. To find the node structure for a specific class without explicitly searching the tree, you can use *SearchClass*.

> *ClassDoc   *node;*

> *node = SearchClass (MakeXmString ("XmText"));*

The parameter must be an XmString. The procedure *MakeXmString* is a convenience function to create XmStrings with the default character set. You should free these XmStrings as usual when no longer needed.

To search for a resource field with a specific name you can use the procedure *FindMatchingFields*. This procedure produces an array of XmStrings which denote the resource fields in which the requested fragment is present.

> *XmString   *string_array;*

int   no_matches;

FindMatchingFields ("fragment", &string_array, &no_matches);

In the example program the string list is used to let the user select one of the entries. If the same field name is found in multiple classes, the name of the class is appended in parentheses to the field name.

Searching for a resource field requires that all class files are read in for the nodes to be filled. Therefore *FindMatchingFields* calls *FillHelpInfo* when necessary.

To find the exact location in the class tree of resource fields in the list, *FindMatchingFields* maintains a table of these locations internally. To retrieve this information for a specific entry in the list you can use *LocateResource.*

XmString   list_entry;
*ClassDoc   *which_node;*
int   which_entry;

LocateResource (list_entry, &which_node, &which_entry);

The entry returned can be used as an index for the array of resource fields in the class node structure. A call to this procedure requires that *FindMatchingFields* has been called before, otherwise the internal table of locations may be undefined.

8.3 The User Interface

This section contains a description of the user interface part of the sample program.

Components

The visible components of the sample program are the main window and three dialog boxes. The main window contains several subcomponents (see Figure 8.3). The program code in file "motifhelp.c" is structured according to this decomposition. The components of the main window and the three dialog boxes are treated as separate objects, i.e. their communication is restricted to defined procedures. Direct access to global variables belonging to another component, or to the widgets implementing them, is avoided. In this way, the implementation of one component can be changed without affecting the others.

Because C does not support this kind of object-oriented programming directly, the compiler cannot enforce the separation and thus some dependency

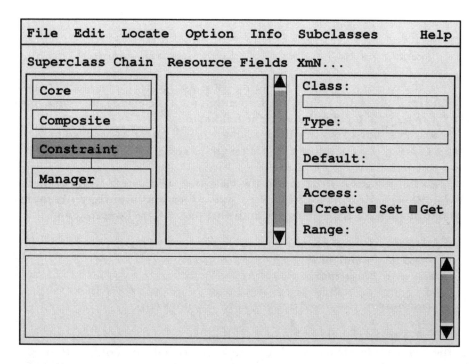

Figure 8.3: Subcomponents of the main window.

may have been overlooked. However, this example clearly shows that object-oriented programming is more a structuring mechanism than a language issue.

The subcomponents of the main window are outlined in Figure 8.3. They form a hierarchy because they are themselves built from widgets. The main window is a container of components and a component itself. It lays out the menu bar, the main form and the help text field. The main form maintains three subcomponents: the superclass chain, a resource field selection list, and the attribute display for a resource field.

The superclass chain component displays the path from the class tree root to some Motif class, i.e. the list of all superclasses of the class at the end of the chain. Therefore the Core class always occupies the top of this chain. One of the classes is always selected. By clicking into another class name, the previously selected one is deselected, just like a radio box.

The resource field selection list displays a scrollable list of all resource fields of the currently selected class. To be more precise, it displays the fields the class defines in addition to its parent classes. To access the fields of the parent class the user simply selects that class. When one of the resource fields is selected, the attributes of this field are displayed in the area to the right. At the same time a descriptive text is displayed in the multi-line text field.

One of the dialogs is used to select a new class as the end of the class chain, the other for locating a resource field. Both contain a selection list and some buttons. The third dialog displays help information about the program.

The Main Procedure

The main procedure is an extension of the template in Chapter 3. Because it is also treated as the essential part of the main window component, the creation of the other components is included in the main procedure.

The first obvious difference from the main procedure in Chapter 3 is that additional parameters are used for *XtOpenDisplay*. An option record with one entry specifies command line options that are recognized in addition to the standard ones managed by the X Toolkit Intrinsics. In this case an option *-dir* followed by a parameter is used to set the location of the help files. The following option record is required:

```
XrmOptionDescRec options [] = {
      {"-dir", "*helpDir", XrmoptionSepArg, ""}
};
```

XrmoptionSepArg denotes that the parameter value follows as the next command line argument, and the empty string is used as a default value for this option.

The mechanism works by transforming the command line parameter into an entry in the resource database. Therefore a corresponding resource database entry for the directory parameter must also be recognized, in this case "helpDir". Because "helpDir" is not a resource field of a widget, the resource database must be queried explicitly for a matching value.

After creating the top-level shell, *XtGetApplicationResources* is used to obtain a value from the resource database.

```
typedef struct {
      String       help_dir;
} AppData, *AppDataPtr;

AppData   data;

static XtResource resources [] = {
      {"helpDir", "Dir", XmRString,
      sizeof (String), XtOffset (AppDataPtr, help_dir),
      XmRString, ""}
};

XtGetApplicationResources (toplevel, &data, resources, XtNumber (resources),
                        NULL, 0);
```

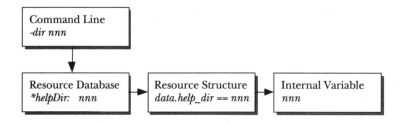

Figure 8.4: Path of command line parameter.

The top-level shell is used to identify the name and class of the application. The *data* record is used to store the value, because the destination location of a resource value is defined in the resource list *resources* as an offset into a structure. The resource list defines the fields whose values are requested. The definition includes the name and class of this field, the resource type and size for automatic conversion (which isn't needed here), the mentioned offset, and a default value.

The value obtained is then used to set the help directory in the "helpbuf" module. To make the mechanism clearer, Figure 8.4 describes the path the command line specification of the help directory takes until it arrives in the "helpbuf" module.

The part of the main procedure following the parameter inquiry creates all the subparts of the main window. The main form and the text field are managed by a paned window to allow individual resizing of both areas. This paned window is used as the work window for a main window widget, which also contains the menu bar. The three dialogs are created as children of the menu bar, because they are considered part of the menu system (they are called by menu entries). Except for the addressing in resource files this has no other consequences, because they are independent pop-up windows.

Before the main loop is entered, the superclass chain is initialized to show the file selection box, which has the largest number of superclasses:

ChangeClassChain (SearchClass (MakeXmString ("FileSelectionBox")));

ChangeClassChain is a procedure belonging to the superclass chain component, and is described below.

The Menu Entries

The menu system of the example program consists of the menu bar and seven pull-down menus. Most of the entries in these menus are used to illustrate typical entries mentioned in the Motif Style Guide. There is no functionality associated with them, and consequently these entries are permanently insensitive. This should be avoided in real application programs (what good are useless menu entries?). However, in the example the additional entries are used to demonstrate the common mnemonic and accelerator specifications.

Because in most menu panes all the entries have a similar function, the menu callbacks in this example are installed as *XmNentryCallbacks* of the row-column, i.e. there is only one callback procedure associated with each menu pane. The index of the menu entry which caused the callback can be calculated by comparing the widget ID in the *call_data* structure with the array of widget IDs for this pane.

The arrays *buttons1* to *buttons7* are therefore defined to store the widget IDs for the buttons of the respective panes after menu creation. The procedure *ButtonIndex* then uses *call_data->widget* (the widget ID of the button whose activation callback was redirected) and searches its position in the array. A menu callback whose function is completely different for each entry looks like this:

```
void HandleLocateMenu (w, client_data, call_data)
      Widget              w;
      caddr_t             client_data;      /* not used */
      XmRowColumnCallbackStruct      *call_data;
{
      switch (ButtonIndex (buttons3, call_data)) {
      case 0:
            PopupClassDialog ();
            break;
      case 1:
            PopupResDialog ();
            break;
      }
}
```

There are seven of these callback procedures in the example program, corresponding to the seven menus.

The callback handler for the "File" menu simply exits, because "Exit" is the only sensitive entry. All the others, like "Save", are meaningless for this program because there are no documents or files to be edited.

Figure 8.5: The "File" menu.

```
┌─────────────────────────────┐
│ Undo      Alt+Backspace      │
│ Cut       Shift+Del          │
│ Copy      Ctrl+Ins           │
│ Paste     Shift+Ins          │
├─────────────────────────────┤
│ Clear                        │
│ Delete                       │
└─────────────────────────────┘
```

Figure 8.6: The "Edit" menu.

The procedure for the "Edit" menu is completely empty, because the Cut & Paste mechanism is not implemented.

The handling code for the "Locate" menu is shown on the previous page: its entries simply pop up a dialog, which installs a new selection on pressing "OK". Connecting the application command as the callback to the "OK" button of a parameter dialog is a common technique.

```
┌──────────────────────────┐
│ Widget Class    F5        │
│ Resource Name   F6        │
└──────────────────────────┘
```

Figure 8.7: The "Locate" menu.

The "Options" menu entries are a special case, because they are toggle buttons, not the usual push buttons. Their setting is used to control the visibility of indiviual entries in the parameter field. For instance, if you are not interested in the resource class specification you can toggle the "Class" entry and this line is unmanaged from the parameter field. The button index is used as the index of the affected parameter field.

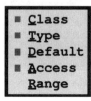

Figure 8.8: The "Options" menu.

Figure 8.9: The "Info" menu.

A similar technique is used for the "Info" menu. Its entries denote the additional sections which are present for the currently selected widget class. Activating an entry causes the help text for this section (e.g. "Description") to be displayed in the text field at the bottom of the main window.

Because not every widget class file contains text for all sections, the sensitivity of the entries is dynamically adjusted by section availability for the current class. In contrast, all other insensitive menu entries in the program are statically determined, i.e. made insensitive at creation (and should really be eliminated, as stated above). Because inapplicable entries are insensitive, the menu callback can be sure that the requested section text is present.

Adjusting the sensitivity of menu entries is performed by the procedure *SetSectionSensitivity*, which must be called whenever another widget class is selected. It uses the bit mask in the class node structure as input.

```
void SetSectionSensitivity (doc)
     ClassDoc   *doc;
{
     int          i, mask;

     mask = 1;
     for (i=0, i<COLOR_SEC; i++) {
            XtSetSensitive (buttons5[i], doc->sections & mask);
            mask += mask;
     }
}
```

SetSectionSensitivity is a good example of the separation of the program code into different objects. *SetSectionSensitivity* is called in only one place, when the selected class is changed. It could equally well be expanded in that place. After all, its body is only four lines long.

However, knowledge about the menu system implementation, for instance that an array stores the widget IDs, will be visible outside the menu system's private area. Should you ever decide to use a different implementation, the whole program must be checked for consequential changes. Including this

```
Arrow Button
Label
List
Scroll Bar
Separator
Text
```

Figure 8.10: The "Subclasses" menu.

procedure in the menu system section and having only a simple interface to the outside ensures easier maintenance for the future.

The "Subclasses" menu is even more dynamic. The number of entries, and the labels on the entries, depend on the currently selected class. This menu contains all subclasses of the selected class in order to allow downward tree traversal. Selecting one of these menu entries selects this subclass as the new end of the class chain.

In common with *SetSectionSensitivity*, the "Subclasses" menu has an associated procedure to configure the menu according to the currently selected class node structure. The menu is created with as many (dummy) entries as the class with the most subclasses needs. In the *SetSubclassesMenu* procedure, the exact number is managed and their labels are set according to information in the class record.

```
void SetSubclassesMenu (doc)
      ClassDoc    *doc;
{
      int         i;
      Args        args[NUM_ARGS];

      XtUnmanageChildren (buttons6, MAX_MENU_BUTTONS);
      for (i=0; i<doc->no_subs; i++) {
            XtSetArg (args[0], XmNlabelString, doc->subs[i]->xm_name);
            XtSetValues (buttons6[i], args, 1);
      }
      XtManageChildren (buttons6, doc->no_subs);
}
```

Again, a simple interface procedure is used to maintain the dependency between the "Subclasses" menu and the currently selected widget class.

The handler procedure for the "Help" menu is also quite simple. Because only one of the several help entries is sensitive, a simple dialog with text from a help file is displayed.

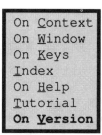

Figure 8.11: The "Help" menu.

Menu Creation

Because all the widgets in the menu system are arranged in a highly regular structure, they are not created individually as most other widgets are. Instead, some procedures are used to create the hierarchy from the specification of all the entry labels, and only the differences are introduced afterwards. However, this might not be economic in a real application, because there could be a larger variety of menu entries than in this simple example.

The procedure *CreateOneMenu* is used to create one menu pane complete with the corresponding cascade button in the menu bar. Necessary parameters are the parent widget (the menu bar), the name of the menu (the label of the cascade button), the array of labels for the menu entries, and the array which will accept the widget IDs of the created buttons. In addition, a parameter decides whether the menu entries are push buttons or toggle buttons.

Following the creation sequence described in Chapter 5, the pane with the buttons is created first, and then the cascade button. The mnemonics are determined heuristically by using the first character of the label, or the first character following a blank (using the *DefaultMnemonic* procedure). However, this is overridden in two special cases in the "Edit" menu.

For performance reasons, gagdets are used for the menu entries. Three possible classes are used: push buttons, toggle buttons (depending on the parameter), and separators (when an empty label is specified).

The complete menu structure is built in *CreateMenus*. The individual panes are created in succession, setting the static sensitivity, any special mnemonics, and some accelerators, as well as the entry callbacks.

Main Form Layout

The main form is an example of use of the form widget. Its sole purpose is to lay out the three subcomponents, each with an additional label. The main form creation procedure creates the top widgets for these six parts, each with the necessary attachments as shown in Figure 8.12.

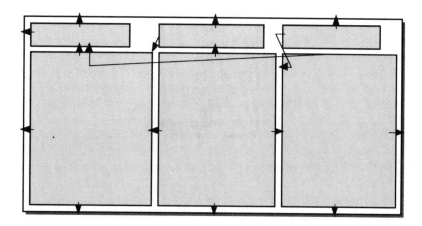

Figure 8.12: Constraints of the main form.

The three parts are attached so that the left and right parts assume their preferred sizes, while the scrolled list in the middle serves as the space buffer on resize. The three labels are left-attached so that they can be aligned with their corresponding parts.

Because the label above the parameter field is used to indicate the resource field name, there is a *SetParamLabel* procedure which sets the field name from the class node structure entry.

Superclass Chain

The superclass chain is the most complicated structure in the example program. In principle, it is a column of toggle buttons without indicator, and arranged as a radio box. Only the currently selected class can be active at a time.

However, this chain represents a path in the class tree, and thus it is possible to change the toggles to represent another path, which may be of different length. Here the same trick is used as in the "Subclasses" menu. The largest possible number of chain elements is created and only the needed ones are managed. Moreover, their labels are changed to reflect the class names in the chain.

To give a better visual representation of a chain, vertically oriented separator gadgets are used between the toggle buttons. This is tricky, because usually in a radio box only toggle buttons are allowed, but as they are never set they do not disturb the operation.

There are two callbacks associated with the toggle buttons in the chain. The arm callback is used to select the corresponding widget class as the current one. Switching is associated with the arm callback to give an instant reaction when the mouse button is pressed instead of waiting until it is released. The other procedure is registered with the value-changed callback and inverts the foreground and background colours of the button to give the selection a better visual appearance on monochrome screens.

Activating a class means updating the other subcomponents. Updates are performed by *ActivateClass*. After filling in the node contents, the resource selection list, the "Info" menu, and the "Subclasses" menu must be updated with the information about the newly activated class.

To change the class chain, either by calling an entry in the "Subclasses" menu, or by selecting a new class through the dialog box, the procedure *ChangeClassChain* is used. After having reset the previously active toggle and unmanaging all toggles, it creates a new chain starting from the new end node of the chain upwards to the root class. The new chain elements are then managed again and the last one activated.

To inhibit resizing after this process (for instance if only shorter class names appear), the resource field *XmNresizeWidth* of the row-column is set after the widget is realized (i.e. after the first time). However, this requires that the first time the chain is populated the longest entry (in this case "FileSelection-Box") is present, otherwise the row-column will not grow wide enough.

For reference from other components, the class chain exports the *ActiveDoc* procedure which returns a pointer to the class node structure of the currently active widget class. This procedure will signal an error if the class chain has not been set up by using *ChangeClassChain* and no active class exists.

So there are three reasons why *ChangeClassChain ("FileSelectionBox")* is called in the main procedure:

- To initialize the active class.
- To have the longest class name considered in the initial geometry calculation.
- To display the longest class chain.

Resource Field Selection List

The resource field selection list uses a list widget inside a scrolled window (an explicitly constructed scrolled list) to display the resource fields of the current class. It uses the single selection model and the single selection callback to fill the parameter field and the text field with information about the selected resource field.

The list items are taken from the class node structure and are set in the procedure *SetResourceSelectionList.*

Parameter Display

The parameter field consists of a row-column widget arranged in a column, with alternating labels and values as elements. The elements for the first three parameters are drawn buttons used to display textual labels; the other two are also row-columns, this time rows with three elements.

Drawn buttons are used for the textual display because they can draw a shadow (in contrast to labels). Input facilities are not needed, so as an alternative you can use a non-editable text.

To display the access flags for the selected resource field, a row of three toggle buttons is used. Their states are set according to the flag bits taken from the class node structure. However, the toggles can be switched by the user (with no effect, but making the toggles insensitive would also grey the labels).

Another approach is used for the range field. Here the three possible ranges ("Special", "Constraint", and "Scrolled") are displayed as drawn buttons, also in a row. Only the relevant range is sensitive, the others are greyed out.

The five parameters can be individually made invisible by unmanaging the two corresponding elements (label and value) of the row-column. This state is toggled by the exported procedure *ParamVisibility*, which is used in the "Options" menu.

The parameter values for the current resource field are set using the procedure *SetParameterField*. This takes a class node structure and an entry index as parameters. The procedure sets all fields even if some of the widgets are unmanaged and thus invisible, because widgets always remember their settings and display the new value when managed again.

Help Text

The help text, the second pane of the paned window inside the main window, is simply a non-editable scrolled text. Its value can be set with *SetHelpText*, using a C string in a buffer.

Class Selection Dialog

The class selection dialog is the simpler of the two selection dialogs. It is used to select a new class as the end of the class chain. The list of classes presented is the result of a *GetClassNames* call.

Both selection dialogs are created at program start-up and are managed on demand. Unmapping the dialog when one of the buttons has been selected is a built-in feature of the selection dialog widget.

For class selection, some standard elements of the selection dialog are removed by ascertaining the relevant child widget IDs and then unmanaging them.

```
Widget     w;

w = XmSelectionBoxGetChild (class_selection_dialog,
                 XmDIALOG_SELECTION_LABEL);
XtUnmanageChild (w);
```

> $w = XmSelectionBoxGetChild \ (class\_selection\_dialog,$
> $\qquad\qquad\qquad\qquad\qquad XmDIALOG\_HELP\_BUTTON);$
> $XtUnmanageChild \ (w);$
>
> $w = XmSelectionBoxGetChild \ (class\_selection\_dialog, \ XmDIALOG\_TEXT);$
> $XtUnmanageChild \ (w);$

The text field together with its label is removed because the item list is rather short, so there is no need to type in the class name as a potential short-cut.

The procedure for selecting a new class is bound to the *XmNokCallback*, which is activated by clicking the "OK" button or double-clicking an entry.

Resource Selection Dialog

The resource selection dialog is more complicated, because its functionality is twofold. It not only permits the selection of a resource field, it also creates a list of matching fields when the fragment of a resource field name is typed in.

On creation the selection dialog is also modified. The "Help" button is unmanaged, but the text field remains—it is used to enter a name or a name fragment. The additional "Apply" button is managed but is normally invisible. The "Apply" button initiates the creation of a matching resource list.

The automatic unmapping of the dialog on a button press is inhibited (via *XmNautoUnmanage*) to prevent the dialog from disappearing when no existing resource field has been selected. Naturally, the "Cancel" button always dismisses the window, so there is a simple *XmNcancelCallback.*

Normally the "OK" button is the default button in a selection dialog, activated by pressing Return in the dialog. This is not desirable when a field fragment has been entered and an item list is not yet present. In this case pressing Return activates the "Apply" action to create the matching list. Therefore the resource selection dialog initially sets the *XmNdefaultButton* to "Apply" and changes this as a result of the Apply callback.

The two major callback routines are *UpdateResList* (connected to the Apply callback) and *SelectRes* (connected to the OK callback). *UpdateResList* uses *Find-MatchingFields* to get a list of matching resource field names. The text value is passed as a field of the selection box callback structure. Depending on whether the match was successful, the default button is set to the "OK" button when there are list items to select.

SelectRes tries to find the entered or selected value in the match list. If the user entered a string not present in the list, this will fail. Otherwise the selected field is displayed (changing the class chain also) and the dialog is unmapped.

The *PopupResDialog* procedure, used as an exported interface to show the resource selection dialog, not only pops up the dialog, but also initalizes the list and text field, because the dialog remembers its state when unmapped.

Help Dialog

The help dialog is simply a multi-line text field inside a bulletin board. The value of the text field is filled with a help text by a pop-up callback procedure. There are no buttons in this dialog, because the dialog can simply be closed through the window manager by double-clicking on the upper left button in the window manager decoration.

Chapter 9

Building
New Widgets

When writing larger programs, the features provided by the Motif widgets are often not sufficient. In many cases it is preferable to construct the additional functionality as one or more new widget classes. In this way some advantages are gained.

Constructing new widgets (by "object-oriented" programming) has the following advantages compared with just "plain programming":

- Many instances with different parameters can be created for a widget class.

- A widget class is largely self-contained and thus can be reused for other software projects.

- Widgets can be automatically configured through the resource database, allowing simple external customization.

However, as you can imagine, it is easier to combine existing building blocks than to build new ones. The process is further complicated by the fact that the X Toolkit Intrinsics are programmed in plain C, which is not well-suited for object-oriented programming. A real object-oriented language would have made writing new widget classes much easier.

Fortunately there are other possibilities for implementing new widget functionality, but without the full integration a new widget class provides. One of these ways, namely the convenience widgets, is already used in Motif, while another method is supported by two extendable widget classes in Motif. The three possibilities discussed in this chapter are:

- *Convenience Widgets.* You can create the impression of a specialized widget class by defining a convenience function to create a widget combination with some preset resource fields.

- *Extendable Widgets.* Motif defines two widget classes which have callbacks to define their behaviour and appearance. By defining appropriate callback functions you can imitate a new primitive widget class to a fairly high degree.

- *New Widget Class.* To extend the Motif functionality seamlessly you have to write your own widget class. This is usually necessary if you want to write your own geometry manager, but it would be better to have access to the Motif source.

If you do not need to have multiple instances of a new widget, you can and should use the strategy presented in the example program in the previous chapter. By grouping together component-related code and variables, and by defining appropriate interface procedures, you at least get a level of abstraction where the implementation details are hidden and can be easily changed locally.

9.1 Convenience Widgets

Several different convenience widgets are already present in Motif. Although they are implemented with different widget classes, they share some common structural properties.

Consider the menu bar, for example. The convenience function *XmCreate-Menubar* creates a row-column widget whose *XmNrowColumnType* field is set to *XmMENU_BAR.* The convenience widget "menu bar" is therefore nothing more than a row-column with a preset value combination of some resource fields.

Another example is the pull-down menu pane. It is a combination of two widgets: a menu shell and a row-column. The shell widget is largely invisible to the programmer, because the row-column expects to have a menu shell parent and sets all necessary adjustments. Combining a widget with a shell is also used to create the different kinds of convenience dialogs.

A more complicated case of widget combination involves the scrolled text and scrolled list widgets. A scrolled window is combined with a text or list widget. In contrast to the shell combinations, you often want to set resource fields of the scrolled window directly. Therefore the combination cannot be invisible—the programmer must be aware that two widgets are involved to set resource fields correctly.

Another problem arises when such a combination is used inside the form widget or another constraint manager. The constraint resource fields must be set for the scrolled window, because it is the direct child of the form. Setting constraints for the text or list is ignored, because they are *not* children of the form.

This is especially confusing because the convenience functions used to create widget combinations can return only one of the widget IDs. The ID returned is generally that of the child, because you can easily access the parent of a widget with *XtParent*, but getting the child ID from the parent is nearly impossible. The constraint resource mechanism is a second reason why you have to be aware of the scrolled window involved.

As a result, to set constraint resource fields for a scrolled text, you have to request the *XtParent* after creation and then set the constraint resource fields with *XtSetValues*. Alternatively, you can create the scrolled window and the text separately—which, by "special magic", has the same effect as the convenience function.

The "special magic" resides in the internal initialization routine of the text widget. This routine detects whether the text is the child of a scrolled window. If it is, it performs all necessary settings for its parent and installs appropriate callback connections.

If you wanted to re-implement such a convenience widget independently, you would have to perform all these initializations in the convenience function. The Motif implementors, however, included the possible combinations in the widget code. Therefore, most of the Motif convenience functions are not strictly necessary.

Example: The Step List Widget

As an example, this section presents a convenience widget called *step list*. It consists of four Motif widgets in combination, connected with appropriate call-backs for communication. It even has the capability to get its own outside resources.

The purpose of a step list is similar to an option menu or a radio box: the user may choose a current setting from a list of possible values. In contrast to these other widgets, the step list displays only one value at a time. The user may step through the values using two arrow buttons at the left side of the current value's display. Figure 9.1 shows a step list widget.

The step list needs the least space of the three alternatives that let the user choose from a set of values. It is especially useful if the set of values has some

Figure 9.1: Example of a step list convenience widget.

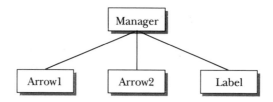

Figure 9.2: Widget tree for step list.

ordering and the user is most likely to select a new value not far from the current one (such as setting a scale factor in discrete steps between 25 and 3200 per cent).

The step list is composed of four different widgets. Two arrow buttons allow the user to switch to the next value in the list in either direction. A label displays an identification of the current value. A drawing area is used as a manager for the collection. The drawing area widget will be explained in Section 9.2 below.

The manager widget in this combination is only used for geometry management. A drawing area was chosen because the form widget (especially in Motif 1.0) cannot fully support the semantics used in the example. Because that may also be the case in one of your applications, the step list illustrates what can be done in a convenience widget in this respect.

The programmer's interface for the step list is simple. The procedure *CreateStepList* is the convenience function to create the step list widget combination. As usual, you can pass an argument list to this procedure. It also takes a callback procedure as an argument to inform the application when the user changes the current value. This callback is passed as a parameter to the creation procedure because there is no way in which a convenience widget can define a new callback to be used with *XtAddCallback*.

Two other procedures, *StepListGetCurrent* and *StepListSetCurrent*, enable the programmer to discover and change the current value. These procedures are necessary because a convenience widget cannot define new resource fields to be used with *XtSetValues* or *XtGetValues*. However, it can define resource fields to be set from the resource database.

Clearly a step list instance needs some permanent private storage, such as the list to choose from, the current value, or the address of the callback procedure. For this purpose a record is allocated for each step list instance on creation, just as instance data are allocated for every widget.

To have it directly accessible, the address of this record is passed to all internal callbacks as *client_data*. It is also stored in the *XmNuserData* resource field of the label, because the label is used as the identifying widget for the whole combination as returned by *CreateStepList*.

The structure for the accompanying record for each step list widget is defined as follows:

```
typedef struct {
    XmStringTable    list;
    int              elements, current;
    Widget           b1, b2, field;
    Dimension        arrow_width;
    XtCallbackProc   call_proc;
    caddr_t          client_data;
} StepRec, *StepRecPtr;
```

The *list* and *elements* fields define the list of possible values, just as in a list widget. One of those elements is designated as the current value. The IDs of the three simple widgets are stored in the record for quick access in callbacks. The record also contains the callback procedure and its client data. The *arrow_width* is used to determine the default geometry of the arrows. It is defined as a geometry resource field and is most often set through the resource database.

Getting Additional Resources

In the previous chapter you have already seen how to obtain values for arbitrary, application-defined resource fields using *XtGetApplicationResources*. These resources appear as additional fields of the application shell and you can specify them as direct attributes of the application's name or class.

You can also get resource values for an arbitrary place in the widget hierarchy using *XtGetSubresources*. These resource values are specified as if they belonged to a subwidget of some widget in the hierarchy. However, this widget is only simulated by the call as far as resource values are concerned.

For the step list widget, *XtGetSubresources* is used to simulate a child of the drawing area manager with a class name "StepList" and with the same name as the label widget. In this way, additional resource values can be set from the resource database separately for every step list in a program.

A resource list definition is required as the primary information concerning which resource fields must be simulated. A resource list has the same structure as the ones used internally in all widget classes:

```
static XtResource item_resources[] = {
    { XmNitems, XmCItems, XmRXmStringTable, sizeof (XmStringTable),
    XtOffset (StepRecPtr, list), XmRImmediate, NULL},
    { XmNitemCount, XmCItemCount, XmRInt, sizeof (int),
    XtOffset (StepRecPtr, elements), XmRImmediate, (caddr_t) 0},
    { XmNarrowWidth, XmCArrowWidth, XmRDimension, sizeof (Dimension),
    XtOffset (StepRecPtr, arrow_width), XmRImmediate, (caddr_t) 16}
};
```

In this case three resource fields are defined. The structure of each entry is as described in Chapter 2. The first three fields for each entry specify the name and class to be used in resource files as well as the type to be used for automatic conversion. You can freely define the first two (but you should use predefined names when they have a suitable meaning). If you need a resource type that is not predefined, you must also provide a conversion procedure.

The size and offset fields are used to identify the memory location where the value is to be stored. The offset calculation macro *XtOffset* needs a pointer to a structure; therefore both *StepRec* and *StepRecPtr* have also been defined.

The last two fields designate a default value to be used when no entry has been found in the resource database. You can either specify an immediate value, as in the example here, or you can use a string or other resource type and have the default value automatically converted. The latter case is demonstrated in the second example, in Section 9.2.

The Step List Creation Procedure

You are now able to understand the first part of the step list creation procedure. First a new record is allocated and the callback information stored. Then the drawing area manager is created. The drawing area supports an *XmNresizeCallback* used for geometry management (more on that later).

```
Widget CreateStepList (parent, name, add_args, num_args, proc, client_data)
        Widget          parent;
        String          name;
        ArgList         add_args;
        Cardinal        num_args;
        XtCallbackProc  proc;
        caddr_t         client_data;
{
        Widget          manager, text, ab1, ab2;
        Arg             args[5];
        StepRec         *rec;
        Dimension          text_height;
        XmFontList      text_font;
        ArgList         merge_args;

        /* init callback record */
        rec = (StepRec*) XtMalloc (sizeof (StepRec));
        rec->current = 1;
        rec->call_proc = proc;
        rec->client_data = client_data;

        /* drawing area as manager */
        XtSetArg (args[0], XmNmarginWidth, 0);
        XtSetArg (args[1], XmNmarginHeight, 0);
```

```
manager = XtCreateManagedWidget ("manager",
                xmDrawingAreaWidgetClass, parent, args, 2);
XtAddCallback (manager, XmNresizeCallback, Resize, rec);
```

The rest of the callback record is either filled with data from the resource database or with default values from the resource list. *XtGetSubresources* simulates a widget with the widget name passed to the creation procedure and the class *STEPPER_CLASS* defined as "StepList".

```
/* initialize the rest of the callback record */
XtGetSubresources (manager, rec, name, STEPPER_CLASS,
                item_resources, XtNumber (item_resources),
                add_args, num_args);
```

In addition, the argument list passed to *CreateStepList* is used to fill the callback record. Usually the programmer sets *XmNitems* and *XmNitemCount* in this argument list, so the record is completely initialized afterwards as far as externally settable fields are concerned.

In the next step the arrow buttons are created, registering their IDs in the callback record. A special callback routine is connected to each arrow button to implement the stepping behaviour. The sensitivity of the two arrow buttons is always adjusted to ensure that a button is insensitive if the last value in that direction has been reached. On creation the sensitivity is accordingly initialized for the first item.

```
/* first scroll button */
XtSetArg (args[0], XmNarrowDirection, XmARROW_UP);
XtSetArg (args[1], XmNwidth, rec->arrow_width);
ab1 = XtCreateManagedWidget ("ab1", xmArrowButtonWidgetClass,
                manager, args, 2);
XtSetSensitive (ab1, False);
XtAddCallback (ab1, XmNactivateCallback, StepUp, rec);
rec->b1 = ab1;

/* second scroll button */
XtSetArg (args[0], XmNarrowDirection, XmARROW_DOWN);
XtSetArg (args[1], XmNwidth, rec->arrow_width);
XtSetArg (args[2], XmNx, rec->arrow_width);
ab2 = XtCreateManagedWidget ("ab2", xmArrowButtonWidgetClass,
                manager, args, 3);
XtSetSensitive (ab2, rec->elements > 1);
XtAddCallback (ab2, XmNactivateCallback, StepDown, rec);
rec->b2 = ab2;
```

The creation of the label field is slightly more complicated. First, the label string is set to the longest item in the list to ensure that the inital size is the maximum needed. To find the longest string, all the strings in the item list must be examined by the function *Longest.*

In proportional fonts, the size of a string does not depend simply on the number of characters. For example, the string "MM" is usually longer than "iii" in a proportional font (as you can see here). Therefore *Longest* needs to know the font, or more exactly, the font list used for the XmStrings. The font list can be found from the label widget, but unfortunately the label does not exist yet.

Therefore the font list that will eventually be used for the label is obtained from the resource database and the argument list. The *GetFontList* procedure uses the same mechanism for obtaining the font list as for obtaining the step list resources.

The second problem is that the argument list passed to *CreateStepList* may also contain arguments for the label, such as spacing. On the other hand some resource fields are determined by the convenience function itself. To handle both these argument lists in one creation step, the argument lists are merged using *XtMergeArgLists.* If a resource field occurs twice in the merged list, the duplicate is not removed, but the last setting takes effect. Therefore the built-in argument list is used as the second parameter to take precedence.

```
/* get the fontlist which will be used in the text display */
text_font = GetFontList (manager, name, "XmDrawnButton");

/* text display (with the longest item) */
XtSetArg (args[0], XmNlabelString,
                Longest (rec->list, rec->elements, text_font));
XtSetArg (args[1], XmNuserData, rec);
XtSetArg (args[2], XmNrecomputeSize, False);
XtSetArg (args[3], XmNx, 2 * rec->arrow_width);
XtSetArg (args[4], XmNpushButtonEnabled, False);

merge_args = XtMergeArgLists (add_args, num_args, args, 5);

text = XtCreateManagedWidget (name, xmDrawnButtonWidgetClass,
                manager, merge_args, num_args + 5);
XtFree (merge_args);
rec->field = text;
```

Just as in the example in the previous chapter a drawn button widget is used to display the current value, because it is able to display a shadow border. The final task of the creation procedure is to align the arrow buttons vertically to the height of the label and to set the label string back to the first item. Because *XmNrecomputeSize* is *False,* setting a shorter label string will not shrink the drawn button.

```
                    /* align text and arrows */
                    XtSetArg (args[0], XmNheight, &text_height);
                    XtGetValues (text, args, 1);
                    XtSetArg (args[0], XmNheight, text_height);
                    XtSetValues (ab1, args, 1);
                    XtSetValues (ab2, args, 1);

                    /* set text to first label */
                    if (rec->elements > 1) {
                            XtSetArg (args[0], XmNlabelString, rec->list[0]);
                            XtSetValues (text, args, 1);
                    }
            }
```

The procedure *GetFontList* is easy to implement. It simply uses an additional structure and a resource list to obtain the same XmFontList value as the label widget will get.

```
    typedef struct {
            XmFontList              fontlist;
    } ResStruct, *ResPtr;


    static XtResource fontlist_resource [] = {
            { XmNfontList, XmCFontList, XmRFontList, sizeof (XmFontList),
            XtOffset (ResPtr, fontlist), XmRString, "fixed"}
    };

    static XmFontList GetFontList (parent, name, class)
            Widget      parent;
            char        *name;
            char        *class;
    {
            ResStruct   res;

            XtGetSubresources (parent, &res, name, class,
                            fontlist_resource, XtNumber (fontlist_resource),
                            NULL, 0);
            return (res.fontlist);
    }
```

Determining the longest item is also not difficult, because you can use the *XmStringWidth* procedure which does the dirty work of summing up the individual character sizes.

```
static XmString Longest (xmlist, no_el, fl)
      XmString          *xmlist;
      int               no_el;
      XmFontList        fl;
{
      int          i, max = 0, maxno = -1, new;
      for (i=0; i<no_el; i++) {
            if (max < (new = XmStringWidth (fl, xmlist[i]))) {
                  max = new; maxno = i;
            }
      }
      if (maxno >= 0)
            return (xmlist[maxno]);
      else
            return NULL;
}
```

Step List Callbacks

There are a number of callbacks connected to the widgets inside the step list. The procedures *StepUp* and *StepDown* handle activation of the two arrows.

If possible they increment or decrement the index of the current item, set the label to this new item, adjust the sensitivity of the arrows if their limits are reached, and activate the registered application callback, if any.

```
static void StepUp (widget, rec, call_data)
      Widget                 widget;
      StepRec                *rec;
      XmAnyCallbackStruct    *call_data;
{
      Arg          args[1];
      int          previous;

      if (rec->current > 1) {
            previous = rec->current;
            rec->current--;
            XtSetArg (args[0], XmNlabelString, rec->list[rec->current-1]);
            XtSetValues (rec->field, args, 1);
            XtSetSensitive (rec->b1, rec->current > 1);
            XtSetSensitive (rec->b2, True);
            CallCallback (rec, call_data->event, previous);
      }
}

static void StepDown (widget, rec, call_data)
      Widget                 widget;
```

```
        StepRec                  *rec;
        XmAnyCallbackStruct  *call_data;
{
        Arg          args[1];
        int          previous;

        if (rec->current < rec->elements) {
                previous = rec->current;
                rec->current++;
                XtSetArg (args[0], XmNlabelString, rec->list[rec->current-1]);
                XtSetValues (rec->field, args, 1);
                XtSetSensitive (rec->b1, True);
                XtSetSensitive (rec->b2, rec->current < rec->elements);
                CallCallback (rec, call_data->event, previous);
        }
}
```

The procedure *CallCallback* finds a suitable callback structure and calls the application-registered routine if a non-*NULL* procedure address was passed on step list creation. The callback structure, together with declarations of exported routines and names of new resource fields, is defined in a separate header file. This header file can also be included in programs using the step list, so that the step list code itself can be compiled into a library.

```
/* StepList.h - header file for stepper widget */

/* new resource names */
#define XmNarrowWidth "arrowWidth"
#define XmCArrowWidth "ArrowWidth"

#define STEPPER_CLASS "StepList"

/* procedures */
Widget CreateStepList ();
void StepListSetCurrent ();
void StepListGetCurrent ();

/* definition of callback structure */

typedef struct {
        int              reason;
        XEvent           *event;
        XmStringTable    list;
        int              elements,
                         current,
                         previous;
} StepListCallbackStruct;
```

The callback structure is modelled on similar structures used in Motif. Even the event record from the arrow button callbacks is passed on.

```
static void CallCallback (rec, event, previous)
      StepRec     *rec;
      XEvent      *event;
      int         previous;
{
      StepListCallbackStruct cb;

      if (rec->call_proc != NULL) {
           cb.reason = XmCR_VALUE_CHANGED;
           cb.event = event;
           cb.list = rec->list;
           cb.elements = rec->elements;
           cb.current = rec->current;
           cb.previous = previous;
           (* rec->call_proc) (rec->field, rec->client_data, &cb);
      }
}
```

Just like the *XmNvalueChangedCallback* of toggle buttons, the step list callback may also be activated when a new current value is set by the program. The event record is *NULL* in this case. Setting a new current item is performed by *StepListSetCurrent.*

```
void StepListSetCurrent (widget, new, call)
      Widget      widget;
      int         new;
      Boolean     call;
{
      StepRec     *rec;
      Arg         args[1];
      int         previous;

      XtSetArg (args[0], XmNuserData, &rec);
      XtGetValues (widget, args, 1);

      if (rec == NULL) return;

      if (new < 1 || new > rec->elements) return;

      previous = rec->current;
      rec->current = new;
      XtSetArg (args[0], XmNlabelString, rec->list[rec->current-1]);
      XtSetValues (rec->field, args, 1);
      XtSetSensitive (rec->b1, rec->current > 1);
```

```
        XtSetSensitive (rec->b2, rec->current < rec->elements);
        if (call) CallCallback (rec->field, NULL, previous);
}
```

Instead of waiting for callbacks your application can also read the current value using *StepListGetCurrent*.

```
void StepListGetCurrent (widget, current_return, label_return)
        Widget      widget;
        int         *current_return;
        XmString    *label_return;
{
        StepRec     *rec;
        Arg         args[1];

        XtSetArg (args[0], XmNuserData, &rec);
        XtGetValues (widget, args, 1);

        *current_return = 0;    /* invalid data */
        if (rec == NULL) return;

        if (rec->current < 1 || rec->current > rec->elements) return;

        *current_return = rec->current;
        *label_return = rec->list[rec->current-1];
}
```

The functionality of the step list widget is now complete. You see that the work is shared between the creation procedure, the internal callbacks, and the exported value-accessing procedures, using a record of common data.

Controlling Geometry Management

A convenience widget usually simulates a primitive widget, disallowing the creation of additional children by the application. Therefore no arbitrary geometry management tasks are required. But even this simplified situation involves several aspects of geometry management:

- The convenience widget must set an appropriate initial size, depending on its own geometry resource fields and the management strategy of its parent.

- If parameters of the widget are changed which affect geometry, requests must be made to acquire the new optimum geometry. Intermittent geometry changes will be neglected in this example because there is nothing like *XtSetValues* for the convenience widget and changes are seldom required "on the fly".

- The convenience widget should react to resize operations of its parent. If it doesn't, an ugly appearance and clipped portions may result that render the widget inoperable.

Setting the initial size is usually the task of the creation procedure. In this case the default size is determined from two sources. The width of the arrow buttons is determined from the simulated resource field *XmNarrowWidth,* and the width of the label field is determined by the longest string. In the first case the width is simply set as a resource field whose default value may be overridden; the second case exploits the fact that, like all label subclasses, the drawn button uses the label string to calculate its initial size, taking into account all necessary spacing resource fields.

As the drawn button also sets its preferred height, the arrow buttons can be adjusted to the same height afterwards.

Both operations depend on the fact that the drawing area, as the parent of the widgets, accepts the initial geometry requests. This is especially important because the children set not only their size but also their position. The x-position is set to multiples of the arrow width so that the widgets exactly touch. The y-position defaults to 0 for all children.

The drawing area not only accepts these geometry requests of its children, but it also adapts its own size to enclose all children exactly. Therefore its width will be exactly the space needed for the two arrows and the preferred width of the label field. Only the *XmNmarginWidth* and *XmNmarginHeight* must be set to 0 because the drawing area tries to enforce a blank margin space around its children by default.

The resource field *XmNrecomputeSize* of the drawn button is set to *False* to prevent resizing when the label is changed during stepping. Otherwise the drawn button would try to reduce its width on shorter items and the drawing area, willingly accepting the change, would also shrink. The desired and actual behaviour is that the size of the label field stays constant except when resized by the step list's parent.

For parent widgets that query their children about their preferred geometry the drawing area always reports its current size as the preferred one. This is a drawback you have to be aware of. If you enclose a step list with some wider widgets in a column, the step list's width will be increased. If the longer items are removed later, the step list will not revert to the optimum size it had at creation, because the drawing area does not know better.

The *XmNresizeCallback* of the drawing area is provided to react to resize operations of the parent. The resize strategy of the step list is simple. If the window is not too small, the arrows remain at a constant width and the label field is resized to fill the remaining space horizontally. If the drawing area is made smaller than three times the initial arrow width, even the arrows are shrunk proportionally to avoid clipping the whole label field.

In the vertical direction the three children are simply clipped if the drawing area is resized smaller than their initial height. Otherwise they are positioned in the middle of the window. Stretching the children vertically is not useful because the stretched arrows would look ugly.

The new geometry settings are performed by the callback procedure *Resize*. First, the new size of the drawing area and the height of the label field are obtained as the basis of the calculations. Then the new geometry resource fields of the children are calculated and set.

Setting the new values initiates geometry requests to confirm with the drawing area that the new values are in fact allowed. This may have the unpleasant effect that the drawing area itself resizes again in response to the request. For example, consider the case where a step list is directly included in a shell window with *XmNallowShellResize* set to *True*.

If the user increases the height of the shell, the drawing area is resized and the *Resize* procedure attempts to move all widgets to a new y-location approximately in the middle of the window. The drawing area accepts that request, but in an attempt to enclose its children exactly resizes itself to approximately half the requested height. This requires a request to the shell, which is granted because of *XmNallowShellResize*. The user will be quite surprised to see the window pop back to half its size when resizing it.

To prevent this effect, the resource field *XmNresizePolicy* of the drawing area is set to *XmRESIZE_NONE*. The drawing area does not then resize itself in response to geometry requests of its children. *XmNresizePolicy* cannot be set at creation because the drawing area would not honour the initial size.

```
static void Resize (widget, rec, call_data)
        Widget                  widget;
        StepRec                 *rec;
        XmAnyCallbackStruct     *call_data;
{
        Arg                     args[3];
        Dimension               width, height, text_height, arrow_width;
        Position                new_y;

        XtSetArg (args[0], XmNwidth, &width);
        XtSetArg (args[1], XmNheight, &height);
        XtGetValues (widget, args, 2);

        if (width < 3 * rec->arrow_width)
                arrow_width = width/3;
        else
                arrow_width = rec->arrow_width;

        XtSetArg (args[0], XmNheight, &text_height);
        XtGetValues (rec->field, args, 1);

        if (height > text_height)
                new_y = (height - text_height)/2;
```

```
        else
                new_y = 0;

        /* stop resizing the drawing area now */
        XtSetArg (args[0], XmNresizePolicy, XmRESIZE_NONE);
        XtSetValues (widget, args, 1);

        /* resize the children */
        XtSetArg (args[0], XmNy, new_y);
        XtSetArg (args[1], XmNwidth, arrow_width);
        XtSetValues (rec->b1, args, 2);

        XtSetArg (args[2], XmNx, arrow_width);
        XtSetValues (rec->b2, args, 3);

        XtSetArg (args[1], XmNwidth, width - 2 * arrow_width);
        XtSetArg (args[2], XmNx, 2 * arrow_width);
        XtSetValues (rec->field, args, 3);
}
```

Except for directly accessing newly-defined resource fields (with *XtGet-Values* or *XtAddCallback* etc.) you can now use the step list widget in your programs like any other convenience widget.

The complete source code for this example, together with a small test program, can be found in Appendix E.

9.2 Using X Primitives

If you want to include more graphical features in your program than simple iconic buttons, you must be prepared to deal with the lower-level X primitives. Because the needs are so diverse among applications in this area, there is no common solution for graphical output in Motif. In the future new widget classes for specific applications may be developed, but for now you must use the Xlib directly.

Xlib programming cannot be covered in any detail in this book. Although you only need a part of the Xlib features to extend Motif applications graphically, you should be prepared to study one of the books listed in Appendix B if you need more than simple variations of the examples in this chapter.

However, this section covers the most important usage of X primitives as far as the user interface is concerned, namely the direct manipulation of iconic objects inside a window. The example implements a window with moveable icons inside, but the mechanism can be applied to create desktop interfaces, directory browsers, rulers for word processing programs with moveable tabulators, and so on.

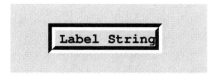

Figure 9.3: Drawn button as a label with default etched shadow.

Extendable Widget Classes

Using X primitives without leaving the Motif framework is enabled by two widget classes whose appearance is completely application-defined. You have encountered both widget classes before, but only in a general sense.

The drawn button widget class is a label subclass with customizable button behaviour (see Figure 9.3). In its default behaviour a drawn button is a label with a shadow. The label behaviour is inherited except for the capability to draw the shadows. The shadow type can be set using *XmNshadowType* (as for the Frame widget).

If the *XmNpushButtonEnabled* resource field is set, the drawn button also acquires the push button behaviour, i.e. the shadows are switched when the button is pressed, and appropriate callbacks are called. Therefore the callbacks *XmNactivateCallback*, *XmNarmCallback*, and *XmNdisarmCallback* are also present.

The primary purpose of the drawn button, however, is to allow the programmer to override the standard appearance of the button face. For this purpose the *XmNexposeCallback* is defined. If there is a procedure connected to it, the normal button face is no longer drawn, except for the shadows. Instead the programmer must paint the interior of the button in the callback procedure, using Xlib routines.

The *XmNexposeCallback* is called whenever an Expose event arrives for the drawn button's window. The Xlib event structure is included in the callback structure, whose address is passed as *call_data*:

```
typedef struct {
        int          reason;
        XEvent       *event;
        Window       window;
} XmDrawnButtonCallbackStruct;
```

You must take care not to overwrite the shadow in the callback routine if you use one (*XmNshadowThickness* not zero), but fortunately the X Window System at least prevents you from inadvertently overwriting other parts of your application area.

XmNshadowType	enum	Type of shadow *XmSHADOW_ETCHED_IN* *XmSHADOW_ETCHED_OUT* *XmSHADOW_IN* *XmSHADOW_OUT*
XmNpushButtonEnabled	Boolean	If push button behaviour
XmNactivateCallback	Callback	When button clicked
XmNarmCallback	Callback	When button goes down
XmNdisarmCallback	Callback	When button goes up
XmNexposeCallback	Callback	For every Expose event
XmNresizeCallback	Callback	When resized through parent

Table 9-1: Drawn button resource fields.

Instead of always inquiring about the current widget size when drawing, you should use the *XmNresizeCallback* to be informed when the size changes. This avoids performance problems because the *XmNexposeCallback* can be called frequently, for instance if other windows on the screen are moved around.

Issues of geometry management have already been discussed in the previous section. Even though you have to manage drawing at the Xlib level, a substantial part of the work is still handled by Motif and the Toolkit Intrinsics.

The drawing area widget is similar to the drawn button, but it is a composite widget and thus has some manager properties instead of the button behaviour. The geometry managing features of the drawing area were exploited in the example in the previous section.

The resource fields *XmNmarginWidth* and *XmNmarginHeight* can be used to ensure a margin around children of the drawing area. All geometry requests which would move a child into this margin will be denied. On the other hand the drawing area tries to enclose all its children with exactly this margin.

The field *XmNresizePolicy* controls how geometry requests of children are handled. The drawing area may refuse all requests that would change its size, it may only grow, or it may adapt to whatever size its children want.

Just like the drawn button, the drawing area provides an *XmNresizeCallback* and an *XmNexposeCallback*. Instead of push button behaviour, the drawing area provides the *XmNinputCallback*, which is called on all keyboard and button

XmNexposeCallback	Callback	For every Expose event
XmNinputCallback	Callback	On keyboard and button events
XmNresizeCallback	Callback	When resized through parent
XmNresizePolicy	enum	How to react to child requests *XmRESIZE_ANY* *XmRESIZE_GROW* *XmRESIZE_NONE*
XmNmarginWidth	short	Margin around children
XmNmarginHeight	short	

Table 9-2: Drawing area resource fields.

events (i.e. KeyPress, KeyRelease, ButtonPress, and ButtonRelease). The drawing area callback structure has the same components as for the drawn button.

Example: Icon Box

The example in this section implements a window with a number of
moveable icons in it. The icons may be used in a program to simulate files in a
directory, an assortment of different applications, or any other application-
specific objects. Depending on your needs, you will certainly modify and extend
this example if you use it in a real program.

Figure 9.4 shows an example of an icon box. A number of advanced techniques are used to give this demonstration a professional look and feel that can
be used for the most sophisticated programs. For example, the icons may overlap one another in their irregular shape. They are automatically equipped with
shadows to make them appear as if they are flying above the ground.

The icons are moveable using the standard dragging technique. An icon is
grabbed by pressing the mouse button while the mouse pointer is over the icon.
The icon then moves with the mouse pointer until the button is released. In the
example the actual icon moves in real-time, without flicker even when crossing
other icons.

The complete source code of this example can be found in Appendix F.
Some parts of it are not repeated in this chapter, either because they do not
introduce anything new, or because they represent standard C programming

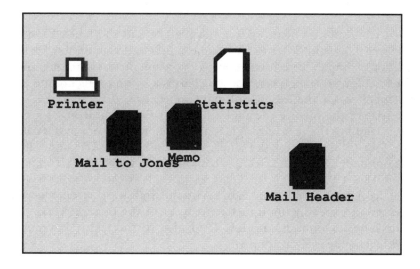

Figure 9.4: Sample icon box window.

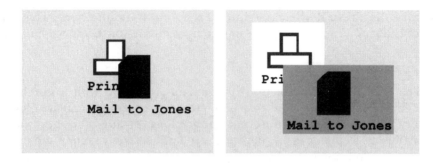

Figure 9.5: Overlapping icons (left) compared with overlapping widgets (right).

without relevance to Motif. In this way the discussion can be kept compact.

It follows from the above description that the icons inside the window cannot be represented by widgets because their shape is irregular. If widgets were used, e.g. a label with a pixmap, the widget background would overlap other icons (see Figure 9.5).

Therefore the icons are implemented using Xlib drawing routines. A drawing area widget is used as the background on which to draw. In a real application the icons would be connected to some application-specific objects; in this example they are simply read from a file.

Just as in the previous example the icon box widget needs a structure with additional data as a basis of the new functionality. The structure associated with the drawing area contains the names, pictures, and positions of all the icons. Because their number is variable, a separate structure is also allocated for each icon.

Each icon consists of two parts: the picture and the label. Both are enclosed by a rectangle in order to have some simple estimate of how far the icon reaches. For example, to test whether two icons might overlap, only the intersection of the four rectangles is checked. This is a common technique to speed up frequent checks at the expense of some unnecessary updating.

The size of the picture rectangle is set globally for all icons as a resource field. The height of the text rectangle is also equal for all icons and is calculated from the font to be used for the labels. The width of the rectangle, however, depends on the length of the string, which may vary widely. The icon geometry is shown in Figure 9.6.

The icon-specific data are stored in the following structure. The coordinates x and y specifiy the upper left corner of the picture rectangle. How much the label extends to the left (and also to the right) is recorded in *string_left*. This value is always positive.

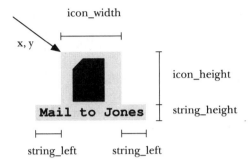

Figure 9.6: Geometry of an icon.

```
typedef struct {
      int          x, y;              /* left upper edge of icon               */
      int          string_left;       /* how much strings extends to left */
      int          higher;            /* next higher stacked icon              */
      XmString     label;             /* label string                         */
      String       class;             /* for selection of pixmap               */
      String       pix_name;          /* name of icon bitmap                   */
      Pixmap       pix;               /* icon pixmap                           */
      String       mask_name;         /* name of mask bitmap                   */
      Pixmap       mask;              /* mask bitmap                           */
      Pixel        foreground;        /* foreground for icon pixmap            */
      Pixel        background;        /* background for icon pixmap            */
} IconRec, *IconRecPtr;
```

The label string is stored as an XmString. The other strings in this structure are used to select the right picture, as each icon may have a different one. A picture is composed of two pixmaps. Each icon may also have different colours, stored in *foreground* and *background*.

In the example, the icon information is simply read from a file. A real application would replace the file by application-specific data. The file contains at least the *label* string and the *class* for each icon. These two strings are then used to simulate a subwidget of the icon box with this name and class to obtain resources for the simulated widget. *XtGetSubresources* is used to obtain values for *pix_name, mask_name, foreground,* and *background.*

In this way you can use the resource mechanism to specify individual pixmaps either for each icon (using its name) or for each class of icons (e.g. for all directories, using its class name). The same applies to the foreground and background colours for these pixmaps.

The input file contains one line for each icon. If you first create such a file by hand, the icons are automatically positioned in a matrix. After having moved some icons, the new positions configuration may be written back to the file. After that, the current positions are included in the file and the icons will occupy their previous positions the next time the file is read.

The structure for the whole icon box is even larger. A number of fields are read in as resources (*pathname, icon_width, icon_height, icon_spacing, columns, fontlist, shadow_off,* and *shadow_color*). The icon records are allocated as one array, whose address is stored in *icons*. The meaning of the other fields will become clear in the discussion.

```
typedef struct {
        String          pathname;       /* pathname where to read info     */
        int             width, height;  /* size of box                     */
        int             icon_width;     /* size of one icon                */
        int             icon_height;
        int             string_height;  /* common height of string box     */
        int             icon_spacing;   /* spacing between icons           */
        int             shadow_off;     /* offset of shadow effect         */
        int             columns;        /* no of icon columns initially    */
        IconRec         *icons;         /* icon array                      */
        int             no_icons;       /* elements in array               */
        int             lowest;         /* index of icon at back of stack  */
        Pixel           shadow_color;   /* color for shadow effect         */
        Pixel           background;     /* pixmap background               */
        Boolean         exposed;        /* to check for first expose       */
        GC              draw_gc;        /* to draw icons into buffer       */
        GC              normal_gc;      /* read-only for other drawing      */
        Pixmap          back;       /* background storage              */
        XmFontList      fontlist;       /* for strings                     */
        int             x_off, y_off;   /* mouse offset when drag-moving   */
        int             moving;         /* index of currently moved icon   */
} BoxRec, *BoxRecPtr;
```

The purpose of the *CreateIconBox* creation procedure is to allocate the records, to create a drawing area widget, to obtain the resources and to connect callbacks to the drawing area. The icon information is read in the procedure *ReadIcons*, which is not described in this chapter.

For all events requiring processing there are appropriate callbacks of the drawing area, except for handling Motion events. Because Motion events may occur very frequently, no widget normally expresses interest in receiving them to avoid wasting bandwidth by sending events which are ignored most of the time.

There are two approaches to handling events that are not normally delivered to the respective widget. You can define your own action procedure for handling the event and then include the action in a translation specification. Using the translation mechanism has the advantage that you can change the triggering event later. For example you can decide in a resource file whether you want the action to be activated by Button1 or Button3. The disadvantage for a convenience widget is that new actions must be registered once only, at program start-up. The icon box widget would have to define an *InitializeIconBox* procedure that the application programmer must not forget to call in his main routine.

The alternative and more basic mechanism is to register an *event handler* procedure directly with the Intrinsics event manager. Using *XtAddEventHandler* you directly specify an event mask containing flags indicating which events the registered procedure shall be called for.

Because it occurs so frequently, a special event mask is provided which indicates that Motion events are only to be sent when one of the mouse buttons is down, i.e. during the dragging process. The icon box creation procedure registers the procedure *HandleMove* using this *ButtonMotionMask*. For other event masks see the appropriate Xlib documentation.

```
Widget CreateIconBox (parent, add_args, num_add_args)
        Widget          parent;
        Arg             add_args[];
        Cardinal        num_add_args;
{
        Widget          area;
        Arg             args[3];
        XmString        face;
        BoxRec          *rec;
        XGCValues            gc_values;
        XmString        dummy;

    rec = (BoxRec *)XtMalloc (sizeof (BoxRec));

    area = XtCreateManagedWidget ("area", xmDrawingAreaWidgetClass,
                        parent, add_args, num_add_args);

    XtGetSubresources (parent, rec, "area", "XmDrawingArea",
                    box_resources, XtNumber (box_resources),
                    add_args, num_add_args);

    dummy = XmStringCreateLtoR ("hg", XmSTRING_DEFAULT_CHARSET);
    rec->string_height = XmStringHeight (rec->fontlist, dummy) + 2;
    XmStringFree (dummy);

    ReadIcons (area, rec);

    XtSetArg (args[0], XmNwidth, rec->width);
    XtSetArg (args[1], XmNheight, rec->height);
    XtSetArg (args[2], XmNuserData, rec);
    XtSetValues (area, args, 3);
```

```
XtAddCallback (area, XmNexposeCallback, ExposeBox, rec);
XtAddCallback (area, XmNinputCallback, HandleButtons, rec);
XtAddEventHandler (area, ButtonMotionMask, False, HandleMove, rec);
XtAddCallback (area, XmNresizeCallback, HandleResize, rec);
XtAddCallback (area, XmNdestroyCallback, DestroyIconBox, rec);

    return area;
}
```

As with most convenience widgets, the main work is done in the callback routines, which will be be discussed in the following section.

Handling the Expose Callback

The most important novelty of the icon box widget compared with the previous example is that the visual appearance is not represented by some appropriately configured primitive widgets but by direct drawing. Widgets handle the drawing in their internal drawing routines. The drawing area widget calls the *XmNexposeCallback* instead.

Drawing window contents in X should always occur in response to Expose events. Expose events are sent whenever a previously occluded area of a window is revealed. Because the X server does not normally save occluded areas, the application must completely redraw this region. The Expose event reports the affected region as a rectangle.

Due to arbitrary overlapping of windows, one operation such as a disappearing window may expose a complex region of a window. Such a situation is shown in Figure 9.7. The complex region is broken down into rectangles by the X server and each rectangle is reported as a separate Expose event.

To avoid leaving garbage on the screen, the X server fills an exposed area with the background of the window (either a solid colour or a pixmap pattern). The drawing procedure may thus assume that the area is already cleared and has a defined background to draw upon.

There are different strategies that deal with how to react to Expose events, differing in performance and the amount of work required.

The simplest strategy is to repaint the whole window. If your drawing procedure does not assume a certain background but only paints over the current contents, as in most cases, it will not matter that some parts of the window were already correct and are drawn unnecessarily.

Because a sequence of Expose events (as described above) is initiated at the same time, it would be wasteful to react to all events in the sequence by repainting the whole window. The events in a sequence are numbered down to zero. Events with non-zero numbers can safely be ignored when the whole window is reconstructed on the last event of the sequence.

Most primitive widgets use this strategy because they are usually small compared with the size of exposed regions. For example it would be slower to

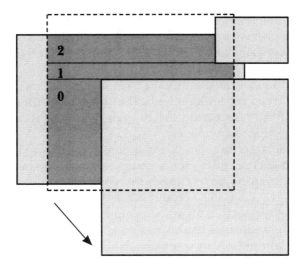

Figure 9.7: Multiple Expose events caused by a single operation.

calculate which characters of a button's label string were affected by an Expose event than to redraw the complete string.

A variation of this strategy tries to reduce the effort for the X server. Drawing in an X window is not only clipped by the window and other over-lapping regions but can also set your own additional clipping region for drawing. For example, when drawing a string you can tell the X server to draw only a certain region, such as the first 10x10 pixels of the label. Although the drawing request includes the whole string, the X server may stop drawing after the first or second character (see Figure 9.8).

The clipping region may be a collection of rectangles and even an arbi-trary set of pixels (this feature will be used again elsewhere in this example).

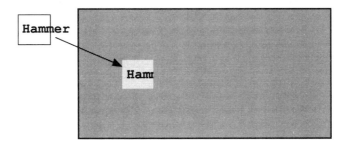

Figure 9.8: Clipping region inside a window.

To exploit the clipping feature an application may collect the rectangles of all the Expose events in a sequence, combine them into a complex region (using some region calculation routines of Xlib), and then use this region as the clipping mask in the final drawing.

If the window contains a number of single objects (such as in this example), the drawing process may be further sped up by checking whether an object to be drawn intersects with the clipping region. If it does not, drawing this object can be skipped completely.

If there are a larger number of small objects in the window you can draw one rectangle on each Expose event, and check each time which objects are affected. Although an object on the border between two rectangles will be drawn twice, this may be faster because it is easier to check whether an object intersects with one rectangle than with a complex region.

A last possibility is used in this example. The complete contents of the window are also kept in a pixmap of the same size as the window, effectively creating invisible background storage. Whenever an Expose event arrives, the exact affected area is copied from the backing pixmap. As this copying takes place in the X server (the pixmap resides in the X server and not in your program), drawing speed may be maximally accelerated by clever hardware and software.

You pay for this performance by increased memory requirements. In this example, however, any other method that ensured smooth movement would be considerably more complicated.

For every Xlib drawing operation you need at least three things: a *display*, a *window*, and a *graphics context*. The display specifies the connection to the X server. You obtain this variable in your standard main routine, but you can ascertain it more conveniently from any widget using *XtDisplay*.

The window of a widget to draw into can be obtained with *XtWindow*. However, the widget must be realized at that time. Therefore the example program waits for the first Expose event before using any operations that require a window.

A graphics context (GC) is a set of parameters residing in the X server which specifies how to perform a drawing operation. A GC resides in the X server to avoid repeatedly sending the parameters over the line with each operation. You must create at least one GC before you can draw.

Creating GCs, and the pixmap to be used as backing storage, is performed in the *InitializeBoxWindow* procedure called on the first Expose event of the drawing area. The first Expose event directly follows the mapping of the window for the first time (after *XtRealize*).

The rest of the callback procedure *ExposeBox* is simple. It copies the rectangle specified in the Expose event from the backing pixmap to the same location in the window, using the procedure *XCopyArea*.

static void ExposeBox (widget, rec, call_data)

```
        Widget                          widget;
        BoxRec                          *rec;
        XmDrawingAreaCallbackStruct     *call_data;
{
        XEvent      *ev = call_data->event;

        if (ev == NULL) return;

        /* create back pixmap if first time */
        if (!rec->exposed)
                InitializeBoxWindow (widget, rec);

        /* copy back to front */
        XCopyArea (XtDisplay (widget), rec->back, XtWindow (widget),
                        rec->normal_gc,
                        ev->xexpose.x, ev->xexpose.y,
                        ev->xexpose.width, ev->xexpose.height,
                        ev->xexpose.x, ev->xexpose.y);
}
```

One further word of explanation: the *XEvent* structure for the event record returned by Xlib and the Motif callbacks and event handlers is a union of different structures, one for each set of events with different attributes. Attributes of an Expose event are accessed under the prefix *ev->xexpose*, while button events use *ev->xbutton* and motion events *ev->xmotion*.

The type of event can be obtained with *ev->type*. Depending on this type you have to use a different prefix for the rest of the structure. The above example relies on the fact that the *XmNexposeCallback* is only called on Expose events (and maybe *NULL* events).

Graphics Contexts

Although X only provides a small number of graphic primitives, these primitives take a large number of parameters. To avoid sending these parameters over the net with each operation, they are bundled into graphics contexts (GCs). GCs reside in the X server just like windows and pixmaps.

Your application may create multiple GCs, each with a different set of parameters. For each drawing primitive you specify which GC to use. You have to provide at least one GC, whose fields you can change between primitives.

Table 9-3 shows all the fields of a GC. Normally you can leave most of them to their default values, and not every operation uses every field of a GC. A full discussion of all the fields, their possible values, and their effect on the drawing operations is beyond the scope of this book.

The fields changed most often are *foreground*, *background*, and *font*. The *function* field determines how the drawn bits are combined with the existing

function	GCFunction	Logical operation to combine bits
plane_mask	GCPlaneMask	Which planes are affected
foreground	GCForeground	Foreground pixel value
background	GCBackground	Background pixel value
line_width	GCLineWidth	Line width in pixels
line_style	GCLineStyle	Line style *LineSolid* *LineOnOffDash* *LineDoubleDash*
cap_style	GCCapStyle	How end points of a path are drawn *CapNotLast* *CapButt* *CapRound* *CapProjecting*
join_style	GCJoinStyle	How lines are joined *JoinMiter* *JoinRound* *JoinBevel*
fill_style	GCFillStyle	How to fill region *FillSolid* *FillTiled* *FillStippled* *FillOpaqueStippled*
fill_rule	GCFillRule	How arbitrary paths are filled *EvenOddRule* *WindingRule*
arc_mode	GCArcMode	How arcs are filled *ArcChord* *ArcPieSlice*
tile	GCTile	Tile pixmap to repeat in drawing
stipple	GCStipple	1bit pixmap for stippling
ts_x_origin	GCTileStipXOrigin	Offset for tile or stipple
ts_y_origin	GCTileStipYOrigin	
font	GCFont	Font ID for text operations
subwindow_mode	GCSubwindowMode	Whether draw over children *ClipByChildren* *IncludeInferiors*
graphics_exposures	GCGraphicsExposures	If GraphicsExposure events are generated
clip_x_origin	GCClipXOrigin	Offset for clipping
clip_y_origin	GCClipYOrigin	
clip_mask	GCClipMask	Bitmap to use for clipping
dash_offset	GCDashOffset	Dash information
dashes	GCDashList	

Table 9-3: Fields of a graphics context.

bits. These *raster operations* are most useful on monochrome screens. For portability you should leave this field to the default value *GXcopy* if possible.

You can create a GC by filling a *XGCValues* structure with the desired values and then call *XCreateGC*. The *XGCValues* structure contains the fields shown in Table 9-3. In the second column of this table a mask bit constant is defined for each field. A logical "or" of the masks for all fields you want to change must be passed to *XCreateGC* to inform the procedure which fields in the structure are valid and which may be uninitialized.

Fields not specified in this mask are ignored in the structure and are set to their default value in the created GC.

The GC you have created is your own, and just as you can freely draw into your windows you can also freely change the fields in the GC whenever you want. If you do not require this ability you can use a similar procedure called *XtGetGC*, which returns a GC that is possibly shared between widgets and thus may not be changed.

The icon box widget needs two GCs: one writable and one read-only. The writable GC is used to draw the icons because each icon may have a different colour. Consequently, the foreground and background colours of this GC are always changed before drawing. The read-only GC is used to draw the strings, which all have the same font and colour.

```
static void CreateGCs (widget, rec)
        Widget          widget;
        BoxRec          *rec;
{
        Arg             args[2];
        Pixel           window_foreground;
        XGCValues       gc_values;

        /* get values from drawing area */
        XtSetArg (args[0], XmNbackground, &rec->background);
        XtSetArg (args[1], XmNforeground, &window_foreground);
        XtGetValues (widget, args, 2);

        /* create writable GC */
        gc_values.foreground = window_foreground;
        gc_values.background = rec->background;
        gc_values.graphics_exposures = False;
        rec->draw_gc = XCreateGC (XtDisplay (widget), XtWindow (widget),
                GCForeground | GCBackground | GCGraphicsExposures,
                &gc_values);

        /* get shareable GC, font is overridden by font_list when drawing */
        gc_values.font = XLoadFont (XtDisplay (widget), "fixed");;
        rec->normal_gc = XtGetGC (widget,
                GCForeground | GCBackground | GCFont | GCGraphicsExposures,
                &gc_values);
}
```

You have to specify a window when creating a GC (*XtGetGC* does this implicitly). This does not mean that the GC can only be used in that window. You can use the GC with any window as the destination, provided the window has the same depth and is on the same screen (depth is explained below).

Initial values for the foreground and background colours are taken from the drawing area. Both GCs set the *graphics_exposures* flag to *False*, specifying that no GraphicsExposure events shall be generated. GraphicsExposure events are used to signal some special cases during *XCopyArea*, but are not used in the example.

A fundamental design decision for every X program is how many GCs to use. Every GC occupies storage in the X server. Therefore the procedure *XtGetGC* tries to share GCs with equal attribute values. Often a number of widgets in a program have the same colour attributes and the probability is high that they can use the same GCs.

On the other hand, frequently changing fields in a GC will affect performance. In this situation it may be better to have a GC for each different combination of attributes.

Most often a compromise between the extremes is needed. In the example program it would be wasteful to use a separate GC for every icon, therefore a single changeable GC is created for drawing all icons.

The Xlib defines different procedures for changing fields in a GC. The general procedure is *XChangeGC*, using a *XGCValues* structure and a mask of desired fields as parameters. It is most useful if you must change a large number of fields at once. For most fields there also exists a single procedure *XSet...* which changes only one field. Both ways are nearly equivalent, however, because Xlib collects a number of consecutive single-field changes into one multi-field change request to the X server.

Pixmaps and Bitmaps

You have already encountered pixmaps as a means of providing iconic labels. But not only can you display a pixmap, you can also draw into it as if it was a window. The only difference is that you cannot directly see the contents of the pixmap on the screen.

Therefore pixmaps and windows are both called *drawables*. The icon box uses a pixmap to draw its image into and then uses this storage to update the window's contents whenever necessary.

Pixmaps can have different depths, depending on the number of bits stored for each pixel. On colour screens 8 bits are most often used to represent one pixel (i.e. 256 different values = 256 simultaneous colours). On a monochrome screen the depth is always 1. Pixmaps with the depth 1 are also called bitmaps because there is exactly one bit per pixel.

Usually all the windows on a screen have the same depth. However, a bitmap can even be created on a colour screen. The contents of the bitmap cannot be copied directly to a window with *XCopyArea*, but there are other ways to use the bitmap. Because of this depth mismatch, a number of programming errors may be undetected on a monochrome machine which will make the program fail on a colour display.

The icon box widget uses three different ways of creating pixmaps. Two ways use a bitmap file specified through the resource mechanism to initialize the contents of the pixmap; the third creates an "empty" pixmap and draws its contents in the application.

When the record for one icon is initialized, the names of two bitmap files are obtained using the resource mechanism. Bitmap files are used because there is currently no standard way to store general pixmaps. A bitmap file can be created using the *bitmap* program. The first bitmap file will be used to initialize a pixmap of the icon's symbol; the other one will be read into a bitmap to specify the shape of the icon. Therefore they must be handled differently.

To obtain a pixmap from a bitmap file you can use the procedure *XmGetPixmap*. You can either pass the full pathname of the file, or the file can be searched in a path specified by the environment variable *XBMLANGPATH*.

To create a pixmap from this file, you also have to supply a foreground and a background colour. Remember that a bitmap has only 1 bit per pixel ("on" or "off"). The "on" pixels will then be replaced by the foreground colour and the "off" pixels by the background colour. *XmGetPixmap* reuses the actual pixmap if it is needed again in the same colours.

```
/* get cached pixmap from Motif */
icon->pix = XmGetPixmap (XDefaultScreenOfDisplay (XtDisplay (widget)),
              icon->pix_name, icon->foreground, icon->background);
```

The Motif widgets obtain their pixmaps in the same way. They provide a resource converter which calls *XmGetPixmap*. None of the predefined converters can be used for the icon box, however, because the predefined converters get their colours from some widget. Instead of writing a new converter, the icon box takes the file names directly from the resource database and converts them before use.

If the bitmap file cannot be found, *XmGetPixmap* returns the constant value *XmUNSPECIFIED_PIXMAP*. This value cannot be used as a pixmap and must be checked before the pixmap is used.

XmGetPixmap always creates a pixmap with the depth taken from the default screen, i.e. the default depth of windows on this screen. All windows of Motif widgets will have this depth. The second pixmap, however, will really be used as a bitmap, therefore it cannot be created using this routine.

Instead the procedure *XReadBitmapFile* creates a bitmap (depth = 1) from the file whose name is supplied. The file must be in the current directory or be specified using the full path, because *XReadBitmapFile* does not search along the *XBMLANGPATH*.

XReadBitmapFile uses an arbitrary window to indicate the screen on which the bitmap will be used. In the example, the window of the widget cannot be used, because the widget is not yet realized when the icon information is

initialized. The default root window of the display, indicating the default
screen, is used instead.

   XReadBitmapFile also does not cache the bitmap, so the array of previously
initialized icons is searched to determine whether the same file has already
been used.

```
/* mask must be bitmap, so get and cache it ourselves */
for (i = 0; i < index; i++ )
        if (strcmp (rec->icons[i].mask_name, icon->mask_name) == 0) {
                icon->mask = rec->icons[i].mask;
                break;
        }
if (i == index)       /* not found */
        if (XReadBitmapFile (XtDisplay (widget),
                             XDefaultRootWindow (XtDisplay (widget)),
                             icon->mask_name, &dummy, &dummy,
                             &icon->mask,
                             &dummy, &dummy) != BitmapSuccess)
                icon->mask = None;
```

   When no file is found, the bitmap is set to the value *None*, which is a valid
pixmap specification in some cases.

   Both procedures mentioned above are a sort of higher-level function,
because they read in the file contents, create a pixmap, and then transport the
contents into the pixmap. Both use the lower-level procedure *XCreatePixmap* internally.

   XCreatePixmap only allocates storage inside the X server and returns the
pixmap as an identification of this area. You must specify width, height, and
depth of the pixmap to be created (in addition to a window indicating the
screen).

   In contrast to a window, a pixmap has no defined background, so the contents of the pixmap are totally undefined after creation. Before drawing into it,
you should first set the background to a defined value—usually with *XFill-
Rectangle*, which fills a rectangle with the foreground colour specified in the GC.

   The procedure *NewBackPixmap* creates a pixmap of the same size and
depth as the icon box window and then draws all icon images into it. It is called
on the first Expose event and whenever the window changes size.

```
static void NewBackPixmap (widget, rec)
        Widget          widget;
        BoxRec          *rec;
{
        Arg             args[1];
        Cardinal        depth;
        int             i;
        XtSetArg (args[0], XmNdepth, &depth);
```

```
    XtGetValues (widget, args, 1);

    /* create backing pixmap */
    rec->back = XCreatePixmap (XtDisplay (widget), XtWindow (widget),
                                    rec->width, rec->height, depth);

    /* initialize pixmap contents */
    XSetForeground (XtDisplay (widget), rec->draw_gc, rec->background);
    XFillRectangle (XtDisplay (widget), rec->back, rec->draw_gc,
                        0, 0, rec->width, rec->height);
    for (i = 0; i < rec->no_icons; i++)
            RedrawIcon (widget, rec, i);
}
```

Icon Box Drawing

Individual icons are drawn using the procedure *RedrawIcon*. This procedure may assume that either the background to draw on has already been cleared or the icon draws over its identical previous image.

Drawing icons is complicated by the fact that icons may overlap and have irregular shapes. Therefore the surroundings of an icon must not be drawn, in order to avoid overwriting underlying icons. The bitmaps drawn with the *bitmap* program are always rectangular. To describe the outline and interior of an icon, a second pixmap is used as a shape mask (see Figure 9.9).

The shape mask exploits the feature that an arbitrary bitmap may be set as the clipping region in a GC. The effect is that only the bits which are set in this mask will really be drawn; the previous contents are untouched where a mask bit is off. Before drawing an icon, its shape is set as the clip mask of the GC and the contents of the icon pixmap are then simply copied. Although the affected area of the copy operation is specified as a rectangle, only the pixels contained in the shape mask are set.

Because of the shape mask, the background colour of an icon need not be the same as the background of the window. Without a shape mask an icon with a different background would stand out as a rectangle, losing most of the

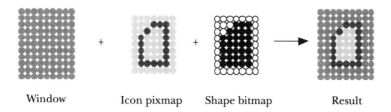

Window   Icon pixmap   Shape bitmap   Result

Figure 9.9: Shape bitmask of an icon used to constrain the icon image in the window.

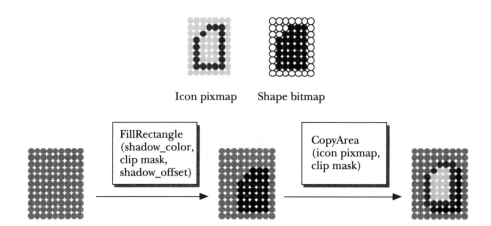

Figure 9.10: Drawing an icon.

aesthetic appeal.

Because the clip mask is smaller than the backing pixmap the icon is drawn in, the GC contains an offset field specifying where the clip mask is to be positioned in the destination drawable. The offset must be set for each icon and is equal to the icon's position, provided the icon and shape bitmaps of one icon have the same size.

The shape mask is also used to draw a shadow behind an icon. For this purpose the clipping offset is slightly increased in both directions, using the *shadow_off* field obtained from the resource database. The clipping area is then filled with the *shadow_color* using *XFillRectangle* (note that *XFillRectangle* is more general than its name implies: it really fills an arbitrary region that is set as the clipping region).

The icon is drawn over its shadow, leaving exactly the right parts of the shadow visible. The whole drawing process is illustrated in Figure 9.10.

The code for *RedrawIcon* looks simpler than the process is. *RedrawIcon* uses a number of single-field changes to the writable *draw_gc*. It also checks whether the icon pixmap has been successfully converted. The mask bitmap need not be checked because it will be *None* in this case. A *None* clipping region switches clipping off, and the mask and shadow simply appear as rectangles.

```
static void RedrawIcon (widget, rec, index)
        Widget      widget;
        BoxRec      *rec;
        int         index;
{
        IconRec     *icon = &rec->icons[index];

        /* set clip mask in gc */
```

```
        XSetClipMask (XtDisplay (widget), rec->draw_gc, icon->mask);

        /* fill shadow */
        XSetClipOrigin (XtDisplay (widget), rec->draw_gc,
                        icon->x + rec->shadow_off, icon->y + rec->shadow_off);
        XSetForeground (XtDisplay (widget), rec->draw_gc, rec->shadow_color);
        XFillRectangle (XtDisplay (widget), rec->back, rec->draw_gc,
                        icon->x + rec->shadow_off, icon->y + rec->shadow_off,
                        rec->icon_width, rec->icon_height);

        /* draw icon */
        XSetClipOrigin (XtDisplay (widget), rec->draw_gc, icon->x, icon->y);
        if (icon->pix != XmUNSPECIFIED_PIXMAP)
             XCopyArea (XtDisplay (widget), icon->pix, rec->back,
                        rec->draw_gc, 0, 0, rec->icon_width, rec->icon_height,
                        icon->x, icon->y);

        /* draw string */
        XmStringDraw (XtDisplay (widget), rec->back,
                      rec->fontlist, icon->label, rec->normal_gc,
                      icon->x - icon->string_left, icon->y + rec->icon_height + 1,
                      rec->icon_width + 2 * icon->string_left,
                      XmALIGNMENT_CENTER,
                      XmSTRING_DIRECTION_L_TO_R,
                      NULL);
}
```

The label is drawn using *XmStringDraw*, the drawing procedure to use for XmStrings. *XmStringDraw* needs a starting position and a width, and allows a shorter text to be centred or otherwise aligned in a larger rectangle. The alignment feature is used by the icon box when a label is shorter than the icon width, because *string_left* is always positive.

XmStringDraw only draws the foreground of the text, i.e. the background shines through between the character strokes. *XmStringDrawImage*, a similar procedure, also paints the background pixels, effectively surrounding the text with a background rectangle.

Other X Graphic Primitives

Before the description of the icon box widget is continued, a number of other X graphic primitives are to be briefly mentioned. Describing these operations in detail is beyond the scope of this book. However, the list will give you a general impression of what is available.

The primitives used to implement the icon box are mostly pixel-oriented. The procedure *XCopyArea* has a cousin *XCopyPlane* which only copies one bit plane into an arbitrary drawable. To erase a window with its defined background you can use *XClearArea* or *XClearWindow*. They are often used to force a redisplay when the picture changes, because erasing the area may generate an Expose event that later triggers the normal drawing procedure to restore the area with the new contents.

Another set of procedures is used for line-oriented drawing. *XDrawPoint* and *XDrawLine* also exist in versions that draw multiple points and lines to save protocol traffic. *XDrawRectangle* and *XDrawArc* draw simple geometric figures. Their axes must be parallel to the coordinate axes; they may not be rotated about arbitrary angles. Rectangles, arcs and polygons can also be filled using the procedures *XFillRectangle*, *XFillArc*, or *XFillPolygon*.

A final set of routines exists for text output. *XDrawString* and *XDraw-ImageString* are comparable to *XmStringDraw* and *XmStringDrawImage*, except that they operate on normal C strings. In X a string must always be drawn in a specific font that defines not only the appearance of the characters but also the size. The characters of a font are stored in pixel format and thus cannot be scaled or rotated.

Direct Manipulation

One of the challenges of graphical user interfaces is to provide objects that the user can manipulate directly. Direct manipulation objects change their appearance not only through commands, but mainly through a process that simulates grabbing and manipulating an object by hand.

In X the mouse is used for direct manipulation. One example is the slider of the Motif scroll bar which can be moved by dragging with the mouse and not only through repeatedly pressing the cursor keys. The illusion of direct manipulation is created by immediate feedback from each small mouse movement.

You have probably experienced situations yourself where the slider is lagging behind the mouse pointer position. When this happens frequently, many people unconsciously compensate for the delay by "dragging harder", as if the delay was caused by a sticky mouse. This example demonstrates that instant feedback is very important for direct manipulation.

Surprisingly, nearly all direct manipulation operations rely on the same simple basic mechanism. The operation starts when a mouse button is pressed with the pointer over some object or a certain part of it. The pointer location determines what kind of process is started. While the button is down, the manipulated object responds to mouse movements by continuously changing one of its parameters, giving visual feedback of what the new value looks like. The process stops when the mouse button is released.

The sequence described above can be used to move objects (like the scroll bar slider), to resize objects (when dragging some sort of handle, like the sash in a paned window), to rotate objects, to draw new objects (between the point first clicked and the current pointer position), and much more.

The first pointer position where the mouse button was pressed plays an important role in the process. First, it determines what operation is started. For example, consider a graphical editor. Depending on whether you click into the middle of the object or in one of the small handles, the object is either moved or resized. Second, the difference between the starting point and the current pointer position is most often the manipulated parameter, for example, for determining how much the object shall be moved.

Frequently the manipulated parameter has only one dimension (for instance a rotation angle), whereas the mouse movement has two. The dependency between the pointer position and the parameter can in this case be described by *constraints* on the feedback. The pointer position is appropriately manipulated before being passed to the feedback routine.

For example, in a scroll bar only one direction of the pointer motion is used to move the slider because the slider is constrained to move in only this direction. A constraint procedure could achieve this effect by simply setting one of the pointer coordinates to its initial value. In this way the feedback procedure need not even be aware of the constraint.

The constraint step can also be used to check for boundary conditions, such as the scroll bar reaching its end position or a moveable icon touching the window borders. It can simply set the coordinate to its maximum value if the real pointer position exceeds the maximum value.

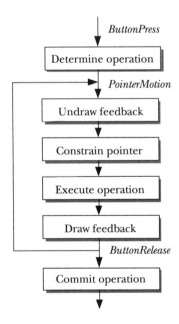

Figure 9.11: Direct manipulation process.

Please note that the constraint procedure only constrains the *internally* used coordinates. The real pointer position should not be manipulated by a program.

The action sequence of the process underlying most direct manipulation operations is illustrated in Figure 9.11.

Because instant feedback is so important to the process, the feedback is often simulated. For example, a moving object must be redisplayed whenever the mouse pointer moves a small number of pixels. Redisplay may be an expensive operation, depending on the number of other objects in the neigh-bourhood, the size of the underlying data structure and the complexity of one object.

To avoid lagging behind the mouse pointer, only a rough indicator such as the outline of the object is really manipulated to give an approximation of the final outcome. In general, using an outline is always better than annoying the user with delays. But as the icon box example demonstrates, it is not too difficult to achieve real feedback with acceptable performance on the X Window System.

When feedback is only simulated, the last step of the direct manipulation process finally performs the parameter change (such as moving the object). With real feedback the state has changed continuously and will already be correct.

On monochrome screens a simple tactic for simulated feedback is to draw an outline using the *GXxor* function in a GC. A property of the "exclusive-or" logical function is that applying it twice will yield the original value. When the pointer moves, the feedback is drawn again at the old position and the previous contents of the window are automatically restored. The outline is then drawn in the new position.

Drawing with "xor" is very fast on monochrome screens, but may not work as intended on colour screens. On a colour screen the "xor" operation trans-forms a pixel value into the value of another colour, more specifically into a colour whose number in the colour map is complementary to its previous number. It does not yield a complementary, or otherwise useful colour, except when the colour map is explicitly set up for this process.

Selecting Icons

The first step in the direct manipulation process after a mouse button has been pressed is to determine which operation to perform. In the case of the icon box widget, the icon to be moved must be determined. For windows and widgets the X server normally determines which window will receive the button-press event.

Because the icons are irregularly shaped, the icon box must itself deter-mine which icon was hit. A correct decision would involve the mask bitmap of an icon and the exact shape of the label text. Because such a check is potentially expensive, applications usually use a set of rectangles instead of the real shape.

Owing to this quick but inaccurate check, even points outside the shape will be considered as belonging to the icon. If these additional points are not too far away, the user will not be confused.

In case of the icon box the two rectangles enclosing the icon and the label are chosen as a basis for hit detection. The procedure *PointInIcon* tests whether a point lies inside one of these two rectangles.

```
Boolean PointInIcon (x, y, icon, w, h, sh)
        int         x;
        int         y;
        IconRec     *icon;
        int         w;
        int         h;
        int         sh;
{
        /* is in icon part ? */
        if (x >= icon->x && x <= icon->x + w &&
                        y >= icon->y && y <= icon->y + h)
                return True;

        /* is in label part ? */
        if (x >= icon->x - icon->string_left &&
                        x <= icon->x + w + icon->string_left &&
                        y >= icon->y + h &&
                        y <= icon->y + h + sh)
                return True;
        /* else false */
        return False;

}
```

The procedure *Hit* calls this test for all icons in the window. Because icons may overlap, there may be more than one icon hit. There must be some way to resolve which icon was meant. A priority is introduced and visually represented by a stacking order among the icons.

An icon stores a reference to the icon with the next-higher priority in the field *higher*. The lowest icon in the ordering is stored in *lowest* in the icon box record. Checking all icons in this order ensures that the last icon to be checked successfully is the one with the highest priority.

```
static int Hit (rec, x, y)
        BoxRec      *rec;
        int         x, y;
{
        int         i, found = -1;
```

```
i = rec->lowest;
do {
        if (PointInIcon (x, y, &rec->icons[i],
                               rec->icon_width, rec->icon_height,
                               rec->string_height))
                found = i;
        i = rec->icons[i].higher;
}
while (i >= 0);
return found;
}
```

The stacking order is changed when an icon is hit. The affected icon is moved to the top of the stack. The reference links must be reordered and the region around the icon must be redrawn to show the icon on top.

```
static void SetOnTop (widget, rec)
        Widget      widget;
        BoxRec      *rec;
{
        int         topindex = rec->moving;
        int         i;
        int         search, previous;

        /* search predecessor */
        for (i = 0; i < rec->no_icons; i++)
                if (rec->icons[i].higher == topindex)
                        previous = i;
                else if (rec->icons[i].higher == -1)
                        rec->icons[i].higher = topindex;
        if (rec->lowest == topindex)
                rec->lowest = rec->icons[topindex].higher;
        else
                rec->icons[previous].higher = rec->icons[topindex].higher;
        rec->icons[topindex].higher = -1;

        /* redraw on top */
        RedrawRegion (widget, rec,
                                rec->icons[topindex].x - rec->icons[topindex].string_left,
                                rec->icons[topindex].y,
                                rec->icon_width + 2 * rec->icons[topindex].string_left,
                                rec->icon_height + rec->string_height);
}
```

The procedure *RedrawRegion*, shown below, redraws a rectangular region, taking into account the stacking order. The icons are drawn from lowest to highest priority, automatically putting icons with higher priority on top of the others.

The procedure *HandleButtons*, connected to the *XmNinputCallback*, starts the direct manipulation process. First, it checks whether it is called for a Button-Press event. Then the affected icon is calculated. If there is an affected icon, the position of the event is recorded as the starting position of the movement process as its offset relative to the icon's origin. Finally the icon is moved to the top.

```
static void HandleButtons (widget, rec, call_data)
        Widget                          widget;
        BoxRec                          *rec;
        XmDrawingAreaCallbackStruct     *call_data;
{
        XEvent    *ev = call_data->event;

        /* activate icon on button press */
        if (ev->xany.type == ButtonPress) {
                rec->moving = Hit (rec, ev->xbutton.x, ev->xbutton.y);
                if (rec->moving < 0) return;
                rec->x_off = ev->xbutton.x - rec->icons[rec->moving].x;
                rec->y_off = ev->xbutton.y - rec->icons[rec->moving].y;
                SetOnTop (widget, rec);
        }
}
```

The rest of the work to move the icon is performed by the event handler for Motion events.

Moving Icons

The key observation for the efficient handling of feedback during the move is that the region affected by a single step is only slightly larger than one icon, because the steps are usually rather small. The affected region is the bounding rectangle of the icon in the old and the new positions, as shown in Figure 9.12. The bounding region is calculated by the *FindInvalidRect* procedure, given the new icon position after the step and the current position contained in the icon box record.

```
static void FindInvalidRect (rec, new_x, new_y, x, y, width, height)
        BoxRec    *rec;
        int       new_x;
        int       new_y;
        int       *x;
        int       *y;
        int       *width;
        int       *height;
```

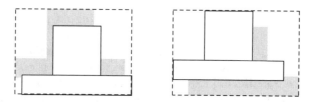

Figure 9.12: Affected regions for positive and negative moves.

```
{
        int          xmove, ymove;
        IconRec      *icon = &rec->icons[rec->moving];

        /* check movement in X direction */
        xmove = new_x - icon->x;
        if (xmove > 0) {
                *x = icon->x - icon->string_left;
                *width = rec->icon_width + xmove + 2 * icon->string_left;
        } else {
                *x = icon->x + xmove - icon->string_left;
                *width = rec->icon_width - xmove + 2 * icon->string_left;
        }

        /* check movement in Y direction */
        ymove = new_y - icon->y;
        if (ymove > 0) {
                *y = icon->y;
                *height = rec->icon_height + rec->string_height + ymove;
        } else {
                *y = icon->y + ymove;
                *height = rec->icon_height + rec->string_height - ymove;
        }
}
```

Redrawing the affected region is only slightly more work than redrawing one icon. Before the affected region can be calculated, the *HandleMove* procedure first constrains the icon position as described above to prevent an icon moving out of the window (the icon would not move out of the window but would disappear because it is clipped).

```
static void HandleMove (widget, rec, ev)
        Widget       widget;
        BoxRec       *rec;
        XEvent       *ev;
```

```
{
    int        new_x, new_y;
    int        x, y, width, height;

    if (rec->moving < 0) return;

    /* constrain motion */
    new_x = ev->xmotion.x - rec->x_off;
    if (new_x < 0)
        new_x = 0;
    if (new_x > rec->width - rec->icon_width)
        new_x = rec->width - rec->icon_width;

    new_y = ev->xmotion.y - rec->y_off;
    if (new_y < 0)
        new_y = 0;
    if (new_y > rec->height - rec->icon_height - rec->string_height)
        new_y = rec->height - rec->icon_height - rec->string_height;

    /* find affected region */
    FindInvalidRect (rec, new_x, new_y, &x, &y, &width, &height);

    /* set new position... */
    rec->icons[rec->moving].x = new_x;
    rec->icons[rec->moving].y = new_y;

    /* ...and redraw region */
    RedrawRegion (widget, rec, x, y, width, height);
}
```

The workhorse in this operation is the procedure *RedrawRegion*. It is optimized to redraw only those icons that are affected by this region (usually only a few).

First, the region is cleared in the back pixmap by filling it with the window's background colour (the clip mask in the *draw_gc* remaining from the last icon drawing must be switched off).

Then all icons are checked in their stacking order to determine whether they intersect with this region, and they are redrawn if they do. The complete icon is redrawn, even the parts outside the affected region, because there is only one clip mask in the GC. If the clip mask had not been used for icon drawing, it could be set to the affected region.

A simple but inaccurate check is used for intersection, using the whole bounding box of the icon, but only a few icons are really drawn whereas all must checked for intersection. Therefore a more accurate test would be slower than redrawing one or two icons unnecessarily.

```
static void RedrawRegion (widget, rec, x, y, width, height)
        Widget      widget;
        BoxRec      *rec;
        int         x, y,
                    width, height;
{
        int         i;

        /* erase invalid rectangle in back pixmap */
        XSetForeground (XtDisplay (widget), rec->draw_gc, rec->background);
        XSetClipMask (XtDisplay (widget), rec->draw_gc, None);
        XFillRectangle (XtDisplay (widget), rec->back, rec->draw_gc,
                        x, y, width, height);

        /* redraw affected icons to back pixmap */
        i = rec->lowest;
        do {
                if (Intersect (x, y, width, height,
                                rec->icons[i].x - rec->icons[i].string_left,
                                rec->icons[i].y,
                                rec->icon_width + 2 * rec->icons[i].string_left,
                                rec->icon_height + rec->string_height))
                        RedrawIcon (widget, rec, i);
                i = rec->icons[i].higher; }
        while (i >= 0);
```

For programs with a larger number of objects you can easily improve the performance by additionally ordering all objects according to their location, so that not all of them need be checked.

Numerous other optimizations are possible (and sometimes necessary) for more specialized applications. This is one of the reasons why a general solution to drawing inside a widget has not appeared to date. You can now imagine what kind of decisions designers of spreadsheets, business graphics packages, and CAD systems face.

Destroying the Icon Box

When the work is done, the working place must be cleaned and all tools restored to their proper locations. All widgets have an *XmNdestroyCallback* for this purpose which will be called when a widget is no longer needed but the program continues to run (when a program exits, all resources in the X server and the program are automatically freed).

There are a number of resources that the icon box widget has allocated which must be freed in this situation. Storage allocated with *XtMalloc* should be freed with *XtFree*. Use *XmStringFree* for XmStrings and *XmFontListFree* for font lists. Resources in the X server should also be freed. Use *XFreePixmap* for pixmaps (if not obtained through *XmGetPixmap*). *XFreeGC* frees a GC and *XtRelease-GC* frees a shared GC.

The icon box saves its current icon positions in a file before being destroyed. The procedure to save this information is also available as an exported procedure.

How to Use the IconBox

Together with the complete code for the icon box widget, you will find a small test program in Appendix F. You have to create some bitmaps and an initialization file containing entries for all the icons you want. Last but not least, you need a resource file specifying the icon colours and which bitmaps to use for which icon.

In reality you would substitute the interface to read the icons from a file by some application-specific routines (e.g. reading real directories and displaying all the files). You might also augment the program by allowing a set of objects to be selected.

To allow selection you have to decide how to represent selected icons, depending on the nature of your application. There would only be a minimal impact on the current code. Only the procedure *RedrawIcon* would have to be changed, using a flag in the icon record to distinguish between normal and selected appearance.

Selecting an icon is a straightforward addition to *HandleButtons*; simply select the clicked icon (and deselect all the others).

You can add a mode to select icons by catching them with a rectangle drawn on the background. This new feature demonstrates how to combine different direct manipulation operations. In this case *HandleButtons* must decide whether a moving operation is started (when an icon is hit) or a selecting rectangle is to be drawn (implying no icon is hit). *HandleMove* must provide different feedback, depending on the mode.

The most ambitious extension would be to allow icons to be moved into other windows (by *drag and drop*). For example, an icon representing a file could be moved above a printer icon in another icon box. Dropping it there would cause the file to be printed.

Implementing this operation is difficult because a widget can normally only draw into its window. There are two possible solutions. First you can create an override shell with a copy of the icon in it and move that. As a separate top-level window it can be moved over the whole screen. However, its rectangular shape would not have a distinctive visual appeal (there is an X extension to support irregularly shaped windows, but it is not supported on all displays).

The other possibility is to draw on the root window. Every client can draw into any window if it knows its window ID. Therefore every client can draw into the root window. Furthermore, you can specify in a GC if you want to draw over child windows, in effect drawing "on top of the screen". However, you must be very careful that other clients do not interfere with your drawing, or else garbage will appear on the screen. Suppressing interference requires the freezing of all applications during the move (you can observe the effect when you move a window with the window manager: the window manager uses a similar mechanism to draw its feedback rectangle).

As you can see, nearly everything is possible with the basic X primitives. Many tasks are made easy by Motif, but there are some desirable features that require considerably more effort and knowledge to implement.

9.3 Writing New Widget Classes

You are now ready to tackle the last problem on the way to becoming an expert Motif programmer: writing your own Motif widget class. Unfortunately, this book can only help you half of the way.

The reason is that you really need the Motif source code to write widget classes. The new widget must work in cooperation with other widgets and there are a lot of private interfaces to be respected. The use of the drawing area widget in the last section has shielded you from these internal interfaces.

The private interfaces are responsible for the difference between application programmers and widget programmers. You should not underestimate the complexity of the private widget interfaces. Looking into the X Toolkit Intrinsics reference manual gives you a rough approximation: about two thirds of this manual cover interfaces of interest to widget programmers only.

Motif also defines a large number of private interfaces. It is promised that these interfaces will be defined and documented in a later Motif release, but they are currently changing as the implementation is improved. The private interface documentation will probably be comparable in size to the current external interface specification.

Implementing new widgets is so complex because every widget class is a subclass of another one and inherits features from this superclass. For example, the push button class is a subclass of label and inherits the label drawing routine (amongst others) from it. Because the inheritance mechanism is programmed in C the programmer must know a good deal about the structure of its superclass.

It is not too difficult to implement a new class as a subclass of Core, the most basic widget class, because the Core class is documented as a standard in the X Toolkit Intrinsics reference. If you follow the Intrinsics specification, the new widget class will work together with Motif widgets, just as X ensures that non-Motif applications will run on the same screen as Motif applications under the Motif window manager.

Mixing widgets of different origins is more of a coexistence than a cooperation. For example, keyboard traversal does not work with non-Motif widgets.

You automatically inherit the Motif features if you make your new widget class a subclass of a Motif class. Therefore you need the internal structure of this class, and thus you need the Motif source code.

The Motif source code is not freely available; you have to obtain a licence from the OSF. For any commercial purpose the cost of a Motif source licence is negligible compared with the cost of making yourself familiar with the internal interfaces—but unfortunately this does not apply if you are hacking for fun.

Subclassing

The first decision to be made in writing a new widget concerns the class to use as the superclass. The decision is easy if you need a slight modification to the behaviour of an existing class. For example, if you need a different appearance of the toggle in a toggle button, you can inherit the toggle button features in your subclass and only re-implement the toggle-drawing parts. In this case you need intimate knowledge of the superclass.

For a more general widget class that does not resemble another Motif widget your choice depends on the category. There is probably no need to create a new shell class, so you can choose between primitive and manager widgets. For both categories there exists a common superclass (Primitive or Manager) that should not be directly instantiated, but is useful for the purpose of inheriting features.

If you need a special kind of manager widget, creating a new widget class is seldom worth the trouble. Manager widgets are often used only once in a program (e.g. the main window). Most of the functionality can be simulated using convenience widgets as described in Section 9.1. Because of this and the complexity of properly implementing geometry management, creating manager widgets is not discussed further in this book.

For primitive widgets the label class is also a useful choice as a superclass. Although there are already a number of label subclasses in Motif, other variations are possible. In this section an *icon widget* is implemented as a subclass of label.

Icon widget development is motivated by the fact that a label can only display either a text or a pixmap. A pixmap used as an icon should be accompanied by an identifying text, because icons are often difficult to decipher on first sight, although they aid memorization later.

To implement an icon with a label surrounded by a shadow in Motif, you need four different widgets: a frame, a row-column, a pixmap label, and a text label. Four widgets are an impressive collection to implement such a simple case, especially if you consider using multiple icons in a palette.

Although the label widget defines resource fields for both string and pixmap, its drawing routine does not draw them both at the same time. The idea is to let the icon widget inherit these fields, but you must change the

Figure 9.13: Sample icon widget.

drawing procedure (remember that the label widget does not draw shadows although the resource fields are present).

The icon widget is not only useful as a static icon, but also with regard to push button or toggle button behaviour. Some simple additions make it possible to add button behaviour by changing the translations of the icon widget. The button behaviour is not as elaborate as in the push button or toggle button classes, especially when a lot of "magic code" is employed for buttons in menus. The icon widget is not useful in menus.

Necessary Header Files

To allow access to private definitions, every widget class defines a private header file in addition to its normal header file for use by application programs. The private header file will be used by subclasses. There is also the general private header file "XmP.h" which contains common definitions for widget writers.

Three files constitute the icon widget implementation: "IconWidget.h" for applications that use the icon widget, "IconWidgetP.h" for possible subclasses (and the icon widget code itself), and "IconWidget.c" which contains the code.

The public header file contains definitions for new resource field names and the exported procedures, i.e. the convenience functions for creation and (possibly) others. It also defines the external class pointer *iconWidgetClass*. The class pointer is used as the central access point. It is passed as a parameter to *XtCreateManagedWidget*. The pointer is stored in the widget's instance record and later used by the X Toolkit Intrinsics to access class-specific behaviour.

The public header file also defines the two C types *IconWidget* and *IconWidgetClass*, which are specialized versions of the general types *Widget* and *WidgetClass*. You can use them to declare variables and parameters which are guaranteed to be an icon widget.

The private header file defines the structure of the icon box class record and the instance record of each icon widget. The structures are used in the implementation module as well as in possible subclasses. Subclasses access features of their superclasses solely through these definitions. The icon widget code accesses fields and procedures of the label class and therefore has to include the "LabelP.h" header.

In extreme cases you can also use a private header to exploit a feature not otherwise accessible (e.g. in a convenience widget). Defeating the information hiding principle in this way cannot be prevented in the C language. However, you must be aware that using the private header file introduces a possible source of portability problems because the internal structures may be changed in future implementations (but then new widget classes will break, too).

Class Record and Instance Record

For every widget class there exists exactly one *class record* that defines the class. The class record contains all parameters of a class (such as the list of newly-defined resource fields) and pointers to procedures implementing the functionality (such as redrawing).

The class record is statically allocated in the widget-defining code. The first entry in the class record is always a pointer to the superclass's class record. In this way a class can access all the features of its superclasses.

Every widget is identified through its *instance record*. The instance record contains the data that have different values among widgets of a class. The structure of this record is the same for all widgets of the same class, but the contents may vary. The instance record is allocated by the X Toolkit Intrinsics when the widget is created.

The instance record is similar to the records allocated for the convenience widgets and is handled similarly (e.g. filling values from the resource database). In fact, the procedures for handling resource fields for convenience widgets are just variations of the code used by the Intrinsics for real widgets.

Because of inheritance, the class and instance records are divided into parts, one for each superclass up to the Core class, and one for the widget class itself. Each part is initialized and managed by the code of the corresponding class. This ensures that a subclass need not know anything about the semantics of these fields. However, the subclass may read the values (and even change them if it knows its parent's rules).

The higher a widget class resides in the class hierarchy, the larger is its part of the class record. The Core part in each class record has the most fields. The reason is that the contents of the class record are variables for generic solutions that need to be modified for subclasses.

For example, there is a field in the Core class part that contains the address of a procedure for redrawing the window's contents. The Core class already handles the receiving and processing of the Expose event. It merges the exposed rectangles into a region. The redrawing procedure is then called at the appropriate time with the region as parameter.

A subclass usually overrides this routine with a private one. However, it also profits from the generic handling performed by the superclass (such as compression of Expose events). The possibility of overriding only strategically selected parts of the superclass functionality is a very powerful feature of object-oriented programming.

The icon widget class does not define any generic behaviour, therefore its part in the class record consists of an extension field only.

```
typedef struct _IconWidgetClassPart
{
        caddr_t extension;
} IconWidgetClassPart;
```

The extension field allows a later revision of the implementation to remain binary-compatible even if new fields are added in this revision (because otherwise all offsets in the record would change by the insertion of a new field). The new fields must be allocated separately and the extension field points to this record. Each part should contain an extension field.

The definition of the class record for the icon widget contains four parts, one each for the Core, XmPrimitive, XmLabel, and IconWidget classes.

```
typedef struct _IconWidgetClassRec
{
        CoreClassPart           core_class;
        XmPrimitiveClassPart    primitive_class;
        XmLabelClassPart        label_class;
        IconWidgetClassPart     icon_class;
} IconWidgetClassRec;

extern IconWidgetClassRec iconWidgetClassRec;
```

The instance record part for the icon widget contains some fields defined as resources (the *offset* between icon and label, *shadow_type*, and the three callbacks for button behaviour). The other fields are private data. The armed state is registered in *armed*, and the *width* and *height* of the pixmap are stored to avoid querying the server each time for this information.

```
typedef struct _IconWidgetPart
{
        short           offset;
        short           width,
                        height;
        unsigned char   shadow_type;
        Boolean         armed;
        XtCallbackList  activate_callback;
        XtCallbackList  arm_callback;
        XtCallbackList  disarm_callback;
} IconWidgetPart;
```

The structure of the instance record also consists of four parts. The exact structure of these parts is defined in the private header files of the superclasses.

```
typedef struct _IconWidgetRec
{
        CorePart                  core;
        XmPrimitivePart           primitive;
        XmLabelPart               label;
        IconWidgetPart            icon;
} IconWidgetRec;
```

The Class Record

The most important part of the code in "IconWidget.c" is the definition of the class record. All the functionality except for the exported creation procedures is accessed through this record.

The class record is statically allocated and filled. For filling the fields you have to know which fields are needed (defined in the private header file) and what are the possible values. The latter information can be obtained for the Core class part from the X Toolkit Intrinsics reference manual. Defining the XmPrimitive and XmLabel parts is more difficult (you have to read the Motif code), but these parts are fortunately not so important.

The first fields of the Core part of the icon widget class record specify a pointer to the superclass record, the name of the class to use in resource specifications, and the size of the instance record.

```
IconWidgetClassRec iconWidgetClassRec =
{
    {
    (WidgetClass) &xmLabelClassRec, /* superclass           */
    "IconWidget",                    /* class_name           */
    sizeof(IconWidgetRec),           /* widget_size          */
```

The following five fields specify how to initialize the class and its instances. There are two procedures that customize class initialization. The first procedure is called exactly once before the new class is used. This procedure can be used to install resource converters and for similar global initializations.

The second procedure is appropriate for initializing fields of the class part. It is called for every subclass, because the class part is duplicated in the subclasses as well.

The second procedure is used to implement inheritance of procedures in the class record. If a class wants to use the same procedure as its superclass (for example, the redrawing procedure), it fills the field with a unique constant which is different from all possible procedure addresses (for example, *XtInherit-*

Expose). During class part initialization, the contents of the field are checked for this special value, and the real address is copied from the superclass.

It is the responsibility of a class to define these constants and to implement the class part initialization procedure for its part of the class record. This procedure is then called for each subclass, and copies the address into the subclass record.

A flag in the class record specifies whether the class has been initialized. It must be defined as *False* in the record allocation.

As the icon widget defines neither resource converters nor inheritable procedures in its class part, both procedures may be specified as *NULL*.

```
NULL,                        /* class_initialize          */
NULL,                        /* class_part_initialize     */
FALSE,                       /* class_initialized         */
```

The third initialization procedure is the most important, as it initializes the contents of the instance record. The Intrinsics only allocate storage and fill fields for which a resource specification exists. The rest of the instance record must be filled by the initialization procedure.

The initialization procedure is *chained*. When creating a new widget, all initialization procedures from all superclasses are called in superclass-to-subclass order. Each initialization procedure is responsible for filling its part in the instance record, but the later procedures may change values of previous parts. The implementation and parameters of the initialization procedure are explained in a section below.

There is also a hook procedure to use the parameter list passed on widget creation to initialize data not resident in the widget record. This hook is rarely used.

```
(XtInitProc) Initialize,     /* initialize                */
NULL,                        /* initialize_hook           */
```

The next procedure is responsible for creating the appropriate X window when a widget is realized. This procedure is usually inherited. It may not be *NULL*.

```
XtInheritRealize,            /* realize                   */
```

Each widget class defines a set of actions that can be used in translations for widgets of this class. The names may be equal to actions in other classes. A matching action declaration is searched in all superclasses starting from the class, and searches among any globally registered actions last. The actions of the icon widget are described in a section below.

```
actionsList,                 /* actions                   */
XtNumber(actionsList),       /* num_actions               */
```

One of the most important entries in the class record is the *resource list*. It specifies which new resource fields a class defines. Its format has already been described in Section 9.1. Because resource fields are inherited, the resource list contains only the new resource fields. However, by repeating a field that has already been defined in a superclass, you can change the default value for this field for the subclass.

For example, the icon widget redefines the shadow thickness to 2. This resource field is already present in the label class, where it has a default value of 0.

```
resources,              /* resources            */
XtNumber(resources),    /* num_resources        */
```

There is a field reserved for internal use by the X Toolkit Intrinsics, whose value can be initialized with the constant *NULLQUARK*.

```
NULLQUARK,              /* xrm_class            */
```

Four flags are contained in the class record to influence event processing for this class. The first three handle event compression. Compression is applied when there are several events in a queue that have arrived but not been processed.

Motion events are good candidates for compression, because they arrive so frequently. To improve feedback a widget should handle only the last motion event in the queue, as the others are already outdated. The technique for compressing Expose events has already been discussed in the previous section. Crossing events can usually be ignored if a widget is crossed quickly. Therefore the icon widget sets all three flags to *True*.

The last flag decides whether visibility of the widget shall be checked using VisibilityNotify events from the X server. This is only useful if redrawing requires much processing power, because unnecessary redrawing can be avoided.

```
TRUE,                   /* compress_motion      */
TRUE,                   /* compress_exposure    */
TRUE,                   /* compress_enterleave  */
FALSE,                  /* visible_interest     */
```

The following fields of the Core class part are procedures which should already be familiar to you, as there are similar callbacks for the drawing area widget (in fact the drawing area executes the callback list from inside these procedures).

The first procedure is called when the widget is destroyed to deallocate any resources the widget had allocated on creation. The icon widget only has to free the three callback lists, as there may be storage allocated for storing the procedures to be called.

The second procedure is called whenever a widget is resized by its parent. The widget can then perform any geometry recalculations. As the icon widget uses the label geometry calculations unchanged, this procedure is inherited.

The third procedure is responsible for redrawing exposed areas of the widget. It is overridden in the icon widget to allow for the displaying of icon and label simultaneously.

```
Destroy,                           /* destroy               */
XtInheritResize,                   /* resize                */
(XtExposeProc) Redisplay,          /* expose                */
```

It has already been mentioned that a widget often needs to intercept *XtSetValues* requests, to check for illegal values and to update any dependent internal fields if necessary. The *SetValues* procedure is mainly responsible for handling the icon widget part of the instance record, but it may also change other fields.

There is also a hook to use for data not allocated in the instance record, a procedure that is called when *XtSetValues* triggered a geometry request that could not be satisfied (almost always inherited), and a hook to get data not in the instance record.

```
(XtSetValuesFunc) SetValues,       /* set_values            */
NULL,                              /* set_values_hook       */
XtInheritSetValuesAlmost,          /* set_values_almost     */
NULL,                              /* get_values_hook       */
```

The next three fields are not very interesting and are initialized in Motif widgets with standard values.

```
NULL,                              /* accept_focus          */
XtVersion,                         /* version               */
NULL,                              /* callback private      */
```

The next field contains the default translation specification for icon widgets.

```
defaultTranslations,               /* tm_table              */
```

The procedure to query the preferred geometry is also inherited from the label class. The last two fields of the Core class part are again uninteresting.

```
XtInheritQueryGeometry             /* query_geometry        */
NULL,                              /* display_accelerator   */
NULL,                              /* extension             */
},
```

The Primitive class part starts with three fields that the label widget already inherits from the Primitive class, so they are inherited by the icon widget, too.

```
{
_XtInherit,                    /* Primitive border_highlight    */
_XtInherit,                    /* Primitive border_unhighlight  */
XtInheritTranslations,         /* translations                  */
```

The next field may contain a procedure used to activate a button through the keyboard. It is omitted here so as not to complicate the example too much (the procedure must set up a timer procedure because when a button is activated through the keyboard there is no event that disarms the button after a short while).

The next two fields are used to give a list of resource fields that must be converted for resolution independence. This list is empty for the icon widget class.

```
NULL,                          /* arm_and_activate    */
NULL,                          /* get resources       */
0,                             /* num get_resources   */
NULL,                          /* extension           */
},
```

The label class part is also quite short. All the fields are inherited using the generic special value _XtInherit.

```
{
_XtInherit,                    /* SetOverrideCallback           */
_XtInherit,                    /* SetWhichButton                */
XtInheritTranslations,         /* menu traversal translations   */
NULL,                          /* extension                     */
},
```

The class record definition ends with the icon widget part, which has only an extension field.

```
{
NULL,                          /* extension                     */
}
};
```

At the end of this enumeration the exported class pointer *iconWidgetClass* is defined as the constant pointer to this record for external access.

WidgetClass iconWidgetClass = (WidgetClass) &iconWidgetClassRec;

The procedures in the class record that are overridden by the icon widget are described in the following sections. The class record also references some substructures that must be defined, namely the default translations, the action list, and the resource list. Defining them is not difficult as you have already encountered them in other contexts.

The default translations only cover crossing events to allow for keyboard traversal (keyboard traversal generates synthetic crossing events).

```
static char defaultTranslations[] =
    "<EnterWindow>:          Enter()          \n\
    <LeaveWindow>:          Leave()";
```

The action list that enumerates all available actions contains some more entries. The actions for the button behaviour are only used when the icon widget is parameterized for button behaviour. As in other Motif widgets, the help callback is not connected by default.

```
static XtActionsRec actionsList[] =
{
        { "Arm",        (XtActionProc) Arm},
        { "Activate",   (XtActionProc) Activate},
        { "Disarm",     (XtActionProc) Disarm},
        { "Enter",      (XtActionProc) Enter},
        { "Leave",      (XtActionProc) Leave},
        { "Help",       (XtActionProc) Help}
};
```

The first entry in the resource list is used to change the default value for the XmNshadowThickness field, which defaults to 0 for labels.

```
static XtResource resources[] =
{
    {
    XmNshadowThickness, XmCShadowThickness, XmRShort, sizeof (short),
    XtOffset (XmPrimitiveWidget, primitive.shadow_thickness),
    XmRImmediate, (caddr_t) 2
    },

    {
    XmNiconOffset, XmCIconOffset, XmRShort, sizeof(short),
    XtOffset (IconWidget, icon.offset),
    XmRImmediate, (caddr_t) 0
    },

    {
    XmNshadowType, XmCShadowType, XmRShadowType,
```

```
        sizeof(unsigned char),
        XtOffset (IconWidget, icon.shadow_type),
        XmRImmediate, (caddr_t) XmSHADOW_OUT
        },


        {
        XmNactivateCallback, XmCCallback, XmRCallback,
        sizeof(XtCallbackList),
        XtOffset (IconWidget, icon.activate_callback),
        XmRPointer, (caddr_t) NULL
        },


        {
        XmNarmCallback, XmCCallback, XmRCallback,
        sizeof(XtCallbackList),
        XtOffset (IconWidget, icon.arm_callback),
        XmRPointer, (caddr_t) NULL
        },


        {
        XmNdisarmCallback, XmCCallback, XmRCallback,
        sizeof(XtCallbackList),
        XtOffset (IconWidget, icon.disarm_callback),
        XmRPointer, (caddr_t) NULL
        },
};
```

The Initialization Procedure

The X Toolkit Intrinsics pass two icon widgets as parameters to the initialization procedure. The first one is a temporary copy containing all the values
as filled from the creation argument list and the resource database. The second
will be the new widget.

You should not change the first widget. It is only a reference to what was
originally requested. When the second widget gets into the hands of the icon
widget initialization procedure, all superclasses have already initialized and
possibly modified their parts of the instance record.

The procedure *Initialize* is rather typical in its behaviour. It first checks the
possible values of the shadow type field. If an illegal value was requested, a
default value is substituted. Some widgets also issue a warning message in this
case.

The second step in the procedure is to initialize fields which are not
accessible as resource fields. The size of the pixmap is obtained from the X
server and the *armed* field is set to *False*.

```
static void Initialize (request, new)
     IconWidget          request, new;

{
     if (new -> icon.shadow_type != XmSHADOW_IN      &&
              new -> icon.shadow_type != XmSHADOW_OUT)
     {
          new -> icon.shadow_type = XmSHADOW_OUT;
     }

     GetPixmapSize (new);
     new->icon.armed = False;
}
```

To obtain the size of the pixmap, the procedure *XGetGeometry* is used. This procedure returns more parameters than are needed. The uninteresting ones are ignored.

```
static void GetPixmapSize (iw)
     IconWidget          iw;
{
     Window     root;
     int        junk, w, h;

     if (iw->label.pixmap != XmUNSPECIFIED_PIXMAP) {
          XGetGeometry (XtDisplay (iw), iw->label.pixmap,
                        &root, &junk, &junk,
                        &w, &h,
                        &junk, &junk);
          iw->icon.width = (short) w;
          iw->icon.height = (short) h;
     }
}
```

The SetValues Procedure

The *SetValues* procedure is similar to *Initialize*, except that there are three parameters. The first parameter is the current widget before changing any field. It should not be modified. The second parameter is the new widget where the changed values have already been set and superclasses have made any modifications they want. The third parameter contains the values from the request.

```
static Boolean SetValues(current, request, neww)
     Widget     current, request, neww;
{
     IconWidget          cur = (IconWidget) current;
```

```
IconWidget       new = (IconWidget) neww;
IconWidget       req = (IconWidget) request;

if (new -> icon.shadow_type != XmSHADOW_IN     &&
        new -> icon.shadow_type != XmSHADOW_OUT)
{
     new -> icon.shadow_type = XmSHADOW_OUT;
}

GetPixmapSize (new);

if (new->icon.shadow_type != cur->icon.shadow_type ||
     new->primitive.highlight_thickness !=
             cur->primitive.highlight_thickness  ||
     new->primitive.shadow_thickness !=
             cur->primitive.shadow_thickness)
{
     return True;
} else {
     return False;
}
}
```

Another difference from the initialization procedure is that a flag must be returned that indicates whether the widget must be redisplayed because of a resource field change. The X Toolkit Intrinsics automatically call the redrawing procedure if *True* is returned.

The Expose Procedure

The procedure *Redisplay* is the main reason why the icon widget has been written. It is rather simple because it uses the label's drawing routine to do most of the work.

The procedure has three parameters: the widget, the event structure of the Expose event, and a region that is present only when event compression for Expose events is requested and is *NULL* otherwise.

The redrawing procedure of the label class is found in the label class record. It is called first, then any additions are drawn on top. First, if a pixmap is present, it is displayed using *XCopyArea*. Then a shadow is drawn. The last step is to highlight the border for the location cursor using some internal Motif routines (this is a standard step for Motif primitive widgets).

```
static void Redisplay(w, event, region)
     Widget        w;
     XEvent        *event;
     Region        region;
```

```
{
    IconWidget        iw = (IconWidget) w;
    short             shad = iw->primitive.shadow_thickness +
                              iw->primitive.highlight_thickness;
    short             avail;


    /* use the label's expose first */
    (* xmLabelClassRec.core_class.expose) (w, event, region);

    /* copy the pixmap into the space left by margin_top */
    if (iw->label.pixmap != XmUNSPECIFIED_PIXMAP) {
        avail = iw->core.width - 2 * shad - 2 * iw->label.margin_width -
                iw->label.margin_left - iw->label.margin_right - iw->icon.width;
        XCopyArea (XtDisplay (w), iw->label.pixmap, XtWindow (w),
                   iw->label.normal_GC, 0, 0,
                   iw->icon.width,
                   iw->icon.height > iw->label.margin_top ?
                        iw->label.margin_top : iw->icon.height,
                   avail/2 + shad +
                        iw->label.margin_width - iw->label.margin_left,
                   iw->label.TextRect.y - iw->icon.height - iw->icon.offset);
    }

    /* draw the shadow */
    DrawShadow (iw, True);

    /* for keyboard traversal */
    if (iw->primitive.highlighted)
        _XmHighlightBorder(w);
    else if (_XmDifferentBackground (w, XtParent (w)))
        _XmUnhighlightBorder(w);
}
```

The drawing procedure makes a number of assumptions about the icon widget. The *XmNlabelType* field must remain at its default value *XmSTRING*, otherwise the pixmap will be displayed twice. This setting was chosen because the label string is more complicated to display than the pixmap and only one of them can be inherited from the label class.

The second reason is that the label will now adjust its geometry according to the label string. Usually the string is wider than the icon, therefore the width will be correct. Otherwise it is up to the programmer to ensure that the icon widget is wide enough for the icon to fit.

The programmer is also responsible for reserving space for the icon vertically, using the resource field *XmNtopMargin*. The icon pixmap is displayed horizontally centred in this top space and above the label string by the distance *XmNiconOffset.*

The situation could be improved if the icon widget checked on initialization and after *XtSetValues* whether there was enough space for the icon. If not, it could increase the top margin or the width. However, this requires that all superclasses must recalculate their layout, effectively forcing a complete resize operation.

In most cases the simpler behaviour will be sufficient, especially if multiple icon widgets are included in a row-column, which may adjust their top margins and widths. You see that it is not easy to make a widget class robust against all external influences.

Please note that the drawing procedure, as for most widgets, does not optimize the redrawing by using the affected region. In most cases the widgets are sufficiently small not to adversely affect performance.

Drawing the shadow is performed by a utility procedure, which is also used to reverse the shadows when a button behaviour is desired. The shadow is drawn "in" when required by the shadow type or when the widget is armed. A parameter flag allows you to distinguish (in the armed state) whether the pointer is inside the window or not. If not, the shadows are drawn normally.

Because shadow drawing is rather complicated, an internal Motif procedure is used to do the dirty work. The parameters are taken from the Primitive instance part.

```
static void DrawShadow (iw, really)
        IconWidget      iw;
        Boolean         really;
{
        Boolean    in = (iw->icon.armed && really) ||
                        iw->icon.shadow_type == XmSHADOW_IN;

        if ((iw->primitive.shadow_thickness) > 0 && XtIsRealized (iw)) {
            _XmDrawShadow (XtDisplay (iw), XtWindow (iw),
                    in ? iw->primitive.bottom_shadow_GC :
                        iw->primitive.top_shadow_GC,
                    in ? iw->primitive.top_shadow_GC :
                        iw->primitive.bottom_shadow_GC,
                    iw->primitive.shadow_thickness,
                    iw->primitive.highlight_thickness,
                    iw->primitive.highlight_thickness,
                    (int)iw->core.width-2*iw->primitive.highlight_thickness,
                    (int)iw->core.height-2*iw->primitive.highlight_thickness);
        }
}
```

Actions

Most of the procedures referenced in the class record deal with the widget's interface to the application. The behaviour in response to events is implemented through action procedures.

The actions installed by default are *Enter* and *Leave*. They handle the highlighting of the widget when the mouse pointer moves into the window. To be effective, the focus policy must be *XmPOINTER*, *XmNhighlightOnEnter* must be *True*, and the *XmNhighlightThickness* must be set to a value greater than zero. The highlighting behaviour is handled by internal Motif procedures.

When the icon widget is armed, the two actions must also handle the reversing of the shadow.

```
static void Enter (iw, event)
    IconWidget        iw;
    XEvent        * event;


{

    _XmPrimitiveEnter (iw, event);

    if (iw->icon.armed)
            DrawShadow (iw, True);
}

static void Leave (iw, event)
    IconWidget        iw;
    XEvent        * event;


{

    _XmPrimitiveLeave (iw, event);

    if (iw->icon.armed)
            DrawShadow (iw, False);
}
```

Three actions are only used for button behaviour. They modify the shadow as appropriate and then call the registered callbacks of their associated callback list. They fill in a structure to be used as *call_data*.

If the callback list is empty a shortcut is taken, although *XtCallCallbackList* would also work in this case. *XFlush* ensures that all drawing requests to the X server are sent out before the callbacks are executed. This is unnecessary if there are no callbacks to execute.

```
static void Arm (iw, event)
    IconWidget        iw;
    XEvent                * event;
```

```
{
        XmAnyCallbackStruct call_value;

        iw->icon.armed = True;
        DrawShadow (iw, True);

        if (iw->icon.arm_callback) {
                XFlush(XtDisplay (iw));
                call_value.reason = XmCR_ARM;
                call_value.event = event;
                XtCallCallbackList (iw, iw->icon.arm_callback, &call_value);
        }
}

static void Disarm (iw, event)
        IconWidget          iw;
        XEvent              * event;

{
        XmAnyCallbackStruct call_value;

        iw->icon.armed = False;
        DrawShadow (iw, True);

        if (iw->icon.disarm_callback) {
                XFlush(XtDisplay (iw));
                call_value.reason = XmCR_DISARM;
                call_value.event = event;
                XtCallCallbackList (iw, iw->icon.disarm_callback, &call_value);
        }
}
```

The *Activate* action also checks if the pointer is inside the window. If it is not, no activation occurs.

```
static void Activate (iw, event)
        IconWidget          iw;
        XEvent              * event;

{
        XmAnyCallbackStruct call_value;

        if ((event->xany.type == ButtonPress || event->xany.type == ButtonRelease)
                        && (event->xbutton.x > iw->core.width ||
                                event->xbutton.y > iw->core.height))
                return;
```

```
        call_value.reason = XmCR_ACTIVATE;
        call_value.event = event;
        XtCallCallbackList (iw, iw->icon.activate_callback, &call_value);
}
```

It is intended that the *Arm* procedure is called on a ButtonPress event, and *Activate* and *Disarm* are called on a ButtonRelease event. Which button is used depends on the translation specification.

The *Help* action simply executes any callbacks connected to the *XmNhelp-Callback* of the Primitive class.

```
static void Help (iw, event)
        IconWidget      iw;
        XEvent          * event;


{

        XmAnyCallbackStruct call_value;

        call_value.reason = XmCR_HELP;
        call_value.event = event;
        XtCallCallbackList (iw, iw->primitive.help_callback, &call_value);
}
```

Convenience Creation

There are two convenience functions used to create icon widgets. The first one creates an icon widget intended as a label, i.e. the shadows are present but there is no button behaviour.

As a further convenience, the name of the pixmap to be used may be passed directly as a parameter, because a pixmap cannot be included as a string in the argument list. The string is converted with *XmGetPixmap* to return a pixmap variable.

```
Widget CreateIconLabel (parent, name, arglist, argcount, pixmap)
        Widget      parent;
        char        *name;
        ArgList     arglist;
        Cardinal    argcount;
        char        *pixmap;


{

        Widget      w;
        Pixmap      pix;
        Arg         args[1];
```

```
w = XtCreateManagedWidget (name, iconWidgetClass,
                                parent, arglist, argcount);

if (pixmap != NULL && pixmap != "") {
    pix = XmGetPixmap (((IconWidget) w)->core.screen,
                    pixmap,
                    ((IconWidget) w)->primitive.foreground,
                    ((IconWidget) w)->core.background_pixel);
        if (pix != XmUNSPECIFIED_PIXMAP) {
            XtSetArg (args[0], XmNlabelPixmap, pix);
            XtSetValues (w, args, 1);
        }
}

return w;   }
```

The second convenience function is similar, but also augments the widget's translations with specifications for the button behaviour. Just as with pixmaps the translations cannot be set directly as a string in the argument list. The string must first be converted to the *XtTranslation* type with *XtParseTranslationTable*.

```
#define BUT_TRANS "#override   \
                <Btn1Down>: Arm()\n<Btn1Up>: Activate() Disarm()"

Widget CreateIconButton (parent, name, arglist, argcount, pixmap)
        Widget      parent;
        char        *name;
        ArgList     arglist;
        Cardinal    argcount;
        char        *pixmap;

{
        Widget            w;
        Pixmap            pix;
        Arg               args[1];
        XtTranslations    parsed = XtParseTranslationTable (BUT_TRANS);

        w = XtCreateManagedWidget (name, iconWidgetClass,
                                        parent, arglist, argcount);

        if (pixmap != NULL && pixmap != "") {
            pix = XmGetPixmap (((IconWidget) w)->core.screen,
                            pixmap,
                            ((IconWidget) w)->primitive.foreground,
                            ((IconWidget) w)->core.background_pixel);
```

```
        if (pix != XmUNSPECIFIED_PIXMAP) {
                XtSetArg (args[0], XmNlabelPixmap, pix);
                XtSetValues (w, args, 1);
        }
}

XtAugmentTranslations (w, parsed);

return w;
}
```

With the push button behaviour the icon widget may also behave like a toggle button if you add the following procedure as the *XmNactivateCallback*:

```
static void ToggleMe (widget, client_data, call_data)
        Widget                  widget;
        caddr_t                 client_data;
        XmAnyCallbackStruct     *call_data;
{
        unsigned char   shadow_type;
        Arg             args[1];

        XtSetArg (args[0], XmNshadowType, &shadow_type);
        XtGetValues (widget, args, 1);

        XtSetArg (args[0], XmNshadowType,
                shadow_type == XmSHADOW_IN ?
                                XmSHADOW_OUT : XmSHADOW_IN);
        XtSetValues (widget, args, 1);
}
```

In this case the current value is represented by the shadow type. The redisplay logic ensures that the shadow is always "in" when the icon widget is armed and the pointer is in the window. Otherwise the current shadow type is displayed.

Chapter 10

Designing an Application

A good program design requires more than putting together some Motif widgets. There are many further questions that must be considered to make your application user-friendly, portable, and adaptable to different needs and environments.

10.1 Interface and Program Structure

Using Motif does not guarantee that your program will be truly user-friendly. While the buttons will always look nice, the reactions to pressing a button may totally confuse the user if your program is not correctly designed. Programmers often underestimate the effort required to restructure a traditional program for a graphical interface. UNIX will not become user-friendly simply by adding Motif.

The key to a friendly user interface is the *principle of least surprise*. Users should not be surprised by the reaction of the program. If they do not know the reaction of the program, they should be able to explore it simply by trying. The principle also requires that similar situations in different programs should show similar behaviour.

The principle of least surprise minimizes the amount of learning necessary to use a program to its full extent. In the early days of personal computing most people used only one or two programs regularly (such as a word processor and a spreadsheet program). Through extensive training they became used to this world of keystroke combinations and quirks. The computer was only used to support a single task.

In these days of distributed computing it is more and more necessary to have more tasks supported by the computer (preparing presentations, making appointments, coordinating project schedules, communicating via different electronic media, analyzing situations, etc.). In these situations the computer must be an assistant, and stay out of the way, because the user is not primarily a computer operator.

In a modern environment there is little time for training and learning (if learning takes too long the computer is simply not used). This is the primary reason why the computer revolution has not been able to rationalize the office environment as it did industry.

Moreover, the computing environment changes frequently as new functions are added, other programs are revised, and new hardware devices appear. It is very unlikely that any user of such a complex system will ever use more than a fraction of the functionality, but each one uses a different fraction. So minimizing the time to learn a new function is far more important than allowing keyboard shortcuts for complex commands (although keyboard shortcuts for mechanisms that are used in all programs are important).

A program design has to consider the following two aspects in order to be easy to learn and use:

- The user must have an intuitive *model* of the program's behaviour. This model should be simple (e.g. no exceptions and special cases). Each part of the model should have a corresponding object in the interface. There should be no hidden states that the user has to remember.

- Each function should be accessible using only the simplest mechanism (menu activation or clicking in an object) to allow exploration. Reading the manual (paper or online) should only be necessary for users unfamiliar with the application area.

A simple but illustrative example is a pocket calculator. Many people have problems with the register(s). These problems occur because the contents of the register are not directly visible. If they were, you could directly observe the effects of the M+/M− keys, thus learning by exploration. An experienced user would be able to hide the register display, but would be able to inspect the value whenever a problem occurred.

Application Models

A user's model of an application is easier to understand if it shares many similarities with other applications. In this section a program model is described that fits nearly all applications. The application's functionality can be expressed in this model—but existing applications must usually be changed to follow this model.

The model presented is consistent with the Motif style guide and is common practice in other graphical user interfaces.

Applications

An application is a single unit of functionality. It is normally not associated with any data or attributes; it represents "pure code". Default settings or other adaptations should be represented by another entity.

An instance of an application is a running process. There may be one process per document, or there may be only one process which handles all documents in a single instance.

The application need not be visible as an object, because you can do nothing with it. It is an unchangeable object. However, the application manifests itself in the appearance and structure of the windows. You should design the windows so that the user may associate them with the correct application. A pleasant icon helps here.

Documents

The data created and manipulated by an application reside in documents. Each document has a specific type, indicating the data structure it uses internally. An application may work on documents with different types, but it usually has one primary type it handles best.

A document that is currently manipulated is associated with its own top-level window and a separate menu bar. As mentioned above, multiple documents of the same application can be handled with a single application instance or a separate process for each document. The user may not be able to see this

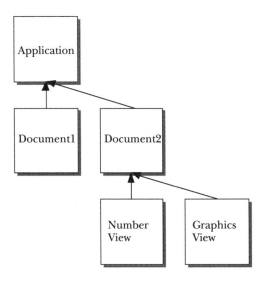

Figure 10.1: Applications, documents, and views.

difference on the screen.

Documents may have an object-oriented substructure, e.g. paragraphs, lines, and characters. Objects may be composite or primitive and have attributes (e.g. font of paragraph etc.)

A document is the smallest entity a user may manipulate on the desktop. In an advanced architecture documents may contain or refer to other documents (e.g. graphics in a text).

Views

The contents of a document are manipulated through a view. The view displays some subset of a document's contents in a certain representation. There may be more than one view on the same document simultaneously, for example to display different sections of a text. The presentation may also differ between multiple views, for example between the page preview and the editing mode of a publishing program.

Commands

Changes in the document are modelled as commands. Commands may be issued by direct manipulation in the view, through activating menu entries or buttons, or through key combinations.

Commands can be complex state transitions, such as hyphenating a document, or simple ones, like inserting a page break. Commands may also have a number of parameters.

Commands are the entities that can be undone. The Undo menu entry will neutralize the effect of the last executed command.

Properties

Simple commands can also be regarded as property changes of a document or a subobject of a document (e.g. a paragraph). Properties are characterized by the fact that changing them can be undone by simply restoring the old value.

Changing properties may have side effects (e.g. for the pagination of a document if the line spacing of a paragraph is changed). However, restoring the original value will also automatically undo all side effects. Correctly maintaining all the dependencies when implementing properties is sometimes difficult, but users find this model particularly easy to understand.

Review of Interface Elements

If your application follows the model described above, you have several possible ways of representing views (with the document substructure), commands, and properties in your user interface. This section describes which widget is suitable for which part of the model.

Menus

The menu system is mainly used to activate the commands of an application. Each menu entry corresponds to one command. During interface design you have to decide how to name and arrange these entries and how to obtain their parameters.

Parameters required by a command are normally entered in a dialog box. The dialog box appears when the menu entry is activated. To signal the presence of a parameter dialog, the menu entry is followed by an ellipsis (...).

The parameter dialog should maintain the parameters that were used for the previous invocation. If a separate dialog box is created for each command requiring parameters, and the dialog is mapped and unmapped on demand, the widgets of the box will maintain the state automatically.

Parameters for a command may also be derived from global properties of the document that are settable elsewhere. However, it is often not obvious to the user that a further parameter is used. Avoid this situation whenever the meaning is not clear to the user.

Menu entries can also be used to change properties by using toggle buttons. The properties may belong to the document or to the currently selected substructure in the view. If the affected object is not obvious, you should look for other possibilities to display and change the value.

If a menu entry represents a property of the currently selected structure, it must change to mirror the current value whenever the selection changes. When multiple objects are selected, there may not be a unique value of this property to reflect in the menu.

Dialogs

Dialog windows are used for three different purposes in the application model presented here:

- To enter parameters for a command.
- To modify properties of objects.
- To receive messages and answer questions.

Parameter Dialogs

A dialog box to enter command parameters is displayed after activating a menu entry. Clicking on its "OK" button is equivalent to actually invoking the menu command, therefore this button may be labelled with the command's name as well.

A parameter dialog should be modeless. There is no reason why other parts of the application cannot be used while parameters are being entered. The menu command will not be executed until the "OK" button is activated; only the parameter values are affected by the user interaction with the dialog box.

The parameter values are preserved until the next activation of the dialog. Therefore "Cancel" simply unmaps the box. All the widgets preserve their state until they are mapped again.

For many commands it is convenient to allow the parameter dialog box to remain present even after the command has been executed. An implementation of this feature is described in Section 7.3. If the dialog stays on the screen the user can quickly repeat the command with slightly different parameters or for a different selected object. If the dialog box is modeless there is really no reason not to implement this feature even if it is never used.

Property Dialogs

A dialog box to display and modify properties is always associated with an identifiable object, except when the properties belong to the document or view. As a convention, a property dialog appears when the corresponding object is double-clicked.

The title of the dialog should identify the object it belongs to. The object should also indicate somehow that a property dialog for it is visible, i.e. that it is "open". If an object has many properties, the top of the dialog should contain an option menu switching between categories to appear in the rest of the box.

The user should be able to open multiple property dialogs for multiple objects simultaneously (X displays usually have sufficient space). Some other systems permit only one property dialog for each kind of object, switching the contents and structure to reflect the properties of the currently selected object at all times. However, you cannot compare two similar objects if this approach is used.

Property dialogs should also be modeless. If any properties of the object are changed by other commands, an open property dialog must immediately reflect the new value. The immediate update feature often requires some effort to implement, but it will greatly benefit the user.

There are two different approaches concerning the handling of property changes through the dialog with respect to when the new value is applied to the object. The simpler approach regards the values in the property dialog as copies of the real property values. The user can edit them at will without affecting the object. The new values are set when the user presses the "Apply" button (which replaces the "OK" button).

This approach is similar to parameter dialogs. You can think of such a property dialog as the parameter dialog for a property-changing command. This approach has the advantage that the user is not likely to change a property accidentally.

The disadvantage is that the direct coupling between the object and the dialog box is lost. For example, when moving an object in a graphical editor you are not required first to determine the new position and then to click "Apply" to actually move the object. A large part of the simplicity of the direct manipulation user interface stems from the fact that changes can easily be undone if required.

Therefore the preferred method for implementing property dialogs is to update the object directly whenever a change occurs, relying on the "Undo" command to correct errors.

Message Dialogs

Message dialogs are used to display messages and ask questions that require a response from the user. Whereas parameter and property dialogs appear on the user's request, message dialogs are initiated by the application and in many cases the user does not expect them to appear.

Message dialogs are mostly modal. They occur in the middle of a program action and execution cannot resume until the user has responded.

A problem with message dialogs is that they are often the result of designing an application from the programmer's point of view rather than the user's. It is easy for a programmer to require user intervention when the program detects some condition deep inside a nested procedure. The user, however, will often be annoyed by modal dialogs because they dictate the interaction sequence.

A typical example is the confirmative "Do you really...?" question just before a delete operation is executed. The message may be appropriate for a first-time user, but an experienced user deleting a number of objects does not want to confirm each one separately. There is a simple remedy for this problem (simple as seen by the user). If the "Undo" operation is properly implemented, perhaps even with the ability to undo more than the last operation, there is no need to confirm the delete.

If you try hard enough, modal dialogs can often be avoided. A principal exception is hardware malfunctions. For instance, you cannot know in advance whether writing a tape will result in a media error. However, you *can* check before the operation whether a tape is inserted and not write-protected.

If you treat the tape drive as a visible object in your program, which clearly displays its state and the state of the tape inserted, it is immediately clear to the user whether the tape is available for a copy operation. This kind of functionality is not easy to implement, but it will make your program truly user-friendly.

Controls

Control areas are used to set and display values in a dialog or document window. It should be clear to the user which internal value a control element corresponds to, whether it mirrors a document property, a property of a document substructure, or a parameter value.

A major task for the interface designer is to decide how to represent a value. For instance, if a property is restricted to a list of possible values, it can be represented by either a list, a radio box, an option menu, a text field etc. Which widget is chosen for the representation depends on the available space and the nature of the possible values.

Another task is to arrange and group the control elements for maximum operating efficiency. The user must be able to grasp the contents of a control area as quickly as possible. Grouping the controls into related topics helps here, as well as the judicious use of frames, surrounding space, and icons. You should avoid being carried away by the Motif 3D effects. Too many shadow lines without clear purpose clutter the screen and destroy the effect.

Buttons

Push buttons play a special role among the widgets for control areas. They are used to map and unmap windows and to execute commands. Although other control area widgets can also execute commands in their callbacks, you should not make use of this feature to avoid confusion. In this way a clear distinction between elements that activate commands (push buttons) and elements that change properties can be maintained.

Buttons can be contained either in the main window or in dialogs. In dialogs their role and position are determined by the type of dialog. If possible you should avoid using more than the standard push buttons in a dialog, because their meaning will be unfamiliar to new users.

Push buttons in a document window are really substitutes for pull-down menu entries. Using push buttons and pull-down menus simultaneously is not recommended. Use accelerators instead if you are concerned about quick access. A simple application with few commands may substitute push buttons for sparsely populated pull-down menus. Push buttons instead of pull-down menus may be used to distinguish applications without documents, such as a system control panel for changing hardware-related settings.

Main Window

The layout of a typical main window with a menu bar and a scrollable view area is defined in the Motif style guide. Some variations have been discussed in Section 5.6.

In addition to a scrollable view a main window may also contain control areas known as *palettes*. They are an alternative to setting document properties in a menu.

Palettes are especially useful to set parameters for direct manipulation commands, such as drawing graphical figures. When initially creating an object, only size and location can be specified directly. All other properties are copied from global settings. Including all global parameters in a palette has the advantage that the user has an accurate overview of the current settings when drawing.

Even though large displays are common, a palette should be designed to be as compact as possible. A useful compromise is to display only the current values, and show a property dialog when the user clicks on the value display. This is a generalization of the technique used in the option menu.

Separation between Functionality and Interface

There are different models that try to describe the boundaries between the purely functional parts of a program and its external presentation through the user interface. The reason for developing such models is clear: only the functional part really requires a programmer, while the interface should in principle be described in other terms.

Unfortunately, reality is different. As you can see from the "motifhelp" example in Chapter 8, many programs are to a large extent composed of interface code. For instance, a graphical editor is mostly interface. Therefore it is wishful thinking to cover all interface programming with a single tool.

In the future more subdivisions must be identified in the interface part of a program. Research in this area has been going on for a long time, but most concepts originate from the world of ASCII terminals and command line interfaces. Nevertheless it is useful to examine present models as a starting point.

The best-known approach is the *Model-View-Controller* (MVC) model used in the Smalltalk-80 system developed at Xerox PARC. The MVC model separates an application interface into three parts: the *model* as the functional part, a *view* as the external representation of the model, and a *controller* that manages the interaction. Figure 10.2 shows this configuration.

Of the three parts, the model is self-contained. It can in principle be executed without direct input or output or any other reference to the view or controller parts. The view depends on the model, because it uses the attributes of the model as a basis for its representation. The view uses a special hook in the model to be informed whenever the model changes (similar to a callback, but in the other direction). The view then redisplays itself accordingly.

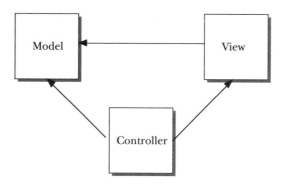

Figure 10.2: Model-View-Controller model.

The controller part is responsible for the interaction. It accepts input and performs any changes in the model and view.

The MVC model resembles the mechanism going on inside a widget if you consider the resource fields as the model, the Expose procedure as the view, and the actions as the controller. However, it is difficult to scale this model to a whole Motif application, because view and controller cannot be clearly separated. Especially in direct manipulation objects, tiny views and controllers exist in each object, but not for the application as a whole.

One thing can be learned from the MVC model, however. The attributes of the model are implemented as *active values*. Changing an attribute inside the model will automatically update the view, although the model does not know anything about the view.

You already know the mechanism to achieve this behaviour: it is simply a value-changed callback in the reverse direction. The view connects a callback procedure to the model which is called when the attribute value in the model changes. The view then reads the relevant attribute values and changes the presentation accordingly.

If you thus equip your interface-independent code with callback capabilities, you end up with three segments of program code as shown in Figure 10.3. The presentation part is composed of widgets (including convenience widgets) and their resource values. The part in the middle consists of callback connections between the two other parts.

Because the interface code is now effectively split into two parts, there is some hope that at least the presentation part can be constructed in ways other than by programming. The UIL is a first step in this direction, but the problem of writing down all the details remains.

Just now the first *interactive design tools* are emerging that allow you to construct the presentation part by direct manipulation. The key to the success of these tools is how they support the interface between the presentation part and the rest of the program. If this interface requires too much additional work, no savings will be achieved.

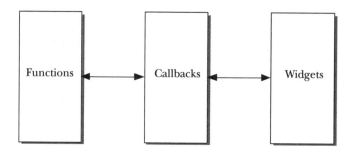

Figure 10.3: Three part division of the program code.

10.2 Portability Issues

Although many portability problems have been solved by using the X Window System as the basis for Motif, some environment dependencies remain. This section outlines the affected areas, while the next section describes how to use the Motif resource mechanisms to solve the problems properly.

Hardware Dependencies

Some portability problems are introduced by different hardware capabilities that cannot be hidden by the X server.

Screen Size and Resolution

The most obvious difference between display devices is their size. Although large megapixel displays are common for workstations, smaller screens are being used more and more with the advent of cheap X terminals and X server support for personal computers.

In the X screen model two variables are affected: the number of pixels a screen supports and the distance between pixels, i.e. the resolution. The number of pixels limits the maximum size of a window (which is specified in pixels). If a window layout developed on one screen is illegible on another, it is a result of different resolutions.

Owing to different screen sizes in pixels you cannot always be certain that a window size will always be completely visible. You have to ensure that the necessary controls stay accessible even if the window is small. This is not simply a nice feature, it is a necessity.

The geometry management facilities of Motif provide a solid foundation on which to build windows that work in different sizes. In very small windows you can always use scrolling.

A good test of your window design is to make the window 500x300 pixels big. This is approximately the maximum window size on a PC screen. Your application should work acceptably with this window size even for longer tasks. Any additional available space should be used to increase the visible area of the view.

Problems with different screen resolutions have mainly to do with font legibility (fonts are discussed below). Because the user will choose a larger font (measured in pixels) on a display with higher resolution in order to achieve the same physical size, the widgets should adapt their size accordingly through geometry management.

If you specify geometry resources explicitly in the program or in an application defaults file, you should use resolution-independent values (see Section 4.2). Resolution-independent resources have one problem, however. If you read a resource field value from one widget and set it in another (as in the resize callback of the step list convenience widget described in Section 9.1), you must ensure that both widgets use the same units.

When drawing with Xlib primitives, you have to be careful on a screen with different resolutions in the X and Y directions (a non-square aspect ratio). Rectangles with equal sides are no longer drawn as squares, and circles appear as ovals. For the purposes of simplicity, X does not compensate for this effect, so you have to scale the coordinates yourself.

Colour

There are considerable differences between monochrome, grey-scale, and colour screens. It is not easy to write a program that performs optimally in all environments.

Except for applications that need colour for their functionality (such as imaging applications), you should use colours only as an additional hint. For example, on a colour screen it is less obtrusive to highlight a selection with a pale yellow or blue background than inverting it as white on black.

You can also use different shades of the same colour to improve the visual appearance of icons, making them more realistic. Shaded colours have the additional advantage that they also work on grey-scale screens and are at least compatible with monochrome screens.

Just like the Motif shadow colours, shades in your program should be derived from a user-settable base colour. Other colours should also be user-settable (see the shadow colour resource in the icon box example in Section 9.2). In this way a program can be appropriately configured for either monochrome or colour settings in an application defaults file.

Keyboard

Sometimes it looks as if workstation manufacturers are trying to differentiate their products by using a different keyboard layout from their competitors. Furthermore, it seems that with every new model a new keyboard is invented.

Through the use of keysyms, X ensures position independence for keys. For instance, it is irrelevant which hardware key generates the Esc keysym. However, you cannot be sure that all keysyms can be generated. You should not rely on a function key as the sole trigger of a command, as some keyboards may not have function keys at all.

You can change the keyboard mapping inside the X server (using the *xmodmap* program, for example). However, this affects all clients at the same time, so it is not a good idea to let a client modify the mapping if it does not find an appropriate key.

In general there should be mouse equivalents for all keyboard functions and vice versa, even if one of the alternatives is more cumbersome than the other. It is not recommended to force the use of either the mouse or the keyboard to achieve a certain result.

Fonts

When your program does not use fonts as parts of its functionality (as is the case when the user may set a specific font for a text document), it should accept any font set by the user or provided as the default on a system. Many fonts are proportional, where different characters have different widths. The Motif widgets adapt themselves to the size of strings in the requested font.

If you require a certain font, you must be aware that the X server determines which fonts are available and that there are no requirements for a minimum font set.

A single font has a certain size, style, and emphasis. Any variation of this font, i.e. any change in the pixel representation of characters, must be a separate font. To account for all these parameters, fonts have long names whose structure is defined in the *X Logical Font Description* (XLFD) standard. This standard ensures that font names are unique. Otherwise it would be possible that a program requesting a certain font on one X server could obtain a completely different font on another.

Sometimes it is necessary to switch to a font variation within a string, for instance to use boldface for emphasis. There is no command to switch to the bold variant of a font, as each variation is a separate font. In Motif you can use XmStrings for this purpose.

The string part to be emphasized is included in the XmString as a component with a different character set name. In the corresponding font list separate fonts can then be specified for the two character sets. See below for a further discussion of XmStrings.

Internationalization

Another source of portability problems are differences in language and scripts, and sometimes even icons, between different countries. Handling these differences will be more and more important in the international marketplace of the future.

XmStrings

XmStrings are designed for text strings including segments in different languages/encodings with different fonts. Different parts of an XmString may even have different writing directions.

An XmString is a sequence of components chosen from the following list of types:

- *Text.* A sequence of characters with no interpretation (no tabs or newline characters).
- *Character set.* An arbitrary identifier to allow association of a font suitable for the encoding.
- *Direction.* Indicating left-to-right or right-to-left writing direction.
- *Separator.* Used to separate multiple lines in one XmString.

No text may precede the first character set identifier, but apart from this there are no restrictions on the composition of XmString components. To create an XmString, you can use the procedure *XmStringCreateLtoR.*

```
char                    *text;
XmStringCharSet         charset;      /* defined as char *    */
XmString                result;

result = XmStringCreateLtoR (text, charset);
```

The *XmStringCreateLtoR* procedure creates a character set and a text component. It also checks for embedded newlines, which are translated into separators. There is a another version of this procedure, called *XmStringCreate*, that does not handle newlines.

To handle other components, you have to create XmStrings consisting of the desired components and then concatenate them. In most cases you can use the procedure *XmStringSegmentCreate*, which creates a text component surrounded by other suitable components.

```
char                    *text;
XmStringCharSet         charset;      /* defined as char *    */
XmStringDirection       direction;
                                 /* XmSTRING_DIRECTION_L_TO_R */
                                 /* XmSTRING_DIRECTION_R_TO_L */
Boolean                 terminating_separator;
XmString                result;

result = XmStringSegmentCreate (text, charset, direction, terminating_separator);
```

You can concatenate these segments using *XmStringConcat.* The procedure allocates space for the result.

```
XmString        s1, s2, result;

result = XmStringConcat (s1, s2);
```

Allocated XmStrings should be freed with *XmStringFree* when no longer used.

There are a number of useful inquiry procedures defined for XmStrings. *XmStringWidth* and *XmStringHeight* return the size of the smallest enclosing rectangle of an XmString. A fontlist parameter is needed to determine the size. *XmStringEmpty* returns *True* if all text segments are empty. *XmStringLineCount* determines the number of lines.

To search for the first text segment in an XmString with a certain character set you can use *XmStringGetLtoR.* In this way you can use an XmString in a context where normal strings are required. The string returned must be freed with *XtFree*.

```
XmString            string;
XmStringCharSet     charset;
char                *text;
Boolean             found;

found = XmStringGetLtoR (string, charset, &text);
```

Two XmStrings can be compared using *XmStringCompare*. Two equal XmStrings are not necessarily binary equal.

```
XmString        s1, s2;
Boolean         equal;

equal = XmStringCompare (s1, s2);
```

As an example, to create a two-line text with a word emphasized through the use of boldface, you can use the following code:

```
XmString        s1, s2, s3;

s1 = XmStringSegmentCreate ("These are ", XmSTRING_DEFAULT_CHARSET,
                            XmSTRING_DIRECTION_L_TO_R, False);
s2 = XmStringSegmentCreate ("bold words", "bold",
                            XmSTRING_DIRECTION_L_TO_R, True);
s3 = XmStringConcat (s1, s2);
XmStringFree (s1); XmStringFree (s2);
s2 = XmStringSegmentCreate ("for emphasis.",
XmSTRING_DEFAULT_CHARSET,
                            XmSTRING_DIRECTION_L_TO_R, False);
s1 = XmStringConcat (s3, s2);
XmStringFree (s2); XmStringFree (s3);
```

If you use this XmString as a label string for a Label widget, the following output will result, provided that an appropriate font list is specified.

These are **bold words**
for emphasis.

To specify a font list in a resource file, you first write the name of the font to be used as the default font for the default character set. Separated from it by a comma you can then list other fonts for other character sets. The following font list is an example:

```
*demo_label.fontList:   8x13, bold=8x13bold
```

Message Strings

Most programs, whether they have a graphical interface or not, contain a large number of strings that are used as menus and messages. The strings must be translated for different countries. To facilitate translation, they should be separate (or at least separable) from the program code.

As a minimum you should define all message strings as preprocessor constants (as in the "motifhelp" example). If necessary, you can later extract all the definitions into a language-specific header file that is translated.

Another method is to set all strings used by widgets in the application defaults resource file. In this way the strings can be translated without recompiling, at a slight performance penalty. Foreign language strings are frequently much longer than the originals. This may also have effects on the geometry, so there may already be a language-specific application defaults file.

As a third alternative you can specify the strings using the UIL. The UIL has some advantages when more than geometric attributes must be changed (for instance the widget hierarchy), but introduces yet another customization file.

There is no complete solution for foreign language translation, because in some cases the code must be changed as well (e.g. different sorting algorithms, date formats, or hyphenation rules). Even simple cases like constructing an informative message (e.g. "There are <n> message(s) waiting for <name>") are highly language-dependent owing to different sentence construction, plural forms etc.

Error Messages

Error messages are a special case of message texts. As explained in Chapter 3 a corresponding text may be obtained from the error database. The error database is handled like the resource database. However, there is no default location where application-specific messages can be read. You have to load a message file in your program.

The following code loads a file and merges its contents into the error database location.

```
XrmDatabase     db;

db = XrmGetFileDatabase ("your_filename");
if (db != NULL)
        XrmMergeDatabase (db, XtAppGetErrorDatabase (context));
```

There is also a system-wide error database that supplies the texts for standard messages. This file, however, is loaded only on demand when the first error message is requested, so it may overwrite your entries.

An error database file for the "motifhelp" example program could look like the following:

       cannotOpen.Main: *Cannot open display.*
       fileOpen.Classfile: *Cannot open "motifhelp.classes".*
       internal.Menu: *Internal error: button not found.*
       internal.Chain: *Internal Error: no active class*
       internal.Section: *Internal error: wrong section number.*

       notFound.Field: *Field %s not found in table.*
       notFound.File: *File %s not found.*

Input Methods

How to enter text is a difficult problem in many languages that do not use the roman alphabet (for instance Chinese). The Motif text widget only supports roman alphabets and only one at a time. For other languages separate *input methods* have to be used. There is work under way to define a framework for substituting different input methods, but there are currently no generally available solutions.

10.3 Using the Motif Resource Mechanisms

Motif defines a variety of mechanisms to adapt a program to specific requirements. There are many different locations that affect a program's behaviour. This section develops some rules for using the resource mechanisms effectively.

The general rule is that the program code should not contain definitions that are not required for program correctness. More specifically, it should only contain the definitions that prevent it from terminating abnormally.

Resource Files

The resource database constructed from several resource files is a powerful tool for customizing an application, especially the presentation aspects such as fonts and colours. Some general guidelines about resource file usage have already been given in Section 2.4.

Planning the Widget Hierarchy

The first step towards effective use of the resource database for a larger program is to document its widget hierarchy. For this it is necessary to have an overview of which resource fields are settable, and how. For an application defaults file all widgets must normally be included, while the hierarchy description for the user may omit some widgets that are not to be changed.

Documenting the hierarchy will force you to choose appropriate widget names that convey some meaning and can be used for identification without access to the source code. If you use the same name for several widgets, these widgets should be sufficiently similar to make individual settings unnecessary.

You should also highlight important subparts of the widget tree to give some hints about when a summary specification is advantageous, such as the background colour for a window.

When defining your own resources or subresources you should look at them from the user's point of view. Programmers often define an option in their code because they are too lazy to analyse the situation. The flag is then only definable in terms of the program logic, and not understandable from the outside. If a choice is really required, an externally understandable redefinition may need some more code, but will benefit the user.

Application Defaults

If there is such a thing as the most important recommendation of this book, it is probably to use an application defaults resource file as much as possible. Including as many details as possible in this file will make your application code shorter and cleaner.

It is a good idea to maintain a separate editor buffer for the application defaults file while coding. You can immediately enter a definition in this file while you write the code to create a widget.

The separate resource file has some disadvantages, however. If you use it extensively, the application will not break without it, but will be largely unusable. Therefore a user must always take care to install the resource file together with the program.

In Motif 1.1 you can specify some resource definitions inside your program that are used when no application defaults file is found, called *fallback resources*. Using fallback resources enables you to define a minimum set of resources to show at least that the program is working. This would not be possible by resources set directly in an argument list, because they cannot be externally overridden, thus they are no longer customizable.

Fallback resources can be defined with *XtAppSetFallbackResources* before calling *XtOpenDisplay*, but only in Motif 1.1. More conveniently, a complete procedure exists in Motif 1.1 to handle all initializations for a Motif program, from initializing the X Toolkit Intrinsics to creating the application shell, including a parameter for fallback resources.

```
String              application_class;
XrmOptionDescList   options;
Cardinal            num_options;
ArgList             args;
Cardinal            num_args;
String              *fallback_resources;
Widget              toplevel;
```

toplevel = XtAppInitialize (NULL, application_class,
                     options, num_options,
                     &argc, argv,
                     fallback_resources,
                     args, num_args);

The fallback resources are a null-terminated array of strings, each string containing a one-line entry in a resource file, for example:

String   fallback_resources [] = {
     ".foobar: oh-uh",*
     *"*obi: 22",*
     NULL
};

When writing an application defaults file you should not prefix the resource specification with the name or class of the program (they are redundant anyway). Otherwise unprefixed resources in the user defaults file will not override similar specifications in the application defaults file.

For example, if the application defaults file specifies a default background colour of green prefixed by its class name:

*CLASS*background: green*

the user is not able to override it with his general preference for blue, because the user's specification will be less specific:

background: blue

The user would be required to override the background specifically for this application class, which would be rather frustrating if more applications and resources are involved.

UIL

The Motif *User Interface Language* (UIL) was designed to allow for the external definition of the widget hierarchy. Resource files can only define resource fields. Because many presentation aspects are affected by the widget hierarchy (see the frame widget, for example), it is often necessary to rearrange the widget hierarchy to change the layout. Changing the widget hierarchy is easier in an external description file than in the program.

The widget hierarchy defined in one or more UIL files is compiled into an internal representation (a UID file) by the *uil* compiler. This internal representation is then read in by the Motif Resource Manager (MRM) at run-time. The MRM creates the widgets from this information, replacing the corresponding widget creation procedures in the program.

The UIL is suitable for foreign versions of a program because translated text can be mixed with other presentation differences in the same file, thus avoiding changes in the program code. The UIL can also be used for *rapid prototyping*, i.e. quickly creating an interface without associated functionality. Lastly, the UIL can be used as an intermediate language for interactive design tools.

However, the UIL is not the best solution for all cases. Introducing yet another external definition mechanism with an associated library is overkill for many applications. It is not clear whether the UIL interface to the program, where the UIL leaves off and the program starts, is anywhere near the optimum. To really define the whole interface the UIL needs more power, but then you are already programming in two different languages.

Furthermore, the UIL in Motif 1.0 had some annoying little problems and unnecessary restrictions, which are being worked upon. In conclusion, you should carefully evaluate whether the additional effort to use the UIL is justified for your projects.

Owing to these problems, the UIL is not described in every detail in this book. Instead, a section from the "motifhelp" example program is implemented using the UIL as a demonstration.

Structure of a UIL program

A UIL program is composed of multiple modules, residing in multiple UIL files. The modules can export and import identifiers, but these facilities are not described here. Only a single module is needed for the example. In addition to defining interfaces between modules, a UIL module can simply include another UIL file.

A module consists of a header followed by a number of sections. There are five types of sections which can be repeated and arranged in any order. The header part of the example module looks like the following:

```
module motifhelp
    names = case_sensitive

include file "XmAppl.uil";
```

The file "XmAppl.uil" contains general constant definitions and the names of the resource fields etc. It is similar in purpose to the C header "Xm.h".

The following types of sections are possible in a UIL file. Each starts with the section type and contains a number of definitions.

- *Object.* An object section contains definitions for widgets with their resource field values, callbacks, and children.

- *Value.* A value section defines constants that can be used in other sections.

- *Procedure.* A procedure section defines the names of procedures that can be used for callbacks. These procedures must be defined by the corresponding C program.

- *Identifier.* An identifier section contains symbolic names for values that are defined by the C program.

- *List.* Complete argument and callback lists can be defined in this section for multiple use.

The object section represents the main contents of a UIL file; the other sections contain supplementary definitions. The object section is a sequence of object definitions of the following form:

```
objectName: WidgetClass {
        controls {
                ...list of child widgets
        };
        arguments {
                ...list of resource field values
        };
        callbacks {
                ...list of callback procedures
        };
};
```

Each list may be omitted if it does not contain entries. The simplest case is a widget with a number of children and no special resource field values, such as the main form widget of the "motifhelp" example:

```
form: XmForm {
        controls {
                XmLabel classLabel;
                XmFrame classFrame;
                XmLabel paramLabel;
                XmFrame paramFrame;
                XmLabel resLabel;
                XmScrolledWindow resRow;
        };
};
```

The UIL requires no ordering between the definition and the application of an identifier, so the referenced child widgets are defined later. The next widget definition contains only resource field values.

```
classLabel: XmLabel {
        arguments {
                XmNlabelString = label_class_chain;
```

```
            XmNresizable = false;
            XmNtopAttachment = XmATTACH_FORM;
            XmNbottomAttachment = XmATTACH_NONE;
            XmNleftAttachment = XmATTACH_FORM;
       };
    };
```

The name *label_class_chain* is a string symbolically defined in a value section. The other values are constants defined in "XmAppl.uil". In addition to symbolic constants you can express values of a number of different types, such as string arrays, font lists, icon bitmaps, colours, character sets, translation tables etc. You can also symbolically reference other widgets, which is convenient for specifying form widget constraints.

```
      classFrame: XmFrame {
            arguments {
                 XmNshadowType = XmSHADOW_IN;
                 XmNtopAttachment = XmATTACH_WIDGET;
                 XmNtopWidget = XmLabel classLabel;
                 XmNbottomAttachment = XmATTACH_FORM;
                 XmNleftAttachment = XmATTACH_FORM;
            };
            controls {
                 XmRowColumn classRow;
            };
      };
```

The *classFrame* is also an example of a specification with both an argument list and a list of children.

In the callback part of a widget specification you can associate callback reasons with procedure names defined in a procedure section.

```
      classRow: XmRowColumn {
            arguments {
                 XmNorientation = XmVERTICAL;
                 XmNspacing = 0;
                 XmNradioBehavior = true;
                 XmNradioAlwaysOne = true;
                 XmNentryAlignment = XmALIGNMENT_CENTER;
            };
            callbacks {
                 XmNcreateCallback =
                      procedure RegisterMainFormWidget (class_row_widget);
            };
      };
```

The value in parentheses is passed as the *client_data* argument to the callback procedure. A speciality of the UIL is that for every widget class, it also supports the *XmNcreateCallback*, whose sole purpose is to obtain the widget ID of a UIL-defined widget inside the program. This mechanism is discussed in detail below.

The remaining object definitions for the main form example do not introduce any new features.

```
!
! param field
!
    paramLabel: XmLabel {
        arguments {
            XmNlabelString = label_empty_name;
            XmNtopAttachment = XmATTACH_FORM;
            XmNbottomAttachment = XmATTACH_NONE;
            XmNleftAttachment = XmATTACH_OPPOSITE_WIDGET;
            XmNleftWidget = XmFrame paramFrame;
            XmNleftOffset = 0;
        };
        callbacks {
            XmNcreateCallback =
                procedure RegisterMainFormWidget (param_label_widget);
        };
    };
    paramFrame: XmFrame {
        arguments {
            XmNshadowType = XmSHADOW_IN;
            XmNtopAttachment = XmATTACH_WIDGET;
            XmNtopWidget = XmLabel classLabel;
            XmNbottomAttachment = XmATTACH_FORM;
            XmNrightAttachment = XmATTACH_FORM;
        };
        controls {
            XmRowColumn paramRow;
        };
    };
    paramRow: XmRowColumn {
        callbacks {
            XmNcreateCallback =
                procedure RegisterMainFormWidget (param_row_widget);
        };
    };

!
! resource selection list
!
```

```
resLabel: XmLabel {
        arguments {
                XmNlabelString = label_res_fields;
                XmNresizable = false;
                XmNtopAttachment = XmATTACH_FORM;
                XmNbottomAttachment = XmATTACH_NONE;
                XmNleftAttachment = XmATTACH_WIDGET;
                XmNleftWidget = XmFrame classFrame;
        };
};
resRow: XmScrolledWindow {
        arguments {
                XmNtopAttachment = XmATTACH_WIDGET;
                XmNtopWidget = XmLabel resLabel;
                XmNbottomAttachment = XmATTACH_FORM;
                XmNrightAttachment = XmATTACH_WIDGET;
                XmNrightWidget = XmFrame paramFrame;
                XmNleftAttachment = XmATTACH_WIDGET;
                XmNleftWidget = XmFrame classFrame;
        };
        callbacks {
                XmNcreateCallback =
                        procedure RegisterMainFormWidget (res_row_widget);
        };
};
```

The value section is used to define constants symbolically for later reference. In this case three strings are defined to have them at hand in one location. Strings that are used for a resource field requiring an XmString are automatically converted.

```
value
        label_class_chain:      "Superclass Chain";
        label_res_fields:       "Resource fields";
        label_empty_name:       "XmN...";
```

The procedure and identifier sections simply define identifiers as known. The real values are later filled in by the C program.

```
procedure
        RegisterMainFormWidget (integer);

identifier
        class_row_widget;
        param_row_widget;
        res_row_widget;
        param_label_widget;
```

This completes the description of the UIL file necessary to implement the main form section of the "motifhelp" demonstration program. The UIL file ends with the following statement.

end module;

You can now compile that program with the *uil* compiler to produce a file with the *uid* extension. The widget creation code (inside the procedure *CreateMainForm*) must then be replaced by MRM calls.

MRM calls

Using the MRM to create a widget hierarchy from a C program consists of four steps in the simplest case:

- Initialize MRM with *MrmInitialize.*
- Open the UID file with *MrmOpenHierarchy.*
- Register program-defined values with *MrmRegisterNames.*
- Create the widget tree with *MrmFetchWidget.*

Normally these steps are part of the main procedure because you will use the UIL throughout your whole program. In this example, however, they are included in the procedure *CreateMainForm*, because only this procedure is reimplemented.

The MRM calls require an additional header file. You must also link your program with the *Mrm* library.

#include <Mrm/MrmPublic.h>

To open the UID file you have to pass a list of filenames that will be opened, because the interface definition may consist of multiple files. In this case, a single filename suffices.

```
MrmHierarchy          mrm_hr;
static char           *db_filename_vec[] =
                          {"main_form.uid"};

MrmInitialize ();
if (MrmOpenHierarchy (XtNumber (db_filename_vec),
                 db_filename_vec,
                 NULL, &mrm_hr) != MrmSUCCESS)
    exit (1);    /* better error */
```

As a result, an identification *mwm_hr* is returned that must be referenced when creating the hierarchy.

In the next step, values must be registered for all names specified in the procedure and identifier sections of the UIL file.

```
static MRMRegisterArg        idlist[] = {
    {"RegisterMainFormWidget",
                    (caddr_t)RegisterMainFormWidget},
    {"param_row_widget",      (caddr_t)&param_row},
    {"res_row_widget",        (caddr_t)&res_row},
    {"class_row_widget",      (caddr_t)&class_row},
    {"param_label_widget",    (caddr_t)&param_label} };
```

```
MrmRegisterNames (idlist, XtNumber (idlist));
```

After this registration step, the symbolic constants contained in the UID file can be resolved. The last step involves the creation of the widgets. As a parameter you must specify which widget in the UID file is intended as the root of the widget tree to be created (you can include multiple widget trees in one file). You must also specify the parent under which the tree is to be created.

```
MrmType               *dummy_class;
```

```
if (MrmFetchWidget (mrm_hr, "form", parent,
                    &form, &dummy_class) != MrmSUCCESS)
    exit (1);    /* better error */
XtManageChild (form);
```

The root widget of the tree is passed as a result. It must be explicitly managed afterwards.

Interfacing C and UIL

The interface between the UIL part and the C program consists of the five symbolic identifiers. Their sole purpose is to inform the C program about the widget IDs it needs. Three of the widget IDs are only needed because their children are created again in C, therefore they are an artifact of the partial use of UIL. However, the *param_label* widget was already needed as a global variable previously, because it is referenced in *SetParamLabel* called from some other callback.

Because the param label is now created by the MRM, the widget ID is not known to the program. A possible solution would be to pass the widget ID as *client_data* to the callback that triggers *SetParamLabel*. Which widget ID to use could then be determined symbolically in the UIL file and *SetParamLabel* would always get the correct widget ID without worries. Unfortunately it is currently not possible to pass widget IDs as callback parameters from the UIL.

Instead you have to use the *XmNcreateCallback* to assign the new widget ID explicitly. This callback is called exactly once for each widget on creation by the MRM. The widget ID passed as the first parameter can then be copied into a global location.

If a single procedure is used for all widgets (and you would not want to define a separate callback procedure for each widget), you must have some way of identifying which widget is created. One possibility is to use integer constants, but these must be defined in both the program and the UIL file.

This example uses a more tricky approach. The four symbolic constants passed to the four different creation callbacks are defined in the program as pointers to widget IDs (see the registration step above). The callback procedure then simply copies the widget ID into the location identified by the passed pointer.

```
Widget      param_label;
Widget      param_row, res_row, class_row;

static void RegisterMainFormWidget (widget, client_data, call_data)
      Widget      widget;
      caddr_t     client_data;
      caddr_t     call_data;
{
      (* ((Widget*) client_data)) = widget;
}
```

The creation callbacks are called during *MrmFetchWidgets*, so the widget IDs have their desired values when *MrmFetchWidget* has finished. They can be used afterwards to create the further subtrees.

The general problem with the UIL approach is that even the most primitive callbacks cannot be expressed in the UIL and that a program using UIL must know a good deal of the widget hierarchy that is not explicit in the code. However, only the future will tell if there are fundamentally better approaches to be found.

Appendices

Appendix A

Glossary
of Terms

Abstract data type—a data type with a set of operations. No other operations can be applied to variables of the type.

Accelerator—a key combination used to activate a menu entry quickly without displaying that menu. More generally: a key combination that, when pressed in one widget, activates actions of another widget.

Application defaults file—a resource file containing default specifications for a certain application. Specified by the programmer, but individual entries can be overridden by the user.

Application Programmers' Interface (API)—the operations a programmer can use to create Motif applications.

Action—a procedure to respond to a special event that can be activated from the translations of a widget.

Argument list—list of resource field/value pairs to supply multiple arguments to a procedure.

Atom—a number uniquely identifying a string inside the X server. Used for communication.

Attachment—a constraint expressed for a child widget of a form widget to make one side stay in a fixed relation to some other point or widget.

Bitmap—a rectangular region of 1-bit pixels. May be a pixmap in the X server or stored in a file.

Button—either a physical button on the mouse, or a widget that simulates a real button on the screen.

Callback—mechanism activating a procedure of the application by a widget under specific conditions.

Callback list—list of procedures to be called when a callback occurs.

Child—window or widget that is contained in, and subordinate to, its parent.

Class—common description for a set of similar objects with equal structures but different attribute values.

Class hierarchy—logical ordering of classes, where a subclass is a specialization of its superclass. Subclasses may inherit, change, or add features.

Click—pressing and releasing a mouse button with no intervening pointer motion.

Client-server model—model where one process (the server) offers services to other processes (clients). Both communicate over some protocol and may reside on different machines in a network.

Clipboard—concept of a storage location hidden to the user which applications may use for temporary storage and exchange of information.

Clipping—ignoring parts of a drawing operation because they lie outside the visible area or the desired clipping region.

Colour database—table of correspondences between colour names and colour values on a specific display.

Colour map—table of correspondences between a limited set of numbers (usually 256) and real colour values (from a much larger range). Used to model hardware limitations for the maximum number of colours that can be displayed simultaneously.

Command line—arguments used to start a program. Available as parameters of the main procedure.

Composite widget—widget that may contain other widgets as children, whose geometries it controls.

Convenience widget—new widget functionality not implemented as a real widget class, instead defining a creation procedure that constructs a widget composition with preset resource fields and connected by call-backs.

Constraint resource fields—resource fields defined by a widget class which can be set differently for each child to specify attributes of this child that are relevant to the parent's function.

Converter—procedure to convert a resource field value from the external string representation used in the resource files and the resource database to the actual coding of the C data type.

Cursor—small graphical symbol on the screen that moves with the mouse or pointing device.

Cut & Paste—two step process to use the clipboard as an intermediate storage location to transfer data from one place to another.

Decoration—area around an application window maintained by the window manager to activate window manager functions.

Dialog box—separate top-level window that appears temporarily to support another window, e.g. for parameter entry and messages.

Direct manipulation—principle that allows graphical objects to be directly moved or reshaped with the mouse instead of by using commands.

Display—a combination of a keyboard, a mouse, and one or more screens controlled by the X server.

Double click—two clicks in rapid succession in the same place.

Drag—pressing and holding a mouse button and then moving the mouse to make some object follow the mouse movement.

Drawable—an object in the X server that can be the target of drawing operations (either a window or a pixmap).

Error database—list of error message texts read at program start-up.

Event—message sent from the X server to the application.

Event-driven—program structure where incoming events determine the flow of control.

Event handler—procedure to react to one or more types of events for a specific widget.

Event loop—"endless" loop to wait for events and handle them as they arrive.

Event mask—specification of which types of events an application wants to receive.

Fallback resources—list of resource specifications that are used when no application default file is found.

Focus—the window/widget which currently receives keyboard events.

Font—name for a typeface in a specific style, size, and emphasis used to map character codes to letters on the screen.

Font list—list of fonts to be used for different character sets in an XmString.

Gadget—a widget without a private X window that relies on its parent widget for event dispatching etc.

Geometry management—process of automatically negotiating size and location of widgets in a hierarchy.

Graphics context—a bundle of attributes for drawing operations, resident in the X server.

Hints—properties attached to a window that may be read by other clients (especially the window manager). They express application desires but need not be obeyed if the other clients do not understand or support this feature.

Icons—small pictures used to represent entities. Icons on the root window managed by the window manager represent top-level windows of applications.

Icon box—window where application icons are collected to save screen space.

Include file—prefabricated C file containing definitions necessary to use a certain part of a library.

Information hiding—principle of hiding implementation details behind a stable and sufficient external interface to enhance modularity.

Inheritance—mechanism to use the functionality of a superclass in a subclass without repeating it.

Insertion cursor—vertical line in a text widget indicating where the next typed character will go.

Instance—a widget of a certain class is called an instance of this class, because the functionality defined in a class is only visible through the behaviour of its instances.

Instance variable—private data associated with an instance of a class.

Inter-client communication conventions (ICCC)—a set of standard rules that govern interaction between clients and between the client and the window manager.

Intrinsics—basic library underlying Motif that implements fundamental mechanisms for constructing widget classes.

Keyboard traversal—*see* traversal.

Keycode—a hardware-specific number associated with a physical key on the keyboard.

Keysym—symbolic identifier for the meaning of a key, such as "Return".

Location cursor—visual identification of which widget or widget part has the focus (i.e. may be controlled) when controlling an application through the keyboard.

Manage—state transition to include a child of a composite widget in layout considerations.

Map—to make a window visible on the screen.

Menu pane—composite widget that contains all the menu entries that appear together.

Method—function of a class with a constant interface that may be implemented differently for different subclasses.

Mnemonic—character abbreviation for a menu command.

Modal—having multiple states in an application where a different and limited set of actions is possible.

Modeless—all controls of an application are available all the time.

Mouse—physical input device to indicate locations.

MRM—Motif Resource Manager. Library to interpret UID files to create widgets.

Object-oriented—partitioning functionality into a set of preferably independent objects. Object-oriented programming usually includes some kind of class hierarchy with inheritance.

Parent—window or widget that controls and encloses others.

Pending delete—if typing will delete the value of a previous selection.

Pixel—a single identifiable location on the screen or in a pixmap. May have a number of different colour values (black and white on a monochrome screen).

Pixmap—rectangular, invisible area of pixels in the X server. A pixmap has a certain depth indicating how many bits are used to represent its colour value.

Pointer—screen feedback of the current mouse position.

Pointer grab—state in which pointer events continue to be sent to a window even if the pointer leaves the window.

Pop-up—window or menu that becomes visible when a mouse button is pressed and disappears when the button is released.

Primitive widget—a widget that has no children. Its appearance is created using basic X drawing mechanisms.

Property—datum attached to a window identified by an arbitrary atom.

Pull-down—menu that appears under a menu bar and can be traversed while the mouse button is pressed.

Realize—process of creating the X window for a widget.

Reparenting—substituting the window manager decoration as a new parent for a top-level window.

Resource—entity stored in the X server and referenced through a symbolic ID (window, pixmap, GC, font). Also used to denote values for widget attributes.

Resource class—class name for a resource field used to specify equal values for a number of related resource fields, e.g. all background colours.

Resource database—database of relevant resource specifications for an application assembled from resource files on program start-up.

Resource field—individual attribute of a widget.

Resource file—file used to supply entries for the resource database.

Resource list—definition of a number of resource fields.

Root window—window representing the screen background and parent of all other windows.

Sash—small knob to adjust the pane size in a paned window.

Save-under—attribute of a window to instruct the X server to save the contents under this window for fast refresh, if possible.

Screen—physical display area. A display may have multiple screens.

Selection—a value available to all clients owned by one client that transfers this value upon request.

Server—*see* X server.

Shadows—areas around a widget drawn in lighter and darker colours to simulate the effect of a light source.

Shell widget—a widget controlling a top-level window. It has no visible appearance but only controls the interaction with the window manager.

Stacking—order in which the children of a window are stacked on one another to determine which one's contents are visible where the windows overlap.

Style guide—rules that define a uniform behaviour of Motif applications.

Subclass—specialization of a class, inheriting features from that class.

Superclass—more general class from which others inherit.

Tab group—a widget or group of widgets that may gain the input focus through the Tab key. Inside the tab group the location cursor can be moved with the arrow keys.

Target—atom to indicate what kind of information is requested from the selection owner about a selection.

Toolkit—objects and functions available to an application programmer.

Top-level window—window that is conceptually a direct child of the root window, but may be reparented by the window manager.

Transient—a window that represents a temporary dialog for another window.

Translation manager—code that maps events to widget actions.

Translations—attribute of a widget that specifies how incoming events are mapped to actions handling them. May be dynamically changed.

Traversal—process to move the input focus among widgets using the keyboard.

Tree—a structure that starts from a root node and branches to other nodes without creating a circle.

UID—user interface database file containing compiled information about a widget hierarchy that MRM may interpret.

UIL—user interface language to express presentation details of a user interface that may be compiled into a UID file.

Widget—basic interface object of the X Toolkit Intrinsics associated with an X window with encapsulated functionality.

Widget class—definition of common behaviour and attributes for widgets.

Widget hierarchy—composition of widgets into composite objects.

Window—rectangular area on the screen that may be used to display information independent of other windows.

Window manager—separate X client process to manage layout among top-level windows.

Window menu—pull-down menu to activate window manager functions.

Window Manager Protocol—defines a situation in which the window manager may send messages to clients and gives the meaning thereof.

XmStrings—special Motif type for strings with parts in different character sets.

X client—application process that uses the services of the X server for input and output.

Xlib—basic C library to support the services defined in the X protocol.

X protocol—protocol whereby X clients and X server communicate.

X server—process exclusively controlling the display hardware and accepting requests from clients.

X terminal—a hardware device that includes the X server, but which may not run clients. The clients must reside on other machines in the network.

X Toolkit Intrinsics—*see* Intrinsics.

X Window System—hardware-independent and network-transparent base layer, offering services to graphical user interfaces.

Appendix B

Further
Literature

Further Reading

For serious work you have to make yourself familiar with Xlib programming. There are two good tutorial books on the subject.

> Adrian Nye, *Xlib Programming Manual*, O'Reilly and Associates 1988, ISBN 0-937175-27-7

> Oliver Jones, *Introduction to the X Window System*, Prentice-Hall 1988, ISBN 0-13-499997-5

The Jones book has fewer examples, but covers more difficult topics.

There are also other books that cover programming with the X Toolkit Intrinsics.

> Adrian Nye, Tim O'Reilly, *X Toolkit Intrinsics Programming Manual*, O'Reilly and Associates 1990, ISBN 0-937175-34-X

> Douglas Young, *X Window System: Programming and Applications With Xt, OSF/Motif Edition*, Prentice-Hall 1990, ISBN 0-13-497074-8

The Young book uses the Motif widgets, but does not address many special Motif features. It contains a large number of examples of the use of Xlib routines together with widgets.

For Reference

Depending on what you received from your manufacturer or software supplier, you also need reference material. This material can be separated into three topics: Xlib, X Toolkit Intrinsics, and Motif.

O'Reilly and Associates, *Xlib Reference Manual*, O'Reilly and Associates 1988, ISBN 0-937175-28-5

Robert Scheifler, James Gettys, Ron Newman, *X Window System: C Library and Protocol reference*, DEC Press 1988, ISBN 1-55558-012-2

The latter is the Xlib "bible" written by the X designers and is the authoritative document. It is a slightly edited version of the manuals on the X11R4 distribution tapes from MIT.

O'Reilly and Associates, *X Toolkit Intrinsics Reference Manual*, O'Reilly and Associates 1990, ISBN 0-937175-33-7

There is a reprint of all the X11R3 manuals available which also contains the X Toolkit Intrinsics manual. The OSF reference manuals for Motif version 1.0 are also available in bound form.

ASP, Inc., *X Manual Set* (3 volumes), Addison-Wesley 1989, ISBN 0-201-17553-3

Open Software Foundation, *Motif Programmer's Reference*, Prentice-Hall 1990, ISBN 0-13-640517-7

For Design Issues

There are a number of books that cover general interface design issues. The most important is, of course, the Motif style guide.

Open Software Foundation, *Motif Style Guide*, Prentice-Hall 1990, ISBN 0-13-640491-X

You can also learn from other user interfaces, such as the Apple Macintosh and the Open Look specifications.

Apple Computer, *Human Interface Guidelines: The Apple Desktop Interface*, Addison-Wesley 1988, ISBN 0-201-17753-6

Sun Microsystems, Inc., *Open Look Graphical User Interface Application Style Guide*, Addison-Wesley 1990, ISBN 0-201-52364-7

Ben Shneiderman has written a general book about Human-Computer Interaction.

Ben Shneiderman, *Designing the User Interface*, Addison-Wesley 1987, ISBN 0-201-16505-8

Appendix C

"Stay Up"
Source Code

The File "StayUp.h"

```
/**********************************/
/* StayUp.h - header file for stay-up library    */
/**********************************/

void MakeDialogStayUp ();
```

The File "StayUp.c"

```
#include <Xm/Xm.h>
#include <X11/Protocols.h>

#define    STAY_UP        "\"Stay Up\"      f.send_msg 4417"
#define    XA_STAY_UP    (Atom)4417

#define XA_MOTIF_WM_MESSAGES XmInternAtom (XtDisplay(message_box), \
        "_MOTIF_WM_MESSAGES", False)
#define XA_WM_DELETE_WINDOW XmInternAtom (XtDisplay(message_box), \
        "WM_DELETE_WINDOW", True)
#define XA_WM_PROTOCOLS    XmInternAtom (XtDisplay(message_box), \
        "WM_PROTOCOLS", True)
```

```
static void DoUnmanage (message_box, client_data, call_data)
     Widget     message_box;
     caddr_t    client_data;
     caddr_t    call_data;
{

     XtUnmanageChild (message_box);
}


static void ReactivateEntry (w, client_data, call_data)
     Widget     w;  /* either message box or shell */
     caddr_t    client_data;
     caddr_t    call_data;
{
     Widget     message_box = (Widget) client_data,
                shell = XtParent (message_box);

     XtAddCallback (message_box, XmNokCallback, DoUnmanage, NULL);

     XmActivateProtocol (shell, XA_MOTIF_WM_MESSAGES, XA_STAY_UP);
     XtRemoveCallback (message_box, XmNcancelCallback,
                     ReactivateEntry, (caddr_t) message_box);
     XmRemoveProtocolCallback (shell, XA_WM_PROTOCOLS,
                     XA_WM_DELETE_WINDOW,
                     ReactivateEntry, (caddr_t) message_box);
}


static void StayUp (w, client_data, call_data)
     Widget     w;
     caddr_t    client_data;
     caddr_t    call_data;
{
     Widget     message_box = (Widget) client_data,
                shell = XtParent (message_box);

     XtRemoveCallback (message_box, XmNokCallback, DoUnmanage, NULL);

     XmDeactivateProtocol (shell, XA_MOTIF_WM_MESSAGES,
                     XA_STAY_UP);
     XtAddCallback (message_box, XmNcancelCallback,
                     ReactivateEntry, (caddr_t) message_box);
     XmAddProtocolCallback (shell, XA_WM_PROTOCOLS,
                     XA_WM_DELETE_WINDOW,
                     Reactivate, (caddr_t) message_box);
}
```

```
void MakeDialogStayUp (message_box)
    Widget      message_box;
{
    Arg         args[2];
    Widget      shell = XtParent (message_box);
    Atom        wm_messages = XA_MOTIF_WM_MESSAGES;

    XtSetArg (args[0], XmNmwmMenu, STAY_UP);
    XtSetArg (args[1], XmNdeleteResponse, XmUNMAP);
    XtSetValues (shell, args, 2);

    XtAddCallback (message_box, XmNokCallback, DoUnmanage, NULL);
    XtAddCallback (message_box, XmNcancelCallback, DoUnmanage, NULL);
    XmAddProtocolCallback (shell, XA_MOTIF_WM_MESSAGES,
                XA_STAY_UP, StayUp, (caddr_t) message_box);
    XmAddProtocols (shell, XA_WM_PROTOCOLS, &wm_messages, 1);
}
```

The File "staytest.c"

```
/* includes */
#include <Xm/Xm.h>
#include <X11/Shell.h>
#include <Xm/PushB.h>
#include <Xm/MessageB.h>

#include "StayUp.h"

/* global definitions */

#define PROGRAM_CLASS "StayUp"
#define ERROR_CLASS      "StayUpError"

#define NUM_ARGS 10

/* error definitions */

#define NErrCannotOpen      "cannotOpen"
#define TErrMain            "Main"

/*************************/

static void StartDialog (widget, client_data, call_data)
    Widget      widget;
    caddr_t     client_data;
    XmAnyCallbackStruct  *call_data;
```

```
{
    XtManageChild ((Widget) client_data);
}


static void CreateMainWindow (parent)
    Widget      parent;
{
    Widget      button, dia;
    Arg         args[NUM_ARGS];
    XmString    face;

    face = XmStringLtoRCreate ("PressMe",
                            XmSTRING_DEFAULT_CHARSET);
    XtSetArg (args[0], XmNlabelString, face);
    button = XtCreateManagedWidget ("button", xmPushButtonWidgetClass,
                            parent, args, 1);
    XmStringFree (face);

    face = XmStringLtoRCreate ("Read Me",
                            XmSTRING_DEFAULT_CHARSET);
    XtSetArg (args[0], XmNmessageString, face);
    dia = XmCreateMessageDialog (button, "dia", args, 1);
    XmStringFree (face);

    MakeDialogStayUp (dia);

    XtAddCallback (button, XmNactivateCallback, StartDialog, (caddr_t) dia);
}

/*****************************/

void main (argc, argv)
    unsigned int    argc;
    char            **argv;
{
    Display         *display;
    XtAppContext    context;
    Widget          toplevel;
    Arg             args[NUM_ARGS];

    /* initialize toolkit */
    XtToolkitInitialize();
    context = XtCreateApplicationContext ();
    display = XtOpenDisplay (
                context,    /* application context           */
                NULL,       /* use DISPLAY from environment  */
                NULL,       /* use last of argv[0] as name   */
```

```
        PROGRAM_CLASS,
        NULL,      /* no additional command line options   */
        0,         /* ditto                                 */
        &argc,
        argv);     /* use and delete standard options       */

if (display == NULL)   /* necessary !      */
    XtErrorMsg (
        NErrCannotOpen, TErrMain,      /* resource name */
        ERROR_CLASS,                   /* resource class   */
        "cannot open display",         /* default message */
        NULL, NULL);                   /* parameters      */

/* create application shell */
XtSetArg (args[0], XmNallowShellResize, True);
toplevel = XtAppCreateShell (
        NULL,                   /* use same program name    */
        PROGRAM_CLASS,   /* repeat class param       */
        applicationShellWidgetClass,
        display,
        args, 1);               /* argument list            */

/* create main window */
CreateMainWindow (toplevel);

/* start loop */
XtRealizeWidget (toplevel);
XtAppMainLoop (context);
}
```

Appendix D

"Motifhelp" Source Code

D.1 Program Source Files

The File "motifhelp.h"

```
#include <Xm/Xm.h>

/************************************************************
* Structure for every class as central reference and node in the class tree
************************************************************/

#define MAX_SUBCLASSES 10
#define MAX_RESOURCES 40

typedef struct _classDoc {
    String          name;
    XmString        xm_name;
    struct _classDoc *super;
    struct _classDoc *subs[MAX_SUBCLASSES];
    int             no_subs;
    int             level;
    Boolean         file_read;
```

```
        /* The following fields are only valid when file-read is True */
        int             no_res;      /* no of fields */
        String          res_name[MAX_RESOURCES],   /* field name      */
                        res_text[MAX_RESOURCES];    /* description text */
        XmString        res_string[MAX_RESOURCES],  /* name           */
                        res_class[MAX_RESOURCES],   /* class name     */
                        res_type[MAX_RESOURCES],    /* resource type  */
                        res_default[MAX_RESOURCES]; /* default value  */
        int             res_access[MAX_RESOURCES],  /* access flags   */
                        res_range[MAX_RESOURCES];
        int             sections;    /* which additional sections are present   */
} ClassDoc;


/* flag bits for access */


#define ACCESS_CREATE   1
#define ACCESS_WRITE    2
#define ACCESS_READ     4


/* possible values for range */


#define RANGE_CONSTRAINT   1
#define RANGE_SCROLLED     2
#define RANGE_SPECIAL      3


/* additional sections, flag bit is (1 << xxx_SEC) */


#define DESCRIPTION_SEC    1
#define BEHAVIOUR_SEC      2
#define CALLBACK_SEC       3
#define TRANSLATION_SEC    4
#define TRAVERSAL_SEC      5
#define COLOR_SEC          6


/************************************************************
 * Procedures defined in helpbuf.c
 ************************************************************/


/*
 * Shorthand utility for creating XmStrings
 */


XmString MakeXmString ();
        /* char    *string;    */


/*
 * Set the directory in which to look for help files
```

```
    */
void SetHelpDir ();
      /* String    help_dir;    */

/*
 * Get the alphabetically sorted list of all class names as a
 * list of XmStrings
 */

XmString *GetClassNames ();
      /* int *no_class_names;        */

/*
 * Get the root node of the class tree (e.g. for traversal)
 */
      ClassDoc *RootClass ();

/*
 * Fill the fields in the node structure if not already read
 */

void FillHelpInfo ();
      /* ClassDoc *doc;        */

/*
 * Read the text of an existing additional section into a buffer
 */

String ReadSection ();
      /* ClassDoc *doc;
      int section;  */

/*
 * Read a section in a specified file
 */

String ReadLongSection ();
      /* char      *file_ending;
      char  *section_name;    */

/*
 * Search the class tree for a node with a specific name
 */

ClassDoc *SearchClass ();
      /* XmString class_name;        */
```

```
/*
 * Find a list of matching fields for name fragment
 * - also store internal info about matches
 */

void FindMatchingFields ();
    /* String    fragment;
       XmString **match_list;
       int      *no_matches;     */

/*
 * Find info about member of current match list
 */

void LocateResource ();
    /* XmString       match_list_entry;
       ClassDoc    **which_doc;
       int      *which_entry;    */

/********************* Error Messages *********************/

#define ERROR_CLASS        "MhelpError"
#define WARN_CLASS         "MhelpWarning"

#define NErrCannotOpen     "cannotOpen"
#define TErrMain           "Main"

#define NErrInternal       "internal"
#define TErrMenu           "Menu"
#define TErrChain          "Chain"

#define NErrFileOpen       "fileOpen"
#define TErrClassfile      "Classfile"
#define TErrSection        "Section"

#define NWarnNFnd          "notFound"
#define TWarnField         "Field"
#define TWarnFile          "File"
```

The File "helpbuf.c"

```
#include "motifhelp.h"
#include <stdio.h>
```

```
/******************* Utility **************************/

XmString MakeXmString (string)
    char  *string;
{
    return XmStringLtoRCreate (string, XmSTRING_DEFAULT_CHARSET);
}

/****************** Information Storage ******************/

/* list of class names as XmStrings for list display and selection */

#define MAX_CLASS_NAMES 50

static XmString    class_name_list[MAX_CLASS_NAMES];
static int         no_class_names = 0;

/* root of class tree */

ClassDoc           *root_class = NULL;

/****************** Sorting ****************************/

#define SORTSIZE 400

static XmString   sortbuf[SORTSIZE];
int               sort_entries;
int               toggle = 0;  /* to deliver different lists to set values */

void InsertItem (item)
    XmString   item;
{
    int        pos, i;
    String     new, old;

    XmStringGetLtoR (item, "", &new);
    for (pos = toggle; pos < sort_entries+toggle; pos++){
        XmStringGetLtoR (sortbuf[pos], "", &old);
        if (strcmp (old, new) >= 0)
            break;
    }
    for (i = sort_entries+toggle; i > pos; i-)
        sortbuf [i] = sortbuf[i-1];
    sort_entries++;
    sortbuf[pos] = item;
}
```

```
XmString *SortStringList (list, no)
    XmString   list[];
    int        no;
{
    int        i;

    if (toggle == 0) toggle = 1; else toggle = 0;
    sort_entries = 0;
    for (i=0; i<no; i++)
        InsertItem (list[i]);
    return &sortbuf[toggle];
}
```

/********************* Help Dir ***************************/

```
#define NAME_BUFLENGTH 200
#define MHELP_PREFIX "motifhelp."

String    dir;

void SetHelpDir (new_dir)
    String    new_dir;
{
    dir = new_dir;
}

FILE *help_open (filename)
    String    filename;
{
    char      namebuffer[NAME_BUFLENGTH];

    strcpy (namebuffer, dir);
    strcat (namebuffer, MHELP_PREFIX);
    strcat (namebuffer, filename);
    return fopen (namebuffer, "r");
}
```

/******************** Initialization *********************/

/* allocate record for new class during initialization */

```
ClassDoc *AllocClassRec (name, parent)
    String     name;
    ClassDoc   *parent;
```

```
{
      ClassDoc   *me = XtNew (ClassDoc);
      int        i;

      me->name = XtMalloc (strlen (name) + 1);
      strcpy (me->name, name);
      me->xm_name = MakeXmString (name);
      me->super = parent;
      if (parent) {
            parent->subs[parent->no_subs] = me;
            parent->no_subs++;
            me->level = parent->level + 1; }
      else
            me->level = 1;
      me->no_subs = 0;
      me->no_res = 0;
      me->sections = 0;
      me->file_read = False;
      return me;
}

/* initialize list of classes and allocate records */

#define BIG_BUFLENGTH 1000

void ReadClassNameList ()
{
      FILE *in;
      char       inbuffer[BIG_BUFLENGTH];
      int        newlinepos;
      ClassDoc   *doc = NULL;
      int        indent, prev_indent=-1;
      XmString   *sortlist;
      int        i;

      in = help_open ("classes");
      if (in == NULL)
            XtErrorMsg (
                  NErrFileOpen, TErrClassfile,  /* resource name      */
                  ERROR_CLASS,                   /* resource class     */
                  "cannot open motifhelp.classes",  /* default message */
                  NULL, NULL);                   /* parameters         */
      no_class_names = 0;
```

```
while (fgets (inbuffer, BIG_BUFLENGTH, in)) {
        /* strip trailing newline */
        newlinepos = strlen (inbuffer)-1;
        if (inbuffer[newlinepos] == '\n') inbuffer[newlinepos] = '\0';
        /* count indentation as level in hierarchy */
        indent=0;
        while (inbuffer[indent] == ' ') indent++;
        /* determine parent by comparing with previous indent */
        while (prev_indent- >= indent) doc = doc->super;
        prev_indent = indent;
        /* allocate */
        doc = AllocClassRec (&inbuffer[indent], doc);
        if (doc->super == NULL) root_class = doc;
        class_name_list[no_class_names++] = doc->xm_name;
}
fclose (in);
sortlist = SortStringList (class_name_list, no_class_names);
for (i = 0; i < no_class_names; i++)
        class_name_list [i] = sortlist [i];
}


/* external interface procedures */

XmString *GetClassNames (no_of_names)
        int     *no_of_names;
{
        if (no_class_names == 0) ReadClassNameList ();
        *no_of_names = no_class_names;
        return class_name_list;
}


ClassDoc * RootClass ()
{
        if (no_class_names == 0) ReadClassNameList ();
        return root_class;
}


/***************** Searching *****************************/

/* recursive search procedure in class tree */

ClassDoc *SearchClassTree (node, name)
        ClassDoc    *node;
        XmString   name;
{
        ClassDoc    *res;
        int            i;
```

```
        if (XmStringCompare (node->xm_name, name)) return node;
        for (i=0; i<node->no_subs; i++)
              if ((res = SearchClassTree (node->subs[i], name)) != NULL)
                    return res;
        return NULL;
}

/* search class tree for named (XmString!) class */

ClassDoc *SearchClass (name)
        XmString   name;
{
        return SearchClassTree (root_class, name);
}

/*********************** File Scanning ********************/

#define BIGBIG_BUFSIZE 40000
#define MAXLINE 200
#define BIGLIMIT BIGBIG_BUFSIZE-MAXLINE

#define MAX_FILENAME 50
#define SMALL_BUFLENGTH 130

#define BLANK ' '
#define TAB '\t'
#define NULLC '\0'
#define NEWLINE '\n'

char        bigbuffer[BIGBIG_BUFSIZE];
char        inbuffer[SMALL_BUFLENGTH];

/* test for containment */

Boolean IsIn (in, str)
        char *in;
        char *str;
{
        char *current = in;

        while (*current != NULLC) {
              if (*current == *str)
                    if (strncmp (current, str, strlen (str)) == 0)
                          return True;
              current++;  }
        return False;
```

```
}

/* find range of following fields from header */

int FindRange (buf)
      char  *buf;
{
      if (IsIn (buf, "Constraint")) return 1;
      if (IsIn (buf, "Scrolled")) return 2;
      if (IsIn (buf, "Special")) return 3;
      return 0;
}


/* extract next table field between tabs */

char *NextInfield (start_pos)
      int    *start_pos;
{
      char  *start = &inbuffer[*start_pos];
      char  *current = start;
      char  last;
      int    len=0;

      while (*current != NEWLINE && *current != TAB &&
                                         *current != NULLC)
            {current++; len++;}
      last = *current;
      *current = NULLC;
      if (last != NULLC) (*start_pos) += len + 1;
      return start;
}



/* Read Single Line Entry in Class Table */

void ReadClassTableEntry (doc, range)
      ClassDoc   *doc;
      int         range;
{
      int         blankpos, entry, newl, val;
      char       *new;

      blankpos = 6;
      entry = doc->no_res;
      new = NextInfield (&blankpos);
      newl = strlen (new) + 1;
      doc->res_name[entry] = XtMalloc (newl);
```

```
            strcpy (doc->res_name[entry], new);
            doc->res_string[entry] =
                    MakeXmString (doc->res_name[entry]);
            doc->res_class[entry] =
                    MakeXmString (NextInfield (&blankpos));
            doc->res_type[entry] =
                    MakeXmString (NextInfield (&blankpos));
            doc->res_default[entry] =
                    MakeXmString (NextInfield (&blankpos));
            new = NextInfield (&blankpos);
            val = 0;
            if (*new == 'C') {val +=1; new++;}
            if (*new == 'S') {val +=2; new++;}
            if (*new == 'G') {val +=4; new++;}
            doc->res_access[entry] = val;
            doc->res_range[entry] = range;
            doc->no_res++;
}


/* read long text section */

void ReadLongText (file)
        FILE *file;
{
        int         count=0;

        while (fgets (&bigbuffer[count], MAXLINE, file)) {
            if (bigbuffer[count] == '#') {
                    strcpy (inbuffer, &bigbuffer[count]);
                    bigbuffer[count] = NULLC;
                    return;      }
            if (count < BIGLIMIT) count += strlen (&bigbuffer[count]);
        }
        inbuffer[0] = NULLC;
}


/* read one section of file */

Boolean ReadResourceText (doc, in)
        ClassDoc    *doc;
        FILE *in;
{
        char        *name = &inbuffer[6];
        int         findex, no_params = 1;
        char        *nameend = &inbuffer[strlen(inbuffer)-1];
```

```
        while (*nameend == NEWLINE || *nameend == TAB ||
                                          *nameend == BLANK)
             nameend–;
        *(++nameend) = NULLC;
        for (findex=0; findex < doc->no_res; findex++)
             if (strcmp (name, doc->res_name[findex]) == 0) break;
        if (findex == doc->no_res) {
             XtWarningMsg (
                  NWarnNFnd, TWarnField,       /* resource name     */
                  WARN_CLASS,                   /* resource class    */
                  "Field %s not found in table",  /* default message */
                  &name, &no_params);            /* parameters       */
             return False;
        }
        ReadLongText (in);
        doc->res_text[findex] = XtMalloc (strlen (bigbuffer) + 1);
        strcpy (doc->res_text[findex], bigbuffer);
        return True;
}

/* compare which sections exist */

#define SECTION0 "DESCRIPTION"
#define SECTION1 "Behavior"
#define SECTION2 "Callback"
#define SECTION3 "Default Translation"
#define SECTION4 "Traversal"
#define SECTION5 "Color"

#define NUM_SECTIONS 6

static String section_headers[] =
    {SECTION0, SECTION1, SECTION2, SECTION3, SECTION4, SECTION5};

/* test whether one of the sections is present */

void CompareSection (doc)
    ClassDoc *doc;
{
    int        i, mask = 1;

    for (i=0; i<NUM_SECTIONS; i++){
        if (strncmp (&inbuffer[3], section_headers[i],
                                      strlen (section_headers[i])) == 0)
             doc->sections += mask;
        mask += mask;
    }
```

```
}

/* read info text of class on demand from separate file */

void FillHelpInfo (doc)
    ClassDoc   *doc;
{
    FILE *in;
    Boolean    res_area, ahead;
    int        newlinepos, range = 0, no_params = 1;
    char       *getres;

    /* test if already read */
    if (doc->file_read) return;
    doc->file_read = True;

    /* filename = motifhelp.<classname> */
    in = help_open (doc->name);
    if (in == NULL) {
        XtWarningMsg (
            NWarnNFnd, TWarnFile,          /* resource name    */
            WARN_CLASS,                    /* resource class   */
            "File %s not found",           /* default message  */
            &(doc->name), &no_params);     /* parameters       */
        return; /* ignore for now */
    }

    res_area = False;
    getres = fgets (inbuffer, SMALL_BUFLENGTH, in);
    while (getres) {
        ahead = False;
        if (res_area) {
            if (strncmp (inbuffer, "#1 ", 3) == 0)
                res_area = False;
            if (strncmp (inbuffer, "#2 ", 3) == 0)
                ahead = ReadResourceText (doc, in);
            if (strncmp (inbuffer, "#3 ", 3) == 0)
                ReadClassTableEntry (doc, range);
            if (strncmp (inbuffer, "#4 ", 3) == 0)
                range = FindRange (inbuffer);}
        else {
            if (strcmp (inbuffer, "#1 New Resources\n") == 0)
                res_area = True;
            if (strncmp (inbuffer, "#1 ", 3) == 0)
                CompareSection (doc);
        }
        if (!ahead) getres = fgets (inbuffer, SMALL_BUFLENGTH, in);
```

```
        }
}

/* read long section into bigbuffer */

String ReadLongSection (ending, section)
        char        *ending;
        char        *section;
{
        FILE *in;
        char        comp[MAX_FILENAME];
        int         complen, no_params = 1;

        /* filename = motifhelp.<classname> */
        in = help_open (ending);
        bigbuffer[0] = NULLC;
        if (in == NULL) {
            XtWarningMsg (
                    NWarnNFnd, TWarnFile,      /* resource name      */
                    WARN_CLASS,                /* resource class     */
                    "File %s not found",       /* default message    */
                    &ending, &no_params);      /* parameters         */
            return; /* ignore for now */
        }

        strcpy (comp, "#1 ");
        strcat (comp, section);
        complen = strlen (comp);
        while (fgets (inbuffer, SMALL_BUFLENGTH, in)) {
            if (strncmp (inbuffer, comp, complen) == 0)
                    {ReadLongText (in); return bigbuffer;}
        }
        return bigbuffer;
}

/* read special labelled section from manual page into bigbuffer */

String ReadSection (doc, section)
        ClassDoc    *doc;
        int         section;
{
        if (section >= 1 && section <= NUM_SECTIONS)
            return ReadLongSection (doc->name, section_headers [section-1]);
        else
            XtErrorMsg (
                    NErrInternal, TErrSection,  /* resource name      */
                    ERROR_CLASS,                /* resource class     */
```

```
                     "wrong section number",      /* default message     */
                     NULL, NULL);                  /* parameters          */
}


/************************** Field Searching ********************/

#define MAX_MATCH 300

struct {
      ClassDoc *doc;
      int        entry;
      int        multiple;
} m_res[MAX_MATCH];

/* table of matching resource fields */

static XmString    show[MAX_MATCH];

static int          no_res_match = 0;

/* find index of selected resource in match table */

void LocateResource (xm, doc, entry)
      XmString   xm;
      ClassDoc    **doc;
      int          *entry;
{
      int          i;

      *doc = NULL;
      for (i=0; i<no_res_match; i++)
            if (XmStringCompare (xm, show[i])) {
                  *doc = m_res [i]. doc;
                  *entry = m_res [i]. entry;
                  return;
            }
}

/* recursively search classes and assemble match table */

void SearchResource (name, doc)
      String      name;
      ClassDoc    *doc;
{
      int          i, j;
```

```
      FillHelpInfo (doc);
      for (i=0; i<doc->no_res; i++)
            if (IsIn (doc->res_name[i], name)) {
                  m_res[no_res_match].doc = doc;
                  m_res[no_res_match].entry = i;
                  m_res[no_res_match].multiple = -1;
                  show[no_res_match] = NULL;
                  for (j=no_res_match-1; j>=0; j--)
                        if (strcmp (m_res[j].doc->res_name[m_res[j].entry],
                                                  doc->res_name[i]) == 0)
                              {m_res[no_res_match].multiple=j; break;}
                  no_res_match++;
            }
      for (i=0; i<doc->no_subs; i++)
            SearchResource (name, doc->subs[i]);
}


/* set representation of matching resource (append classname) */

void SetShow (index, multi)
      int         index;
      Boolean     multi;
{
      char        buffer[SMALL_BUFLENGTH];

      strcpy (buffer, m_res[index].doc->res_name[m_res[index].entry]);
      if (multi) {
            strcat (buffer, " <");
            strcat (buffer, m_res[index].doc->name);
            strcat (buffer, ">");
      }
      show[index] = MakeXmString (buffer);
}



/* create match table for incomplete specification */

void FindMatchingFields (name, list, no_fields)
      String      name;
      XmString    **list;
      int         *no_fields;
{
      int         i, j;

      for (i=0; i<no_res_match; i++) XmStringFree (show[i]);
      no_res_match = 0;
      SearchResource (name, root_class);
```

```
        for (i=no_res_match-1; i>=0; i-)
            if (show[i] == NULL)   if (m_res[i].multiple >= 0) {
                j = i;
                while (j>=0) {SetShow (j, True); j=m_res[j].multiple;}
            }
            else
                    SetShow (i, False);
        *no_fields = no_res_match;
        *list = SortStringList (show, no_res_match);
}
```

The File "motifhelp.c"

```
/*************************************************************
 *
 *      motifhelp.c
 *
 *      Displays Information about Motif Widget Classes
 *
 *      Author:
 *      Thomas Berlage, GMD
 *      P.O. Box 1240
 *      D-5205 Sankt Augustin 1
 *      Phone: +49 (2241) 14-0
 *      Email: berlage@gmdzi.gmd.de
 *
 *      Version 1.2
 *      05.07.90
 *
 *************************************************************/

#include "motifhelp.h"

#include <stdio.h>
#include <strings.h>

#include <Xm/Xm.h>
#include <X11/Shell.h>
#include <Xm/MainW.h>
#include <Xm/Text.h>
#include <Xm/RowColumn.h>
#include <Xm/BulletinB.h>
#include <Xm/CascadeB.h>
#include <Xm/CascadeBG.h>
#include <Xm/DrawnB.h>
#include <Xm/Frame.h>
```

```
#include <Xm/Form.h>
#include <Xm/Label.h>
#include <Xm/LabelG.h>
#include <Xm/List.h>
#include <Xm/MessageB.h>
#include <Xm/PanedW.h>
#include <Xm/PushB.h>
#include <Xm/PushBG.h>
#include <Xm/SelectioB.h>
#include <Xm/ScrolledW.h>
#include <Xm/ToggleB.h>
#include <Xm/ToggleBG.h>
#include <Xm/Separator.h>
#include <Xm/SeparatoG.h>
#include <Xm/PanedW.h>


/***************** Forward Declarations *******************/

/* menu system */
Widget CreateMenus ();
void SetSectionSensitivity ();
void SetSubclassesMenu ();

/* main form */
void CreateMainForm ();

/* superclass chain */
void CreateClassChain ();
void ChangeClassChain ();
ClassDoc *ActiveDoc ();

/* resource selection list */
void CreateSelectionList ();
void SetResourceSelectionList ();
void SelectResourceEntry ();

/* parameter field */
void CreateParameterField ();
void ParamVisibility ();
Boolean ParamIsVisible ();
void SetParameterField ();

/* help text area */
void CreateHelpText ();
void SetHelpText ();

/* class selection dialog */
```

```
void CreateClassSelectionDialog ();
void PopupClassDialog ();

/* resource selection dialog */
void CreateResSelectionDialog ();
void PopupResDialog ();

/* help dialog */
void CreateHelpDialog ();
void PopupHelpDialog ();

/********************** Global Data *************************/

#define NUM_ARGS 10        /* max. size of argument list in this program */
#define SMALL_BUFLENGTH 130


/*********************** Main Program *********************/

#define PROGRAM_CLASS "Mhelp"

#define MAIN_TITLE  "Motif Help Browser"

/* structure for additional application resources */

typedef struct {
     String        help_dir;
} AppData, *AppDataPtr;

static XtResource resources [] = {
     {"helpDir", "Dir", XmRString, sizeof (String),
      XtOffset (AppDataPtr, help_dir), XmRString, ""}
};

/* additional command line options */

XrmOptionDescRec options [] = {
     {"-dir", "*helpDir", XrmoptionSepArg, ""}
};


/* main program */

main (argc, argv)
     unsigned int      argc;
     char              **argv;
{
```

```
Display          *display;
XtAppContext     context;
AppData          data;
Arg              args[NUM_ARGS];
Widget           toplevel, bar, main_w, menu,pane;
Widget           frame1, form;

/* initialize toolkit */
XtToolkitInitialize();
context = XtCreateApplicationContext ();
display = XtOpenDisplay (
           context,      /* application context                    */
           NULL,         /* use DISPLAY from environment           */
           NULL,         /* use last of argv[0] as name            */
           PROGRAM_CLASS,
           options,      /* additional command line options        */
           XtNumber (options),
           &argc,
           argv);        /* use and delete standard options        */

if (display == NULL)      /* necessary !    */
     XtErrorMsg (
           NErrCannotOpen, TErrMain,      /* resource name     */
           ERROR_CLASS,                   /* resource class    */
           "cannot open display",         /* default message   */
           NULL, NULL);                   /* parameters        */

/* create application shell */
XtSetArg (args[0], XmNtitle, MAIN_TITLE);
toplevel = XtAppCreateShell (
           NULL,                      /* use same program name   */
           PROGRAM_CLASS,   /* repeat class param      */
           applicationShellWidgetClass,
           display,
           args, 1);                  /* argument list           */

/* read additional resources */
XtGetApplicationResources (toplevel, &data, resources,
                     XtNumber (resources), NULL, 0);
SetHelpDir (data.help_dir);

/* create main window */
main_w = XtCreateManagedWidget ("main", xmMainWindowWidgetClass,
                     toplevel, NULL, 0);

/* create menus */
bar = CreateMenus (main_w);
```

```
        /* create paned window */
        pane = XtCreateManagedWidget ("pane", xmPanedWindowWidgetClass,
                            main_w, args, 0);

        /* create selection pane ... */
        CreateMainForm (pane);

        /* create text pane ... */
        CreateHelpText (pane);

        XmMainWindowSetAreas (main_w, bar, NULL, NULL, NULL, pane);

        /* create dialog shells */
        CreateClassSelectionDialog (bar);
        CreateResSelectionDialog (bar);
        CreateHelpDialog (bar);

        /* set initial class */
        ChangeClassChain (SearchClass (MakeXmString ("FileSelectionBox")));

        /* start loop */
        XtRealizeWidget (toplevel);
        XtAppMainLoop(context);
}

/*********************** Menus ***************************/

/* widget ID's for all the menu buttons */

#define MAX_MENU_BUTTONS 8

static Widget       buttons1[MAX_MENU_BUTTONS],
                    buttons2[MAX_MENU_BUTTONS],
                    buttons3[MAX_MENU_BUTTONS],
                    buttons4[MAX_MENU_BUTTONS],
                    buttons5[MAX_MENU_BUTTONS],
                    buttons6[MAX_MENU_BUTTONS],
                    buttons7[MAX_MENU_BUTTONS];


/* identify button index from callback */

int ButtonIndex (buttons, call_data)
        Widget                      buttons[MAX_MENU_BUTTONS];
        XmRowColumnCallbackStruct   *call_data;
{
```

```
    int         i;

    for (i=0; i<MAX_MENU_BUTTONS; i++)
        if (buttons[i] == call_data->widget) return i;
    XtErrorMsg (
        NErrInternal, TErrMenu,     /* resource name     */
        ERROR_CLASS,                /* resource class    */
        "button not found",         /* default message   */
        NULL, NULL);                /* parameters        */
    return -1;
}


/*** File Menu ***/

void HandleFileMenu (w, client_data, call_data)
    Widget                          w;
    caddr_t                         client_data;
    XmRowColumnCallbackStruct       *call_data;
{
    exit (0);
}


/*** Edit Menu ***/

void HandleEditMenu (w, client_data, call_data)
    Widget                          w;
    caddr_t                         client_data;
    XmRowColumnCallbackStruct       *call_data;
{
}


/*** Locate Menu ***/

void HandleLocateMenu (w, client_data, call_data)
    Widget                          w;
    caddr_t                         client_data;
    XmRowColumnCallbackStruct       *call_data;
{
    switch (ButtonIndex (buttons3, call_data)) {
        case 0:
            PopupClassDialog ();
            break;
        case 1:
            PopupResDialog();
            break;
    }
}
```

```
/*** Option Menu ***/

void HandleOptionMenu (w, client_data, call_data)
      Widget                           w;
      caddr_t                          client_data;
      XmRowColumnCallbackStruct        *call_data;
{
      int    who = ButtonIndex (buttons4, call_data);

      ParamVisibility (who, ! ParamIsVisible (who));
}


/*** Info Menu ***/

void HandleInfoMenu (w, client_data, call_data)
      Widget                           w;
      caddr_t                          client_data;
      XmRowColumnCallbackStruct        *call_data;
{
      Arg          args[NUM_ARGS];
      String       buffer;

      buffer = ReadSection (ActiveDoc (), ButtonIndex (buttons5, call_data) + 1);
      SetHelpText (buffer);
}

/* Adjust sensitivity of menu buttons to reflect which sections exist */

void SetSectionSensitivity (doc)
      ClassDoc    *doc;
{
      int          i, mask;

      mask = 1;
      for (i=0; i<COLOR_SEC; i++) {
            XtSetSensitive (buttons5[i], doc->sections & mask);
            mask+= mask;
      }
}


/*** Subclasses Menu ***/

void HandleSubclassMenu (w, client_data, call_data)
      Widget                           w;
      caddr_t                          client_data;
      XmRowColumnCallbackStruct        *call_data;
{
```

```
        int          chosen_entry = ButtonIndex (buttons6, call_data);
        ClassDoc    *doc = ActiveDoc ();

        ChangeClassChain (doc->subs [chosen_entry]);
}


/* Build a new subclasses menu for the current class */

void SetSubclassesMenu (doc)
        ClassDoc    *doc;
{
        int          i;
        Arg          args[NUM_ARGS];

        XtUnmanageChildren (buttons6, MAX_MENU_BUTTONS);
        for (i=0; i<doc->no_subs; i++) {
            XtSetArg (args[0], XmNlabelString, doc->subs[i]->xm_name);
            XtSetValues (buttons6[i], args, 1);
        }
        XtManageChildren (buttons6, doc->no_subs);  }

/*** Help Menu ***/

void HandleHelpMenu (w, client_data, call_data)
        Widget                        w;
        caddr_t                       client_data;
        XmRowColumnCallbackStruct    *call_data;
{
        Arg   args[NUM_ARGS];
        String buffer;

        buffer = ReadLongSection ("help", "Version");
        PopupHelpDialog (buffer);
}


/******************** Menu Creation **************************/

/* labels for the menus */

#define FILE_MENU              "File"
#define EDIT_MENU              "Edit"
#define LOCATE_MENU            "Locate"
#define OPTIONS_MENU           "Options"
#define INFO_MENU              "Info"
#define SUBCLASSES_MENU        "Subclasses"
#define HELP_MENU              "Help"
```

```
static String       menu1[] =
      {"New", "Open...", "Save", "Save As...", "Print...", "Exit"};

static String       menu2[] =
      {"Undo", "Cut", "Copy", "Paste", "", "Clear", "Delete"};

static String       menu3[] =
      {"Widget Class...", "Resource Name..."};

static String       menu4[] =
      {"Class", "Type", "Default", "Access", "Range"};

static String       menu5[] =
      {"Description", "Behaviour", "Callback", "Translations", "Traversal",
       "Color"};

static String       menu6[] = /* only placeholders */
      {"1", "2", "3", "4", "5", "6", "7", "8"};

static String       menu7[] =
      {"On Context", "On Window", "On Keys", "Index", "On Help",
       "Tutorial", "On Version"};

/* determine default mnemonic */

#define BLANK ' '
#define NULLC '\0'

char DefaultMnemonic (label)
      String      label;
{
      char  *pos = label;

      while (*pos != NULLC)
              if (*pos++ == BLANK) return *pos;
      return *label;
}

/* create one pulldown menu */

Widget CreateOneMenu (parent, name, labels, num_labels, buttons, is_toggle)
      Widget      parent;
      char        *name;
      char        *labels[];
      int         num_labels;
      Widget      buttons[10];
      Boolean     is_toggle;
```

```
{
    Widget      shell, casc;
    Arg         args[NUM_ARGS];
    int         row;
    XmString    buffer;

    /* create pulldown menu */
    shell = XmCreatePulldownMenu (parent, name, NULL, 0);

    /* create buttons */
    for (row = 0; row < num_labels; row++) {
        if (strlen (labels[row]) == 0) {
            buttons[row] =
                    XmCreateSeparatorGadget (shell, "msep", NULL, 0); }
        else {
            buffer = MakeXmString (labels[row]);
            XtSetArg (args[0], XmNlabelString, buffer);
            XtSetArg (args[1], XmNmnemonic,
                DefaultMnemonic (labels[row]));
            if (is_toggle) {
                XtSetArg (args[2], XmNset, True);
                buttons[row] =
                    XmCreateToggleButtonGadget (shell, "mtoggle",
                                                        args, 3);}
            else {
                buttons[row] =
                    XmCreatePushButtonGadget (shell, "mbutton",
                                                        args, 2);
            }
            XmStringFree (buffer);
        }
    }

    /* manage all buttons */
    XtManageChildren (buttons, num_labels);

    /* create cascade button */
    buffer = MakeXmString (name);
    XtSetArg (args[0], XmNlabelString, buffer);
    XtSetArg (args[1], XmNmnemonic, *name);
    XtSetArg (args[2], XmNsubMenuId, shell);
    casc = XtCreateManagedWidget ("casbutton",
                    xmCascadeButtonWidgetClass, parent, args, 3);
    XmStringFree (buffer);

    if (strcmp (name, HELP_MENU) == 0) {
        XtSetArg (args[0], XmNmenuHelpWidget, casc);
```

```
            XtSetValues (parent, args, 1);
      }

      return shell;
}


/* set accelerator for button */            Keys  string

void SetAccelerator (button, acc, acc_text)
      Widget      button;
      char        *acc;
      char        *acc_text;
{
      Arg         args[NUM_ARGS];
      XmString    s;

      s = MakeXmString (acc_text);
      XtSetArg (args[0], XmNaccelerator, acc);
      XtSetArg (args[1], XmNacceleratorText, s);
      XtSetValues (button, args, 2);
      XmStringFree (s);
}


/* create all menus */

Widget CreateMenus (parent)
      Widget      parent;
{
      Widget      bar, menu;
      int         i;
      Arg         args[NUM_ARGS];

      bar = XmCreateMenuBar (parent, "bar", NULL, 0);
      XtManageChild (bar);

      /* create file menu */
      menu = CreateOneMenu (bar, FILE_MENU,
                            menu1, XtNumber (menu1), buttons1, False);
      XtAddCallback (menu, XmNentryCallback, HandleFileMenu, NULL);
      XtSetSensitive (buttons1[0], False);
      XtSetSensitive (buttons1[1], False);
      XtSetSensitive (buttons1[2], False);
      XtSetSensitive (buttons1[3], False);
      XtSetSensitive (buttons1[4], False);
```

```
/* create edit menu */
menu = CreateOneMenu (bar, EDIT_MENU,
                      menu2, XtNumber (menu2), buttons2, False);
XtAddCallback (menu, XmNentryCallback, HandleEditMenu, NULL);
XtSetSensitive (buttons2[0], False);
SetAccelerator (buttons2[0], "Meta<Key>Backspace:", "Alt+Backspace");
XtSetSensitive (buttons2[1], False);
SetAccelerator (buttons2[1], "Shift<Key>Delete:", "Shift+Del");
XtSetArg (args[0], XmNmnemonic, 't');
XtSetValues (buttons2[1], args, 1);
XtSetSensitive (buttons2[2], False);
SetAccelerator (buttons2[2], "Ctrl<Key>Insert:", "Ctrl+Ins");
XtSetSensitive (buttons2[3], False);
SetAccelerator (buttons2[3], "Shift<Key>Insert:", "Shift+Ins");
XtSetSensitive (buttons2[5], False);
XtSetArg (args[0], XmNmnemonic, 'e');
XtSetValues (buttons2[5], args, 1);
XtSetSensitive (buttons2[6], False);

/* create locate menu */
menu = CreateOneMenu (bar, LOCATE_MENU,
                      menu3, XtNumber (menu3), buttons3, False);
XtAddCallback (menu, XmNentryCallback, HandleLocateMenu, NULL);
SetAccelerator (buttons3[0], "<Key>F5:", "F5");
SetAccelerator (buttons3[1], "<Key>F6:", "F6");

/* create options menu */
menu = CreateOneMenu (bar, OPTIONS_MENU,
                      menu4, XtNumber (menu4), buttons4, True);
XtAddCallback (menu, XmNentryCallback, HandleOptionMenu, NULL);

/* create info menu */
menu = CreateOneMenu (bar, INFO_MENU,
                      menu5, XtNumber (menu5), buttons5, False);
XtAddCallback (menu, XmNentryCallback, HandleInfoMenu, NULL);
XtSetArg (args[0], XmNmnemonic, 'l');
XtSetValues (buttons5[3], args, 1);

/* create subclasses menu */
menu = CreateOneMenu (bar, SUBCLASSES_MENU,
                      menu6, XtNumber (menu6), buttons6, False);
XtAddCallback (menu, XmNentryCallback, HandleSubclassMenu, NULL);

/* create help menu */
menu = CreateOneMenu (bar, HELP_MENU,
                      menu7, XtNumber (menu7), buttons7, False);
XtAddCallback (menu, XmNentryCallback, HandleHelpMenu, NULL);
```

```
        XtSetSensitive (buttons7[0], False);
        XtSetSensitive (buttons7[1], False);
        XtSetSensitive (buttons7[2], False);
        XtSetSensitive (buttons7[3], False);
        XtSetSensitive (buttons7[4], False);
        XtSetSensitive (buttons7[5], False);

        return bar;
}


/****************** Main Form *******************************/

#define LABEL_CLASS_CHAIN    "Superclass Chain"
#define LABEL_RES_FIELDS     "Resource Fields"
#define LABEL_EMPTY_NAME     "XmN..."

Widget      param_label;


void CreateMainForm (parent)
        Widget      parent;
{
        Arg         args[NUM_ARGS];
        XmString    s;
        int         n;
        Widget      form;
        Widget      class_label, res_label;
        Widget      class_row, res_row, param_row;
        Widget      class_frame, param_frame;

        form = XtCreateManagedWidget ("form", xmFormWidgetClass, parent,
                                        args, 0);

        /* create XmString for label */
        s = MakeXmString (LABEL_CLASS_CHAIN);
        /* set up arguments for label widget */
        n=0;
        XtSetArg (args[n], XmNlabelString, s); n++;
        XtSetArg (args[n], XmNresizable, False); n++;
        XtSetArg (args[n], XmNtopAttachment, XmATTACH_FORM); n++;
        XtSetArg (args[n], XmNbottomAttachment, XmATTACH_NONE); n++;
        XtSetArg (args[n], XmNleftAttachment, XmATTACH_FORM); n++;
        class_label = XtCreateManagedWidget ("listLabel", xmLabelWidgetClass,
                                        form, args, n);
        XmStringFree (s);
```

```
n=0;
XtSetArg (args[n], XmNtopAttachment, XmATTACH_WIDGET); n++;
XtSetArg (args[n], XmNtopWidget, class_label); n++;
XtSetArg (args[n], XmNbottomAttachment, XmATTACH_FORM); n++;
XtSetArg (args[n], XmNleftAttachment, XmATTACH_FORM); n++;
XtSetArg (args[n], XmNshadowType, XmSHADOW_IN); n++;
class_frame = XtCreateManagedWidget ("classFrame",
                                xmFrameWidgetClass, form, args, n);
n=0;
XtSetArg (args[n], XmNorientation, XmVERTICAL); n++;
XtSetArg (args[n], XmNspacing, 0); n++;
XtSetArg (args[n], XmNradioBehavior, True); n++;
XtSetArg (args[n], XmNradioAlwaysOne, True); n++;
XtSetArg (args[n], XmNentryAlignment, XmALIGNMENT_CENTER);
n++;
class_row = XtCreateManagedWidget ("classRow",
                            xmRowColumnWidgetClass, class_frame, args, n);
CreateClassChain (class_row);
XmAddTabGroup (class_row);

/* create status pane ... */
n=0;
XtSetArg (args[n], XmNtopAttachment, XmATTACH_WIDGET); n++;
XtSetArg (args[n], XmNtopWidget, class_label); n++;
XtSetArg (args[n], XmNbottomAttachment, XmATTACH_FORM); n++;
XtSetArg (args[n], XmNrightAttachment, XmATTACH_FORM); n++;
XtSetArg (args[n], XmNshadowType, XmSHADOW_IN); n++;
param_frame = XtCreateManagedWidget ("pFrame", xmFrameWidgetClass,
                            form, args, n);


n=0;
param_row = XtCreateManagedWidget ("pRow",
                            xmRowColumnWidgetClass, param_frame, args, n);

/* create XmString for label */
s = MakeXmString (LABEL_EMPTY_NAME);
/* set up arguments for label widget */
n=0;
XtSetArg (args[n], XmNlabelString, s); n++;
XtSetArg (args[n], XmNtopAttachment, XmATTACH_FORM); n++;
XtSetArg (args[n], XmNbottomAttachment, XmATTACH_NONE); n++;
XtSetArg (args[n], XmNleftAttachment,
                        XmATTACH_OPPOSITE_WIDGET); n++;
XtSetArg (args[n], XmNleftWidget, param_frame); n++;
XtSetArg (args[n], XmNleftOffset, 0); n++;
param_label = XtCreateManagedWidget ("pLabel",
                        xmLabelWidgetClass, form, args, n);
```

```
        XmStringFree (s);

        CreateParameterField (param_row);

        /* create XmString for label */
        s = MakeXmString (LABEL_RES_FIELDS);
        /* set up arguments for label widget */
        n=0;
        XtSetArg (args[n], XmNlabelString, s); n++;
        XtSetArg (args[n], XmNresizable, False); n++;
        XtSetArg (args[n], XmNtopAttachment, XmATTACH_FORM); n++;
        XtSetArg (args[n], XmNbottomAttachment, XmATTACH_NONE); n++;
        XtSetArg (args[n], XmNleftAttachment, XmATTACH_WIDGET); n++;
        XtSetArg (args[n], XmNleftWidget, class_frame); n++;
        res_label = XtCreateManagedWidget ("listLabel",
                            xmLabelWidgetClass, form, args, n);
        XmStringFree (s);

        /* set up arguments for scrolled window */
        n=0;
        XtSetArg (args[n], XmNtopAttachment, XmATTACH_WIDGET); n++;
        XtSetArg (args[n], XmNtopWidget, res_label); n++;
        XtSetArg (args[n], XmNbottomAttachment, XmATTACH_FORM); n++;
        XtSetArg (args[n], XmNrightAttachment, XmATTACH_WIDGET); n++;
        XtSetArg (args[n], XmNrightWidget, param_frame); n++;
        XtSetArg (args[n], XmNleftAttachment, XmATTACH_WIDGET); n++;
        XtSetArg (args[n], XmNleftWidget, class_frame); n++;
        /* create scrolled window */
        res_row = XtCreateManagedWidget ("resSW",
                            xmScrolledWindowWidgetClass, form, args, n);

        CreateSelectionList (res_row);
}

void SetParamLabel (doc, entry)
        ClassDoc    *doc;
        int         entry;
{
        Arg         args[NUM_ARGS];
        XmString    s;
        char        strbuf[SMALL_BUFLENGTH];

        strcpy (strbuf, "XmN");
        strcat (strbuf, doc->res_name[entry]);
        s = MakeXmString (strbuf);
        XtSetArg (args[0], XmNlabelString, s);
        XtSetValues (param_label, args, 1);
```

```
        XmStringFree (s);
}

/******************* Superclass Chain ************************/

/* superclass chain parameters */

#define MAX_CLASS_DEPTH 11
#define MAX_CLASS_WIDGETS 2*MAX_CLASS_DEPTH-1

/* alternating buttons and separators */

static Widget      class_chain[MAX_CLASS_WIDGETS];
static ClassDoc    *cl_docs[MAX_CLASS_WIDGETS];

/* the activated (pressed) class or -1 */

static int         active_class;

/* forward declarations for this section */

void ArmClass ();
void ActivateClass ();

/* report the active class node */

ClassDoc *ActiveDoc ()
{
    if (active_class >= 0)
        return cl_docs[active_class];
    else
        XtErrorMsg (
            NErrInternal, TErrChain,    /* resource name    */
            ERROR_CLASS,                /* resource class   */
            "no active class",          /* default message  */
            NULL, NULL);                /* parameters       */
}

/* Callback for inverting foreground and background */

void InvertToggle (w, client_data,  call_data)
    Widget     w;
    caddr_t    client_data;
    XmToggleButtonCallbackStruct    *call_data;
{
    Arg        args[NUM_ARGS];
    Pixel      fg, bg;
```

```
        XtSetArg (args[0], XmNforeground, &fg);
        XtSetArg (args[1], XmNbackground, &bg);
        XtGetValues (w, args, 2);
        XtSetArg (args[0], XmNforeground, bg);
        XtSetArg (args[1], XmNbackground, fg);
        XtSetValues (w, args, 2);
}


/* arm callback procedure for drawn button */

void ArmClass (w, client_data, call_data)
        Widget      w;
        caddr_t     client_data;
        caddr_t     call_data;
{
        Arg         args[NUM_ARGS];
        int         index = (int) client_data;

        ActivateClass (index);
}


/* create widgets for class chain */

void CreateClassChain (parent)
        Widget      parent;
{
        int   i;
        Arg   args[NUM_ARGS];

        for (i=0; i<MAX_CLASS_DEPTH; i++) {
                XtSetArg (args[0], XmNindicatorOn, False);
                XtSetArg (args[1], XmNshadowThickness, 2);
                XtSetArg (args[2], XmNfillOnSelect, True);
                class_chain[2*i] =
                        XtCreateWidget ("chain", xmToggleButtonWidgetClass,
                                        parent, args, 3);
                XtAddCallback (class_chain[2*i], XmNarmCallback, ArmClass, 2*i);
                XtAddCallback (class_chain[2*i], XmNvalueChangedCallback,
                                        InvertToggle, NULL);
                XtSetArg (args[0], XmNorientation, XmVERTICAL);
                class_chain [2*i+1] =
                        XtCreateWidget ("c_sep", xmSeparatorGadgetClass,
                                        parent, args, 1);
        }
        active_class = -1;
}
```

```
/* make one widget the active class */

void ActivateClass (chain_pos)
      int            chain_pos;
{
      ClassDoc    *doc;

      active_class = chain_pos;
      /* read help if necessary */
      doc = cl_docs[active_class];
      FillHelpInfo (doc);
      /* set the selection list contents */
      SetResourceSelectionList (doc);
      /* sensitivity in info menu */
      SetSectionSensitivity (doc);
      /* create subclasses menu */
      SetSubclassesMenu (doc);
      /* clear help text */
      SetHelpText ("");
}


/* build new superclass chain to a newly selected widget class */

void ChangeClassChain (class_doc)
      ClassDoc    *class_doc;
{
      int            i, level;
      Boolean     is_set;
      Arg           args[NUM_ARGS];
      Widget       parent_row = XtParent (class_chain[0]);

      /* inhibit resize */
      if (XtIsRealized (parent_row)) {
            XtSetArg (args[0], XmNresizeWidth, False);
            XtSetValues (parent_row, args, 1);
      }
      /* first unmanage all */
      XtUnmanageChildren (&class_chain[1], MAX_CLASS_WIDGETS-1);
      if (active_class >= 0)
            InvertToggle (class_chain[active_class], NULL, NULL);
      /* set button labels downwards from level */
      level = class_doc->level;
      for (i=level-1; i>=0; i--) {
            XtSetArg (args[0], XmNlabelString, class_doc->xm_name);
            is_set = (level == i+1 ? True : False);
            XtSetArg (args[1], XmNset, is_set);
```

```
                XtSetValues (class_chain [2*i], args, 2);
                cl_docs[2*i] = class_doc;
                class_doc = class_doc->super;
        }
        /* manage rest and activate last one */
        if (level > 0) {
                XtManageChildren (class_chain, 2*level-1);
                InvertToggle (class_chain[2*level-2], NULL, NULL);
                ActivateClass (2*level-2);
        }
}


/***************** Resource Selection List *********************/

/* widget for the selection */

static Widget      res_list;

/* callback for list selection */

void GetResourceHelp ();

/* create the selection list */

void CreateSelectionList (parent)
        Widget      parent;
{
        int         n;
        XmString    s;
        Arg         args[NUM_ARGS];
        Widget      s_bar;

        /* create list widget */
        XtSetArg (args[0], XmNscrollBarDisplayPolicy, XmSTATIC);
        XtSetArg (args[1], XmNselectionPolicy, XmSINGLE_SELECT);
        res_list = XtCreateManagedWidget ("list", xmListWidgetClass, parent,
                                          args, 2);
        XmAddTabGroup (res_list);
        XtAddCallback (res_list, XmNsingleSelectionCallback,
        GetResourceHelp, NULL);

        XtSetArg (args[0], XmNverticalScrollBar, &s_bar);
        XtGetValues (res_list, args, 1);
        if (s_bar != NULL) XmAddTabGroup (s_bar);
}
```

```
/* select a resource entry by program */

void SelectResourceEntry (doc, entry)
      ClassDoc    *doc;
      int         entry;
{
      Arg          args[NUM_ARGS];

      XtSetArg (args[0], XmNselectedItems, &doc->res_string[entry]);
      XtSetArg (args[1], XmNselectedItemCount, 1);
      XtSetValues (res_list, args, 2);
      SetHelpText (doc->res_text[entry]);
      SetParameterField (doc, entry);
}


/* Set the list of resource names */

void SetResourceSelectionList (doc)
      ClassDoc    *doc;
{
      Arg          args[NUM_ARGS];

      XtSetArg (args[0], XmNitems, doc->res_string);
      XtSetArg (args[1], XmNitemCount, doc->no_res);
      XtSetValues (res_list, args, 2);
}


/* Display corresponding help text and parameters */

void GetResourceHelp (w, client_data, call_data)
      Widget      w;
      caddr_t     client_data;
      XmListCallbackStruct *call_data;
{
      ClassDoc    *doc = ActiveDoc ();

      SetHelpText (doc->res_text[call_data->item_position - 1]);
      SetParameterField (doc, call_data->item_position - 1);
}
```

```
/********************* Parameter Field **********************/

#define NUM_CAT 5
#define NUM_CHOICES 3

static String text_fields[] =
        {"Class: ", "Type: ", "Default: ", "Access: ", "Range: "};
static String access_enum[] = {"Create", "Set", "Get"};
static String range_enum[] = {"Constraint", "Scrolled", "Special"};

static Widget prompt_w[NUM_CAT], value_w[NUM_CAT];
static Widget access_choices[NUM_CHOICES], range_choices[NUM_CHOICES];

#define MIDDLE_POS 60

/* create parameter fields */

void CreateParameterField (parent)
        Widget      parent;
{
        int         i, j, n;
        XmString    s;
        Arg         args[NUM_ARGS];

        for (i=0; i<NUM_CAT; i++) {

                /* create label part */
                s = MakeXmString (text_fields[i]);
                n=0;
                XtSetArg (args[n], XmNlabelString, s); n++;
                XtSetArg (args[n], XmNalignment, XmALIGNMENT_BEGINNING);
                n++;
                prompt_w[i] = XtCreateWidget ("prompt", xmLabelGadgetClass,
                                        parent, args, n);
                XmStringFree(s);

                /* create value part */
                if (i==NUM_CAT-2) {
                        /* create first choice */
                        n=0;
                        XtSetArg (args[n], XmNpacking, XmPACK_COLUMN); n++;
                        XtSetArg (args[n], XmNorientation, XmHORIZONTAL); n++;
                        XtSetArg (args[n], XmNentryAlignment,
                                        XmALIGNMENT_CENTER); n++;
                        value_w[i] = XtCreateWidget ("access",
                                        xmRowColumnWidgetClass,
                                        parent, args, n);
```

```
            for (j=0; j<NUM_CHOICES; j++) {
                s = MakeXmString (access_enum[j]);
                XtSetArg (args[0], XmNlabelString, s);
                access_choices[j] = XtCreateWidget ("choice",
                                    xmToggleButtonGadgetClass,
                                    value_w[i], args, 1);
                XmStringFree (s);
            }
            XtManageChildren (access_choices, NUM_CHOICES);}

        else if (i==NUM_CAT-1) {
            n=0;
            XtSetArg (args[n], XmNpacking, XmPACK_COLUMN); n++;
            XtSetArg (args[n], XmNorientation, XmHORIZONTAL); n++;
            XtSetArg (args[n], XmNentryAlignment,
                                    XmALIGNMENT_CENTER); n++;
            value_w[i] = XtCreateWidget ("range",
                                    xmRowColumnWidgetClass,
                                    parent, args, n);
            for (j=0; j<NUM_CHOICES; j++) {
                s = MakeXmString (range_enum[j]);
                XtSetArg (args[0], XmNlabelString, s);
                range_choices[j] = XtCreateWidget ("choice",
                                    xmDrawnButtonWidgetClass,
                                    value_w[i], args, 1);
                XmStringFree (s);
            }
            XtManageChildren (range_choices, NUM_CHOICES);}

        else {
            /* create text field */
            s = MakeXmString (" ");
            n=0;
            XtSetArg (args[n], XmNalignment,
                                    XmALIGNMENT_BEGINNING); n++;
            XtSetArg (args[n], XmNshadowThickness, 2); n++;
            XtSetArg (args[n], XmNlabelString, s); n++;
            value_w [i] = XtCreateWidget ("value",
                                    xmDrawnButtonWidgetClass,
                                    parent, args, n);
            XmStringFree (s);
        }
    }
    XtManageChildren (value_w, NUM_CAT);
    XtManageChildren (prompt_w, NUM_CAT);
}
```

```
/* fill in parameters according to information in doc node */

void SetParameterField (doc, entry)
     ClassDoc   *doc;
     int        entry;
{
     Arg        args[NUM_ARGS];
     int        i, mask, acc;

     SetParamLabel (doc, entry);

     XtSetArg (args[0], XmNlabelString, doc->res_class[entry]);
     XtSetValues (value_w[0], args, 1);
     XtSetArg (args[0], XmNlabelString, doc->res_type[entry]);
     XtSetValues (value_w[1], args, 1);
     XtSetArg (args[0], XmNlabelString, doc->res_default[entry]);
     XtSetValues (value_w[2], args, 1);
     acc = doc->res_access[entry];
     mask = 1;
     for (i=0; i<NUM_CHOICES; i++) {
          XtSetArg (args[0], XmNset, acc&mask);
          XtSetValues (access_choices[i], args, 1);
          mask+=mask;
     }
     for (i=0; i<NUM_CHOICES; i++) {
          XtSetSensitive (range_choices[i], i == doc->res_range[entry]-1);
     }
}

/* return visibility of one parameter */

Boolean ParamIsVisible (index)
     int    index;
{
     return XtIsManaged (prompt_w [index]);
}

/* change visibility of one parameter */

void ParamVisibility (index, on)
     int        index;
     Boolean    on;
{
     if (on) {
          XtManageChild (prompt_w[index]);
          XtManageChild (value_w[index]);}
     else {
```

```
            XtUnmanageChild (prompt_w[index]);
            XtUnmanageChild (value_w[index]);}
}


/************************ Help Text ************************/

static Widget      helptext;

void CreateHelpText (parent)
      Widget      parent;
{
      Arg         args[NUM_ARGS];
      Widget      h_sb, v_sb;

      XtSetArg (args[0], XmNeditable, False);
      XtSetArg (args[1], XmNeditMode, XmMULTI_LINE_EDIT);
      helptext = XmCreateScrolledText (parent, "helptext", args, 2);
      XtManageChild (helptext);

      XtSetArg (args[0], XmNverticalScrollBar, &v_sb);
      XtSetArg (args[1], XmNhorizontalScrollBar, &h_sb);
      XtGetValues (XtParent (helptext), args, 2);
      if (v_sb != NULL) XmAddTabGroup (v_sb);
      if (h_sb != NULL) XmAddTabGroup (h_sb);
}


void SetHelpText (text)
      String      text;
{
      Arg         args[NUM_ARGS];

      XtSetArg (args[0], XmNvalue, text);
      XtSetValues (helptext, args, 1);
}


/****************** Class Selection Dialog ********************/

#define LIST_LABEL "Motif Classes"
#define LIST_TITLE "Widget Class Selection"

static Widget      class_selection_dialog;

void SelectClass ();
```

```
/* create class selection dialog */

void CreateClassSelectionDialog (parent)
       Widget      parent;
{
       Arg         args[NUM_ARGS];
       XmString    s1, s2;
       Widget      w;
       XmString    *class_names;
       int         no_class_names;

       s1 = MakeXmString (LIST_LABEL);
       s2 = MakeXmString (LIST_TITLE);
       class_names = GetClassNames (&no_class_names);
       XtSetArg (args[0], XmNlistItems, class_names);
       XtSetArg (args[1], XmNlistItemCount, no_class_names);
       XtSetArg (args[2], XmNlistLabelString, s1);
       XtSetArg (args[3], XmNdialogTitle, s2);
       class_selection_dialog = XmCreateSelectionDialog (parent, "seldia",
                                             args, 4);
       XmStringFree (s1);
       XmStringFree (s2);
       XtAddCallback (class_selection_dialog, XmNokCallback, SelectClass, NULL);

       /* manually remove unwanted children */
       w =  XmSelectionBoxGetChild (class_selection_dialog,
                                 XmDIALOG_SELECTION_LABEL);
       XtUnmanageChild (w);
       w = XmSelectionBoxGetChild (class_selection_dialog,
                                 XmDIALOG_HELP_BUTTON);
       XtUnmanageChild (w);
       w = XmSelectionBoxGetChild (class_selection_dialog,
                                 XmDIALOG_TEXT);
       XtUnmanageChild (w);
}

/* reset class dialog before pop-up */

void PopupClassDialog ()
{
       XtManageChild (class_selection_dialog);
}

/* select a new class as chain endpoint */

void SelectClass (w, client_data, call_data)
       Widget      w;
```

```
        caddr_t     client_data;
        XmSelectionBoxCallbackStruct *call_data;
{
        ClassDoc    *doc = SearchClass (call_data->value);
        if (doc == NULL) return;
        ChangeClassChain (doc);
}


/****************** Resource Selection Dialog *******************/

#define RESL_LABEL          "Matching Resource Fields"
#define WORK_LABEL          "Enter part of Resource Name:"

#define RES_TITLE           "Resource Selection"
#define APPLY_LABEL         "Search"

static Widget       res_selection_dialog;

/* callback for selecting one of the matching resources */

static void SelectRes (w, client_data, call_data)
        Widget      w;
        caddr_t     client_data;
        XmSelectionBoxCallbackStruct        *call_data;
{
        ClassDoc    *doc;
        int         entry;

        if (call_data->value != NULL) {
                LocateResource (call_data->value, &doc, &entry);
                if (doc != NULL) {
                        XtUnmanageChild (w);
                        ChangeClassChain (doc);
                        SelectResourceEntry (doc, entry);
                }
        }
}


/* callback for manual pop-down of dialog */

static void DiaDown (w, client_data, call_data)
        Widget      w;
        caddr_t     client_data;
        caddr_t     call_data;
{
        XtUnmanageChild (w);
}
```

```
/* callback for creating list of matching resources */

static void UpdateResList (w, client_data, call_data)
    Widget       w;
    caddr_t      client_data;
    XmSelectionBoxCallbackStruct      *call_data;
{
    Arg          args[NUM_ARGS];
    Widget       wid;
    String       seg;
    XmString     *match_res;
    int          no_match;

    XmStringGetLtoR (call_data->value, XmSTRING_DEFAULT_CHARSET,
                                       &seg);
    FindMatchingFields (seg, &match_res, &no_match);
    XtSetArg (args[0], XmNlistItems, match_res);   XtSetArg (args[1],
                                       XmNlistItemCount, no_match);
    XtSetValues (res_selection_dialog, args, 2);

    if (no_match > 0) {
        wid = XmSelectionBoxGetChild (w, XmDIALOG_OK_BUTTON);
        XtSetArg (args[0], XmNdefaultButton, wid);
        XtSetValues (w, args, 1);}
    else {
        wid = XmSelectionBoxGetChild (w, XmDIALOG_APPLY_BUTTON);
        XtSetArg (args[0], XmNdefaultButton, wid);
        XtSetValues (w, args, 1);
    }
}


/* create the resource selection dialog */

void CreateResSelectionDialog (parent)
    Widget       parent;
{
    Arg          args[NUM_ARGS];
    XmString     s1, s2, s3, s4;
    Widget       w;

    s1 = MakeXmString (RESL_LABEL);
    s2 = MakeXmString (WORK_LABEL);
    s3 = MakeXmString (RES_TITLE);
    s4 = MakeXmString (APPLY_LABEL);
    XtSetArg (args[0], XmNlistLabelString, s1);
    XtSetArg (args[1], XmNautoUnmanage, False);
    XtSetArg (args[2], XmNselectionLabelString, s2);
```

```
        XtSetArg (args[3], XmNdialogTitle, s3);
        XtSetArg (args[4], XmNapplyLabelString, s4);
        res_selection_dialog = XmCreateSelectionDialog (parent, "resdia",
                                    args, 5);
        XmStringFree (s1); XmStringFree (s2);
        XmStringFree (s3); XmStringFree (s4);
        XtAddCallback (res_selection_dialog, XmNokCallback, SelectRes, NULL);
        XtAddCallback (res_selection_dialog, XmNapplyCallback,
                                    UpdateResList, NULL);
        XtAddCallback (res_selection_dialog, XmNcancelCallback,
                                    DiaDown, NULL);
        w = XmSelectionBoxGetChild (res_selection_dialog,
                                    XmDIALOG_APPLY_BUTTON);
        XtManageChild (w);
        w = XmSelectionBoxGetChild (res_selection_dialog,
                                    XmDIALOG_HELP_BUTTON);
        XtUnmanageChild (w);
        XtSetArg (args[0], XmNdefaultButton, w);
        XtSetValues (res_selection_dialog, args, 1);
}

/* reset resource dialog before pop-up */

void PopupResDialog ()
{
        Widget      w;
        Arg         args[NUM_ARGS];
        XmString    s;

        w = XmSelectionBoxGetChild (res_selection_dialog,
                                    XmDIALOG_APPLY_BUTTON);
        s = MakeXmString ("");
        XtSetArg (args[0], XmNdefaultButton, w);
        XtSetArg (args[1], XmNlistItems, NULL);
        XtSetArg (args[2], XmNlistItemCount, 0);
        XtSetArg (args[3], XmNtextString, s);
        XtSetValues (res_selection_dialog, args, 4);
        XmStringFree (s);
        XtManageChild (res_selection_dialog);
}

/********************* Help Dialog *************************/

#define HELP_TITLE "Help Text"

static Widget      help_dialog;
```

```
/* create help dialog */

void CreateHelpDialog (parent)
      Widget      parent;
{
      Arg            args[NUM_ARGS];
      XmString    s1;

      s1 = MakeXmString (HELP_TITLE);
      XtSetArg (args[0], XmNdialogTitle, s1);

      help_dialog = XmCreateMessageDialog (parent, "helpdia", args, 1);
      XmStringFree (s1);
}

/* pop up the help dialog */

void PopupHelpDialog (buffer)
      String      buffer;
{
      Arg            args[NUM_ARGS];
      XmString    s;

      s = MakeXmString (buffer);
      XtSetArg (args[0], XmNmessageString, s);
      XtSetValues (help_dialog, args, 1);
      XmStringFree (s);
      XtManageChild (help_dialog);
}
```

D.2 Support Files

The File "motifhelp.classes"

```
Object
 Core
  Primitive
   ArrowButton
  Label
   CascadeButton
   DrawnButton
   PushButton
   ToggleButton
```

List
ScrollBar
Separator
Text
Composite
Constraint
Manager
BulletinBoard
Form
MessageBox
SelectionBox
Command
FileSelectionBox
DrawingArea
Frame
PanedWindow
RowColumn
Scale
ScrolledWindow
MainWindow
Shell
OverrideShell
MenuShell
WMShell
VendorShell
TopLevelShell
ApplicationShell
TransientShell
DialogShell
Gadget
ArrowButtonGadget
LabelGadget
CascadeButtonGadget
PushButtonGadget
ToggleButtonGadget
SeparatorGadget

The File "motifhelp.help"

#1 Version
This is MotifHelp, a program to display information about the Motif
Widget Classes. The information presented is extracted from the
Motif Reference Manuals and is copyrighted by OSF.

This is a first demonstration version of this program.

Author: Thomas Berlage
GMD
P.O. Box 1240
W-5205 Sankt Augustin 1
Germany
email: berlage@gmdzi.gmd.de

Any suggestions, hints and error reports are welcome. This program
is not guaranteed to work.

The File "motifhelp.FileSelectionBox"

#1 NAME
XmFileSelectionBox

this info not used
#1 SYNOPSIS
not used
#1 DESCRIPTION
This section describes the widget class in general.

#1 Classes
not used

#1 New Resources
This section is not used, but indicates the start of a section
where individual resource field entries are found.

#4 XmFileSelectionBox Resource Set
Sections headers with #4 are analysed for range.
i.e. whether 'Constraint', 'Scrolled' or 'Special' appears.

following are the table entries, separated with tabs

#3 XmNdirMask	*XmCDirMask*	*XmString*	*"*"*	*CSG*
#3 XmNdirSpec	*XmCDirSpec*	*XmString*	*NULL*	*CSG*
#3 XmNfileSearchProc	*XmCFileSearchProc*	*XtProc*	*see below*	*CSG*
#3 XmNfilterLabelString	*XmCFilterLabelString*	*XmString*	*"File Filter"*	*CSG*
#3 XmNlistUpdated	*XmCListUpdated*	*Boolean*	*True*	*CSG*

afterwards the individual descriptions usually follow

#2 XmNdirMask
Description text for this field may follow.

#2 XmNdirSpec
Description text for this field may follow.

#2 XmNfileSearchProc
Description text for this field may follow.

#2 XmNfilterLabelString
Description text for this field may follow.

#2 XmNlistUpdated
Description text for this field may follow.

#1 Inherited Resources
This section with all its entries is ignored, because this
information is currently extracted from the file of the superclass.
However, this does not take into account any default values
which may have been overridden in this class!

#1 Callback Information
Another section which is used when present.

#1 Behavior
Another section which is used when present.

#1 Default Translations
Another section which is used when present.

D.3 Help File Generation

The File "motifhelp.gensource"

SOURCE="/vol/Motif/src/doc/man/source"
MH="motifhelp.gen1 $SOURCE"
echo "Generating Source of Motifhelp Files"
$MH Object Object
$MH RectObj RectObj
$MH WindowObj WindowObj
$MH Core Core
$MH XmPrimitive Primitive
$MH XmArrowButA ArrowButton
$MH XmLabel Label
$MH XmCascadeBA CascadeButton
$MH XmDrawnButt DrawnButton

```
$MH XmPushButtA PushButton
$MH XmToggleBuA ToggleButton
$MH XmList List
$MH XmScrollBaA ScrollBar
$MH XmSeparatoA Separator
$MH XmText Text
$MH Composite Composite
$MH Constraint Constraint
$MH XmManager Manager
$MH XmBulletinB BulletinBoard
$MH XmForm Form
$MH XmMessageBA MessageBox
$MH XmSelectioA SelectionBox
$MH XmCommand Command
$MH XmFileSeleA FileSelectionBox
$MH XmDrawingAr DrawingArea
$MH XmFrame Frame
$MH XmPanedWind PanedWindow
$MH XmRowColumn RowColumn
$MH XmScale Scale
$MH XmScrolledA ScrolledWindow
$MH XmMainWindA MainWindow
$MH Shell Shell
$MH OverrideShe OverrideShell
$MH XmMenuShell MenuShell
$MH WMShell WMShell
$MH VendorShell VendorShell
$MH TopLevelShe TopLevelShell
$MH Application ApplicationShell
$MH TransientSh TransientShell
$MH XmDialogShe DialogShell
$MH XmGadget Gadget
$MH XmArrowButB ArrowButtonGadget
$MH XmLabelGadg LabelGadget
$MH XmCascadeBB CascadeButtonGadget
$MH XmPushButtB PushButtonGadget
$MH XmToggleBuB ToggleButtonGadget
$MH XmSeparatoB SeparatorGadget
```

The File "motifhelp.gen1"

```
rm -f motifhelp.$3
echo "$1/$2.3X -> motifhelp.$3"
sed -f motifhelp.sed $1/$2.3X >motifhelp.$3
```

The File "motifhelp.sed"

```
/^\.mc/d
1,$s/\\f.//g
1,$s/\\(em/-/g
1,$s/\.SH/\#1/
1,$s/\.SS \"\(.*\)\"/\#1 \1/
1,$s/\.IP.*\"X\(.*\)\".*/\#2 X\1/
1,$s/\.IP.*X\([a-zA-Z]*\).*/\#2 X\1/
1,$s/\.IP.*\"\(.*\)\".*/\1/
1,$s/^\.*//
1,$s/^\(XmN.*   X.*[CSG]\)$/#3 \1/
/^center/d
/^cB/d
/^lB/d
/^lp8/d
/^Name.*Class.*Type/d
/^\_/d
1,$s/^\([A-Za-z]* .*Resource Set\)/#4 \1/
1,$s/^\(.*Special Menu Resource\)/#4 \1/
```

Appendix E

"Step List"
Source Code

The File "StepList.h"

```
/*********************************************/
/* StepList.h - header file for stepper widget        */
/*********************************************/

/* new resource names */

#define XmNarrowWidth "arrowWidth"
#define XmCArrowWidth "ArrowWidth"

#define STEPPER_CLASS "StepList"

/* procedures */

Widget CreateStepList ();
void StepListSetCurrent ();
void StepListGetCurrent ();
```

```
/* definition of callback structure */

typedef struct {
      int              reason;
      XEvent           *event;
      XmStringTable    list;
      int              elements,
                       current,
                       previous;
} StepListCallbackStruct;

/********************************************/
```

The File "StepList.c"

```
#include <Xm/Xm.h>
#include <Xm/ArrowB.h>
#include <Xm/DrawnB.h>
#include <Xm/DrawingA.h>

#include "StepList.h"

/***************** Common information for stepper ***************/

/*_____*/
/* record associated with widget */
/*_____*/

typedef struct {
      XmStringTable    list;
      int              elements, current;
      Widget           b1, b2, field;
      Dimension        arrow_width;
      XtCallbackProc   call_proc;
      caddr_t          client_data;
} StepRec, *StepRecPtr;;

/*_____*/
/* resource list for items */
/*_____*/

static XtResource item_resources[] = {
      { XmNitems, XmCItems, XmRXmStringTable, sizeof (XmStringTable),
      XtOffset (StepRecPtr, list), XmRImmediate, NULL},
```

```
        { XmNitemCount, XmCItemCount, XmRInt, sizeof (int),
        XtOffset (StepRecPtr, elements), XmRImmediate, (caddr_t) 0},
        { XmNarrowWidth, XmCArrowWidth, XmRDimension, sizeof (Dimension),
        XtOffset (StepRecPtr, arrow_width), XmRImmediate, (caddr_t) 16}
};


/*_____*/
/* definitions to prefetch fontList info */
/* (before widget is created)          */
/*_____*/

typedef struct {
        XmFontList      fontlist;
} ResStruct, *ResPtr;

static XtResource fontlist_resource [] = {
        { XmNfontList, XmCFontList, XmRFontList, sizeof (XmFontList),
        XtOffset (ResPtr, fontlist), XmRString, "fixed"}
};



/********************* Stepper callbacks *********************/

/*_____*/
/* call application callback */
/*_____*/

static void CallCallback (rec, event, previous)
        StepRec     *rec;
        XEvent      *event;
        int         previous;
{
        StepListCallbackStruct cb;

        if (rec->call_proc != NULL) {
                cb.reason = XmCR_VALUE_CHANGED;
                cb.event = event;
                cb.list = rec->list;
                cb.elements = rec->elements;
                cb.current = rec->current;
                cb.previous = previous;
                (* rec->call_proc) (rec->field, rec->client_data, &cb);
        }
}
```

```
/*_____*/
/* StepUp callback */
/*_____*/

static void StepUp (widget, rec, call_data)
        Widget                  widget;
        StepRec                 *rec;
        XmAnyCallbackStruct     *call_data;
{
        Arg         args[1];
        int         previous;

        if (rec->current > 1) {
                previous = rec->current;
                rec->current--;
                XtSetArg (args[0], XmNlabelString, rec->list[rec->current-1]);
                XtSetValues (rec->field, args, 1);
                XtSetSensitive (rec->b1, rec->current > 1);
                XtSetSensitive (rec->b2, True);
                CallCallback (rec, call_data->event, previous);
        }
}


/*_____*/
/* StepDown callback */
/*_____*/

static void StepDown (widget, rec, call_data)
        Widget                  widget;
        StepRec                 *rec;
        XmAnyCallbackStruct     *call_data;
{
        Arg         args[1];
        int         previous;

        if (rec->current < rec->elements) {
                previous = rec->current;
                rec->current++;
                XtSetArg (args[0], XmNlabelString, rec->list[rec->current-1]);
                XtSetValues (rec->field, args, 1);
                XtSetSensitive (rec->b1, True);
                XtSetSensitive (rec->b2, rec->current < rec->elements);
                CallCallback (rec, call_data->event, previous);
        }
}
```

```
/*_____*/
/* resize callback */
/*_____*/

static void Resize (widget, rec, call_data)
        Widget                  widget;
        StepRec                 *rec;
        XmAnyCallbackStruct     *call_data;
{
        Arg                 args[3];
        Dimension           width, height, text_height, arrow_width;
        Position            new_y;

        XtSetArg (args[0], XmNwidth, &width);
        XtSetArg (args[1], XmNheight, &height);
        XtGetValues (widget, args, 2);

        if (width < 3 * rec->arrow_width)
                arrow_width = width/3;
        else
                arrow_width = rec->arrow_width;

        XtSetArg (args[0], XmNheight, &text_height);
        XtGetValues (rec->field, args, 1);

        if (height > text_height)
                new_y = (height - text_height)/2;
        else
                new_y = 0;

        /* stop resizing the drawing area now */
        XtSetArg (args[0], XmNresizePolicy, XmRESIZE_NONE);
        XtSetValues (widget, args, 1);

        /* resize the children */
        XtSetArg (args[0], XmNy, new_y);
        XtSetArg (args[1], XmNwidth, arrow_width);
        XtSetValues (rec->b1, args, 2);

        XtSetArg (args[2], XmNx, arrow_width);
        XtSetValues (rec->b2, args, 3);

        XtSetArg (args[1], XmNwidth, width - 2 * arrow_width);
        XtSetArg (args[2], XmNx, 2 * arrow_width);
        XtSetValues (rec->field, args, 3);
}
```

```
/********************* Creation procedure **********************/


/*_____*/
/* find the longest XmString of the list */
/*_____*/

static XmString Longest (xmlist, no_el, fl)
        XmString        *xmlist;
        int             no_el;
        XmFontList      fl;
{
        int                 i, max = 0, maxno = -1, new;

        for (i=0; i<no_el; i++) {
                if (max < (new = XmStringWidth (fl, xmlist[i]))) {
                        max = new; maxno = i;
                }
        }
        if (maxno >= 0)
                return (xmlist[maxno]);
        else
                return NULL;
}


/*_____*/
/* prefetch fontList */
/*_____*/

static XmFontList GetFontList (parent, name, class)
        Widget      parent;
        char        *name;
        char        *class;
{
        ResStruct   res;

        XtGetSubresources (parent, &res, name, class,
                        fontlist_resource, XtNumber (fontlist_resource),
                        NULL, 0);
        return (res.fontlist);
}


/*_____*/
/*** creation procedure ***/
/*_____*/

Widget CreateStepList (parent, name, add_args, num_args, proc, client_data)
        Widget              parent;
```

```
    String          name;
    ArgList         add_args;
    Cardinal        num_args;
    XtCallbackProc  proc;
    caddr_t         client_data;
{
    Widget          manager, text, ab1, ab2;
    Arg             args[5];
    StepRec         *rec;
    Dimension       text_height;
    XmFontList      text_font;
    ArgList         merge_args;

    /* initialize callback record */
    rec = (StepRec*) XtMalloc (sizeof (StepRec));
    rec->current = 1;
    rec->call_proc = proc;
    rec->client_data = client_data;

    /* drawing area as manager */
    XtSetArg (args[0], XmNmarginWidth, 0);
    XtSetArg (args[1], XmNmarginHeight, 0);
    manager = XtCreateManagedWidget ("manager",
                        xmDrawingAreaWidgetClass, parent,
                        args, 2);
    XtAddCallback (manager, XmNresizeCallback, Resize, rec);

    /* initialize the rest of the callback record */
    XtGetSubresources (manager, rec, name, STEPPER_CLASS,
                item_resources, XtNumber (item_resources),
                add_args, num_args);

    /* first scroll button */
    XtSetArg (args[0], XmNarrowDirection, XmARROW_UP);
    XtSetArg (args[1], XmNwidth, rec->arrow_width);
    ab1 = XtCreateManagedWidget ("ab1", xmArrowButtonWidgetClass,
                        manager, args, 2);
    XtSetSensitive (ab1, False);
    XtAddCallback (ab1, XmNactivateCallback, StepUp, rec);
    rec->b1 = ab1;

    /* second scroll button */
    XtSetArg (args[0], XmNarrowDirection, XmARROW_DOWN);
    XtSetArg (args[1], XmNwidth, rec->arrow_width);
    XtSetArg (args[2], XmNx, rec->arrow_width);
    ab2 = XtCreateManagedWidget ("ab2", xmArrowButtonWidgetClass,
                        manager, args, 3);
```

```
        XtSetSensitive (ab2, rec->elements > 1);
        XtAddCallback (ab2, XmNactivateCallback, StepDown, rec);
        rec->b2 = ab2;

        /* get the fontlist which will be used in the text display */
        text_font = GetFontList (manager, name, "XmDrawnButton");

        /* text display (with the longest item) */
        XtSetArg (args[0], XmNlabelString,
                            Longest (rec->list, rec->elements, text_font));
        XtSetArg (args[1], XmNuserData, rec);
        XtSetArg (args[2], XmNrecomputeSize, False);
        XtSetArg (args[3], XmNx, 2 * rec->arrow_width);
        XtSetArg (args[4], XmNpushButtonEnabled, False);

        merge_args = XtMergeArgLists (add_args, num_args, args, 5);
        text = XtCreateManagedWidget (name, xmDrawnButtonWidgetClass,
                            manager, merge_args, num_args + 5);
        XtFree (merge_args);
        rec->field = text;

        /* align text and arrows */
        XtSetArg (args[0], XmNheight, &text_height);
        XtGetValues (text, args, 1);
        XtSetArg (args[0], XmNheight, text_height);
        XtSetValues (ab1, args, 1);
        XtSetValues (ab2, args, 1);

        /* set text to first label */
        if (rec->elements > 1) {
                XtSetArg (args[0], XmNlabelString, rec->list[0]);
                XtSetValues (text, args, 1);
        }
}


/******************** Access current item **********************/

/*_____*/
/*** change current item ***/
/*_____*/

void StepListSetCurrent (widget, new, call)
        Widget      widget;
        int         new;
        Boolean     call;
```

```
{
    StepRec    *rec;
    Arg        args[1];
    int        previous;

    XtSetArg (args[0], XmNuserData, &rec);
    XtGetValues (widget, args, 1);

    if (rec == NULL) return;

    if (new < 1 || new > rec->elements) return;

    previous = rec->current;
    rec->current = new;
    XtSetArg (args[0], XmNlabelString, rec->list[rec->current-1]);
    XtSetValues (rec->field, args, 1);
    XtSetSensitive (rec->b1, rec->current > 1);
    XtSetSensitive (rec->b2, rec->current < rec->elements);
    if (call) CallCallback (rec->field, NULL, previous);
}


/*_____*/
/*** get current item ***/
/*_____*/

void StepListGetCurrent (widget, current_return, label_return)
    Widget     widget;
    int        *current_return;
    XmString   *label_return;
{
    StepRec    *rec;
    Arg        args[1];

    XtSetArg (args[0], XmNuserData, &rec);
    XtGetValues (widget, args, 1);

    *current_return = 0;    /* invalid data */
    if (rec == NULL) return;

    if (rec->current < 1 || rec->current > rec->elements) return;

    *current_return = rec->current;
    *label_return = rec->list[rec->current-1];
}
```

The File "steptest.c"

```
/* includes */
#include <Xm/Xm.h>
#include <X11/Shell.h>

#include "StepList.h"

/* global definitions */

#define PROGRAM_CLASS  "Stepper"
#define ERROR_CLASS    "StepperError"

#define NUM_ARGS 10

/* error definitions */

#define NErrCannotOpen    "cannotOpen"
#define TErrMain          "Main"

/* main window creation */

static void PrintCurrent (widget, client_data, call_data)
     Widget     widget;
     caddr_t    client_data;
     StepListCallbackStruct *call_data;
{
     printf ("step from %d to %d .\n", call_data->previous, call_data->current);
}

/* must be static because it is not copied in CreateStepList */
XmString   array[3];

static void CreateMainWindow (toplevel)
     Widget     toplevel;
{
     Arg   args[2];

     array[0] = XmStringCreateLtoR ("——",
                         XmSTRING_DEFAULT_CHARSET);
     array[1] = XmStringCreateLtoR ("hello you all",
                         XmSTRING_DEFAULT_CHARSET);
     array[2] = XmStringCreateLtoR ("there",
                         XmSTRING_DEFAULT_CHARSET);
```

```
        XtSetArg (args[0], XmNitems, array);
        XtSetArg (args[1], XmNitemCount, 3);
        CreateStepList (toplevel, "list", args, 2, PrintCurrent, NULL);
}


/****************************/

void main (argc, argv)
        unsigned int    argc;
        char  **argv;
{
        Display            *display;
        XtAppContext       context;
        Arg                args[NUM_ARGS];
        Widget             toplevel;

        /* initialize toolkit */
        XtToolkitInitialize();
        context = XtCreateApplicationContext ();
        display = XtOpenDisplay (
                context,     /* application context              */
                NULL,        /* use DISPLAY from environment     */
                NULL,        /* use last of argv[0] as name      */
                PROGRAM_CLASS,
                NULL,        /* no additional command line options */
                0,           /* ditto                           */
                &argc,
                argv);       /* use and delete standard options  */

        if (display == NULL)   /* necessary !     */
                XtErrorMsg (
                        NErrCannotOpen, TErrMain,     /* resource name */
                        ERROR_CLASS,                  /* resource class */
                        "cannot open display",        /* default message*/
                        NULL, NULL);                  /* parameters    */

        /* create application shell */
        XtSetArg (args[0], XmNallowShellResize, True);
        toplevel = XtAppCreateShell (
                NULL,                /* use same program name    */
                PROGRAM_CLASS,       /* repeat class param       */
                applicationShellWidgetClass,
                display,
                args, 1);            /* argument list            */

        /* create main window */
        CreateMainWindow (toplevel);
```

```
/* start loop */
XtRealizeWidget (toplevel);
XtAppMainLoop (context);
}
```

Appendix F

"Icon Box" Source Code

The File "IconBox.h"

```
/*******************************************************/
/*    IconBox.h - header file for IconBox
/*******************************************************/

/* new resource fields */

#define XmNiconBitmap        "iconBitmap"
#define XmNiconMask          "iconMask"
#define XmNiconForeground    "iconForeground"
#define XmNiconBackground    "iconBackground"
#define XmNpathname          "pathname"
#define XmNiconWidth         "iconWidth"
#define XmNiconHeight        "iconHeight"
#define XmNiconSpacing       "iconSpacing"
#define XmNshadowOffset      "shadowOffset"
#define XmNshadowColor       "shadowColor"

#define XmCIconBitmap        "IconBitmap"
#define XmCIconMask          "IconMask"
#define XmCPathname          "Pathname"
#define XmCIconWidth         "IconWidth"
```

```
#define XmCIconHeight        "IconHeight"
#define XmCIconSpacing       "IconSpacing"
#define XmCShadowOffset      "ShadowOffset"
#define XmCShadowColor       "ShadowColor"
```

```
/* procedures */
```

```
Widget CreateIconBox ();
void   SaveIconBox ();
```

```
/*************************************  .  *************************/
```

The File "IconBox.c"

```
#include <stdio.h>
```

```
#include <Xm/Xm.h>
#include <Xm/DrawingA.h>
```

```
#include "IconBox.h"
```

```
/******************** Record for each icon ********************/
```

```
typedef struct {
        int        x, y;              /* left upper edge of icon          */
        int        string_left;       /* how much strings extends to left */
        int        higher;            /* next higher stacked icon         */
        XmString   label;             /* label string                     */
        String     class;             /* for selection of pixmap          */
        String     pix_name;          /* name of icon bitmap              */
        Pixmap     pix;               /* icon pixmap                      */
        String     mask_name;         /* name of mask bitmap              */
        Pixmap     mask;              /* mask bitmap                      */
        Pixel      foreground;        /* foreground for icon pixmap       */
        Pixel      background;        /* background for icon pixmap       */
} IconRec, *IconRecPtr;
```

```
/******************** Icon box data record ********************/
```

```
typedef struct {
        String     pathname;          /* pathname where to read info      */
        int        width, height;     /* size of box                      */
        int        icon_width;        /* size of one icon                 */
        int        icon_height;
```

```
        int          string_height;   /* common height of string box      */
        int          icon_spacing;    /* spacing between icons             */
        int          shadow_off;      /* offset of shadow effect           */
        int          columns;         /* no of icon columns initially      */
        IconRec      *icons;          /* icon array                        */
        int          no_icons;        /* elements in array                 */
        int          lowest;          /* index of icon at back of stack    */
        Pixel        shadow_color;    /* color for shadow effect           */
        Pixel        background;      /* pixmap background                 */
        Boolean      exposed;         /* to check for first expose         */
        GC           draw_gc;         /* to draw into buffer               */
        GC           normal_gc;       /* read-only for other drawing       */
        Pixmap       back;            /* background storage                */
        XmFontList   fontlist;        /* for strings                       */
        int          x_off, y_off;    /* mouse offset when drag-moving     */
        int          moving;          /* index of currently moved icon     */
} BoxRec, *BoxRecPtr;

/****************** Resource list for icon record ****************/

static XtResource icon_resources [] = {
        { XmNiconBitmap, XmCIconBitmap, XmRString, sizeof (Pixmap),
        XtOffset (IconRecPtr, pix_name), XmRString, ""},
        { XmNiconMask, XmCIconMask, XmRString, sizeof (String),
        XtOffset (IconRecPtr, mask_name), XmRString, ""},
        { XmNiconForeground, XmCForeground, XmRPixel, sizeof (Pixel),
        XtOffset (IconRecPtr, foreground), XmRString, "black"},
        { XmNiconBackground, XmCBackground, XmRPixel, sizeof (Pixel),
        XtOffset (IconRecPtr, background), XmRString, "white"}
};

/****************** Resource list for box record ******************/

static XtResource box_resources[] = {
        { XmNpathname, XmCPathname, XmRString, sizeof (String),
        XtOffset (BoxRecPtr, pathname), XmRString, "dir"},
        { XmNiconWidth, XmCIconWidth, XmRInt, sizeof (int),
        XtOffset (BoxRecPtr, icon_width), XmRImmediate, (caddr_t) 40},
        { XmNiconHeight, XmCIconHeight, XmRInt, sizeof (int),
        XtOffset (BoxRecPtr, icon_height), XmRImmediate, (caddr_t) 40},
        { XmNiconSpacing, XmCIconSpacing, XmRInt, sizeof (int),
        XtOffset (BoxRecPtr, icon_spacing), XmRImmediate, (caddr_t) 10},
        { XmNshadowOffset, XmCShadowOffset, XmRInt, sizeof (int),
        XtOffset (BoxRecPtr, shadow_off), XmRImmediate, (caddr_t) 3},
        { XmNcolumns, XmCColumns, XmRInt, sizeof (int),
        XtOffset (BoxRecPtr, columns), XmRImmediate, (caddr_t) 5},
        { XmNshadowColor, XmCShadowColor, XmRPixel, sizeof (Pixel),
```

```
        XtOffset (BoxRecPtr, shadow_color), XmRString, "gray50"},
        { XmNfontList, XmCFontList, XmRFontList, sizeof (XmFontList),
        XtOffset (BoxRecPtr, fontlist), XmRString, "fixed"}
};
```

```
/******************** Create box and read icons ********************/
```

```
/*_____*/
/* forward declarations for callbacks */
/*_____*/
```

```
static void ExposeBox ();
static void HandleButtons ();
static void HandleMove ();
static void HandleResize ();
static void DestroyIconBox ();
```

```
/*_____*/
/* temporary structure for icons read from file */
/*_____*/
```

```
typedef struct {
        char        *n;        /* name of icon                        */
        char        *c;        /* class that may determine pixmap */
        int         x, y;      /* position if not -1                  */
} TempRec;
```

```
/*_____*/
/* initialize one icon record */
/*_____*/
```

```
static void InitIcon (widget, temp, rec, index)
        Widget      widget;
        TempRec     *temp;
        BoxRec      *rec;
        int         index;
{
        IconRec     *icon = &rec->icons[index];
        int         dummy, i;

        /* get resources for icon record */
        XtGetSubresources (widget, icon, temp->n, temp->c,
                        icon_resources, XtNumber (icon_resources), NULL, 0);

        /* set label and its offset to the left of icon */
        icon->label = XmStringCreateLtoR (temp->n,
```

```
                                        XmSTRING_DEFAULT_CHARSET);
     icon->string_left = ((int) XmStringWidth (rec->fontlist, icon->label) -
                                        rec->icon_width + 1) / 2;
     if (icon->string_left < 0) icon->string_left = 0;
     icon->class = temp->c;

     /* calculate initial position */
     if (temp->x < 0) {
          icon->x = (index % rec->columns) *
                (rec->icon_width + rec->icon_spacing) +
                rec->icon_spacing/2;
          icon->y = (index / rec->columns) *
                (rec->icon_height + rec->string_height + rec->icon_spacing) +
                rec->icon_spacing/2;
     } else {
          icon->x = temp->x;
          icon->y = temp->y;
     }

     /* icons are read in stacking order */
     icon->higher = index + 1;

     /* get cached pixmap from Motif */
     icon->pix = XmGetPixmap (XDefaultScreenOfDisplay (XtDisplay (widget)),
                    icon->pix_name, icon->foreground, icon->background);

     /* mask must be bitmap, so get and cache it ourselves */
     for (i = 0; i < index; i++ )
          if (strcmp (rec->icons[i].mask_name, icon->mask_name) == 0) {
                icon->mask = rec->icons[i].mask;
                break;
          }
     if (i == index)      /* not found */
          if (XReadBitmapFile (XtDisplay (widget),
                    XDefaultRootWindow (XtDisplay (widget)),
                    icon->mask_name, &dummy, &dummy, &icon->mask,
                    &dummy, &dummy) != BitmapSuccess)
                icon->mask = None;
}


/*_____*/
/* read the icon information from a file */
/*_____*/

static void ReadIcons (widget, rec)
     Widget      widget;
```

```
    BoxRec      *rec;
{
    FILE *fp;
    char        nbuf[100], cbuf[100];
    int         xbuf, ybuf;
    int         w = 0, h = 0;
    TempRec     tmp[400];
    int         no, i;

    fp = fopen (rec->pathname, "r");
    if (fp == NULL) return;

    no = 0;
    while (fscanf (fp, " %s", nbuf) != EOF) {
        xbuf = -1; ybuf = -1;
        /* check for window size */
        if (strlen (nbuf) == 1 && nbuf[0] == '#')
            fscanf (fp, " %d %d %s", &w, &h, nbuf);
        /* test whether position information has been written */
        if (strlen (nbuf) == 1 && nbuf[0] == ':')
            fscanf (fp, " %d %d %s %s", &xbuf, &ybuf, nbuf, cbuf);
        else
            fscanf (fp, " %s", cbuf);
        /* copy into tmp array */
        tmp[no].x = xbuf;
        tmp[no].y = ybuf;
        tmp[no].n = XtMalloc (strlen (nbuf) + 1);
        strcpy (tmp[no].n, nbuf);
        tmp[no].c = XtMalloc (strlen (cbuf) + 1);
        strcpy (tmp[no].c, cbuf);
        no++;
    }
    fclose (fp);

    /* allocate icon records and initialize */
    rec->icons = (IconRec*) XtCalloc (no, sizeof (IconRec));
    for (i = 0; i < no; i++) {
        InitIcon (widget, &tmp[i], rec, i);
    }
    rec->no_icons = no;
    rec->lowest = 0;
    rec->icons[no-1].higher = -1;

    /* set initial size of window */
    if (w > 0 && h > 0) {
        rec->width = w;
        rec->height = h;
```

```
        } else {
            rec->width = (rec->columns + 1) *
                            (rec->icon_width + rec->icon_spacing);
            rec->height = (((no - 1)/ rec->columns) + 2) *
                            (rec->icon_height + rec->string_height + rec->icon_spacing);
        }
    }
}

/*_____*/
/*** Exported creation procedure ***/
/*_____*/

Widget CreateIconBox (parent, add_args, num_add_args)
        Widget          parent;
        Arg             add_args[];
        Cardinal        num_add_args;
{
        Widget          area;
        Arg             args[3];
        XmString        face;
        BoxRec          *rec;
        XGCValues       gc_values;
        XmString        dummy;

        rec = (BoxRec *)XtMalloc (sizeof (BoxRec));

        area = XtCreateManagedWidget ("area", xmDrawingAreaWidgetClass,
                            parent, add_args, num_add_args);

        XtGetSubresources (parent, rec, "area", "XmDrawingArea",
                            box_resources, XtNumber (box_resources),
                            add_args, num_add_args);

        dummy = XmStringCreateLtoR ("hg", XmSTRING_DEFAULT_CHARSET);
        rec->string_height = XmStringHeight (rec->fontlist, dummy) + 2;
        XmStringFree (dummy);

        ReadIcons (area, rec);

        XtSetArg (args[0], XmNwidth, rec->width);
        XtSetArg (args[1], XmNheight, rec->height);
        XtSetArg (args[2], XmNuserData, rec);
        XtSetValues (area, args, 3);

        XtAddCallback (area, XmNexposeCallback, ExposeBox, rec);
        XtAddCallback (area, XmNinputCallback, HandleButtons, rec);
        XtAddEventHandler (area, ButtonMotionMask, False, HandleMove, rec);
```

```
     XtAddCallback (area, XmNresizeCallback, HandleResize, rec);
     XtAddCallback (area, XmNdestroyCallback, DestroyIconBox, rec);

     return area;
}


/******************* Handling expose through back pixmap ************/

/*_____*/
/* redraw one icon to back pixmap */
/*_____*/

static void RedrawIcon (widget, rec, index)
     Widget     widget;
     BoxRec     *rec;
     int        index;
{
     IconRec    *icon = &rec->icons[index];

     /* set clip mask in gc */
     XSetClipMask (XtDisplay (widget), rec->draw_gc, icon->mask);

     /* fill shadow */
     XSetClipOrigin (XtDisplay (widget), rec->draw_gc,
                     icon->x + rec->shadow_off, icon->y + rec->shadow_off);
     XSetForeground (XtDisplay (widget), rec->draw_gc, rec->shadow_color);
     XFillRectangle (XtDisplay (widget), rec->back, rec->draw_gc,
                     icon->x + rec->shadow_off, icon->y + rec->shadow_off,
                     rec->icon_width, rec->icon_height);

     /* draw icon */
     XSetClipOrigin (XtDisplay (widget), rec->draw_gc, icon->x, icon->y);
     if (icon->pix != XmUNSPECIFIED_PIXMAP)
         XCopyArea (XtDisplay (widget), icon->pix, rec->back,
                     rec->draw_gc, 0, 0, rec->icon_width, rec->icon_height,
                     icon->x, icon->y);

     /* draw string */
     XmStringDraw (XtDisplay (widget), rec->back,
                     rec->fontlist, icon->label, rec->normal_gc,
                     icon->x - icon->string_left, icon->y + rec->icon_height + 1,
                     rec->icon_width + 2 * icon->string_left,
                     XmALIGNMENT_CENTER,
                     XmSTRING_DIRECTION_L_TO_R,
                     NULL);
}
```

```
/*_____*/
/* create GCs */
/*_____*/

static void CreateGCs (widget, rec)
        Widget          widget;
        BoxRec          *rec;
{
        Arg             args[2];
        Pixel           window_foreground;
        XGCValues       gc_values;

        /* get values from drawing area */
        XtSetArg (args[0], XmNbackground, &rec->background);
        XtSetArg (args[1], XmNforeground, &window_foreground);
        XtGetValues (widget, args, 2);

        /* create writable GC */
        gc_values.foreground = window_foreground;
        gc_values.background = rec->background;
        gc_values.graphics_exposures = False;
        rec->draw_gc = XCreateGC (XtDisplay (widget), XtWindow (widget),
                GCForeground | GCBackground | GCGraphicsExposures,
                &gc_values);

        /* get shareable GC, font is overridden by fontlist, but must be initialized */
        gc_values.font = XLoadFont (XtDisplay (widget), "fixed");
        rec->normal_gc = XtGetGC (widget,
                GCForeground | GCBackground | GCFont | GCGraphicsExposures,
                &gc_values);
}

/*_____*/
/* create back pixmap and initialize */
/*_____*/

static void NewBackPixmap (widget, rec)
        Widget          widget;
        BoxRec          *rec;
{
        Arg             args[1];
        Cardinal        depth;
        int             i;

/       XtSetArg (args[0], XmNdepth, &depth);
        XtGetValues (widget, args, 1);
```

```
        /* create back pixmap */
        rec->back = XCreatePixmap (XtDisplay (widget), XtWindow (widget),
                                   rec->width, rec->height, depth);

        /* initialize pixmap contents */
        XSetForeground (XtDisplay (widget), rec->draw_gc, rec->background);
        XFillRectangle (XtDisplay (widget), rec->back, rec->draw_gc,
                        0, 0, rec->width, rec->height);
        for (i = 0; i < rec->no_icons; i++)
                RedrawIcon (widget, rec, i);
}


*_____*/
/* create back pixmap on first expose */
/*_____*/

static void InitializeBoxWindow (widget, rec)
        Widget          widget;
        BoxRec          *rec;
{
        CreateGCs (widget, rec);
        NewBackPixmap (widget, rec);
        rec->exposed = True;
}


/*_____*/
/* test whether two rectangles intersect */
/*_____*/

static Boolean Intersect (x1, y1, w1, h1, x2, y2, w2, h2)
        int    x1, y1, w1, h1, x2, y2, w2, h2;
{
        if (x1 + w1 < x2 || y1 + h1 < y2) return False;
        if (x1 > x2 + w2 || y1 > y2 + h2) return False;
        return True;
}


/*_____*/
/* redraw partial region of back pixmap and refresh window */
/*_____*/

static void RedrawRegion (widget, rec, x, y, width, height)
        Widget          widget;
        BoxRec          *rec;
        int             x, y, width, height;
{
```

```
int         i;

/* erase invalid rectangle in back pixmap */
XSetForeground (XtDisplay (widget), rec->draw_gc, rec->background);
XSetClipMask (XtDisplay (widget), rec->draw_gc, None);
XFillRectangle (XtDisplay (widget), rec->back, rec->draw_gc,
                    x, y, width, height);

/* redraw affected icons to back pixmap */
i = rec->lowest;
do {
      if (Intersect (x, y, width, height,
                   rec->icons[i].x - rec->icons[i].string_left,
                   rec->icons[i].y,
                   rec->icon_width + 2 * rec->icons[i].string_left,
                   rec->icon_height + rec->string_height))
             RedrawIcon (widget, rec, i);
        i = rec->icons[i].higher; }
while (i >= 0);

/* refresh window of drawing area */
XCopyArea (XtDisplay (widget), rec->back, XtWindow (widget),
                 rec->normal_gc, x, y, width, height, x, y);
}


/*_____*/
/* simple expose procedure */
/*_____*/


static void ExposeBox (widget, rec, call_data)
      Widget                          widget;
      BoxRec                          *rec;
      XmDrawingAreaCallbackStruct     *call_data;
{
      XEvent      *ev = call_data->event;

      if (ev == NULL) return;

      /* create back pixmap if first time */
      if (!rec->exposed)
             InitializeBoxWindow (widget, rec);

      /* copy back to front */
      XCopyArea (XtDisplay (widget), rec->back, XtWindow (widget),
                    rec->normal_gc,
                    ev->xexpose.x, ev->xexpose.y,
                    ev->xexpose.width, ev->xexpose.height,
```

```
                              ev->xexpose.x, ev->xexpose.y);
}


/******************* Handle button-down *******************/

/*_____*/
/* test whether point in icon or in label part */
/*_____*/

Boolean PointInIcon (x, y, icon, w, h, sh)
        int         x;
        int         y;
        IconRec     *icon;
        int         w;
        int         h;
        int         sh;
{
        /* is in icon part ? */
        if (x >= icon->x && x <= icon->x + w &&
                    y >= icon->y && y <= icon->y + h)
            return True;
        /* is in label part ? */
        if (x >= icon->x - icon->string_left &&
                        x <= icon->x + w + icon->string_left &&
                        y >= icon->y + h &&
                        y <= icon->y + h + sh)
            return True;
        /* else false */
        return False;
}


/*_____*/
/* which icon was hit ? */
/*_____*/

static int Hit (rec, x, y)
        BoxRec      *rec;
        int         x, y;
{
        int         i, found = -1;

        i = rec->lowest;
        do {
                if (PointInIcon (x, y, &rec->icons[i],
                                rec->icon_width, rec->icon_height,
                                rec->string_height))
                    found = i;
```

```
                        i = rec->icons[i].higher;
                }
        while (i >= 0);
        return found;
}


/*_____*/
/* move icon on top */
/*_____*/

static void SetOnTop (widget, rec)
        Widget          widget;
        BoxRec          *rec;
{
        int             topindex = rec->moving;
        int             i;
        int             search, previous;

        /* search predecessor */
        for (i = 0; i < rec->no_icons; i++)
                if (rec->icons[i].higher == topindex)
                        previous = i;
                else if (rec->icons[i].higher == -1)
                        rec->icons[i].higher = topindex;
        if (rec->lowest == topindex)
                rec->lowest = rec->icons[topindex].higher;
        else
                rec->icons[previous].higher = rec->icons[topindex].higher;
        rec->icons[topindex].higher = -1;

        /* redraw on top */
        RedrawRegion (widget, rec,
                        rec->icons[topindex].x - rec->icons[topindex].string_left,
                        rec->icons[topindex].y,
                        rec->icon_width + 2 * rec->icons[topindex].string_left,
                        rec->icon_height + rec->string_height);
}


/*_____*/
/* handle input callback */
/*_____*/

static void HandleButtons (widget, rec, call_data)
        Widget                          widget;
        BoxRec                          *rec;
        XmDrawingAreaCallbackStruct     *call_data;
{
```

```
    XEvent      *ev = call_data->event;

    /* activate icon on button press */
    if (ev->xany.type == ButtonPress) {
            rec->moving = Hit (rec, ev->xbutton.x, ev->xbutton.y);
            if (rec->moving < 0) return;
            rec->x_off = ev->xbutton.x - rec->icons[rec->moving].x;
            rec->y_off = ev->xbutton.y - rec->icons[rec->moving].y;
            SetOnTop (widget, rec);
    }
}


/********************** Handle resize callback ******************/

static void HandleResize (widget, rec, call_data)
    Widget                             widget;
    BoxRec                             *rec;
    XmDrawingAreaCallbackStruct        *call_data;
{
    Arg  args[2];

    XtSetArg (args[0], XmNwidth, &rec->width);
    XtSetArg (args[1], XmNheight, &rec->height);
    XtGetValues (widget, args, 2);

    XFreePixmap (rec->back);
    NewBackPixmap (widget, rec);
}



/********************** Handle movement ********************/

/*_____*/
/* find rectangle invalidated by move */
/*_____*/

static void FindInvalidRect (rec, new_x, new_y, x, y, width, height)
    BoxRec      *rec;
    int         new_x;
    int         new_y;
    int         *x;
    int         *y;
    int         *width;
    int         *height;
{
    int         xmove, ymove;
    IconRec     *icon = &rec->icons[rec->moving];
```

```
        /* check movement in X direction */
        xmove = new_x - icon->x;
        if (xmove > 0) {
                *x = icon->x - icon->string_left;
                *width = rec->icon_width + xmove + 2 * icon->string_left;
        } else {
                *x = icon->x + xmove - icon->string_left;
                *width = rec->icon_width - xmove + 2 * icon->string_left;
        }

        /* check movement in Y direction */
        ymove = new_y - icon->y;
        if (ymove > 0) {
                *y = icon->y;
                *height = rec->icon_height + rec->string_height + ymove;
        } else {
                *y = icon->y + ymove;
                *height = rec->icon_height + rec->string_height - ymove;
        }
}


/*_____*/
/* handle motion events */
/*_____*/

static void HandleMove (widget, rec, ev)
        Widget          widget;
        BoxRec          *rec;
        XEvent          *ev;
{
        int             new_x, new_y;
        int             x, y, width, height;

        if (rec->moving < 0) return;

        /* constrain motion */
        new_x = ev->xmotion.x - rec->x_off;
        if (new_x < 0)
                new_x = 0;
        if (new_x > rec->width - rec->icon_width)
                new_x = rec->width - rec->icon_width;
        new_y = ev->xmotion.y - rec->y_off;
        if (new_y < 0)
                new_y = 0;
        if (new_y > rec->height - rec->icon_height - rec->string_height)
                new_y = rec->height - rec->icon_height - rec->string_height;
```

```
        /* find affected region */
        FindInvalidRect (rec, new_x, new_y, &x, &y, &width, &height);

        /* set new position... */
        rec->icons[rec->moving].x = new_x;
        rec->icons[rec->moving].y = new_y;

        /* ...and redraw region */
        RedrawRegion (widget, rec, x, y, width, height);
}

/******************** Exit and destroy cleanup **************/

/*_____*/
/* write new state back to file */
/*_____*/

static void WriteIcons (rec)
        BoxRec      *rec;
{
        int          i;
        FILE *fp;
        String       name;

        fp = fopen (rec->pathname, "w");
        if (fp == NULL) return;

        fprintf (fp, "# %d %d\n", rec->width, rec->height);
        i = rec->lowest;
        do {
                XmStringGetLtoR (rec->icons[i].label,
                                 XmSTRING_DEFAULT_CHARSET,
                                 &name);
                fprintf (fp, ": %d %d %s %s\n",
                             rec->icons[i].x, rec->icons[i].y,
                             name, rec->icons[i].class);
                i = rec->icons[i].higher;}
        while (i >= 0);
}

/*_____*/
/*** exported save procedure ***/
/*_____*/

void SaveIconBox (widget)
        Widget       widget;
```

```
{
        Arg         args[1];
        BoxRec      *rec;
        XtSetArg (args[0], XmNuserData, &rec);
        XtGetValues (widget, args, 1);
        WriteIcons (rec);
}


/*_____*/
/* handle destroy callback */
/*_____*/

static void DestroyIconBox (widget, rec, call_data)
        Widget      widget;
        BoxRec      *rec;
        caddr_t     call_data;
{
        int         i, j;

        /* write new state to file */
        WriteIcons (rec);

        /* free pixmaps */
        for (i = 0; i < rec->no_icons; i++) {
                for (j = 0; j < i; j++)
                        if (strcmp (rec->icons[i].mask_name,
                                        rec->icons[j].mask_name) == 0)
                                break;
                if (i == j && rec->icons[i].mask != None)
                        XFreePixmap (XtDisplay (widget), rec->icons[i].mask);
        }

        /* free records */
        for (i = 0; i < rec->no_icons; i++) {
                XtFree (rec->icons[i].mask_name);
                XtFree (rec->icons[i].pix_name);
                XmStringFree (rec->icons[i].label);
        }

        XtFree (rec->pathname);
        XmFontListFree (rec->fontlist);
        XFreeGC (XtDisplay (widget), rec->draw_gc);
        XtReleaseGC (widget, rec->normal_gc);
        XFreePixmap (XtDisplay (widget), rec->back);
        XtFree (rec->icons);
        XtFree (rec);
}
```

The File "boxtest.c"

```
/* includes */
#include <Xm/Xm.h>
#include <X11/Shell.h>

/* HACK */
#define XA_WM_PROTOCOLS \
        XmInternAtom(XtDisplay(toplevel),"WM_PROTOCOLS",FALSE)
/* !!!IMPORTANT!!! */
#include <X11/Protocols.h>

#include "IconBox.h"

/* global definitions */

#define PROGRAM_CLASS "IconBox"
#define ERROR_CLASS    "IconBoxError"

#define NUM_ARGS 10

/* error definitions */

#define NErrCannotOpen    "cannotOpen"
#define TErrMain          "Main"

/****************************/

void EndProgram (widget, client_data, call_data)
     Widget     widget;
     caddr_t    client_data;
     caddr_t    call_data;
{
     SaveIconBox ((Widget) client_data);
     exit (0);
}

void main (argc, argv)
     unsigned int    argc;
     char            **argv;
{
     Display         *display;
     XtAppContext    context;
     Arg             args[NUM_ARGS];
     Widget          toplevel, box;
```

```
/* initialize toolkit */
XtToolkitInitialize();
context = XtCreateApplicationContext ();
display = XtOpenDisplay (
            context,    /* application context                */
            NULL,       /* use DISPLAY from environment       */
            NULL,       /* use last of argv[0] as name        */
            PROGRAM_CLASS,
            NULL,       /* no additional command line options */
            0,          /* ditto                              */
            &argc,
            argv);      /* use and delete standard options    */

if (display == NULL)    /* necessary !      */
    XtErrorMsg (
            NErrCannotOpen, TErrMain,      /* resource name */
            ERROR_CLASS,                   /* resource class  */
            "cannot open display"      ,   /* default message */
            NULL, NULL);                   /* parameters      */

/* create application shell */
XtSetArg (args[0], XmNallowShellResize, True);
XtSetArg (args[1], XmNdeleteResponse, XmDO_NOTHING);
toplevel = XtAppCreateShell (
            NULL,                /* use same program name */
            PROGRAM_CLASS,   /* repeat class param        */
            applicationShellWidgetClass,
            display,
            args, 2);            /* argument list         */

/* create main window */
box = CreateIconBox (toplevel, args, 0);

XmAddWMProtocolCallback (toplevel,
        XmInternAtom (display, "WM_DELETE_WINDOW", True),
        EndProgram, (caddr_t) box);
/* start loop */
XtRealizeWidget (toplevel);
XtAppMainLoop (context);
}
```

Appendix G

"Icon Widget"
Source Code

The File "IconWidget.h"

```
#ifndef _IconWidget_h
#define _IconWidget_h

#ifndef NeedFunctionPrototypes
#define NeedFunctionPrototypes 0
#endif

#include <Xm/Xm.h>


#define XmNiconOffset  "iconOffset"
#define XmCIconOffset       "IconOffset"


extern WidgetClass iconWidgetClass;

typedef struct _IconWidgetClassRec * IconWidgetClass;
typedef struct _IconWidgetRec       * IconWidget;

Widget CreateIconLabel (
#if NeedFunctionPrototypes
```

```
        Widget      /* parent   */,
        char*       /* name     */,
        ArgList     /* arglist  */,
        Cardinal    /* argcount */,
        char*       /* pixmap   */
#endif
);

Widget CreateIconButton (
#if NeedFunctionPrototypes
        Widget      /* parent   */,
        char*       /* name     */,
        ArgList     /* arglist  */,
        Cardinal    /* argcount */,
        char*       /* pixmap   */
#endif
);


#endif /* _IconWidget_h */
/* DON'T ADD ANYTHING AFTER THIS #endif */
```

The File "IconWidgetP.h"

```
#ifndef _IconWidgetP_h
#define _IconWidgetP_h


#include "IconWidget.h"
#include <Xm/XmP.h>


/*    Icon class structure      */

typedef struct _IconWidgetClassPart
{
        caddr_t extension;
} IconWidgetClassPart;


/*    Full class record declaration for Icon class      */

typedef struct _IconWidgetClassRec
{
        CoreClassPart          core_class;
```

```
        XmPrimitiveClassPart    primitive_class;
        XmLabelClassPart        label_class;
        IconWidgetClassPart     icon_class;
} IconWidgetClassRec;

extern IconWidgetClassRec iconWidgetClassRec;


/*      The icon widget instance record     */

typedef struct _IconWidgetPart
{
        short           offset;
        short           width,
                        height;
        unsigned char   shadow_type;
        Boolean         armed;
        XtCallbackList  activate_callback;
        XtCallbackList  arm_callback;
        XtCallbackList  disarm_callback;
} IconWidgetPart;


/*      Full instance record declaration    */

typedef struct _IconWidgetRec
{
        CorePart                core;
        XmPrimitivePart         primitive;
        XmLabelPart             label;
        IconWidgetPart          icon;
} IconWidgetRec;

#ifndef XtSpecificationRelease
#define XtCallCallbackList(w,cb,cd)      XtWidgetCallCallbacks (cb,cd)
#endif

#endif /* _IconWidgetP_h */
/* DON'T ADD ANYTHING AFTER THIS #endif */
```

The File "IconWidget.c"

```
#include <X11/Intrinsic.h>
#include <X11/IntrinsicP.h>
#include <Xm/Xm.h>
```

```
#include <Xm/XmP.h>
#include <Xm/Label.h>
#include <Xm/LabelP.h>
#include "IconWidget.h"
#include "IconWidgetP.h"


/*    Static routine definitions      */

static void       Initialize ();
static Boolean    SetValues ();
static void       Redisplay ();
static void       Destroy ();

static void       Arm ();
static void       Activate ();
static void       Disarm ();
static void       Enter ();
static void       Leave ();
static void       Help();

static void       GetPixmapSize ();
static void       DrawShadow ();


/*    Default translation table and action list    */

static char defaultTranslations[] =
    "<EnterWindow>:        Enter()           \n\
    <LeaveWindow>:         Leave()";

static XtActionsRec actionsList[] =
{
    { "Arm",        (XtActionProc) Arm},
    { "Activate",   (XtActionProc) Activate},
    { "Disarm",     (XtActionProc) Disarm},
    { "Enter",      (XtActionProc) Enter},
    { "Leave",      (XtActionProc) Leave},
    { "Help",       (XtActionProc) Help}
};

static XtResource resources[] =    {
    {
    XmNshadowThickness, XmCShadowThickness, XmRShort, sizeof (short),
    XtOffset (XmPrimitiveWidget, primitive.shadow_thickness),
    XmRImmediate, (caddr_t) 2
    },
```

```
    {
    XmNiconOffset, XmCIconOffset, XmRShort, sizeof(short),
    XtOffset (IconWidget, icon.offset),
    XmRImmediate, (caddr_t) 0
    },

    {
    XmNshadowType, XmCShadowType, XmRShadowType,
    sizeof(unsigned char),
    XtOffset (IconWidget, icon.shadow_type),
    XmRImmediate, (caddr_t) XmSHADOW_OUT
    },

    {
    XmNactivateCallback, XmCCallback, XmRCallback, sizeof(XtCallbackList),
    XtOffset (IconWidget, icon.activate_callback),
    XmRPointer, (caddr_t) NULL
    },

    {
    XmNarmCallback, XmCCallback, XmRCallback, sizeof(XtCallbackList),
    XtOffset (IconWidget, icon.arm_callback),
    XmRPointer, (caddr_t) NULL
    },

    {
    XmNdisarmCallback, XmCCallback, XmRCallback, sizeof(XtCallbackList),
    XtOffset (IconWidget, icon.disarm_callback),
    XmRPointer, (caddr_t) NULL
    },
    };


/*    The IconWidget class record definition    */

IconWidgetClassRec iconWidgetClassRec =
{
    {
    (WidgetClass) &xmLabelClassRec, /* superclass              */
    "IconWidget",                   /* class_name              */
    sizeof(IconWidgetRec),          /* widget_size             */
    NULL,                           /* class_initialize        */
    NULL,                           /* class_part_initialize   */
    FALSE,                          /* class_initialized       */
    (XtInitProc) Initialize,        /* initialize              */
    NULL,                           /* initialize_hook         */
```

```
XtInheritRealize,                   /* realize                      */
actionsList,                        /* actions                      */
XtNumber(actionsList),              /* num_actions                  */
resources,                          /* resources                    */
XtNumber(resources),                /* num_resources                */
NULLQUARK,                          /* xrm_class                    */
TRUE,                               /* compress_motion              */
TRUE,                               /* compress_exposure            */
TRUE,                               /* compress_enterleave          */
FALSE,                              /* visible_interest             */
Destroy,                            /* destroy                      */
XtInheritResize,                    /* resize                       */
(XtExposeProc) Redisplay,           /* expose                       */
(XtSetValuesFunc) SetValues,        /* set_values                   */
NULL,                               /* set_values_hook              */
XtInheritSetValuesAlmost,           /* set_values_almost            */
NULL,                               /* get_values_hook              */
NULL,                               /* accept_focus                 */
XtVersion,                          /* version                      */
NULL,                               /* callback private             */
defaultTranslations,                /* tm_table                     */
XtInheritQueryGeometry              /* query_geometry               */
NULL,                               /* display_accelerator          */
NULL,                               /* extension                    */
},

{
_XtInherit,                         /* Primitive border_highlight   */
_XtInherit,                         /* Primitive border_unhighlight */
XtInheritTranslations,              /* translations                 */
NULL,                               /* arm_and_activate             */
NULL,                               /* get resources                */
0,                                  /* num get_resources            */
NULL,                               /* extension                    */
},

{
_XtInherit,                         /* SetOverrideCallback      */
_XtInherit,                         /* SetWhichButton               */
XtInheritTranslations,              /* menu traversal translation   */
NULL,                               /* extension                    */
},

{
NULL,                               /* extension                    */
}
};
```

```
WidgetClass iconWidgetClass = (WidgetClass) &iconWidgetClassRec;


/**********************************************************
 *
 *      Initialize
 *      Get geometry if pixmap already there
 *
 **********************************************************/

static void Initialize (request, new)
        IconWidget          request, new;

{
        if (new -> icon.shadow_type != XmSHADOW_IN      &&
                    new -> icon.shadow_type != XmSHADOW_OUT)
        {
            new -> icon.shadow_type = XmSHADOW_OUT;
        }

        GetPixmapSize (new);
        new->icon.armed = False;
}

/**********************************************************
 *
 *      GetPixmapSize
 *      Get geometry if pixmap already there
 *
 **********************************************************/

static void GetPixmapSize (iw)
        IconWidget          iw;
{
        Window      root;
        int         junk, w, h;

        if (iw->label.pixmap != XmUNSPECIFIED_PIXMAP) {
            XGetGeometry (XtDisplay (iw), iw->label.pixmap,
                            &root, &junk, &junk,
                            &w, &h,
                            &junk, &junk);
            iw->icon.width = (short) w;
            iw->icon.height = (short) h;
        }
}
```

```
/**********************************************************
*
*       Redisplay
*       Handle expose events
*
**********************************************************/

static void Redisplay(w, event, region)
        Widget      w;
        XEvent      *event;
        Region      region;
{
        IconWidget          iw = (IconWidget) w;
        short               shad = iw->primitive.shadow_thickness +
                                    iw->primitive.highlight_thickness;
        short               avail;


        /* use the label's expose first */
        (* xmLabelClassRec.core_class.expose) (w, event, region);

        /* copy the pixmap into the space left by margin_top */
        if (iw->label.pixmap != XmUNSPECIFIED_PIXMAP) {
                avail = iw->core.width - 2 * shad - 2 * iw->label.margin_width -
                        iw->label.margin_left - iw->label.margin_right - iw->icon.width;
                XCopyArea (XtDisplay (w), iw->label.pixmap, XtWindow (w),
                        iw->label.normal_GC, 0, 0,
                        iw->icon.width,
                        iw >icon.height > iw->label.margin_top ?
                                iw->label.margin_top : iw->icon.height,
                        avail/2 + shad +
                                iw->label.margin_width - iw->label.margin_left,
                        iw->label.TextRect.y - iw->icon.height - iw->icon.offset);
        }

        /* draw the shadow */
        DrawShadow (iw, True);

        /* for keyboard traversal */
        if (iw->primitive.highlighted)
                _XmHighlightBorder(w);
        else if (_XmDifferentBackground (w, XtParent (w)))
                _XmUnhighlightBorder(w);
}
```

```
/****************************************************
 *
 *      DrawShadow
 *
 ****************************************************/

static void DrawShadow (iw, really)
    IconWidget      iw;
    Boolean     really;
{
    Boolean     in = (iw->icon.armed && really) ||
                        iw->icon.shadow_type == XmSHADOW_IN;

    if ((iw->primitive.shadow_thickness) > 0 && XtIsRealized (iw)) {
        _XmDrawShadow (XtDisplay (iw), XtWindow (iw),
                in ? iw->primitive.bottom_shadow_GC :
                        iw->primitive.top_shadow_GC,
                in ? iw->primitive.top_shadow_GC :
                        iw->primitive.bottom_shadow_GC,
                iw->primitive.shadow_thickness,
                iw->primitive.highlight_thickness,
                iw->primitive.highlight_thickness,
                (int)iw->core.width-2*iw->primitive.highlight_thickness,
                (int)iw->core.height-2*iw->primitive.highlight_thickness);

    }
}




/****************************************************
 *
 *      SetValues
 *      Update geometry, pixmap might have changed
 *
 ****************************************************/

static Boolean SetValues(current, request, neww)
    Widget      current, request, neww;
{
    IconWidget          cur = (IconWidget) current;
    IconWidget          new = (IconWidget) neww;
    IconWidget          req = (IconWidget) request;
```

```
if (new -> icon.shadow_type != XmSHADOW_IN       &&
        new -> icon.shadow_type != XmSHADOW_OUT)
{
    new -> icon.shadow_type = XmSHADOW_OUT;
}

GetPixmapSize (new);

if (new->icon.shadow_type != cur->icon.shadow_type ||
        new->primitive.highlight_thickness !=
            cur->primitive.highlight_thickness   ||
        new->primitive.shadow_thickness !=
            cur->primitive.shadow_thickness)
{
    return True;
} else{
    return False;
}
}


/**********************************************************
 *
 *    Destroy
 *    Clean up allocated resources when the widget is destroyed.
 *
 **********************************************************/

static void Destroy (iw)
    IconWidget      iw;

{

    XtRemoveAllCallbacks (iw, XmNactivateCallback);
    XtRemoveAllCallbacks (iw, XmNarmCallback);
    XtRemoveAllCallbacks (iw, XmNdisarmCallback);
}



/**********************************************************
 *
 *    Enter
 *
 **********************************************************/

static void Enter (iw, event)
    IconWidget      iw;
    XEvent     * event;
```

```
{
      _XmPrimitiveEnter (iw, event);

      if (iw->icon.armed)
            DrawShadow (iw, True);
}

/***********************************************************
 *
 *    Leave
 *
 ***********************************************************/

static void Leave (iw, event)
      IconWidget        iw;
      XEvent            *event;

{
      _XmPrimitiveLeave (iw, event);

      if (iw->icon.armed)
            DrawShadow (iw, False);
}

/***********************************************************
 *
 *    Arm
 *
 ***********************************************************/

static void Arm (iw, event)
      IconWidget        iw;
      XEvent            *event;

{
      XmAnyCallbackStruct call_value;

      iw->icon.armed = True;
      DrawShadow (iw, True);

      if (iw->icon.arm_callback) {
            XFlush(XtDisplay (iw));
            call_value.reason = XmCR_ARM;
            call_value.event = event;
            XtCallCallbackList (iw, iw->icon.arm_callback, &call_value);
      }
}
```

```
/***************************************************************
 *
 *   Activate
 *
 ***************************************************************/

static void Activate (iw, event)
        IconWidget      iw;
        XEvent          *event;

{

        XmAnyCallbackStruct call_value;

        if ((event->xany.type == ButtonPress || event->xany.type == ButtonRelease)
                && (event->xbutton.x > iw->core.width ||
                        event->xbutton.y > iw->core.height))
            return;

        call_value.reason = XmCR_ACTIVATE;
        call_value.event = event;
        XtCallCallbackList (iw, iw->icon.activate_callback, &call_value);
}

/***************************************************************
 *
 *   Disarm
 *
 ***************************************************************/

static void Disarm (iw, event)
        IconWidget      iw;
        XEvent          *event;

{

        XmAnyCallbackStruct call_value;

        iw->icon.armed = False;
        DrawShadow (iw, True);

        if (iw->icon.disarm_callback) {
            XFlush(XtDisplay (iw));
            call_value.reason = XmCR_DISARM;
            call_value.event = event;
            XtCallCallbackList (iw, iw->icon.disarm_callback, &call_value);
        }
}
```

```
/**********************************************************
 *
 *    Help
 *    This function processes Function Key 1 press
 *
 **********************************************************/

static void Help (iw, event)
     IconWidget      iw;
     XEvent          *event;

{

     XmAnyCallbackStruct call_value;

     call_value.reason = XmCR_HELP;
     call_value.event = event;
     XtCallCallbackList (iw, iw->primitive.help_callback, &call_value);
}



/**********************************************************
 *
 *    CreateIconLabel
 *    Create an instance of an icon as label
 *
 **********************************************************/

Widget CreateIconLabel (parent, name, arglist, argcount, pixmap)
     Widget      parent;
     char        *name;
     ArgList     arglist;
     Cardinal    argcount;
     char        *pixmap;

{

     Widget      w;
     Pixmap      pix;
     Arg         args[1];

     w = XtCreateManagedWidget (name, iconWidgetClass,
                                parent, arglist, argcount);

     if (pixmap != NULL && pixmap != "") {
          pix = XmGetPixmap (((IconWidget) w)->core.screen,
                             pixmap,
                             ((IconWidget) w)->primitive.foreground,
                             ((IconWidget) w)->core.background_pixel);
```

```
            if (pix != XmUNSPECIFIED_PIXMAP) {
                  XtSetArg (args[0], XmNlabelPixmap, pix);
                  XtSetValues (w, args, 1);
            }
      }

      return w;    }

/**********************************************************
 *
 *      CreateIconButton
 *      Create an instance of an icon as button
 *
 **********************************************************/

#define BUT_TRANS  \
      "#override <Btn1Down>: Arm()\n<Btn1Up>: Activate() Disarm()"

Widget CreateIconButton (parent, name, arglist, argcount, pixmap)
      Widget        parent;
      char          *name;
      ArgList       arglist;
      Cardinal      argcount;
      char          *pixmap;

{
      Widget            w;
      Pixmap            pix;
      Arg               args[1];
      XtTranslations    parsed = XtParseTranslationTable (BUT_TRANS);

      w = XtCreateManagedWidget (name, iconWidgetClass,
                                 parent, arglist, argcount);

      if (pixmap != NULL && pixmap != "") {
            pix = XmGetPixmap (((IconWidget) w)->core.screen,
                              pixmap,
                              ((IconWidget) w)->primitive.foreground,
                              ((IconWidget) w)->core.background_pixel);
            if (pix != XmUNSPECIFIED_PIXMAP) {
                  XtSetArg (args[0], XmNlabelPixmap, pix);
                  XtSetValues (w, args, 1);
            }
      }

      XtAugmentTranslations (w, parsed);
```

```
        return w;
}
```

The File "icontest.c"

```
/* includes */
#include <Xm/Xm.h>
#include <X11/Shell.h>
#include <Xm/RowColumn.h>

#include "IconWidget.h"

/* global definitions */

#define PROGRAM_CLASS   "Icon"
#define ERROR_CLASS     "IconError"

#define NUM_ARGS 10

/* error definitions */

#define NErrCannotOpen    "cannotOpen"
#define TErrMain          "Main"

/************************/

static void PressMe (widget, client_data, call_data)
     Widget               widget;
     caddr_t              client_data;
     XmAnyCallbackStruct *call_data;
{
     XBell (XtDisplay (widget), 100);
}

static void ToggleMe (widget, client_data, call_data)
     Widget               widget;
     caddr_t              client_data;
     XmAnyCallbackStruct *call_data;
{
     unsigned char    shadow_type;
     Arg              args[NUM_ARGS];

     XtSetArg (args[0], XmNshadowType, &shadow_type);
     XtGetValues (widget, args, 1);
```

```
        XtSetArg (args[0], XmNshadowType,
        shadow_type == XmSHADOW_IN ?
                              XmSHADOW_OUT : XmSHADOW_IN);
        XtSetValues (widget, args, 1);
}

static void CreateMainWindow (parent)
        Widget      parent;
{
        Widget      row, label, button, toggle;
        Arg         args[NUM_ARGS];
        XmString    face;

        XtSetArg (args[0], XmNorientation, XmHORIZONTAL);
        XtSetArg (args[1], XmNpacking, XmPACK_COLUMN);
        row = XtCreateManagedWidget ("row", xmRowColumnWidgetClass, parent,
                              args, 2);

        face = XmStringLtoRCreate ("Label",
                              XmSTRING_DEFAULT_CHARSET);
        XtSetArg (args[0], XmNlabelString, face);
        label = CreateIconLabel (row, "label", args, 1,
                              "/home/berlage/bitmaps/gredit");
        XmStringFree (face);

        face = XmStringLtoRCreate ("PressMe",
                              XmSTRING_DEFAULT_CHARSET);
        XtSetArg (args[0], XmNlabelString, face);
        button = CreateIconButton (row, "button", args, 1,
                              "/home/berlage/bitmaps/gredit");
        XtAddCallback (button, XmNactivateCallback, PressMe, NULL);
        XmStringFree (face);

        face = XmStringLtoRCreate ("ToggleMe",
                              XmSTRING_DEFAULT_CHARSET);
        XtSetArg (args[0], XmNlabelString, face);
        toggle = CreateIconButton (row, "toggle", args, 1,
                              "/home/berlage/bitmaps/gredit");
        XtAddCallback (toggle, XmNactivateCallback, ToggleMe, NULL);
        XmStringFree (face);

}
```

```
/*****************************/

void main (argc, argv)
      unsigned int      argc;
      char  **argv;
{
      Display           *display;
      XtAppContext      context;
      Arg               args[NUM_ARGS];
      Widget            toplevel;

      /* initialize toolkit */
      XtToolkitInitialize();
      context = XtCreateApplicationContext ();
      display = XtOpenDisplay (
              context,     /* application context               */
              NULL,        /* use DISPLAY from environment      */
              NULL,        /* use last of argv[0] as name       */
              PROGRAM_CLASS,
              NULL,        /* no additional command line options */
              0,           /* ditto                             */
              &argc,
              argv);       /* use and delete standard options   */

      if (display == NULL)   /* necessary !    */
          XtErrorMsg (
              NErrCannotOpen, TErrMain,      /* resource name */
              ERROR_CLASS,                   /* resource class  */
              "cannot open display",         /* default message*/
              NULL, NULL);                   /* parameters    */

      /* create application shell */
      XtSetArg (args[0], XmNallowShellResize, True);
      toplevel = XtAppCreateShell (
              NULL,                /* use same program name  */
              PROGRAM_CLASS,       /* repeat class param     */
              applicationShellWidgetClass,
              display,
              args, 1);            /* argument list          */

      /* create main window */
      CreateMainWindow (toplevel);

      /* start loop */
      XtRealizeWidget (toplevel);
      XtAppMainLoop (context);
}
```

Index

475